MILITARY
JOURNAL
of the
AMERICAN
REVOLUTION

MILITARY JOURNAL

OF THE

AMERICAN REVOLUTION,

From the commencement to the disbanding of the

AMERICAN ARMY;

Comprising a detailed account of the principal events and

BATTLES OF THE REVOLUTION,

WITH THEIR EXACT DATES,

And a Biographical Sketch of the most Prominent Generals.

BY JAMES THACHER, M. D.,

Surgeon in the American Revolutionary Army.

CORNER HOUSE

HISTORICAL PUBLICATIONS

Gansevoort, New York   12831

1998

New materials copyright © 1998 by
Corner House Historical Publications
All Rights Reserved

This soft cover edition printed by:

Corner House Historical Publications
14 Catherine Street: PO Box 207
Gansevoort, NY 12831

The most recent impression of the soft-cover edition
is indicated by the number below:

10 9 8 7 6 5 4 3 2 1

ISBN: 0-87928-124-3   Soft cover   1998

The Corner House Historical Publications edition is an
unabridged reprint of the edition published in 1862 by
Hurlbut, Williams & Co., Hartford, CT. The first edition
was published in 1823 by Richardson & Lord, Boston and a
later edition was published in 1827 by Cottons & Barnard,
Boston. The Corner House edition includes a new
biosketch of the author and a listing of illustrations. Printed
on acid free paper in the United States of America.

PREFACE.

"HISTORY," says a late elegant writer, "presents no struggle for liberty which has in it more of the moral sublime than that of the American Revolution. It has been of late years too much forgotten in the sharp contentions of party; and he who endeavors to withdraw the public mind from the debasing conflicts, and to fix it on the grandeur of that epoch, which, magnificent in itself, begins now to wear the solemn livery of antiquity, as it is viewed through the deepening twilight of more than half a century, certainly performs a meritorious service, and can scarcely need justification."

The American Revolution, conducted, as it was, by a band of brave and heroic spirits, animated by the highest and noblest motives, should never be forgotten. The peaceful possession of the rich inheritance they bequeathed to posterity, obtained at so much sacrifice, should enshrine their memory in the heart of every free citizen; and cause the story of their deeds to be perused with new and ever increasing interest.

What can be better calculated to stir the mighty pulsations of a nation's heart, and fill it with patriotic enthusiasm, than the recital of those glorious achievements of gallant spirits, upon our own soil, for the priceless legacy of *Liberty* and *Freedom?*

And who can better bring before us the events and transactions of that important period,—that memorable struggle, than one who daily witnessed its thrilling scenes, and made with an impartial hand their daily record?

PREFACE.

The narrations in this "Journal" are invested, with peculiar interest, from the fact that its author himself mingled in the varied scenes of the Revolution, observed the different phases of military life ; was personally acquainted with the characters he presents; and therefore gives us the truthful results of his own observation, greatly heightened in beauty and interest, by the attractive style which he employs, and the ease and grace with which he presents them. It is richly interspersed with sentiment, enlivened by anecdote, and abounds in rare and valuable information, such as can not fail of being regarded by every one who has a heart to appreciate the glorious privileges of this our dear-bought heritage.

Let one apply himself to the perusal of these deeply interesting pages, and the love of liberty will grow stronger in his heart, and on its altar the fires of patriotism will grow brighter and purer!

Let him look at the illustrious characters who played their part so effectually on the broad theatre of the Revolution, as they are here portrayed, and learn what mighty results, *holy purpose*, coupled with *invincible energy*, can work out.

Let him peruse these "Annals" of the ever memorable contest, with devout admiration, and sincere gratitude to those heroic men, who, under providence, wrought the sublime achievement of our "National Independence," and think,

"It is to the virtues of such souls, man owes
His portion in the good that Heaven bestows."

CONTENTS.

CONTENTS.

CONTENTS. ix

CONTENTS.

CONTENTS.

REVOLUTIONARY ANNALS.

APPENDIX.

BIOGRAPHICAL SKETCHES.

ROKEBY, YORKSHIRE, FROM THE WEST.

ILLUSTRATIONS

ABOUT THE AUTHOR

Dr. James Thacher, M.D. was born in Massachusetts in 1754 near Boston and died in 1844. His schooling was minimal with only a five-year apprenticeship and no formal higher education. Thacher sought a medical staff position at the Provincial Hospital in Cambridge after the Battle of Breed's Hill, June 17, 1775. His name was put on a list of sixteen medical candidates for examination by a board of medical officers. On July 10, Thacher was one of ten selected for the surgeon's mate position. He received his appointment from the Provincial Congress and began his career on July 15 with the Continental Army.

He served at the hospital in Cambridge, Massachusetts until February 18, 1776 when he was assigned to Colonel Whitcomb's Regiment stationed at the barracks on Prospect Hill. After the siege, Whitcomb's Regiment was ordered to Fort Ticonderoga. Thacher left Boston on August 20 and rejoined the Regiment there on September 6.

Thacher was assigned to the Northern Department and served in the Saratoga Campaign, July - October, 1777. After the close of the campaign, he served in various hospitals until November 1778 when he accepted a position as Surgeon with Colonel Gibson's 1st Virginia Regiment. On June 24, 1779, he resigned his position with Gibson's Regiment to accept a position with Colonel Jackson's Regiment stationed at Providence, Rhode Island. He continued to serve with Jackson's Regiment until July 1781, when he was assigned Surgeon to the newly formed Corps of Light Infantry commanded by Colonel Alexander Scammel. Thacher arrived at Yorktown on September 27 and participated in the siege and surrender.

He closed his military career on January 1, 1783 and returned to Plymouth, Massachusetts where he practiced and taught medicine. He received an honorary M.D. degree from Harvard and was a fellow of the American Academy of Arts and Sciences. Thacher also turned to scientific and historical writing in addition to the preparation of his military journal which was first published in 1823. Publications to his credit include *American Modern Practice* (1818-1826), *American Medical Biography* (1828), *Management of Bees* (1829) and *History of Plymouth* (1832).

GEORGE WASHINGTON.

MILITARY JOURNAL.—1775.

January.—At the precise period when my medical studies and education are completed, under the patronage of Dr. Abner Hersey of Barnstable, and I am contemplating the commencement of a new career in life, I find our country about to be involved in all the horrors of a civil war. A series of arbitrary and oppressive measures, on the part of the mother-country, has long been advancing to that awful crisis, when an appeal to the power of the sword becomes inevitable. The event of this mighty struggle is to decide an affair of infinite magnitude, not merely as it respects the present generation, but as it will affect the welfare and happiness of unborn millions. The great fundamental principle, in the present controversy, is the right which is claimed by the Parliament of Great Britain, to exercise dominion, as the only supreme and uncontrollable legislative power over all the American Colonies. "Can they make laws to bind the colonies in all cases whatever; levy taxes on them without their consent; dispose of the revenues, thus raised, without their control; multiply officers at pleasure, and assign them fees, to be paid without, nay, contrary to and in direct violation of acts of our provincial assemblies, and approved by the crown? Can they enlarge the power of admiralty courts; divert the usual channels of justice; deprive the colonists of trial by a jury of their countrymen; in short, break down the barriers which their forefathers have erected against arbitrary power, and enforce their edicts by fleets and armies?" Then indeed are we reduced to a state of abject slavery; and all resistance to acts of Parliament may justly be called by the name of treason and rebellion. "The people of these colonies consider themselves as British subjects, entitled to all the rights and privileges of Freemen. It is inseparably essential to the

freedom of a people, and the undoubted right of Englishmen, that no taxes be imposed on them but with their
own consent, given personally or by their representatives.
From their local circumstances, the colonies cannot be
represented in the house of commons of Great Britain;
the only representatives of the people of the colonies are
the persons chosen therein by themselves; and no taxes
ever can be constitutionally imposed on them, but by their
respective legislatures." All acts of Parliament therefore,
for raising a revenue in America, are considered as de-
priving us of our property, without our consent, and consequently as a palpable infringement of our ancient rights
and privileges. They are unconstitutional and arbitrary
laws, subversive of the liberties and privileges secured to
us by our royal charters. It is not consistent with the
principles which actuate the American people, ever tamely
to submit to such a degrading system of government; not,
however, from a want of loyalty to our king, nor from an
undue impatience of subordination or legal restraint; for
in a quiet submission and demeanor to constitutional authority, and in zeal and attachment to our king, we dare
to vie with any of our fellow-subjects of Great Britain;
but it is an innate love of liberty, and our just rights, that
impels us to the arduous struggle. In no country, it is
asserted, is the love of liberty more deeply rooted, or the
knowledge of the rights inherent to freemen more generally diffused, or better understood, than among the British
American Colonies. Our religious and political privileges
are derived from our virtuous fathers; they were inhaled
with our earliest breath; and are, and will I trust ever
be, implanted and cherished in the bosom of the present
and future generations. These are the prevalent sentiments in New England at this eventful crisis, and all the
other provinces, Georgia excepted, are known to be in
unison with us in the resolution, to oppose with all our
power every violation of our just rights and privileges.
We are not, however, authorized, even in the most glorious
of causes, to expect a perfect unanimity among a people.
Numerous are the springs of men's actions; and diversity
of sentiment and views are characteristic of human nature.
Accordingly we find a small minority in our country who
are inimical to the common cause, and who are continually

opposing every proceeding of the majority. These people are doubtless actuated by various motives; a few, comparatively, influenced by principle; some by a spirit of timidity, or the absurd doctrine of passive obedience and non-resistance; others, from the strength of their passions, and weakness of judgment, are biassed and led astray by designing demagogues. There are, however, those who are vile enough to prostrate all honor and principle with the sordid view of office and preferment:

"For 'tis their duty, all the learned think,
T' espouse that cause by which they eat and drink."

Those disaffected individuals, who still adhere to the royal cause, have received the epithet of *Tories;* the very name is extremely abhorrent to the people in general, and they are subjected to such rigorous discipline as to prevent them from doing injury to the great cause of our country. The great majority of the people are happily united in the resolution to oppose, to the uttermost, the wicked attempts of the English cabinet. This class of people have assumed the appellation of *Whigs;* but by our enemies are stigmatized by the name of *Rebels.* If, as we affirm, the British government have ceased to rule agreeably to the principles of our constitution, and our royal charter, and have assumed to themselves the high prerogative of despotic sway, then are we absolved from our allegiance and duties as British subjects. A contract abrogated by one party, can no longer be binding on the other. If we are menaced with royal power and authority, we justify ourselves in defending our indefeasible rights against despotism and tyrannical oppression. Cowards alone will bend to unjust power, and slaves and sycophants only will yield both soul and body to the disposal of tyrannical masters. Should our efforts, under God, be crowned with the desired success, we shall obtain the honor of rescuing ourselves and posterity from vassalage; but if compelled to succumb under royal power, then will ours be the rebel's fate, the scaffold and the gibbet will be glutted with their devoted victims. We cannot justly be accused of a rash precipitance of proceeding; for petitions and memorials, couched in the most loyal and humble language, have been at various periods presented to our royal sovereign,

and his parliament, praying for a redress of grievances;
but they are deaf to all our complaints and supplications,
and the coercive arm of power is suspended over us,
threatening implacable vengeance.

Among the odious acts of the British Parliament they
passed one which imposed a duty on the article of tea, and
several cargoes of this commodity were shipped to America
to obtain the duty and a market. On the arrival of the
tea ships at Boston great indignation was excited among
the people; town meetings were called to devise some
legal measures to prohibit the landing of the odious article.
It was universally understood that if the tea was once
landed, and stored, it would by some means come to a
market, and the duty to the government be secured. In
order to defeat this object a number of persons in disguise
entered the ships at the wharves, broke open three hundred and forty-two chests of tea, and discharged their contents into the water at the dock. This was on the 16th
December, 1773. When intelligence of this summary
proceeding reached England, it was condemned by the
government as enormously criminal. They menaced our
province with the most exemplary vengeance, and Parliament soon passed the Boston Vindictive Port Bill as a part
of their coercive system, so that merely the name of tea
is now associated with ministerial grievances, and tea
drinking is almost tantamount to an open avowal of tory-
ism. Those who are anxious to avoid the odious epithet
of enemies to their country, strictly prohibit the use of tea
in their families, and the most squeamish ladies are compelled to have recourse to substitutes, or secretly steal
indulgence in their favorite East India beverage.

March.—For the purpose of enforcing submission to the
cruel mandates of the royal government, a reïnforcement
of the British army has arrived at Boston; and General
Gage is appointed Governor and Commander in Chief.
An armed fleet also occupies the harbor; and the whole
port is closed against all but British vessels. In short,
the horrors of civil war seem stalking, with rapid strides,
towards our devoted country. The people have resorted
to the expedient of abolishing all the courts of justice
under the new regulations. In our shire towns the populace have collected in sufficient numbers to bar the doors

MAJOR GENERAL ISRAEL PUTNAM.

of the court houses, and prohibit the entrance of judges
and officers; the jurors are so intimidated, or zealous in
the good cause, that in general they refuse to take the oath,
or to act in any manner under the new modification of
government; and the clerks of courts, who have issued
warrants by which the jurors are summoned, have in many
instances been compelled to acknowledge their contrition,
and to publish in the newspapers, a full recantation. At
the regular term of the Court of Common Pleas at Barnstable in September last, I witnessed the following prompt
procedure. A body of about twelve hundred men assembled and obstructed the passage to the court-house door.
The leader of this assemblage was Dr. Nathaniel Freeman,
a bold son of liberty, of Sandwich. Colonel James Otis,
the chief justice of the court, preceded by the sheriff,
approached; and the venerable chief justice demanded
admission. Dr. Freeman replied that it was the intention
of the people to prevent the court's being opened to exercise those unconstitutional powers with which they are
invested by Parliament. The chief justice, in his majesty's name, commanded them to disperse, and permit the
court to enter and proceed to business. But his majesty's
name had lost its power; it can have no charms with the
sons of liberty. The venerable judge then said he had
acquitted himself of his duty, and retired. This proceeding had been discussed and concerted prior to the court
term; and Colonel Otis himself, a stanch whig, was, it is
believed, not only apprized of, but actually acquiesced in,
this bold measure. This excellent man is now advanced
to about seventy-four years in life; he is considered as
possessing sound sense and good judgment; and as being
of the purest integrity. He has been, for many years, the
leading law character in the Old Colony, and a member
of his majesty's council of the province; but his patriotism
and zeal in the cause of our country have rendered him
and his family exceedingly odious to Governor Hutchinson
and other adherents of the crown. Colonel Otis is the
parent of that great champion, and able advocate for liberty
and the rights of man, James Otis, jun. Esq. This gentleman is now in a melancholy state of mental derangement; and all New England is deploring the irreparable
loss of the talents, eloquence, and patriotic services of this

justly celebrated character. Colonel Otis has two other sons, Joseph and Samuel Allen Otis, who are active whigs; and a daughter, married to James Warren, Esq. of Plymouth, who is now President of our provincial Congress. Though no judicial courts are in existence, few crimes are committed; all is peace, order and regularity. The people are their own rulers, and never was there less need of penal laws. Trivial disputes are mutually adjusted or decided by reference; pecuniary demands are suspended, and the simple recommendations of Congress, and of our committees of safety, receive that cheerful acquiescence which is scornfully denied to the coercive edicts emanating from despotic power. For

"Freedom has a thousand charms, to show
That slaves, howe'er contented, never know."

We have a provincial Congress in session at Concord, consisting of delegates elected by the people, and also a grand Continental Congress at Philadelphia, composed of characters highly distinguished for political wisdom, rigid patriotism and public virtue.

The public indignation is now greatly excited by the following shameful transaction. The people from the country, whose business called them into Boston, were suspected by the officers of purchasing guns from their soldiers. In order to furnish an opportunity to inflict punishment and to raise occasion for a serious quarrel, Lieutenant Colonel Nesbit of the forty-seventh regiment ordered a soldier to offer a countryman an old rusty musket. A man from Billerica was caught by this bait, and purchased the gun for three dollars. The unfortunate man was immediately seized by Nesbit, and confined in the guard-house all night. Early next morning they stripped him entirely naked, covered him over with warm tar, and then with feathers, placed him on a cart, and conducted him through the streets as far as liberty-tree, where the people began to collect in vast numbers; and the military, fearing for their own safety, dismissed the man, and retreated to their barracks. The party consisted of about thirty grenadiers with fixed bayonets, twenty drums and fifes playing the Rogues' March, headed by the redoubtable Nesbit with a drawn sword! What an honorable deed for a British field officer and grenadiers! The selectmen of Billerica remonstrated with General Gage respecting this outrage, but obtained no satisfaction.

April 21st.—Intelligence is now received that the British regulars have marched out of Boston, and actually commenced hostilities against our people at Lexington. For the purpose of ascertaining the particular facts, I have been desired to wait on Colonel Otis, at his mansion in this town. It was in the evening, when I found this dignified patriot in his easy-chair, with several of his neighbors listening with agitated spirits to some account of this first most awful tragedy. The good old gentleman had received a letter containing a statement of some particulars, and with manifest trepidation he said to this effect: "The British troops marched to Lexington and Concord last Wednesday, the 19th instant, for the purpose of destroying some of our military stores; our militia collected and met them at Lexington; the regulars soon commenced firing on them; our people returned the fire; a smart skirmish ensued, and several men were killed on both sides. The British were compelled to retreat, in some confusion, to Boston; and our people pursued and harassed them. The fearful day has arrived! a civil war has actually commenced in our land. We must be prepared for the worst, and may God preserve and protect our country." This tragical event seems to have electrified all classes of people; the brave are fired with manly resentment, the timid overwhelmed in despair; the patriotic whigs sorrowing over public calamities, while the tories indulge the secret hope, that the friends of liberty are about to receive their chastisement. The sword is now unsheathed, and our friends are slaughtered by our cruel enemies; expresses are hastening from town to town, in all directions through the country, spreading the melancholy tidings and inspiriting and rousing the people *To Arms! To Arms!* The people of New England have taken the alarm, and their hearts are animated even to enthusiasm. There is an enthusiasm in religion, in politics, in military achievements, and in gallantry and love, and why not an enthusiasm in the love of country? No species of enthusiasm surely can be more laudable, or more honorable. Never was a cause more just, more sacred than ours; we are commanded to defend the rich inheritance bequeathed to us by our virtuous ancestors; and it is our bounden duty to transmit it uncontaminated to posterity; we must fight valiantly therefore, for our lives and property, for our *holy religion*, for our honor, and for our dearest friends. We are not born to be slaves, and are resolved to live and die free; appealing to the Sovereign Ruler of the Universe for the justice of our cause, and relying on his Almighty arm for protection and support. A certain number of active men, in every town, have formed themselves into military companies, under the name of *minute-men;* they are daily practising the manual exercise, and are held in constant readiness to march against the enemy at a moment's warning. We await with trembling expectation the issue of every hour.

Authenticated accounts are now received of the battle at Lexington. On Tuesday evening, 18th instant, General Gage despatched, with as much secrecy as possible, a detachment consisting of eight or nine hundred regulars, under the command of Lieutenant-Colonel Smith, for the purpose of destroying some military stores which our people had deposited at Concord, about eighteen miles from Boston. Having arrived at Lexington, six miles short of Concord, they were met by a company of militia, of about one hundred men, who, having taken the alarm, began to assemble from different towns before daylight. They were assembled near the church, about sunrise; when the British advanced in quick march to within a few rods, Major Pitcairn called out, "*Disperse, you Rebels! throw down your arms and disperse.*" Their small number would not admit of opposition, and while they were dispersing, the regulars huzzaed, and immediately one or two pistols were fired by the officers, and four or five muskets by the soldiers; when a pretty general discharge from the whole party followed, by which eight of our people were killed and seven wounded. The British now renewed their march to Concord, where they destroyed a few articles of stores and sixty barrels of flour. Here they were met by about one hundred and fifty militia-men, on whom they fired, and killed two and wounded others. Our militia and minute-men were now collecting in considerable numbers, and being justly enraged they made a bold and furi-

ous attack on the enemy, and drove them in *quick march*
to Lexington. General Gage having received intelligence
of the critical situation of his troops, immediately ordered
out Lord Percy, with a large rëinforcement, with two field
pieces. He marched over the neck through Roxbury, his
music playing by way of contempt and derision the tune
of " *Yankee doodle.*" This timely rëinforcement joined the
party under command of Colonel Smith at Lexington,
which formed a force of about eighteen hundred men.
They soon deemed it prudent to commence their march
to Boston, the provincial militia and minute-men, continually increasing in numbers, pursued and flanked them
with the hope of cutting off their retreat. A constant
skirmishing ensued; the provincials concealed themselves
behind stone walls, and with a sure aim thinned their
enemies' ranks, and occasioned among them great confusion. On their side, they could only keep up a scattering
fire, without effect, frequently firing over the stone walls,
when there was not a man to be seen behind them. The
great object of the British, was to effect a safe retreat to
Boston; but, to avenge themselves, they burnt and plundered houses, destroyed property, and actually murdered
several innocent unarmed persons. The situation of the
king's forces was, during the day, extremely hazardous;
and it is considered wonderful that any of them escaped.
Worn down and almost exhausted with fatigue, and their
ammunition nearly expended, they had become nearly
defenceless when they reached Charlestown, in the evening, after a loss of two hundred and seventy-three men,
killed, wounded and prisoners. The loss on the side of
the Provincials is eighty-eight in the whole. The British
officers have received a specimen of *Yankee courage,* which
they have hitherto affected to hold in the most sovereign
contempt; they have ascertained, by fatal experience, that
the people of New England will bid defiance to their veteran regulars, and fight courageously in defence of their
rights. It is truly said to be matter of astonishment and
chagrin, that after all their glorying, their veteran troops
have been compelled to flee before a comparatively small
number of undisciplined *Yankees.* The origin of this term,
so frequently employed by way of reproach to the New
England people, is said to be as follows: A farmer, by

name Jonathan Hastings, of Cambridge, about the year 1713, used it as a cant, favorite word, to express excellency when applied to any thing; as a Yankee good horse, Yankee cider, &c., meaning an excellent horse and excellent cider. The students at college, having frequent intercourse with Mr. Hastings, and hearing him employ the term on all occasions, adopted it themselves, and gave him the name of Yankee Jonathan; this soon became a cant word among the collegians to express a weak, simple, awkward person, and from college it was carried and circulated through the country, till, from its currency in New England, it was at length taken up and unjustly applied to the New Englanders in common, as a term of reproach. It was in consequence of this that a particular song, called " *Yankee doodle*," was composed in derision of those scornfully called Yankees.*

May.—Since the catastrophe at Lexington, our Provincial Congress have addressed the several towns of the colony in a circular letter, in the following impressive language: "We conjure you by all that is dear, by all that is sacred, that you give all assistance possible in forming the army. Our all is at stake. Death and devastation are the certain consequences of delay. Every moment is infinitely precious. An hour lost may deluge your country in blood, and entail perpetual slavery on the few of your posterity who may survive the carnage. We beg and entreat, as you will answer it to your country, to your consciences, and, above all, as you will answer it to God himself, that you will hasten and encourage, by all possible means, the enlistment of men to form the army, and send them forward to head-quarters at Cambridge, with that expedition which the vast importance and instant urgency of the affair demands."

It is scarcely possible to describe the zeal and military ardor which pervades New England since the battle at Lexington. It is supposed that nearly forty thousand men have been in arms with the design of investing the town of Boston, and avenging themselves on the enemy

---

* There appears some incongruity in the above definition of the word Yankee. The following is supposed by some to be the origin from which it is derived: "Yankee is the Indian corruption of *English. Yenglees, Yangles, Yankles,* and finally *Yankee.*"

for their late slaughter of our brethren. The universal voice is "*starve them out.*" Drive them from the town, and let his majesty's ships be their only place of refuge. Our Provincial Congress have resolved that an army of thirty thousand men be immediately raised and established. A considerable number have already enlisted, and being formed into regiments, have taken their station at Cambridge and Roxbury. The country militia, in great numbers, have arrived from various parts of New England; and the town of Boston is now invested on all sides, and thus is the whole royal army reduced to the humble condition of a besieged garrison. The situation of the inhabitants is deplorable; a considerable proportion of the most affluent have removed into the country; but others, from various circumstances, are compelled to remain and suffer all the calamities of a besieged town and precarious subsistence. Instances indeed are not wanting of members of families being torn from each other, women and children flying from their husbands and parents, under the most afflictive and destitute circumstances.

We are now experiencing a singular kind of interregnum in our province; more than a year has elapsed without any legal government, or any regular administration of law and justice.—No crimes, however, of an atrocious nature have, we believe, been perpetrated; all classes of people appear to be submissive, under the influence of the principles of moral rectitude and common justice; and the resolutions and recommendations of Congress have all the weight and efficacy of laws. Our domestic tranquillity is in some measure interrupted by a restless spirit among the tories; but the great body of the community are actuated by the glorious cause of our country's freedom. The maxim adopted by our enemies is, "*Divide and conquer.*" We enjoin the command, "*Unite and be invincible.*" It is considered infinitely important to encourage and promote a more perfect union among the colonies, and harmony and unanimity among the people. "*Liberty or death,*" "*Unite or die,*" are the mottoes which blazon the chronicles of the day, and embellish the military standards of almost every militia company. The man who does not acquiesce in the theme of liberty is marked by the vigilant eye of suspicion, or stigmatized as an enemy to his country. Liberty-poles are erected in almost every town and village; and when a disaffected tory renders himself odious, by any active conduct, with the view of counteracting the public measures, he is seized by a company of armed men, and conducted to the liberty-pole, under which he is compelled to sign a recantation, and give bonds for his future good conduct. In some instances, of particular stubbornness and obstinacy, individuals have been imprisoned or their names have been published in the newspapers as enemies to their country. It has indeed unfortunately happened, that a few individuals, in consequence of their own indiscretion, have been the subjects of a more rigorous procedure. Having fallen into the hands of those whose zeal has transported them beyond the bounds of moderation, they have received from the rabble a coat of tar and feathers, and in this predicament have been exposed to the scoffs and ridicule of the populace. Such examples have the effect of striking terror into the hearts of all the disaffected, and of restraining the whole party from acting against the general sense of the people. The tories make bitter complaints against the discipline which they receive from the hands of the whigs; their language is, "You make the air resound with the cry of liberty, but subject those who differ from you to the humble condition of slaves, not permitting us to act, or even think, according to the dictates of conscience." The reply is, "It is one of the first principles of a free government, that the majority shall bear rule; our majority is immensely large; we have undertaken the hazardous task of defending the liberties of our country against the mighty power of Great Britian; and hold ourselves responsible for our conduct. If you possess not patriotism and courage enough to unite your efforts with ours, it is our duty to put it out of your power to injure the common cause. If we are successful, your party and posterity will participate in the important advantages to be derived from our efforts. If our party should be crushed, then will yours in turn become triumphant." A small number of our tories have abandoned their homes, their families and property, and resorted to the standard of their royal master in Boston; consoling themselves in the confident expectation of an ample reward, and a triumphant restoration. The clergymen of New England are, almost without excep-

BENJAMIN FRANKLIN.

tion, advocates of whig principles; there are a few instances only of the separation of a minister from his people, in consequence of a disagreement in political sentiment. The tories censure, in a very illiberal manner, the preacher who speaks boldly for the liberties of the people, while they lavish their praises on him who dares to teach the absurd doctrine, that magistrates have a divine right to do wrong, and are to be implicitly obeyed. It is recommended by our Provincial Congress, that on other occasions than the Sabbath, ministers of parishes adapt their discourses to the times, and explain the nature of civil and religious liberty, and the duties of magistrates and rulers. Accordingly, we have from our pulpits the most fervent and pious effusions to the throne of Divine Grace in behalf of our bleeding, afflicted country. A zealous divine, who has been compelled to abandon the people of his charge in Boston, on one occasion used, in the pulpit at P***, the following emphatical language: "Oh! Lord, if our enemies will fight us, let them have fighting enough. If more soldiers are on their way hither, sink them, O Lord, to the bottom of the sea." Every heart seemed ready to respond, "Amen, yea, let them have fighting enough."

June 14th.—General Gage has issued a proclamation declaring the province of Massachusetts Bay to be in a state of rebellion, offering a pardon to all who will resort to his standard, and denouncing the penalty of martial law on all those who refuse to submit to his authority, or who shall be found aiding or corresponding with such as he has designated as unpardonable rebels and traitors. He has been pleased to proscribe by name, Mr. John Hancock and Mr. Samuel Adams, as objects of his exemplary vengeance. Yet, singular at it may appear, this same authorized governor, and general-in-chief of the royal army, is now cooped up in the town of Boston, panting for a country airing, of which he is debarred by his denounced rebels.

We are again shocked by intelligence that a terrible battle has been fought between the British regulars and the American soldiers, on Bunker, or rather Breed's hill, in Charlestown, near Boston, on the 17th instant. The report states that the whole town of Charlestown is burnt to ashes by the enemy, and that Dr. Joseph Warren, lately

appointed major-general in our army, is killed; and that
several hundreds of our soldiers are killed and wounded.
The battle, it is said, was extremely severe and destructive;
but the provincial troops displayed the greatest courage
and bravery, in the face of the regulars, and have obtained
immortal honor. The British were several times defeated
before they took possession of our works, and have suffered a loss of more than a thousand of their best troops;
among whom are a large proportion of their most valuable officers. They are now taught that Americans can bid
defiance to royal regulars, when called to defend their
freedom. The situation of our country is truly deplorable, a civil war at our doors; our neighbors, our fathers
and brothers, called from their families to encounter an
inexorable enemy, consisting indeed of brethren and kin-
dred; our domestic peace and welfare cruelly interrupted,
and the aspect of our public affairs gloomy in the extreme.
All New England has become a theatre of military array;
and every member of the community manifests the deepest
concern for the great calamities with which the country is
afflicted, by the tyrannical measures of a corrupt administration. In the favor of Heaven and the wisdom of our
Congress we repose all our hope and confidence. Participating, I trust, in the glorious spirit of the times, and
contemplating improvement in my professional pursuits,
motives of patriotism and private interest prompt me to
hazard my fortune in this noble conflict with my brethren
in the provincial army. From the critical and embarrassed
situation of our country, numerous and almost insurmountable difficulties are opposed to my view; and I am too
young to possess a maturity of judgment, but yet unable
to resist the impulse of enthusiasm which characterizes
the times. My friends afford me no encouragement, alleging that, as this is a civil war, if I should fall into the
hands of the British, the gallows will be my fate. The
terrors of the gallows are not to be conquered, but I must
indulge the hope that I may escape it. Hundreds of my
superiors may take their turn before mine shall come. The
tories assail me with the following powerful arguments:
"Young man, are you sensible you are about to violate
your duty to the best of kings, and run headlong into destruction? Be assured that this rebellion will be of short

duration. The royal army is all-powerful, and will, in a few months, march through the country and bring all to subjection; for they are experienced in war and expert in discipline. Their fleet is able to destroy every seaport town and beat down all our cities. There remains no rational alternative but a reconciliation and renewed obedience to our lawful government; or we shall soon experience their just vengeance. What is your army but an undisciplined rabble? Can they stand against an army of regulars? Where are your cannon, your fire-arms, your bayonets, and all your implements of war? Above all, where is your treasure, and where can you look for a barrel of gunpowder? The whole country can scarcely afford a sufficiency for a battle of an hour." Not a small portion of their reasoning I feel to be just and true. I am not certain, however, but much of it may prove erroneous. The result of the late battle at Charlestown should convince the most incredulous tory that our soldiers will face the regular troops, and we are blessed with the smiles of Heaven on our exertions. It would be presumption in me to determine as to possibilities and prospects; but the voice of liberty cannot be stifled, while the welfare and happiness of more than three millions of people now in America, and of unborn millions, are involved in the issue. Our rulers are the most competent judges, and under their banners I shall venture, I hope not rashly, to enlist, and trust my destiny in the hands of a kind and overruling Providence. My contemplated enterprise, it is true, requires the experience and resolution of riper years than twenty-one, and qualifications, which I do not possess, to ingratiate myself with strangers and those in authority. Having consulted Joseph Otis, Esq. of Barnstable, on this occasion, he immediately applauded my enterprise, and politely furnished me with a letter to his brother-in-law, James Warren, Esq. of Plymouth, who is President of our Provincial Congress at Watertown. Imagination could not fail to paint my prospects in bright colors, and I proceeded, July the 3d, with alacrity to the seat of Congress. I was not disappointed in my interview with Mr. Warren; my letter procured for me a favorable and polite reception. He honored me with his friendship and kind assistance, and introduced me to his lady, whose father's

family and my own, have for many years been on terms
of friendly intercourse. The office which I solicit is one
in the medical department, in the provincial hospital at
Cambridge. A medical board, consisting of Drs. Holton
and Taylor, are appointed to examine the candidates; and
they added my name to the list for examination, on the
10th instant. This state of suspense continuing several
days, excites in my mind much anxiety and solicitude,
apprehending that my stock of medical knowledge, when
scanned by a learned committee, may be deemed inadequate, and all my hopes be blasted. While on my journey,
a visit of a few days to my friends at Plymouth gave me
an opportunity to pay my respects to the *rock* which received the first footsteps of our venerated forefathers.
The inhabitants of this ancient town, from a reverence
for the memory of the virtuous band of brothers from
whom we derive our origin, have lately, with commendable zeal and much labor, split off the upper portion of
the rock, and removed it to a public square near the church
and court-house. This rock, with its associations, would
seem almost capable of imparting that love of country,
and that moral virtue, which our times so much require.
We seem holding converse with the celestial spirits, and
receiving monition from those who are at rest in their
graves. Have these ancient sages bequeathed their mantle
to posterity? Can we set our feet on their rock without
swearing, by the spirit of our fathers, to defend it and
our country? If we reflect on their matchless enterprise,
their fortitude, and their sufferings, we must be inspired
with the spirit of patriotism, and the most invincible heroism. Unappalled by the dangers of unknown seas, and
the perils and the hardships of a savage wilderness, they
left their native country, and undertook a settlement which
promises, through ages, to remain the rich abode of knowledge, religion, virtue and freedom. Let us, then, cherish
a becoming sense of the exalted privileges inherited from
our ancestors, and resolve to defend them against all attempts of a corrupt administration.

July.—I improve the interim of my suspense to record
an authentic narrative of the *battle on Breed's hill*, on the
17th of June. Intelligence had been received that it was
he intention of General Gage to post a part of his troops,

within a few days, on a promontory just at the entrance of the peninsula at Charlestown, called Bunker's hill. It was deemed important that our troops should possess themselves of this eminence, before the enemy could occupy it. Accordingly orders were given to Colonel Prescott, a veteran of the last war, with one thousand men, to march silently in the evening of 16th of June, and throw up some intrenchments on the height of Bunker's hill. By some mistake they took possession of Breed's hill, which, being about one-fourth of a mile nearer Boston, was less capable of being defended. From some cause, the detachment was always delayed in their labor, till twelve o'clock; but such was their alacrity, that before day-light they had formed a small redoubt and some imperfect line of defence. About four o'clock in the morning the British were astonished to behold the works which had been thrown up in a single night, within a short distance of their vessels, without giving the least alarm. They immediately commenced a tremendous cannonade from their shipping, their floating batteries, and from all their fortifications, which could have a bearing on the American works. Bombs and shot were incessantly rolling among the provincials during the forenoon, till the royal grenadiers and light infantry could be prepared to make their formidable attack; yet one man only was killed; and the Americans courageously persevered in strengthening their works. They received in the course of the forenoon a small reïnforcement, which augmented their number to about fifteen hundred, and this was not much exceeded during the day of battle. It was by an unaccountable error that those people, who had been laboring all the night, were not relieved by others, nor even furnished with provisions before the battle. Generals Putnam, Warren and Pomeroy, animated and encouraged the troops with their presence. At about one o'clock, 17th of June, the royal forces were observed to cross the river from Boston, and land on the shore at Charlestown; at the head of these veterans were Major-General Howe and Brigadier-General Pigot; their force consisted of about three thousand men, well provided with field-artillery. They formed in two lines, their officers haranguing them probably in such language as this: "Those cowardly rebels must and shall be put to flight. See the

dastardly Yankees with rusty guns and scarcely a bayonet
among them. March on, my lads, march on! show them
that you are Britons; show them these dazzling arms and
bayonets bright and sharp, and you shall soon see them
take to their heels and run." Hear the voice of Putnam,
of Prescott and Warren: "See, my brave soldiers, that
phalanx approaching; these lines must and shall be defended; these are the cruel enemies to your freedom; they
have come to enslave you; remember their barbarous murders of our friends at Lexington; fight manfully, and
they shall be vanquished; reserve your fire till their near
approach; then with a sure aim cut them down, and the
victory shall be ours." The regulars deliberately advance
to the attack, the grenadiers in front. The Americans
reserve their fire till the enemy are within eight or ten
rods, that they may do effectual execution; when, by a
general discharge of musketry and field-artillery, several
officers and men are seen to fall, "their ranks are thinned;
see the ground covered with the slain; see those wounded
officers borne off the field." The conflict becomes close,
and such are the fatal effects of the incessant and furious
discharge of our musketry, that the regulars retreat in
disorder, and many of them flee even to their boats. The
officers, greatly agitated, pursue their men, and threaten
them with their swords; with great difficulty they are
rallied, and commanded to advance again to the attack.
The provincials are prepared, and when sufficiently near,
a deadly fire from their ranks puts the enemy a second
time to flight, leaving such numbers of dead and wounded
that several of their officers exclaim, "It is downright
butchery to lead the men on afresh against the lines." At
this critical moment Major-General Clinton, who till now
had been a spectator with General Burgoyne on Copp's hill
in Boston, passed over and entered the field, just in time
to unite his efforts with those of the other officers for the
purpose of forcing the regulars to renew the attack. The
Americans still remain firm and courageous at their posts;
but unfortunately it was now discovered that their powder
was nearly expended, and another supply could not be
procured. The enemy now change the position of their
cannon, and place them in a situation to rake the inside
of our breastwork in its whole course, which at length

obliges the provincials to retire within their little redoubt. The firing from the British ships, and other armed vessels and batteries, is now pushed to the utmost extremity; the regulars are impelled forward by their officers, and our redoubt is attacked on three sides at the same time. Our brave men continue their resistance, and actually confront the enemy with the butt-end of their muskets after they had entered the fort. A party of our men under command of Captain Knowlton had taken up a post and rail fence, and placing it against another, filled the vacancy with newly mowed hay, which served as a slight defence. The British light infantry attempted to force this little party from their stand, and by this means to cut off the retreat of our troops. In this they displayed the greatest bravery, but their opposers poured forth their reserved and formi dable fire in such a manner as to produce astonishing execution, and to arrest their progress, till the whole of the Americans could effect a retreat. The narrow neck of land over which alone the provincials could retire, was so securely guarded by a man of war and two floating batteries, as to render it extremely hazardous to pass over; but notwithstanding their incessant firing, our loss there was quite inconsiderable. The provincials were obliged to leave five pieces of field-artillery in the hands of the enemy, finding it impossible to remove them. But a loss infinitely to be lamented, and which occasions universal grief and sorrow, is that of Major-General Joseph War- ren. This distinguished patriot and hero was, but a few days before, appointed by Congress to the rank of major- general in our army. Such was his zeal and ardor, that he rushed into the battle foremost in danger with his musket, and encouraged the soldiers by his example, till near the close of the battle, when he received a fatal shot, and immediately expired. The loss at this crisis of a man possessing so much public virtue and military ardor is almost irreparable. But the valor with which he is signalized reflects glory on his memory. It yet remains to mention that on this ever-memorable day, just at the commencement of the battle, General Howe ordered the handsome town of Charlestown to be set on fire, that the smoke might conceal their manœuvres. The town con- sisted of upwards of three hundred dwelling-houses, some of them elegant, and about two hundred buildings of other descriptions, which contained property and goods to a large amount, belonging to the distressed inhabitants of Boston. Fire was communicated to a number of houses, which, being wafted by the wind, soon reached the sacred temple, when the flames issued from its lofty spire; while from the conflagration and the embattled field, smoke mingled with smoke in majestic columns, and ascended to the clouds. This, with the roaring of cannon, sheets of fire from the musketry, and the awful slaughter, formed a spectacle which for sublimity and grandeur has never perhaps been exceeded. This most dreadful scene, with all its concomitant horrors, was within view of a vast concourse of agonized spectators, posted on the tops of houses and steeples in Boston, and on numerous surrounding hills, hundreds of whom were trembling for the fate of a parent, a husband or a brother. Well might a devout person exclaim, "Good Heavens! what a scene do I behold! what carnage of the human race! what sacrifice of precious life. My God! stay thy hand, restrain a further effusion of human blood, spare the innocent, let punishment fall on the heads of the guilty. Is there not some hidden curse in reserve for our country's foes!" At the head of the British army General Howe advanced with undaunted bravery, continually pressing into the most exposed situation. It is truly wonderful that he escaped with only a wound in his foot. The valiant Major Pitcairn, who was so conspicuously active at Lexington, was among the first who mounted our breastworks, and at the moment when he was heard to exclaim, "the day is ours," the fatal ball pierced his body and he fell. His son, a captain, received him in his arms, with all the ardor of filial love and tender sympathy, and bore him to the boat, where he expired. On the American side, Generals Putnam, Warren, Pomeroy, and Colonel Prescott were emphatically the heroes of the day, and their unexampled efforts were crowned with glory. The incomparable Colonel Prescott marched at the head of the detachment, and though several general officers were present, he retained the command during the action. He displayed a native daring bravery altogether unrivalled, and infused the conquering spirit of a soldier into the hearts of all who were under his command, and

JOHN HANCOCK.

crowned himself with immortal honor. Colonel John Stark commanded a regiment from New Hampshire, and signalized himself by his active bravery. His very valiant Major McClary was killed by a cannon-ball while recrossing Charlestown neck, which is lamented as a public loss. On this never-to-be-forgotten occasion a fair opportunity was presented for the trial of the courage and prowess of the people of New England, when contending for their constitutional freedom. They marched to the field as an undisciplined, inexperienced body of yeomanry, rather than as professed warriors; a large majority of them carrying ordinary fire-arms, unprovided with bayonets, and habited in the style of country laborers. It was their lot to contend with an army of disciplined veterans, professedly experienced in the art of warfare, uniformly clothed and armed, and commanded by generals whose names, even in Europe, are little less than a host.

The comparative force of the two armies was about two to one against the provincials, besides the royal artillery, ships, and other armed vessels. What in fact is the result of this most unequal combat? Certain it is, that on the first and the second onset, the veterans were fairly repulsed, and whatever advantage was ultimately obtained, was at the expense of some of their most valuable officers and the flower of the British grenadiers and light infantry. These two corps, at the moment of their first onset, lost three-fourths of their number; of one company five, and of another, fourteen only escaped. The remarkable disparity of loss is a clear demonstration of the superior advantage on our side. It is an ascertained fact, that of the enemy nineteen commissioned officers were killed and seventy wounded; and their total loss, according to General Gage, was one thousand and fifty-four. Of the provincials, the killed and dead of their wounds, are one hundred and thirty-nine. Other wounded, two hundred and seventy-eight. Prisoners by the enemy, thirty-six. Total, four hundred and fifty-three. The provincials have much reason to triumph on the successful issue of this first general conflict with veteran troops; it must tend greatly to increase their confidence in their own powers, and give them a serious impression that we are favored with the smiles of Heaven. Had our troops been furnished

3

with a sufficient quantity of ammunition, the enemy must
have suffered a total defeat. After our troops retreated,
the regulars took possession of their dear-bought Bunker's
hill, and immediately fortified themselves there. It is
said that some of the veteran British officers, who have
been in some hard-fought battles in Europe, observed, that
they had never witnessed any one equal in severity to that
on Breed's hill. It is presumed they will no longer apply
the term poltroons to American soldiers. A considerable
number of tories, whose zeal for the royal cause led them
into battle, were killed or wounded. Our army has taken
post at Cambridge and Roxbury, in such a manner as to
invest the town of Boston. Our general officers are Generals Ward, Pomeroy, Thomas and Heath, of Massachusetts colony, and General Putnam from Connecticut.

On the day appointed, the medical candidates, sixteen
in number, were summoned before the board for examination. This business occupied about four hours; the subjects were anatomy, physiology, surgery and medicine.
It was not long after, that I was happily relieved from
suspense, by receiving the sanction and acceptance of the
board, with some acceptable instructions relative to the
faithful discharge of duty, and the humane treatment of
those soldiers who may have the misfortune to require
my assistance. Six of our number were privately rejected
as being found unqualified. The examination was in a
considerable degree close and severe, which occasioned
not a little agitation in our ranks. But it was on another
occasion, as I am told, that a candidate under examination
was agitated into a state of perspiration, and being required
to describe the mode of treatment in rheumatism, among
other remedies he would promote a sweat, and being asked
how he would effect this with his patient, after some hesitation he replied, "I would have him examined by a
medical committee." I was so fortunate as to obtain the
office of surgeon's mate in the provincial hospital at Cambridge, Dr. John Warren being the senior surgeon. He
was the brother and pupil of the gallant General Joseph
Warren, who was slain in the memorable battle on Breed's
hill. This gentleman has acquired great reputation in his
profession, and is distinguished for his humanity and attention to the sick and wounded soldiers, and for his

amiable disposition. Having received my appointment by the Provincial Congress, I commenced my duty in the hospital, July 15th. Several private, but commodious, houses in Cambridge are occupied for hospitals, and a considerable number of soldiers who were wounded at Breed's hill, and a greater number of sick of various diseases, require all our attention. Dr. Isaac Foster, late of Charlestown, is also appointed a senior hospital surgeon; and his student, Mr. Josiah Bartlet, officiates as his mate; Dr. Benjamin Church is director-general of the hospital.

I am informed that General George Washington arrived at our provincial camp, in this town, on the 2d July; having been appointed, by the unanimous voice of the Continental Congress at Philadelphia, general and commander-in-chief of all the troops raised, and to be raised, for the defence of the United Colonies, as they are now termed. They are, New Hampshire, Massachusetts, Rhode Island, Connecticut, New York, New Jersey, Pennsylvania, Delaware, Maryland, Virginia, North Carolina, South Carolina, and Georgia. General Washington is a native of Virginia; he was in General Braddock's defeat in 1755, and having had considerable experience in the wars with the French and Indians on the frontiers of that colony, in former years, he is supposed to possess ample qualifications for the command of our army, and the appointment gives universal satisfaction. Such is his disinterested patriotism, that he assured Congress, on his appointment, that he should receive from the public, for his military services, no other compensation than the amount of his necessary expenses. He has been received here with every mark of respect, and addressed by our Provincial Congress in the most affectionate and respectful manner. All ranks appear to repose full confidence in him as commander-in-chief; it is the fervent prayer of the religiously disposed, that he may be instrumental in bringing this unhappy controversy to an honorable and speedy termination. He is accompanied by General Lee and General Gates; two gentlemen who have held commissions in the royal army. The former is now appointed major-general, and the latter adjutant-general, by our Continental Congress. General Washington has established his head-quarters in a convenient house, about half a mile from Harvard College, and in the vicinity of our hospital. The provincial army is encamped in various parts of this town and Roxbury, and some works have been erected on Prospect hill, and on an eminence near Roxbury church, within cannon-shot of Boston. The amount of our forces I have not ascertained; but we are daily increasing in numbers, both of militia and enlisted soldiers. The operations of the war have interrupted the progress of education at college; the students have returned to their homes, and the college buildings are occupied by our soldiery.

July 20th.—This day is devoted to a Public Fast throughout the United Colonies, by the recommendation of Congress, to implore the Divine benediction on our country; that any further shedding of blood may be averted; and that the calamities with which we are afflicted may be removed. This is the first general or Continental Fast ever observed since the settlement of the colonies. I have been much gratified this day with a view of General Washington. His excellency was on horseback, in company with several military gentlemen. It was not difficult to distinguish him from all others; his personal appearance is truly noble and majestic; being tall and well proportioned. His dress is a blue coat with buff-colored facings, a rich epaulette on each shoulder, buff under dress, and an elegant small sword; a black cockade in his hat.

August.—The firing of cannon is now frequently practised from our works at Prospect hill and Winter hill, advantageous eminences in full view and within cannon-shot of the enemy's camp on Bunker's hill; and some shot are returned from the enemy; but without any considerable loss. At Roxbury also our people have fortified several hills, and breastworks are thrown up across the main street, within half a mile of the British lines; from which cannon-shot and some bomb-shells are every day thrown into Boston. The enemy fire their cannon-shot into Roxbury, and several have passed through the church; but little damage has yet been sustained, and our soldiers become so familiarized to the sight of cannon-shot rolling among them, that they manifest little or no fear of the consequences. The right wing of our army at Roxbury is commanded by Major-General Ward; and the left at Prospect hill, by Major-General Lee.

CAPTAIN BENJAMIN CHURCH.

The Continental Congress having voted, "That a sum not exceeding two millions of Spanish milled dollars be emitted by them in bills of credit for the defence of America," gold and silver soon disappeared, and paper bills now circulate instead of specie.

Several companies of riflemen, amounting, it is said, to more than fourteen hundred men, have arrived here from Pennsylvania and Maryland; a distance of from five hundred to seven hundred miles. They are remarkably stout and hardy men; many of them exceeding six feet in height. They are dressed in white frocks, or rifle-shirts, and round hats. These men are remarkable for the accuracy of their aim; striking a mark with great certainty at two hundred yards distance. At a review, a company of them, while on a quick advance, fired their balls into objects of seven inches diameter, at the distance of two hundred and fifty yards. They are now stationed on our lines, and their shot have frequently proved fatal to British officers and soldiers who expose themselves to view, even at more than double the distance of common musket-shot.

October.—An event of considerable importance has occurred, which occasions much surprise and speculation. Dr. Benjamin Church has long sustained high reputation as a patriot and son of liberty. He has, for some time, been a member of our House of Representatives; and has been appointed surgeon-general and director of our hospitals. This gentleman has just been detected in a traitorous correspondence with the enemy in Boston. A letter in cipher, written by him, was intrusted to the care of a female, with whom he was well acquainted, to be conveyed to Boston. On examination, the woman absolutely refused to reveal the name of the writer, till she was terrified by the threats of severe punishment; when she named Dr. Church, he was greatly agitated and confounded, manifested marks of guilt, and made no attempt to vindicate himself. But after the letter was deciphered, and he had taken time to reflect, he used all his powers of persuasion to make it appear that the letter contained no information that would injure the American cause; and made a solemn appeal to Heaven that it was written for the purpose of procuring some important intelligence from the enemy. He was tried, convicted, and expelled from the House of Repre-

sentatives; and Congress afterwards resolved, "that he
be closely confined in some secure jail in Connecticut,
without the use of pen, ink, or paper; and that no person
be allowed to converse with him, except in the presence
and hearing of a magistrate, or the sheriff of the county."*

I have just returned from a ramble to Roxbury, with a
view of meeting with a only person with whom i am acquainted,
I returned after a slight view of the lines and the church
in that town, which is pierced through in many places by
cannon-shot from the enemy.

10*th*.—General Gage has sailed for England; and the
command of the army, has devolved on General William
Howe. He has issued a proclamation, prohibiting all
persons attempting to quit the town, without a written
license, on penalty of military execution, if taken, and if
they escape they are to be proceeded against as traitors,
and their effects to be forfeited; and also declaring, that
if any, who are licensed to depart, attempt carrying away
more than five pounds in specie, they shall forfeit the
whole sum discovered, beside suffering fine and imprisonment. Such is the wretched condition of the Bostonians
since their native town has been converted into a royal
garrison. It is recollected that in April last, it was agreed
between General Gage and a committee of the town, that
on the inhabitants in general surrendering up their fire-
arms to the care of the selectmen, all such inhabitants as
were desirous of removing out of town, should have this
liberty, with their families and effects. The town voted
to comply with this proposal, and General Gage on his
part confirmed the same. It was also stipulated, that those
persons in the country who should incline to remove into
Boston should be permitted to change their residence without molestation. The fire-arms were accordingly surrendered, and some of the inhabitants were allowed to depart;
but it was not long before General Gage found various
pretences to violate his stipulation, and prohibited any
further removals; in consequence of which, many families
were compelled to a cruel separation; husbands and wives,

* Dr. Church was finally permitted to depart from the country. He
and his family embarked for the West Indies; the vessel foundered at
sea, and all were lost.

parents and children, were separated, and the aged and infirm left without protection.

The term for which the continental soldiers enlisted will expire in a few weeks, and it is understood that the recruits for a future army will be enlisted to serve to the 1st of December next, unless sooner discharged, as hopes are yet entertained that a settlement of our difficulties with Great Britain may be effected. Reports are in circulation that an attack on the town of Boston is contemplated; or, that the plan has been agitated and is relinquished, till our people can pass over on the ice. The public appear to be impatient to have our inveterate enemies expelled from our territories.

November.—Our hospitals are considerably crowded with sick soldiers from camp; the prevailing diseases are autumnal fevers and dysenteric complaints, which have proved fatal in a considerable number of instances. It is highly gratifying to observe, that these brave men, while in the service of their country, receive in sickness all the kind attention from physicians and nurses, which their circumstances require; they have the prayers and consolations of pious clergymen, and are destitute of nothing but the presence of their dearest friends to alleviate their sufferings.

I am sorry to have occasion to notice in my journal the following occurrence. The body of a soldier has been taken from the grave, for the purpose, probably of dissection, and the empty coffin left exposed. This affair occasions considerable excitement among our people; both resentment and grief are manifested; as it seems to impress the idea that a soldier's body is held in no estimation after death. Such a practice, if countenanced, might be attended with serious consequences as it respects our soldiers. Much inquiry has been made, but without success, for the discovery of the persons concerned; and the practice in future is strictly prohibited by the commander-in-chief.

The joyful intelligence is now announced in the public papers, that Captain Manly, of Marblehead, commander of one of our privateers, has captured an English ship, bound to Boston, loaded with ordnance stores, of immense value at the present time. Among the ordnance is a large brass mortar on a new construction, and a number of pieces of fine brass cannon. There are small arms, ammunition, utensils, &c. &c. in great abundance. An invoice, it is said, could scarcely be formed of articles better suited to our wants and circumstances. Several other store vessels have been taken by our privateers, with cargoes of provision and various kinds of stores, to a very considerable amount, which greatly augments the distresses of the troops and people in Boston, and affords us a very opportune and essential supply. It is now represented that the distresses of the inhabitants and troops in Boston exceed the possibility of description. They are almost in a state of starvation, for the want of food and fuel. The inhabitants, totally destitute of vegetables, flour and fresh provisions, have actually been obliged to feed on horse flesh; and the troops confined to salt provisions; by means of which they have become very sickly. They have taken down a number of houses, removed the pews from the church, and are digging up the timber at the wharves for fuel.

December 2d.—I visited the park of artillery, and was much gratified to find a collection of ordnance far exceeding my expectations, and such as is supposed by some to be adequate to our present exigence. I had a view of the large brass mortar taken by Captain Manly; it is now called the *Congress*, and will soon be prepared to speak in strong terms to its former masters.

4th.—A considerable number of Connecticut troops have left our service and returned home; no persuasion could induce them to continue in service after their time of enlistment had expired. Enlisting officers are distributed in various parts of New England; but it is reported that voluntary enlistments go on slowly. The people seem to be unwilling to engage in the public service, and require higher wages. The spirit of patriotism appears in some degree to have subsided, and the militia are to be employed.

11th.—A party of militia, said to be about two thousand, have arrived in camp; and information is received that three thousand more are on their march. A few enlisted soldiers have arrived; but so destitute are they of firearms, that it has been found necessary to take the arms by force from the soldiers who retire, paying for them, in order to supply the recruits.

MAJOR GENERAL RICHARD MONTGOMERY.

18th.—The Americans have advanced and *broken* ground at Lechmere's Point, within half a mile of Boston; which occasioned a severe cannonade from the enemy; but they persevered in their work, and suffered but an inconsiderable loss. It is stated, from the minutes of some person, that from Breed's hill battle to the 25th instant, the British have thrown upwards of two thousand shot and shells. By the whole firing, on Cambridge side, they killed only seven, and on Roxbury side five, just a dozen in the whole. At this rate, how many shot and bombs will it require to subdue the whole of his majesty's rebellious subjects?

January, 1776.—At the close of the last year, as is now reported, our army was reduced to a very critical situation, being obliged to substitute new-raised troops and militia in the place of those who had been in service five or six months; and this exchange was made within musket-shot of the enemy's lines. During part of this period, our numbers were not sufficient to man the lines, nor was there powder enough in camp to furnish four rounds a man. Before our privateers had fortunately captured some prizes with cannon and other ordnance, our army before Boston had, I believe, only four small brass cannon and a few old honey-comb iron pieces with their trunnions broken off; and these were ingeniously bedded in timbers in the same manner as that of stocking a musket. These machines were extremely unwieldy and inconvenient, requiring much skill and labor to elevate and depress them. Had the enemy been made acquainted with our situation, the consequences might have been exceedingly distressing.

25th.—The newspapers announce the most painful intelligence from our army in Canada. General Montgomery, the commander, made a desperate, but unsuccessful, assault on the city of Quebec, on the 31st ultimo. The event has proved most fatal and disastrous. General Montgomery and his aid-de-camp, with several other officers, were slain. Colonel Arnold, the second in command, heroically passed the first barrier with his small party, and received a wound in his leg. About three hundred of the continental troops were made prisoners, and about sixty killed and wounded. We remain unacquainted with further particulars. The death of General

Montgomery is universally deplored. In the public papers we have the following account of this brave officer. "He was a captain of grenadiers in the 17th regiment of British troops, of which General Monckton was colonel. He served the last war in the expeditions in the West Indies and America, and returned with his regiment to England. In 1772 he quitted his regiment, though in a fair way of preferment. Whilst in America he imbibed an affection for this country—he had, while in the king's service, declared his disapprobation of the sentiments of the ministry, and viewed America as the rising seat of arts and freedom."

February 9th.—A very considerable firing was heard last evening from Boston; it was occasioned by a detach-ment of one hundred men, under the command of Major Knowlton, who made an incursion into Charlestown, for the purpose of burning a number of houses, to deprive the enemy of their use. He effected the object of his expedition by burning about ten houses in the possession of the enemy, and returned in less than two hours, bringing off some muskets, without the loss of a single man either killed or wounded.

14th.—The following anecdote is worth notice; it ap-pears by extracts from letters written by the officers who are the subjects of it. Some British officers, soon after General Gage arrived at Boston, while walking on Beacon hill in the evening, were frightened by noises in the air, which they took to be the whizzing of bullets. They left the hill with great precipitation, and reported that they were shot at with air-guns, and wrote frightful accounts of the affair to their friends in England. The whizzing noise which so alarmed these valiant officers, could be no other than the buzzing of bugs and beetles while flying in the air.

16th.—It might be supposed that the melancholy aspect of the times, and the dreadful disappointments and priva-tions of the British officers and tories in Boston, would afford matter for the most serious consideration, and effect-ually check every emotion bordering on levity and amuse-ment. We find, however, that they do not deny them-selves balls and theatrical amusements, for they say in the language of the poet,

> "What need of piping for the songs and sherry,
> When our own mis'ries can make us merry."

It is asserted from Boston, that on the evening when Major Knowlton set fire to the houses in Charlestown, 8th instant, the farce of "*The Blockade of Boston*," of which General Burgoyne is the reputed author, was to be performed. The figure designed to burlesque General Washington was dressed in an uncouth style, with a large wig and long rusty sword, attended by his orderly-sergeant in his country dress, having on his shoulder an old rusty gun, seven or eight feet long. At the moment this figure appeared on the stage, one of the regular sergeants came running on the stage, threw down his bayonet, and exclaimed, "The Yankees are attacking our works on Bunker's hill." Those of the audience who were unacquainted with the different parts, supposed that this belonged to the farce; but when General Howe called out, *Officers to your alarm posts*, they were undeceived; all was confusion and dismay; and among the ladies, shrieking and fainting ensued. How pure the satisfaction to a great mind employed in burlesquing those Yankees by whom they are besieged!

18*th*.—Dr. John Morgan of Philadelphia is appointed by Congress director-general of our hospitals, instead of Dr. Church, removed. Since his arrival here, a new and systematic arrangement in the medical department has taken place; the number of surgeon's mates in the hospital is to be reduced, and vacancies in regiments are to be supplied. I have been subjected to another examination by Dr. Morgan, and received from him the appointment of surgeon's mate to Dr. David Townsend, in the regiment commanded by Colonel Asa Whitcomb, stationed in the barracks on Prospect hill.

22*d*.—Our regiment, according to orders, marched to Roxbury, and took quarters in the large and elegant house formerly belonging to Governor Shirley. Great preparations are making in our army for some important event. Several regiments of militia have arrived from the country; and orders have been received for surgeons and mates to prepare lint and bandages, to the amount of two thousand, for fractured limbs and other gun-shot wounds. It is, however, to be hoped that not one-quarter of the number will be required, whatever may be the nature of the occasion. Great activity and animation are observed among our officers and soldiers, who manifest an anxious desire to have a conflict with the enemy. Either a general assault on the town of Boston, or the erection of works on the heights of Dorchester, or both, is generally supposed to be in contemplation.

March 2*d.*—A very heavy discharge of cannon and mortars commenced from all our works at Cambridge and Roxbury.

3*d.*—The firing from our works continues, but the great brass mortar, the *Congress*, and two others, have unfortunately burst; which is exceedingly regretted.

4*th.*—The object in view is now generally understood to be the occupying and fortifying of the advantageous heights of Dorchester. A detachment of our troops is ordered to march for this purpose this evening; and our regiment, with several others, has received orders to march at four o'clock in the morning, to relieve them. We are favored with a full bright moon, and the night is remarkably mild and pleasant; the preparations are immense; more than three hundred loaded carts are in motion. By the great exertions of General Mifflin, our quarter-master-general, the requisite number of teams has been procured. The covering party of eight hundred men advance in front. Then follow the carts with the intrenching tools; after which, the working party of twelve hundred, commanded by General Thomas, of Kingston. Next in the martial procession are a train of carts, loaded with fascines and hay, screwed into large bundles of seven or eight hundred weight. The whole procession moved on in solemn silence, and with perfect order and regularity; while the continued roar of cannon serves to engage the attention and divert the enemy from the main object.

5*th.*—At about four o'clock our regiment followed to the heights of Dorchester, as a relief party. On passing Dorchester neck I observed a vast number of large bundles of screwed hay, arranged in a line next the enemy, to protect our troops from a raking fire, to which we should have been greatly exposed, while passing and repassing. The carts were still in motion with materials; some of them have made three or four trips. On the heights we found two forts in considerable forwardness, and sufficient for a defence against small arms and grape-shot. The amount of labor performed during the night, considering the earth is frozen eighteen inches deep, is almost incredible. The enemy having discovered our works in the morning, commenced a tremendous cannonade from the forts in Boston, and from their shipping in the harbor. Cannon-shot are continually rolling and rebounding over the hill; and it is astonishing to observe how little our soldiers are terrified by them. During the forenoon we were in momentary expectation of witnessing an awful scene; nothing less than the carnage of Breed's hill battle was expected. The royal troops are perceived to be in motion, as if embarking to pass the harbor, and land on Dorchester shore, to attack our works. The hills and elevations in this vicinity are covered with spectators to witness deeds of horror in the expected conflict. His Excellency General Washington is present, animating and encouraging the soldiers, and they in return manifest their joy, and express a warm desire for the approach of the enemy; each man knows his place, and is resolute to execute his duty. Our breastworks are strengthened, and among the means of defence are a great number of barrels, filled with stones and sand, arranged in front of our works; which are to be put in motion and made to roll down the hill, to break the ranks and legs of the assailants as they advance. These are the preparations for blood and slaughter. Gracious God! if it be determined in thy Providence that thousands of our fellow-creatures shall this day be slain, let thy wrath be appeased, and in mercy grant that victory be on the side of our suffering, bleeding country!

The anxious day has closed, and the enemy has failed to molest us. From appearances, however, there are strong reasons to suppose that they have only postponed their meditated work till another day. It is presumed that the martial fire, which has been enkindled in the breasts of our soldiery, will not be extinguished during the night, and that they will not rest quietly under their disappointment. Early in the morning of the 6th, our regiment was relieved from its tour of duty, and I bade adieu to Dorchester heights, without being called to dress a single wound. Not more than two or three men were killed or wounded during the twenty-four hours. Some of the British troops were seen to embark, and pass down towards the castle last evening, to be in readiness, it was supposed, in conjunction with others, to attack our works this morning; but a most violent storm came on in the night, and still continuing, obliges General Howe to abandon his enterprise, and thus has a kind Providence seen fit to frustrate a design, which must have been attended with immense slaughter and bloodshed. General Howe must now be sensible of his exposed situation, and be convinced of the immediate necessity of evacuating the town of Boston, if he would prevent the sacrifice of his fleet and army.

7th.—There are strong indications in Boston that the king's troops are preparing to evacuate the town; and that no attempt will be made to dispossess our people of the works which we have constructed on Dorchester heights.

8th.—A flag of truce has come out of Boston with a message from the selectmen; acquainting General Washington that General Howe has come to the determination to evacuate the town; and that he would leave it standing, provided his army should be permitted to retire without being molested. At the same time intimating, as is reported, that in case he should be attacked by our army, the town should be set on fire in different places, in order to secure his retreat. We are unacquainted with the determination of his excellency respecting this proposition; but it is well known that he has been in favor of making an attack on the town; and that the necessary preparations were made, and the plan arranged, to be put in execution in the event of the enemy's meditated attack on our works at Dorchester heights. Four thousand troops, the first division commanded by General Sullivan, the second by General Greene, were ordered to be in readiness, and in case the enemy had advanced and been defeated on the heights of Dorchester, this force, at a given signal, was to have rushed into the town and taken possession.

It is credibly reported from Boston, that on the morning when the British officers discovered our newly-erected works, which, on account of a fog, loomed to great advantage, and appeared larger than the reality, General Howe, on viewing them, was heard to say in astonishment, " know not what I shall do: the rebels have done more in one night than my whole army would have done in weeks." His admiral soon assured him that if the rebels were permitted to hold possession, he should not be able to keep a single ship in the harbor in safety.

Nothing of consequence occurred to observation till Sunday morning, March 17th, when at an early hour it was perceived that the royal army commenced their embarkation on board of transports. In the course of the forenoon we enjoyed the unspeakable satisfaction of beholding their whole fleet under sail, wafting from our shores the dreadful scourge of war. It was in the power of the provincials by a cannonade to have annoyed the enemy's shipping and transports as they passed Dorchester heights, and to have occasioned great embarrassment and destruction among them; but no orders were given for this purpose, and they were suffered to pass unmolested. By this event we are happily relieved of a force consisting of seven thousand five hundred and seventy-five regulars, exclusive of the staff, which, with the marines and sailors, may be estimated at about ten thousand in the whole. This force greatly exceeds the five regiments with which General Grant vauntingly boasted in England that he could march successfully from one end of the American continent to the other. A considerable number of tories, who had joined the royal standard, took passage with their families on board of the transports with the army, and bade adieu to their native country, without knowing what part of the world is to be their destiny.

Immediately after the enemy sailed from Boston harbor, General Washington ordered the major part of his army to march to New York, to secure that city against the apprehended invasion of General Howe. It was not till Wednesday, the 20th, that our troops were permitted to enter the town, when our regiment, with two or three others, were ordered to march in, and take up our quarters, which were provided for us in comfortable houses. While marching through the streets, the inhabitants appeared at their doors and windows; though they manifested a lively joy on being liberated from a long imprisonment, they were not altogether free from a melancholy gloom which ten tedious months' siege has spread over their countenances. The streets and buildings present a scene which reflects disgrace on their late occupants, exhibiting a deplorable desolation and wretchedness.

22*d.*—A concourse of people from the country are crowding into town, full of friendly solicitude, and it is truly interesting to witness the tender interviews and fond embraces of those who have been long separated, under ircumstances so peculiarly distressing. But it is particularly unfortunate on this occasion, that the small-pox is lurking in various parts of the town; which deters many from enjoying an interview with their friends. The parents and sister of my friend Dr. Townsend have continued in town during the siege; being introduced to the family by the Doctor, I received a kind and polite invitation to take up my abode with them, where I am enjoying the kindest attentions and civilities. I accompanied several gentlemen to view the British fortifications on Roxbury neck, where I observed a prodigious number of little military engines called caltrops, or crow-feet, scattered over the ground in the vicinity of the works to impede the march of our troops in case of an attack. The implement consists of an iron ball armed with four sharp points about one inch in length, so formed that which way soever it may fall one point still lies upwards to pierce the feet of horses or men, and are admirably well calculated to obstruct the march of an enemy.

23*d.*—I went to view the Old South Church, a spacious brick building near the centre of the town. It has been for more than a century consecrated to the service of religion, and many eminent divines have in its pulpit labored in teaching the ways of righteousness and truth. But during the late siege the inside of it was entirely destroyed by the British, and the sacred building occupied as a riding-school for Burgoyne's regiment of dragoons. The pulpit and pews were removed, the floor covered with earth, and used for the purpose of training and exercising their horses. A beautiful pew, ornamented with carved work and silk furniture, was demolished; and by order of an officer, the carved work, it is said, was used as a fence for a hog-sty. The North Church, a very valuable building, was entirely demolished, and consumed for fuel. Thus are our houses, devoted to religious worship, profaned and destroyed by the subjects of his royal majesty. His excellency the commander-in-chief has been received by the inhabitants with every mark of respect and gratitude; and a public dinner has been provided for him. He requested the Rev. Dr. Eliot, at the renewal of his customary Thursday Lecture, to preach a thanksgiving sermon, adapted to the joyful occasion. Accordingly on the 28th, this pious divine preached an appropriate discourse from Isaiah xxxiii. 20, in presence of his excellency and a respectable audience.

29th.—The Massachusetts House of Representatives and Council presented his excellency a respectful and affectionate address; and received from him a reply no less respectful and satisfactory.

One of our soldiers found a human skeleton in complete preparation, left by a British surgeon, which I have received as an acceptable present.

April 8th.—I attended at the Stone Chapel, where were performed the funeral solemnities over the remains of that patriot and hero Major-General Joseph Warren. The remains were taken from the earth at Breed's hill, placed in an elegant coffin, and brought into the chapel, where, in the presence of a numerous assembly, a eulogy was pronounced by Perez Morton, Esq., a young lawyer of abilities. The ceremony was conducted by the society of Free Masons, of which the deceased was grand master. A grand procession was formed, and the remains having received the customary masonic honors, were deposited in the vault under the chapel. This proceeding was to me a pleasing novelty, and in the view of the public, a grateful tribute to the memory of a beloved fellow-citizen.

> "Let laurels, drench'd in pure Parnassian dews,
> Reward his mem'ry, dear to every muse,
> Who, with a courage of unshaken root,
> In honor's field advancing his firm foot,
> Plants it upon the line that justice draws,
> And will prevail or perish in her cause.
> 'Tis to the virtues of such men man owes
> His portion in the good that Heaven bestows.
> And when recording History displays
> Feats of renown, though wrought in ancient days;
> Tells of a few stout hearts, that fought and died
> Where duty placed them, at their country's side;
> The man that is not moved with what he reads,
> That takes not fire at their heroic deeds,
> Unworthy of the blessings of the brave,
> Is base in kind, and born to be a slave."—COWPER.

4

May.—As the small-pox is in many parts of the town among both the inhabitants and soldiers, I was advised by my friends to have recourse to inoculation for my own safety, though contrary to general orders. I was accordingly inoculated by my friend Dr. John Homans, and have passed through the disease in the most favorable manner, not suffering one day's confinement.

June 13*th.*—The harbor of Boston has not been entirely cleared of British shipping since the town was evacuated. A fifty-gun ship and several other vessels still occupy the the lower harbor, near Nantasket. A number of provincial troops and volunteers are now ordered on an expedition, under command of General Benjamin Lincoln, with heavy cannon, for the purpose of driving them from the harbor. A part of our regiment being ordered on the expedition, we embarked at the Long Wharf, and landed on Long Island, and immediately made arrangements for a cannonade. A few shot soon convinced the commodore of his danger; he returned the fire with some spirit; but having received a shot through his upper works, he soon got under sail and hastily departed. Thus is the port of Boston again opened by our own authority, after being closed during two years by virtue of an act of the British Parliament.

20*th.*—The removal of the British armed vessels from Nantasket has been productive of very favorable consequences. Three days after their departure two transports from Scotland bound to Boston, unapprised of the event, entered Nantasket road, and were accosted by a discharge of cannon from an American battery before they were undeceived. In this situation it was impossible for them to escape, and several of our privateers made their appearance, and commanded them to strike their flag. This being refused, a smart action ensued, and continued about an hour and a half, when they were obliged to yield and strike to the privateers. On board the transports Major Menzies and eight others were killed, and seventeen wounded. Lieutenant-Colonel Archibald Campbell, two hundred and sixty-seven Highlanders, and forty-eight others, were made prisoners. Major Menzies has been buried here with the honors of war.

July 3*d.*—Orders are given to inoculate for the small-

pox, all the soldiers and inhabitants in town, as a general
infection of this terrible disease is apprehended. Dr.
Townsend and myself are now constantly engaged in this
business.

12th.—Melancholy accounts have been received respecting the situation of our army in Canada; they are subjected to very great hardships, sufferings, and privations.
Destitute of the necessary supplies of provisions and stores,
exhausted by fatigue, and reduced by sickness, with the
small-pox attended by unexampled mortality, they are in
a state but little short of desperation. In addition to all
their sufferings, they now have to deplore the loss of their
valuable commander, Major-General John Thomas. This
gentleman was a native of Kingston, Massachusetts. He
was in military service in former wars against the French
and Indians, where he acquired a high degree of reputation. He was among the first to espouse the cause of his
country in a military character in 1775, and during the
siege of Boston, and on the heights of Dorchester, he was
distinguished as an active, vigilant and brave officer. In
March, 1776, he was promoted by Congress from a brigadier to the rank of major-general, and by them appointed
to command our forces in Canada. On his arrival there
he found innumerable difficulties to encounter; the small-
pox frequently breaking out among the troops, and the
soldiers being in the practice of inoculating themselves, to
the great injury of the public service. The general deemed
it necessary, for the safety of the army, to prohibit the
practice of inoculating, and not excepting himself from
the injunction, he unfortunately received the infection,
which proved fatal to him, and deprived the public of a
valuable general officer. He was held in universal respect
and confidence as a military character, and his death is
deeply deplored throughout the army.

The very important intelligence from Philadelphia is
now proclaimed, that on the 4th instant, the American
Congress declared the thirteen United Colonies, "*Free,
Sovereign, Independent States.*" The subject has for some
time agitated the public mind, and various opinions have
been entertained relative to this momentous transaction.
Opinions of much weight and authority have been and
still are in collision, and it has been considered very

doubtful whether the grand object would be accomplished at the present time. Objections, however, have yielded to imperious necessity, and a new epoch for United America has now commenced. We are now, in the 16th year of the reign of his Majesty King George the Third, absolved from all allegiance to the British crown; and all political connexion between us, as subjects, and his government is totally and for ever dissolved, unless indeed Providence shall so order, that we shall be again reduced to a state of dependence and vassalage.

18th.—This day the declaration of American Independence has been proclaimed in form from the balcony of the state-house in this town. On this most joyful occasion Colonels Whitcomb and Sargeant's regiments were paraded under arms in King street; and also a detachment from the Massachusetts regiment of artillery with two field-pieces. A number of the members of our council and house of representatives, the magistrates, clergymen, selectmen, and a large number of other gentlemen of Boston, and of the neighboring towns, assembled in the council-chamber. At one o'clock the declaration was proclaimed by Colonel Thomas Crafts, and was received with great joy. Three huzzas from the concourse of people were given, after which thirteen pieces of cannon were fired from Fort hill and from Dorchester neck, the Castle, Nantasket, &c. The detachment of artillery in King street, discharged their cannon thirteen times; which was followed by the two regiments in thirteen separate divisions; all corresponding to the number of the American United States; after which, the gentlemen in the council chamber partook of a collation, and a number of appropriate toasts were proclaimed by the president of the council.

This highly important transaction of our Congress is the theme of every circle and topic of universal discussion, and it receives the sanction and approbation of a large majority of the community. When we reflect on the deranged condition of our army, the great deficiency of our resources, and the little prospect of foreign assistance, and at the same time contemplate the prodigious powers and resources of our enemy, we may view this measure of Congress as a prodigy. The history of the world cannot furnish an instance of fortitude and heroic magnanimity

THOMAS JEFFERSON.

parallel to that displayed by the members, whose signatures are affixed to the declaration of American Independence. Their venerated names will ornament the brightest pages of American history, and be transmitted to the latest generations. The instrument was signed by John Hancock, Esq. as President, and by fifty-four others, delegates from the thirteen United States. The Congress have in their declaration recited the grievances and oppressions, for which we could not obtain redress; and proclaimed to the world the causes which impelled them to a separation from the crown of Great Britain. A sensible and popular writer, in a production entitled "*Common Sense*," argues the necessity of the measure from the following considerations. "We had no credit abroad because of our *rebellious dependency*. Our ships could obtain no protection in foreign ports, because we afforded them no justifiable reason for granting it to us. The calling of ourselves subjects, and at the same time fighting against the prince we acknowledge, was a dangerous precedent to all Europe. If the grievances justified our taking up arms, they justified our separation; if they did not justify our separation, neither could they justify our taking arms. All Europe was interested in reducing us as rebels, and all Europe, or the greater part at least, is interested in supporting us in our independent state. At home our condition was still worse; our currency had no foundation; and the state of it would have ruined whig and tory alike. We had no other laws than a kind of moderated passion; no other civil power than an honest mob; and no other protection than the temporary attachment of one man to another. Had independency been delayed a few months longer, this continent would have been plunged into irretrievable confusion; some violent for it, some against it—all in the greatest cabal; the rich would have been ruined, and the poor destroyed. The *necessity* of being independent would have brought it on in a little time, had there been no rupture between Britain and America. The increasing importance of commerce—the weight and perplexity of legislation—and the enlarged state of European politics, would clearly have shown to the continent the impropriety of continuing subordinate; for after the coolest reflection on the matter, this must be allowed, 'that Britain

was too jealous of America to govern it justly; too igno
rant of it to govern it well; and too distant from it to
govern it at all.'" The author of *Common Sense* is Mr.
Thomas Paine, lately from England. I am credibly informed that the following anecdote occurred on the day
of signing the declaration. Mr. Harrison, a delegate from
Virginia, is a large portly man—Mr. Gerry of Massachusetts is slender and spare. A little time after the solemn
transaction of signing the instrument, Mr. Harrison said
smilingly to Mr. Gerry, "When the hanging scene comes
to be exhibited, I shall have the advantage over you, on
account of my size. All will be over with me in a moment, but you will be kicking in the air half an hour after
I am gone."

20*th*.—It appears, by the public papers, that a detachment from the British army of two thousand eight hundred men, under the command of Major-General Clinton,
Lord Cornwallis, and a fleet consisting of two line of battle
ships, frigates, and other armed vessels, amounting to
forty or fifty, have lately made a furious attack on the town
of Charleston, South Carolina. Major-General Lee, who
commands our army in that quarter, has written to Congress a particular statement of the engagement, which, he
says, continued for twelve hours without intermission.
The enemy was twice repulsed with great loss; and the
Carolina troops and militia have gained the highest honor
by their brave and intrepid conduct. Colonel Moultrie,
in a particular manner, is deserving of the highest praise.
But the British fleet has suffered a loss almost beyond
example. Their ships shattered almost to total ruin, and
one frigate of twenty-eight guns was blown up by her own
crew. A number of officers were killed and wounded,
and the number of men is said to be one hundred and
seventy-nine killed, and two hundred and sixty wounded.
Not one man, who was quartered at the beginning of the
action on the Bristol's quarter-deck, escaped being killed
or wounded. Lord Campbell, the late governor of that
colony, being a volunteer on board, received a mortal
wound; and the Commodore, Sir Peter Parker, had a
material part of his breeches torn away, and was otherwise
wounded. The whole of the British forces displayed the
greatest courage and bravery. In a southern newspaper
are inserted the following lines on Sir Peter's disaster:

"If honor in the breech is lodged,
        As Hudibras hath shown,
    It may from hence be fairly judged
        Sir Peter's honor's gone."

The English Parliament, doubting the competency of
their own powers to subjugate the United Colonies, have
resorted to the assistance of foreign troops to prosecute
their sanguinary purposes. They have actually entered
into treaty with several German princes to furnish seventeen thousand men, to aid in the great work of reducing
the Americans to the same degraded state of vassalage
with these hirelings themselves. The terms stipulated in
the treaties are, that besides the wages to be paid these
foreigners, Parliament engages to pay for every soldier
who shall not return, thirty pounds sterling; and for every
disabled soldier fifteen pounds sterling! These mercenary
troops, it is said in England, are to "assist in forcing the
rebels to ask mercy." It has been asserted in the House
of Lords, that the expense to England for these foreign
troops cannot be less than one million five hundred thousand pounds for one year! There is now the clearest
evidence, that the British ministry are wofully disappointed
in their expectations respecting the spirit and temper of
the American people. They had entertained no idea that
the colonists would proceed to such daring enormity as to
spurn their mighty power and authority. They appear
now determined by their augmented forces to crush at a
blow all opposition to their mandates, and to coerce the
rebels into a sense of duty to their king. It is estimated
that a force exceeding forty thousand men is to be employed in America the present year. His majesty has
appointed the two brothers, Lord Howe and General
Howe, commissioners for restoring peace to the colonies,
and for granting pardon to such of his majesty's subjects,
now in rebellion, as shall deserve the royal clemency.
Besides the two commissioners, they are about to send on
the same service a combination of Hessians, Brunswickers,
Waldeckers, English, Scotch, and Irish. The Scots may
perhaps come prepared with the following advice:

    "O learn from our example and our fate,
    Learn wisdom and repentance ere too late."

The following transaction is now a subject of newspaper

discussion and of general conversation. Admiral Lord
Howe arrived off the city of New York, not long since,
to take the command of the British fleet; on his arrival
he proclaimed to the public that he and his brother General
Howe were appointed his majesty's commissioners,
with full powers to grant pardons to all or to any town,
county, or district, who may have departed from their
allégiance and duty to his majesty, &c., and who are willing
by a speedy return to reap the benefit of the royal favor.
These royal commissioners despatched Colonel Patterson,
adjutant-general of the British army, to General Washington,
at New York, with letters respecting their mission;
but as the letters were not directed in a manner expressive
of his official station, his excellency refused to receive
them; but treated Colonel Patterson with much politeness,
and dismissed him. The conduct of General Washington
in this interview received the approbation of Congress,
and they resolved, "that he had acted with a dignity becoming
his character." They further resolved, "that no
letters or messages be received on any occasion whatever
from the enemy, by the commander-in-chief or others, the
commanders of the American army, but such as shall be
directed to them in the characters they respectively sustain."
It was not many days after this that Colonel Patterson
again waited on General Washington, and on this
occasion he addressed him by the title of excellency; and
in the name of the commissioners apologized for any deficiency
in point of respect or punctilio, and assured· him
that they had the highest personal respect for General
Washington, and did not mean to derogate from his rank;
that the letter, of which he was now the bearer from the
commissioners, was directed to George Washington, Esq.,
&c. &c. &c., which they hoped would remove all difficulties;
as the three *et ceteras* might be understood to imply every
thing that ought to follow. To this the general replied,
that though it was true the three *et ceteras* might mean
every thing, it was also true they might *mean any thing*,
and as Congress had approved of his conduct in the first
interview, he could not enter into any new treaty without
fresh authority, and declined receiving the letter; adding
that he should absolutely decline any letter directed to
him as a private person, when it related to his public sta-

tion. Colonel Patterson said, Lord and General Howe were invested with exceedingly great powers, and were very desirous of being the medium of an accommodation of difficulties. The general replied, he had read the act of Parliament, and found they were merely empowered to grant pardons. The Americans had committed no wrong, and therefore wanted no pardons; we were only defending what we deemed our indisputable rights. Colonel Patterson seemed confused, and replied that this would open a wide field for argument. The adjutant-general conducted with the greatest attention and politeness; and manifested great solicitude that the letter might be received, and that the interview might be productive of favorable results. He expressed strong acknowledgments for the favor done him, in omitting the usual ceremony of blinding his eyes, when passing our works. General Washington invited him to partake of a collation provided for him, and he was introduced to our general officers. After many compliments and polite expressions, he departed with saying, "Has your excellency no commands to my Lord or General Howe?" "None, sir," replied the general, "but my particular compliments to both of them."

This event furnishes an irrefragable testimony of the manly firmness of mind and dignity of conduct of our commander-in-chief; and is calculated to impress the English commanders with a just sense of his exalted merit and character.

August 1st.—The continental army, under the immediate command of General Washington, is stationed at New York; and it is expected that the British army, under command of General Howe, will endeavor to take possession of that city the present season.

5th.—Colonel Whitcomb's regiment, consisting of five hundred men, has now gone through the small-pox in this town by inoculation, and all, except one negro, have recovered.

7th.—This regiment, with Colonel Sargeant's, are preparing to march to Ticonderoga. A number of teams are procured to transport the baggage and stores, and this morning, at seven o'clock, they marched out of town with colors displayed and drums beating. Being myself indisposed, I am permitted to tarry in town till my health is restored, and in the mean time I am directed to take charge of the sick soldiers that remain here.

20th.—Having recovered my health, and being prepared to follow our regiment, I am this day to bid adieu to the town of Boston, where I have resided very pleasantly for the last five months. I am destined to a distant part of our country, and know not what suffering and hazards I shall be called to encounter, while in the discharge of my military duty. I shall commence my journey in company with Lieutenant Whiting and fourteen men who were left here as invalids.

September.—We took our route through Worcester, Springfield, Charlestown, in New Hampshire, and over the Green Mountains to Skeensboro'; which is the place of rendezvous for the continental troops and militia destined to Ticonderoga. Here boats are provided at the entrance of Lake Champlain, which are continually passing to and from this place. We embarked on the 6th instant, and with good oarsmen and sails we arrived the same day, and joined our regiment here, a distance of thirty miles. While on our march, we received alarming reports respecting some military operations between our army, commanded by General Washington, and the British, · under command of General Howe, on Long Island, near New York. The report states that our army has suffered a complete defeat with great loss, and that two of our general officers are taken prisoners. The inhabitants through the country are in great alarm; but have not obtained the particulars; as the account at present is vague, and somewhat contradictory, we hope and trust that a particular detail will prove the event to be more favorable to our cause.

Soon after my arrival here, a soldier had the imprudence to seize a rattlesnake by its tail; the reptile threw its head back and struck its fangs into the man's hand. In a few moments a swelling commenced, attended with severe pain. It was not more than half an hour, when his whole arm to his shoulder was swollen to twice its natural size, and the skin became of a deep orange color. His body, on one side, soon became affected in a similar manner, and a nausea at his stomach ensued. The poor man was greatly and justly alarmed; his situation was very critical. Two medical men, beside myself, were in close attendance for several hours. Having procured a quantity of olive oil, we directed the patient to swallow it in large and repeated doses, till he had taken one quart; and at the same time we rubbed into the affected limb a very large quantity of mercurial ointment. In about two hours we had the satisfaction to perceive the favorable effects of the remedies. The alarming symptoms abated, the swelling and pain gradually subsided, and in about forty-eight hours he was happily restored to health.   •

10th.—I have omitted to record the following incidents, till I could ascertain the particulars of the reports.

We learn by accounts from New York that, some time since, a plot of a most atrocious nature was detected in that city. A gang of tories had associated for the purpose of joining the British army; and had concerted a plan, it is said, to assassinate his Excellency General Washington and some other officers; and while our army were engaged with the enemy, to blow up our magazines, &c. The mayor of the city, and an armorer who was employed in making rifles for the tories, and several others, were taken into custody, and committed to close prison. The mayor, on examination, confessed that he received money from Governor Tryon to pay the armorer for the rifles. Two of his excellency's guards were confederate; and a third, to whom the secret was confided, honestly disclosed the information. Several of these miscreants were tried and convicted, and two or three were executed. Another vile plot has been discovered in the city of Albany. By the confession of two tories, the plan was to set the city on fire, and to blow up the magazine. Some of the incendiaries were apprehended, and the meditated plot frustrated. We have now ample evidence, that the tories are the most virulent and implacable of our enemies; and it is to be considered as a remarkable interposition of Providence, that their vile machinations are so frequently defeated. Internal secret enemies are always more dangerous than avowed foes in the field; and so numerous and active are the tories in the vicinity of our main army, that it has been found necessary to adopt coercive measures, and to compel them to take the oath of allegiance, as prescribed by our Congress, or to depart from our territories.

12th.—I must not omit to notice another instance of villany in a German by the name of Ledwitz. By his solicitation he was appointed lieutenant-colonel in our army, and he has been detected in a traitorous correspondence with Governor Tryon of New York. He entrusted his letter to one Steen, an honest German, to be conveyed to New York; but he considered it his duty to expose the perfidy, and delivered it to General Washington. In his letter he first presents his compliments in a formal manner to Lord Howe, and then proceeds to profess a consciousness that the world will censure him for his treachery, in corresponding with the enemy of those in whose service he is employed, but apologizes by asserting that he had been forced to accept his commission, for fear of ruin to himself and family; and as he had engaged, through compulsion, by a rebellious mob, he can be under no obligation to be faithful in their service. Besides this, he adds, he had previously taken Governor Tryon's advice, and had promised to do all he could in his new capacity for his majesty's service. He then asserts that a person who is a friend to the king, though an interested one, had offered to furnish him with weekly returns of the strength and detail of the continental army, for the sum of four thousand pounds sterling, to be paid in advance in gold; but that he had agreed with him to render that service for two thousand pounds, which sum, he requested, might be immediately conveyed to him. By this criminal act the perfidious wretch had forfeited his life, according to the articles of war; but on his trial by a court martial, his life was saved by the casting vote of a militia officer, who pretended some scruples of conscience; he was, however, cashiered, and declared incapable of holding any military office in the service of the United States.

15th.—I have now ascertained, by accounts published, that the battle on Long Island took place on the 27th of August. The British and Hessian army, supposed to amount to twenty-four thousand, landed on the island under cover of their shipping. The continental army consisted of ten thousand five hundred and fourteen effectives only; and these were so situated, that but a small part could be brought into action; the conflict therefore was extremely unequal. In point of numbers, of discipline,

ATTEMPT TO ASSASSINATE WASHINGTON.

èxperience in war, and of artillery, the enemy possessed the most decided advantage; besides the important assistance afforded by a powerful fleet. The very judicious plan of attack by the British generals was carried into execution with irresistible ardor and impetuosity. The Americans defended themselves with great bravery, till a considerable number of them were completely surrounded and the remainder dispersed. The palm of victory was on the side of the enemy; and our loss is very considerable. Major-General Sullivan and Lord Stirling were obliged to surrender as prisoners; and our total loss is supposed to be not less than one thousand or twelve hundred in killed, wounded, and missing. The enemy suffered very severely.

After this unfortunate skirmishing, our army retreated within their lines at Brooklyn, and were exposed to the greatest hazard; our troops, fatigued and discouraged by defeat, a superior enemy in their front, and a powerful fleet about to enter the East River with a view of effectually cutting off their retreat; but an interposition of Providence, and the wisdom and vigilance of the commander-in-chief, preserved our army from destruction. Having resolved to withdraw his army from its hazardous position, General Washington crossed over to the island in the night of the 29th of August, and personally conducted the retreat in so successful a manner, under the most embarrassing circumstances, that it is considered as a remarkable example of good generalship. A circumstance which is remarked as manifestly providential, is, that a thick fog enveloped the whole of Long Island in obscurity about two o'clock in the morning, while on the side of the enemy at New York, the atmosphere was perfectly clear. Thus by a providential interposition of an unusual fog, our army, consisting of nine thousand men, in one night embarked under great disadvantages, and with their baggage, provisions, stores, horses, and the munitions of war, crossed a river, a mile or more wide, and landed at New York undiscovered and without material loss. The enemy were so near, that they were heard at work with their pick-axes, and in about half an hour after, the fog cleared off and the enemy were seen taking possession of the American lines.

20th.—General Washington, finding the city of New

York untenable, has removed his whole army about nine
miles up the country; which he effected in safety, though
uuder a heavy cannonade from the British shipping.—
General Howe with his army took immediate possession
of the city. Major-General Sullivan, who was captured
on Long Island, has been permitted to return on his parole;
and is charged with a message to Congress from Lord
Howe. The purport of the message is, that his lordship,
as commissioner, could not treat with .Congress, as such;
but is desirous of a conference with some of the members,
as private gentlemen. Congress could not consider themselves justified in sending any of their members in their
private character; but ever desirous of establishing peace
on reasonable terms, offered to send a committee to inquire whether his lordship had any authority to treat with
persons authorized by Congress for this purpose, and what
that authority was, and to hear such propositions as he
should think proper to make respecting the same. They
accordingly made choice of Dr. Benjamin Franklin, John
Adams, Esq. and Edward Rutledge, Esq., who had an interview with Lord Howe on Staten Island. The first proposition from his lordship was, that the colonies should return
to their allegiance and obedience to the government of
Great Britain. The committee expressed their opinion,
that a return to the domination of Great Britian was not
to be expected. They mentioned the repeated humble
petitions of the colonies to the king and parliament, which
had been treated with contempt, and answered with additional injuries; the unexampled patience we had shown under their tyrannical government, and that it was not till the
last act of Parliament, which denounced war against us, and
put us out of the king's protection, that we declared our
independence; *and that it is not now in the power of Congress to agree that the people should return to their former dependent state.* The committee reported to Congress that
it did not appear that his lordship's commission contained
any other authority of importance than what is expressed
in the act of Parliament, namely, that of granting pardons, with such exceptions as the commissoners shall think
proper to make, and of declaring America, or any part of
it, to be in the king's peace on submission. The committee conducted the business with great judgment, and in a

manner becoming the dignity of their character. The Congress adopted no other measures on this occasion; and the British commissioners, finding that the United States could not relinquish their independency, published their declaration to the people at large, recommending to them "to reflect seriously on their present conduct and expectations, and to judge for themselves, whether it is more consistent with their honor and happiness to offer up their lives as a sacrifice to the unjust and precarious cause in which they are engaged, or to return to their allegiance, accept the blessings of peace, and be secured in the free enjoyment of their liberties and property." Had the declaration of independence been deferred but a few weeks longer, this proceeding of the commissioners might have been productive of consequences exceedingly disastrous to our country. It would probably have increased the number of opposers to the measure, and occasioned the greatest confusion and embarrassment. It was undoubtedly their object, by a specious prospect of reconciliation, to create a division among the colonies and people, and thereby paralyze their exertions and preparations for war. But at the present time, the declaration of the king's commissioners is not calculated to effect the great purpose which they have in view; the people at large have become too wise to be duped and cajoled out of their freedom. They repose unbounded confidence in the wisdom of the Congress of their choice; and have no disposition to counteract their views or embarrass their counsels. The number of individuals, who have accepted of the proffered conditions, is supposed to be very inconsiderable; and by far the largest portion of them are in the city of New York and its immediate vicinity. By a flag from New York we learn that, about five days after the British army took possession of that city, a destructive fire broke out, and raged with such violence, that about one thousand houses, some of the most superb buildings, being about one-quarter of the whole city, were consumed. Some suspicions were entertained that this disaster was occasioned by American emissaries, and several persons had been treated with great cruelty, though no proof was produced against them. There is on the contrary much reason to conclude that the conflagration was merely accidental.

We have the information that, before our army evacuated the city of New York, General Howe's army landed,
under cover of five ships of war, the British and Hessians
in two separate divisions. So soon as this was announced
to our commander-in-chief, by a heavy cannonade from
the men of war, he instantly rode toward our lines; but
he was astonished and mortified to find that the troops
which had been posted there, and also two brigades which
had been ordered to support them, were retreating in great
confusion and disorder. He made every effort to rally
them, but without success; they were so panic-struck that
even the shadow of an enemy seemed to increase their
precipitate flight. His excellency, distressed and enraged,
drew his sword and snapped his pistols, to check them;
but they continued their flight without firing a gun; and
the general, regardless of his own safety, was in so much
hazard, that one of his attendants seized the reins, and
gave his horse a different direction. The following fact
is of considerable interest:

When retreating from New York, Major-General Putnam, at the head of three thousand five hundred continental troops, was in the rear, and the last that left the city.
In order to avoid any of the enemy that might be advancing in the direct road to the city, he made choice of a
road parallel with and contiguous to the North River, till
he could arrive at a certain angle, whence another road
would conduct him in such a direction as that he might
form a junction with our army. It so happened that a
body of about eight thousand British and Hessians were
at the same moment advancing on the road, which would
have brought them in immediate contact with General
Putnam, before he could have reached the turn into the
other road. Most fortunately, the British generals, seeing
no prospect of engaging our troops, halted their own, and
repaired to the house of a Mr. Robert Murray, a Quaker
and friend of our cause; Mrs. Murray treated them with
cake and wine, and they were induced to tarry two hours
or more, Governor Tryon frequently joking her about her
American friends. By this happy incident General Putnam, by continuing his march, escaped a rencounter with
a greatly superior force, which must have proved fatal to
his whole party. One half-hour, it is said, would have

LORD HOWE.

been sufficient for the enemy to have secured the road at
the turn, and entirely cut off General Putnam's retreat.
It has since become almost a common saying among our
officers, that Mrs. Murray saved this part of the American army.

I have collected from the preceding pages of my Journal
some observations relative to the formation and character
of our army. After the battle at Lexington, such was the
enthusiasm for the cause of liberty, and so general and
extensive the alarm, that thousands of our citizens, who
were engaged in the cultivation of their farms, spontane-
ously rushed to the scene of action; and an army was
assembled almost without the efforts of public authority.
At this most eventful period, it was the fond hope of a
large proportion of our patriotic leaders, that the controversy with our parent-country would yet be compromised
on honorable and equitable terms. Though the haughty
Britons had unsheathed the sword, and shed the blood of
their brethren, it was impossible to endure the idea that
our loyal and humble supplications to the king could any
longer be contemptuously rejected; more especially after
a complete union of all the colonies in a determined opposition to their tyrannical measures was clearly demonstrated. Calculating therefore that the services of an army
would be required for a short period only, and the troops
in the field consisting chiefly of minute-men, volunteers
and militia, it was a considerable time before they were
regularly organized into regiments and brigades. In many
instances the soldiers were indulged the privilege of choosing their own officers; the consequence was, as might be
expected, that the choice did not fall on the most respectable and meritorious, but on those who were the most
popular among the lower class; and these too frequently
proved unqualified to discharge their military duties in a
manner creditable to themselves or advantageous to the
public service. Nor was it to be expected that this description of people could appreciate the importance of the
great desiderata in all armies, discipline and subordination.
It has been found, by sad experience, that but little dependence can be placed on an army of militia, and those whose
term of service is so short that they are almost continually
fluctuating from camp to their farms, and in whom the

5

noble spirit of patriotism is in a considerable degree extinguished. There is another evil of a very serious complexion which has manifested itself in our camp. Since
the troops from the Southern states have been incorporated
and associated in military duty with those from New England, a strong prejudice has assumed its unhappy influence,
and drawn a line of distinction between them. Many of
the officers from the South are gentlemen of education,
and unaccustomed to that equality which prevails in New
England; and, however desirable, it could scarcely be
expected that people from distant colonies, differing in
manners and prejudices, could at once harmonize in friendly
intercourse. Hence we too frequently hear the burlesque
epithet of *Yankee* from one party, and that of *Buck-skin*,
by way of retort, from the other. The troops which compose the continental army being enlisted for a few months
only, their time of service will soon expire. Congress,
being apprised of the absolute necessity of a permanent
army, have lately resolved, "to raise a standing army to
consist of about seventy-five thousand men, to serve for
the term of three years, or during the war." These troops,
when raised, are to be systematically arranged on the continental establishment, and according to their apportion-
ment, the quota of Massachusetts is fifteen battalions, or
about twelve thousand men. To encourage enlistments,
each soldier is to receive a bounty of twenty dollars, besides
his wages and allowance of rations, and one hundred acres
of land, if he serve during the war. The officers are to
receive land in proportion to their respective ranks, from
two hundred to five hundred acres. Their monthly pay
is to be as follows:

Colonel, a month,	$75 00	Lieutenant,	$27 00
Lieutenant-Colonel,	60 00	Ensign,	20 00
Major,	50 00	Sergeant-Major,	9 00
Chaplain,	33 33	Quarter-Master Sergeant,	9 00
Surgeon,	33 33	Drum-Major,	8 00
Surgeon's-Mate,	18 00	Fife-Major,	8 33
Adjutant,	40 00	Sergeant,	8 00
Quarter-Master,	27 50	Corporal,	7 33
Regimental Pay-Master,	26 67	Drummer and Fifer,	7 33
Captain,	40 00	Privates,	6 67

Each commissioned officer is allowed the privilege of
taking a soldier from the ranks for a waiter, and he is ex-
empted from camp and other duty, except in time of action.

The officers are also allowed a number of rations in proportion to their rank. A surgeon draws three, and a mate two rations. One pound of beef or pork; one pound of bread or flour a day; a small quantity of vegetables, when to be had; one gill of rum or whiskey a day; a small quantity of vinegar, salt, soap and candles, a week, constitute a ration.

Ticonderoga is situated on an angle of land forming the western shore of Lake Champlain; or rather what is called South Bay; being the inlet into the lake. It is about twelve miles south of the old fortress at Crown Point; and about one hundred and ten miles north of Albany. This point of land is surrounded on three sides by water, and on the north-west side it is well defended by the old French lines and several block-houses. The works at this place were originally erected by the French, in 1756, and the post was considered of high importance by both the French and English, as commanding the pass direct from Canada to the provinces of New York and New England. In the war between the English and French, in the year 1759, it was surrendered to General Amherst, which was a prelude to the conquest of Canada by the English and Provincial army. In 1775, after the commencement of hostilities at Lexington, this post was taken from the English, by a small party of militia volunteers under command of Colonel Allen and Colonel Arnold, which put the Provincials in possession of a large number of cannon, mortars and other ordnance; a part of which was transported to Cambridge during the siege of Boston. On the east side of South Bay, directly opposite to Ticonderoga, is a high circular hill, on the summit of which our army has erected a strong fort, within which is a square of barracks. This is called Mount Independence. A communication is maintained between the two places by a floating bridge thrown across the lake, which is about four hundred yards wide. The army stationed at this post at present is supposed to consist of about eight or ten thousand men, and Major-General Gates is commander-in-chief. We have a naval armament on Lake Champlain, below this garrison, which is commanded by the intrepid General Arnold; General Waterbury is second in command. The British have also a naval armament, of superior force, at the head of which

is the celebrated Sir Guy Carleton. Preparations are
making on both sides for a vigorous combat to decide
which power shall have dominion on the lake Should
Sir Guy Carleton be able to defeat our fleet, it is supposed
that he will pursue his victorious career by an attempt to
possess himself of this garrison; and our troops are making
the utmost exertion to put our works in the best possible
state of defence. Each regiment has its alarm-post assigned, and they are ordered to repair to it, and to man the
lines at day-light every morning. Among our defensive
weapons are poles, about twelve feet long, armed with
sharp iron points, which each soldier is to employ against
the assailants when mounting the breastworks. We are
happy to learn from head-quarters that the two continental
generals, taken in the action on Long Island, Lord Stirling
and Major-General Sullivan, have returned to our camp;
being exchanged for General Prescott, captured in Canada,
and Governor Brown, who was brought off from New
Providence by one of our armed vessels.

October.—By some gentlemen from head-quarters, near
New York, we are amused with an account of a singular
machine, invented by a Mr. D. Bushnell of Connecticut,
for the purpose of destroying the British shipping by
explosion. This novel machine was so ingeniously constructed, that, on examination, Major-General Putnam
was decidedly of opinion that its operations might be
attended with the desired success; accordingly he encouraged the inventor, and resolved to be himself a spectator
of the experiment on the British shipping in New York
harbor. Mr. Bushnell gave to his machine the name of
American Turtle or Torpedo. It was constructed on the
principles of submarine navigation, and on trial it has been
ascertained that it might be rowed horizontally, at any
given depth under water, and the adventurer, concealed
within, might rise or sink, as occasion requires. A *magazine* of *powder* was attached to it in such a manner as to
be screwed into the bottom of the ship; and being now
disengaged from the machine, the operator retires in safety,
leaving the internal clock-work in motion; and at the
distance of half an hour, or an hour, the striking of a gun
lock communicates fire to the powder, and the explosion
takes place. It was determined to make the experiment

with this machine in the night, on the ship Eagle, of sixty-four guns, on board of which admiral Lord Howe commanded. General Putnam placed himself on the wharf to witness the result. Mr. Bushnell had instructed his brother in the management of the Torpedo with perfect dexterity; but being taken sick, a sergeant of a Connecticut regiment was selected for the business, who, for want of time, could not be properly instructed. He, however, succeeded so far as to arrive in safety with his apparatus under the bottom of the ship, when the screw, designed to perforate the copper sheathing, unfortunately struck against an iron plate, near the rudder, which, with the strong current and want of skill in the operator, frustrated the enterprise; and, as day-light had begun to appear, the sergeant abandoned his magazine, and returned in the Torpedo to the shore. In less than half an hour a terrible explosion from the magazine took place, and threw into the air a prodigious column of water, resembling a great water-spout, attended with a report like thunder. General Putnam and others, who waited with great anxiety for the result, were exceedingly amused with the astonishment and alarm which this secret explosion occasioned on board of the ship. This failure, it is confidently asserted, is not to be attributed to any defect in the principles of this wonderful machine; as it is allowed to be admirably calculated to execute destruction among the shipping.

10th.—By intelligence from our fleet, on the lake, we are in daily expectation of a decisive naval action, as the British are known to have a superior force; our officers, here, I understand, are full of anxiety respecting the important event. Great confidence is reposed in the judgment and bravery of General Arnold, whom General Gates has appointed to command our fleet.

15th.—I have now to record an account of a naval engagement between the two fleets on Lake Champlain. The British, under command of Sir Guy Carleton, advanced on the 11th instant, and found our fleet in a line of battle prepared for the attack. A warm action soon ensued, and became extremely close and severe, with round and grape shot, which continued about four hours. Brigadier-General Waterbury, in the Washington galley, fought with undaunted bravery, till nearly all his officers were killed and wounded, and his vessel greatly injured; when General Arnold ordered the remaining shattered vessels to retire up the lake, towards Crown Point, in order to refit. On the 13th, they were overtaken by the enemy, and the action was renewed, in which was displayed the greatest intrepidity on both sides. The Washington galley, being crippled in the first action, was soon obliged to strike and surrender. General Arnold conducted during the action with great judgment, firmness and gallantry, obstinately defending himself against a superior force, both in numbers and weight of metal. At length, however, he was so closely pressed that his situation became desperate, and he run his own vessel, the Congress galley, on shore, which with five gondolas were abandoned and blown up. Out of sixteen of our vessels, eleven were taken or destroyed, five only arrived safe at this place. Two of the enemy's gondolas were sunk by our fleet, and one blown up with sixty men. Their loss in men is supposed to be equal to our own, which is estimated at about one hundred. A large number of troops were on board the British fleet, consisting of regulars, Canadians and savages, which have been landed on each side of the lake, and it is now expected that Sir Guy Carleton, at the head of his army, reported to be about ten thousand strong, will soon invest this post. By order of General Gates, our commander, the greatest exertions are constantly making, by strengthening our works, to enable us to give them a warm reception; and our soldiery express a strong desire to have an opportunity of displaying their courage and prowess; both officers and men are full of activity and vigilance.

18th.—It is now ascertained that the British army and fleet have established themselves at Crown Point, and are strengthening the old fortifications at that place. Some of their vessels have approached within a few miles of our garrison, and one boat came within cannon-shot distance of our lower battery, in order to reconnoitre and sound the channel; but a few shot having killed two men, and wounded another, soon obliged her to retire. All our troops are ordered to repair to their alarm posts, and man the lines and works; every morning, our continental colors are advantageously displayed on the ramparts, and our cannon and spears are in readiness for action.

20th.—Ever since the defeat of our fleet we have been providentially favored with a strong southerly wind, which has prevented the enemy's advancing to attack our lines, and afforded us time to receive some reïnforcements of militia, and to prepare for a more vigorous defence. It seems now to be the opinion of many of our most judicious officers, that had Sir Guy Carleton approached with his army, immediately after his victory on the lake, the struggle must have been most desperate, and the result precarious; but we now feel more confidence in our strength.

Several letters, lately received from Canada, acknowledge that no man ever manœuvred with more dexterity, fought with more bravery, or retreated with more firmness, than did General Arnold on the 11th and 12th instant. After making every effort to compensate, by the advantage of situation, for the inferiority of force, and seeing his own vessel, and the rest, torn to pieces by the superior weight of metal, and the execution of the enemy's howitzers, he set fire to his vessel, and would not quit her till she was so completely in flames that it was impossible for the enemy to strike her colors on their arrival, and they were left flying among the flames to the last. This, says one of the letters, was supporting a point of honor in a manner almost romantic; yet so it was.

November 1st.—The enemy remain at Crown Point, and evince no disposition to molest our garrison, having probably discovered that our means of defence are too formidable for them to encounter. General Gates has now ordered a detachment of troops to march towards Crown Point, to reconnoitre their position, or to attack them. A report was soon returned that the whole fleet and army have abandoned Crown Point, and retired into Canada, where they will probably occupy their winter-quarters in peace, and it is not probable that Sir Guy Carleton intends to invest our garrison, at this advanced season, unless, however, he should attempt it by marching his army over the ice, when the lake is frozen, which will probably be very practicable.

15th.—Ticonderoga is situated in about latitude forty-four degrees. I have no means in possession of ascertaining the precise degree of cold; but we all agree that it is colder here than in Massachusetts at the same season. The earth has not yet been covered with snow, but the frost is so considerable that the water of the lake is congealed, and the earth is frozen. We are comfortably situated in our barracks; our provisions are now good, and having no enemy near enough to alarm or disturb us, we have nothing of importance to engage our attention. Our troops are quite healthy, a few cases of rheumatism and pleurisy comprise our sick-list, and it is seldom that any fatal cases occur.

December 10*th.*—Intelligence has lately arrived at head-quarters here, that a British fleet, and a detachment of five or six thousand of the royal army have taken possession of Newport, in Rhode Island, without any opposition; many of the inhabitants being friendly to the royal cause, they were received as friends. By letters from officers, and by other information from our main army, we learn with sorrow that our affairs in that quarter are in a most deplorable and almost desperate situation. Since the evacuation of New York, several battles and skirmishes have taken place between the two armies, with considerable loss on both sides; but his excellency the commander-in-chief has constantly avoided a general action. Fort Washington and Fort Lee have fallen into the hands of the enemy, with a considerable number of prisoners; and our army being reduced to the lowest ebb, discouraged and dispirited, are retreating through the Jerseys, and the enemy in close pursuit. The continental army has even crossed the Delaware, and left the whole state of Jersey in the possession of the royal army.

20*th.*—Another disaster of much importance is the capture of Major-General Lee; on the 13th instant, marching at the head of his division to join the main army, he very incautiously took up his lodgings at a house three or four miles from his troops. Information of this was, by some tories, communicated to Colonel Harcourt of the British light-horse, who resolved to attempt his capture. Accordingly, with a detachment of dragoons, he speedily surrounded the house; made General Lee his prisoner, and not permitting him time to take his cloak and hat, mounted him on a horse, and in triumph conveyed him to New York. The loss of this favorite general officer, it is feared, will be attended with very serious consequences, as respects the American cause. He was from his youth an officer in the British service, where he sustained a reputation of the highest grade, as a brave and skilful warrior. Having adopted our country, and become a zealous advocate for its liberties, he had acquired the confidence and highest regard of the public, and was exalted to the rank of second in command in our army.

Such is now the gloomy aspect of our affairs that the whole couutry has taken the alarm; strong apprehensions are entertained that the British will soon have it in their power to vanquish the whole of the remains of the continental army. The term of service of a considerable part of our troops has nearly expired, and new recruits do not arrive in sufficient numbers to supply their places. His Excellency General Washington is continually making every possible effort to produce a change of circumstances more auspicious to our country. The critical and distressing situation in which he is placed is sufficient to overwhelm the powers of any man of less wisdom and magnanimity than our commander-in-chief. He has the confidence and the affection of the officers and soldiers of the whole army; and there is not perhaps another man to be found so well calculated to discharge the duties of his important and responsible station. It is generally agreed by our officers that, in his retreat through the Jerseys and over the Delaware, under the most pressing difficulties, he displayed the talents and wisdom characteristic of a great military commander, possessing unfailing resources of mind. While retreating through the Jerseys with an army not exceeding three thousand five hundred men, and deeming our cause as almost desperate, he said to Colonel Reed, passing his hand over his throat, "My neck does not feel as though it was made for a halter: we must retire to Augusta county in Virginia, and if overpowerd we must pass the Alleghany mountains." General Washington at this time was suffering the most agonizing distress for the fate of his army and his country.

The king's commissioners, flushed with the success of the royal army, have availed themselves of the occasion, and put forth another proclamation, granting pardons to all those who shall within sixty days subscribe a declaration to remain peaceable, not to take up arms, nor encourage others to act against the king's authority; and at the same time, they charge and command all who are assembled in arms against his majesty to disband, and all under the names of general and Provincial Congress committees, &c. to desist from their *treasonable* practices, and relinquish their usurped power within sixty days from the date of the proclamation.

This production, couched in the haughty style of royal authority, demands submission of those who have long since been compelled to abjure all allegiance to the British crown. How far the people of this continent may be disposed to retrace their steps, to abandon the government of their choice, relinquish their independence and succumb to arbitrary power, is a point to be decided within sixty days. However apparently forlorn is our situation, we presume to hope that his majesty's commissioners will not realize their sanguine expectations, though British clemency on the one hand, and the gallows on the other, may be the alternative. The Congress resolved, on the 12th instant, that it be recommended to all the United States as soon as possible to appoint a day of fasting and humiliation. This is according to the custom of our pious ancestors in times of imminent dangers and difficulties. Considering the rapid movements of the enemy, and knowing it to be their intention to possess themselves of the city of Philadelphia, the Congress have resolved to retire to Baltimore in Maryland. They have also ordered, that hand-bills be circulated through the states with the view of rousing the whole people to a sense of the impending danger, and the calamities that will ensue should the enemy succeeded in the attempt to get possession of the capital.

26*th*.—A singular kind of riot took place in our barracks last evening, attended by some unpleasant consequences. Colonel A. W. of Massachusetts, made choice of his two sons, who were soldiers in his regiment, to discharge the menial duties of waiters, and one of them having been brought up a shoe-maker, the colonel was so inconsiderate as to allow him to work on his bench in the same room with himself. The ridiculous conduct has for some time drawn on the good old man the contemptuous sneers of the gentlemen officers, especially those from Pennsylvania. Lieutenant-Colonel C. of Wayne's regiment, being warmed with wine, took on himself the task of reprehending the "Yankee" colonel for thus ·degrading his rank. With this view he rushed into the room in the evening, and soon despatched the shoe-maker's bench; after which, he made an assault on the colonel's person, and bruised him severely. The noise and confusion soon collected a number of officers and soldiers, and it was a considerable time before the rioters could be quelled. Some of the soldiers of Colonel Wayne's regiment actually took to their arms and dared the *Yankees*, and then proceeded to the extremity of firing their guns. About thirty or forty rounds were aimed at the soldiers of our regiment, who were driven from their huts and barracks, and several of them were severely wounded. Colonel C., in making an assault on a superior officer, and encouraging a riot, is guilty of one of the highest crimes in our articles of war. It was in the power of Colonel W., and in fact it was his duty, to bring the audacious offenders to exemplary punishment; but, as if to complete the disgrace of the transaction, Colonel C. sent some soldiers into the woods to shoot a fat bear, with which he made an entertainment, and invited Colonel W. and his officers to partake of it; this effected a reconciliation; and Colonel W. was induced to overlook the high-handed assault on his own person and on the lives of his soldiers. Our colonel is a serious, good man, but is more conversant with the economy of domestic life than the etiquette practised in camp.

January 5th.—At the close of the last year, the situation of our main army was gloomy and discouraging: a large proportion of the troops had retired from service, as their term of enlistment expired, and the small remains of our army was retreating before the enemy, and passed the Delaware for safety. It is now announced in our general orders, to our inexpressible joy and satisfaction, that the scene is in some degree changed, the fortune of war is reversed, and Providence has been pleased to crown the efforts of our commander-in-chief with a splendid victory. His excellency, having obtained information that the advanced party of the enemy, consisting of about fifteen hundred Hessians and British light-horse, under command of Colonel Rahl, was stationed at the village of Trenton, concerted a plan for taking them by surprise. For this purpose he made choice of Christmas night, under the idea that in consequence of the festivity, they might be less vigilantly guarded. At this time the whole force under his immediate command did not exceed three thousand men. At the head of about two thousand four hundred men, one division being commanded by General Greene and the other by General Sullivan, he crossed the river Delaware in boats, in the night of the 25th of December, during a severe storm of snow and rain. The passage of the boats was rendered extremely difficult and hazardous by the ice, and part of the troops and cannon actually failed in the attempt. Having landed on the Jersey shore, he had nine miles to march, and he reached the village about seven o'clock in the morning with such promptitude and secrecy, as to attack the enemy almost as soon as his approach was discovered. A smart firing ensued, which continued but a few minutes, when the enemy, finding themselves surrounded, threw down their arms and surrendered as prisoners. Colonel Rahl, the commanding officer, was mortally wounded, and seven other officers were wounded and left at Trenton on their parole. About thirty-five soldiers were killed, sixty wounded, and nine hundred and forty-eight, including thirty officers, were taken prisoners, amounting in all to one thousand and forty-eight. Of the Continentals not more than ten, it is supposed, were killed and wounded. General Washington recrossed the Delaware the same day in triumph, bringing off six excellent brass cannon, about one thousand two hundred small arms, and three standards, with a quantity of baggage, &c. This very brilliant achievement is highly honorable to the commander-in-chief, and to all that were engaged in the enterprise. We are sanguine in the hope that this most auspicious event will be productive of the happiest effects, by inspiriting our dejected army, and dispelling that panic of despair into which the people have been plunged. General Washington allowed the Hessian prisoners to retain their baggage, and sent them into the interior of Pennsylvania, ordering that they be treated with favor and humanity. This conduct, so contrary to their expectations, excited their gratitude and veneration for their amiable conqueror, whom they styled, "*a very good rebel.*"

BATTLE OF TRENTON.

15th.—By some friends from the main army, and from current report, it appears that the British, having overrun the Jerseys, considered the Continental army as on the point of annihilation, and flattered themselves that what they term the rebellion, is effectually crushed. In their march through the Jerseys they have committed such licentious ravages and desolation, as must be deemed disgraceful by all civilized people; an indiscriminate robbery and plundering mark every step of their progress; rapine and murder, without distinction of friend or foe, age or sex, has been put in practice with an inexorable spirit, and countenanced by officers of rank and distinction. Even those unfortunate inhabitants who have been deluded by their promises, and received printed protections, are equally sufferers by these cruel and atrocious wretches. Hundreds of inhabitants, both male and female, have been deprived of their dwellings and sustenance, stripped of their clothing, and exposed to the inclemency of the winter, and to personal insult and abuse of almost every description. But their wicked career is about to be checked. Providence will not suffer such enormities to be perpetrated with impunity. Those miserable inhabitants, whose lives have been spared, are driven to desperation, and feel that they have no hope but in the extirpation of their cruel enemies. The people who have been subdued have, with a noble spirit, risen on their conquerors, and are resolved to revenge the injuries which they have suffered.

We are now informed of another very important advantage which General Washington has gained over the royal army by means of a well-concerted stratagem. After his success at Trenton, General Washington received considerable reïnforcements of troops from Virginia and Maryland, and some regiments of militia, which enabled him again to cross the Delaware into the Jerseys and face the enemy. While at Trenton, Lord Cornwallis advanced to attack him, and a severe cannonade commenced. In the evening, General Washington ordered a great number of fires to be lighted up, and leaving a sufficient number of men to keep them burning during the night, to deceive the enemy, stole a march with his main army, taking a circuitous route, and, at nine o'clock the next morning, attacked three regiments of the British who were posted

at Princeton, routed them, and drove them from their redoubts. By this masterly manœuvre, the enemy lost about
five hundred in killed, wounded and prisoners. The loss
on our side is very inconsiderable in point of numbers,
but we have to lament the death of Brigadier-General
Mercer, a brave officer, who commanded the Virginia militia. The fact is published, that after General Mercer surrendered himself, the enemy, deaf to the voice of humanity,
stabbed him with their bayonets, and with the butt end
of a musket battered and disfigured his face in a savage
manner. It is to be remarked, that on this memorable
occasion Lord Cornwallis was completely out-generaled;
while he was expecting to find the Continental army at
their lighted fires at Trenton, he was astonished and confounded to hear the firing occasioned by this same army,
beating up their quarters twelve miles in his rear. His
lordship immediately repaired by a forced march to Princeton, but arrived too late to retaliate on his vigilant
antagonist, who had taken up his route to Morristown.
Finding that the Continentals were out of his reach, his
lordship proceeded without halting to Brunswick. Strat-
agems in war, when wisely concerted, and judiciously executed, are considered as characterizing a military genius
of superior order, and is a quality of inestimable value in
every commander. It is often exultingly remarked in our
camp, that Washington was born for the salvation of his
country, and that he is endowed with all the talents and
abilities necessary to qualify him for the great undertaking.
The militia of Jersey, immediately on their being liberated
from the control of the British, flew to arms, exasperated
and stimulated by a recollection of their sufferings, and
have become their most bitter and determined enemies;
and are very active and vigilant in harassing them on all
occasions, keeping a continual watch, and cutting off small
parties whenever opportunities offer. It is gratifying to
the army that Congress have conferred on their General-
issimo more ample powers, and appointed him *Dictator* for
the *limited* term of six months; to reform and new-model
the military arrangements, in such manner as he may
judge most advantageous for the public service. Much
good is expected to result from this measure.

　　30*th*.—It is with infinite satisfaction we learn that the

royal army has been compelled to quit almost every part of the Jerseys, and that our army is pursuing them from post to post, and they find no security but in the vicinity of their shipping.

General Washington has issued a proclamation, commanding all persons having taken the oath of allegiance to Great Britain, and accepted protections and certificates, to deliver up the same, and take the oath of allegiance to the United States—granting at the same time full liberty to all those who prefer the protection of Great Britain to the freedom and happiness of their country, forthwith to withdraw themselves and families to the enemy's lines.

The winter hitherto has been mild and temperate; Lake Champlain is now frozen over, and the ice is about one foot thick; the earth is covered with snow, but the storms have not been very violent, and the cold not so intense as might be expected in a northern climate. There have been frequent instances of persons being detected lurking about the country who are employed by the enemy in enlisting soldiers for the tory regiments in New York. In order effectually to prevent this nefarious conduct, every person of this description who may fall into our hands is to be tried by a court martial, and if found guilty, will be executed as a spy. A few days since one Daniel Strong was found lurking about our army at Peekskill, and on examination enlisting orders were found sewed in his clothes; he was immediately tried as a spy from the enemy, sentenced to suffer death, and was executed accordingly.

February.—The present unfortunate situation of General Lee, who is in close confinement in the provost prison, in New York, affords a topic for general conversation both in and out of the army. A correspondence between General Washington and General Howe has taken place relative to the subject, from which it appears that General Lee receives the most rigid and ungenerous treatment, under the absurd pretence that he is a deserter from the British service, when it is well known that he resigned his commission long before he received an appointment in our army. As we have not in our possession any British officers of equal rank, General Washington has proposed to make an exchange of six Hessian field-officers for General Lee, that being considered as the usual proportion for the disparity of rank. This proposal being rejected, his excellency next required of General Howe, that General Lee should receive from his hands treatment suitable to his rank, and such as the custom of all armies has prescribed for prisoners of war. If this should be refused, General Howe was assured, that the unpleasant expedient of retaliation should be immediately adopted. This unhappy affair soon arrested the attention of Congress, and they resolved "that General Washington inform General Howe, that should the proffered exchange of General Lee not be accepted, and the ill treatment of him be continued, the principle of retaliation shall occasion five of the Hessian field-officers, together with Lieutenant-Colonel A. Campbell, or any other officers that are or may be in our possession, equivalent in number or quality, to be detained in order that the same treatment which General Lee shall receive may be exactly inflicted on their persons." The result of this unfortunate business is, that the threatened retaliation has been resorted to on our part, and that Lieutenant-Colonel Campbell and five Hessian field-officers are committed to prison, and subjected to the same rigorous treatment which it has been ascertained is inflicted on the person of General Lee. Lieutenant-Colonel Campbell, being on parole near Boston, is confined in the jail at Concord. In a letter to General Howe, which has been published, after acknowledging the liberal and generous attention which he had previously received, he describes his present condition as being most horrid, and in his view altogether unjustifiable. It remains therefore with General Howe to afford to Colonel Campbell all the relief which he desires, and extend to him all the comforts and privileges which his rank demands, by first relaxing his severity, and complying with the rules of war, as respects General Lee; it being the determination of our government to place the British prisoners in precisely the same circumstances with our prisoners in their custody. My leisure hours permit me to advert to another subject which excites the interest and the inexpressible indignation of every American. I allude to the abominable conduct of the British commanders towards our unfortunate officers and soldiers, who, by the fortune of war, have fallen into their hands. In all countries and armies, prisoners of war

BRIGADIER GENERAL HENRY LEE.

have a just claim on the duties of humanity; from the moment of their captivity hostilities should cease, the sword should be sheathed; being themselves disarmed, no arm can of right be lifted against them, and while they conduct in a manner becoming their condition, they are entitled to the customary immunities and to be treated with lenity. Among the savage tribes we know their captives are tortured by fire, by the scalping-knife, and the tomahawk, but we are yet, and, for the honor of human nature, hope we ever shall remain, unacquainted with any civilized nation, except the English, who devote their captives to various forms of destruction. It would seem that the application of the term rebel to our prisoners, is sufficient to reconcile the consciences of their victors to inflict on them the most unprecedented cruelties. The following is a brief summary of the systematic method adopted and practised for their destruction, as taken from the New London Gazette, from General Washington's letter of complaint to General Howe, and from the verbal statement of the officers and soldiers who have returned from New York by exchange. They were crowded into the holds of prison-ships, where they were almost suffocated for want of air, and into churches, and open sugar-houses, &c., without covering or a spark of fire. Their allowance of provisions and water for three days, was insufficient for one, and in some instances, they were for four days entirely destitute of food. The pork and bread, for they had no other sustenance, and even the water allowed them, were of the worst possible quality, and totally unfit for human beings. A minute detail of their dreadful sufferings would only serve to harrow up the feelings of surviving friends; as a gross outrage against the principles of humanity, suffice it to say, that in consequence of the most barbarous treatment, died within a few weeks, not less than fifteen hundred American soldiers, brave young men, the pride and shield of our country. After death had released the sufferers, their bodies were dragged out of the prisons, and piled up without doors, till enough were collected for a cart-load, when they were carted out and tumbled into a ditch, and slightly covered with earth. Besides the above diabolical treatment, the prisoners were continually insulted and tantalized by the British officers and malicious tories, cursing

6

and swearing at them as rebels, saying, "this is the just punishment of your rebellion; nay, you are treated too well for rebels, you have not received half you deserve, and half you shall receive; but if you will enlist in his majesty's service, you shall have victuals and clothing enough." Thus these callous-hearted Englishmen meanly endeavored to augment the royal army by the enlistment of American prisoners, or to diminish the number of their opposers; but such was the integrity and patriotism of these men, that hundreds submitted to death rather than become rebels to their native country. In one instance, four of our wounded officers, of respectable rank, were put into a common dirt-cart, and conveyed through the streets of New York as objects of derision, reviled as rebels, and treated with the utmost contempt.* But, it may be inquired, if I mean to describe the British commanders as transformed into demons?

I only record notorious facts, and it is not my journal, but the faithful and impartial pages of history that will transmit to posterity this stigma on the English character. Gracious Heavens! are these the people from whom we derive our origin, and who are inviting the Americans to a reconciliation? A more dreadful curse can scarcely be denounced! It is worthy of observation, that the British and Hessian prisoners in our hands were treated in a manner directly the reverse of that just described, and they never found cause to complain. It is some satisfaction to find, that since the brilliant success of our army in the Jerseys, and a considerable number of British and Hessians having fallen into our hands, the cruel severities inflicted on our

* A friend who was unfortunately a prisoner in New York, has recently favored me with the following facts: In 1776, a number of prisoners were made by the British in our retreat from Long Island. Among others, a Lieutenant Dunscomb, of New York. He and his fellow-officers were ordered before the commanding-general, who, in harsh language, reproached them for their crime of rebellion and its necessary consequences. A gentleman present, began to plead their youth as an apology. It won't do, said General Howe, you shall all be hanged! "Hang, and be d—d," said Dunscomb. They hanged no one that I know of, but they played the fool by going through the farce of making them ride with a rope round their necks seated on coffins to the gallows. Otho Williams, subsequently adjutant-general to the southern army, and a most worthy and amiable gentleman, I particularly know was treated in this manner.

prisoners have been in some degree mitigated. To the foregoing unparalleled catalogue of criminal proceedings, I have to add, from another writer, that the enemy wantonly destroyed the New York water-works, an elegant public library at Trenton, and the grand orrery made by the celebrated Rittenhouse, which was placed in the college at Princeton, a piece of mechanism which the most untutored savage, staying the hand of violence, would have beheld with wonder and delight. Thus are our cruel enemies warring against liberty, virtue and the arts and sciences. To make war against literature and learning is the part of barbarians. I cannot resist the temptation to transcribe a few paragraphs from an elegant speech of Governor Livingston to the general assembly of the state of New Jersey, March the 5th. "They have plundered friends and foes; effects, capable of division, they have divided; such as were not, they have destroyed: they have warred on decrepid old age, warred on defenceless youth; they have committed hostilities against the professors of literature and the ministers of religion, against public records and private monuments; books of improvement, and papers of curiosity; and against the arts and sciences. They have butchered the wounded, asking for quarter; mangled the dead, weltering in their blood; refused to the dead the rites of sepulture; suffered prisoners to perish for want of sustenance; insulted the persons of females; disfigured private dwellings of taste and elegance, and, in the rage of impiety and barbarism, profaned edifices dedicated to Almighty God."

Lake Champlain is now open, and free from ice in its whole extent, and the hostile Indians begin to lurk about our lines, laying wait for their prey. A party of these savages in the British interest, a few days since, discovered about thirty of our unarmed recruits on their way to join their corps at Fort George; they immediately made their attack, killed and tomahawked some, made several prisoners, and escaped towards Canada; a few of these men fortunately escaped, and several that were wounded were brought into our lines. Colonel Whitcomb with a party of continentals was ordered to pursue the Indians; he overtook part of them, and killed several, but the prisoners were carried off beyond his reach.

An enterprise of little importance has lately been put in execution by a detachment of royalists from New York. Their object was to destroy some stores which were deposited at Peekskill. General McDougal, who had the command of the post, with a small number of men, found it prudent to retire, and the enemy accomplished in part the object of the expedition. Lieutenant-Colonel Willet, however, with only sixty men, came on them by surprise, when a skirmish ensued, which obliged them to retire with great precipitation on board their vessels in the North River, after having suffered a considerable loss.

April 1st.—The term of service of Colonel Whitcomb's regiment having expired, they have now left the service, and returned to New England. Having received an invitation from Dr. Jonathan Potts, the surgeon-general in this department, to accept the office of surgeon's-mate in the general hospital, I have received the said appointment, and commenced my official duties accordingly at this place; Dr. D. Townsend being at the same time appointed senior surgeon. We find here about eighty soldiers laboring under various diseases, and eight or ten that have been cruelly wounded by the savages who have been skulking in the woods in the vicinity. In our retired situation here, we are unacquainted with any military transactions in other quarters till they transpire in the public papers.

May.—It is just announced that the enemy have undertaken an expedition to Danbury, in Connecticut, for the purpose of destroying a magazine of stores at that place. Governor Tryon, a major-general of the Provincial troops in New York, was the commander of the detachment, consisting of one thousand eight hundred men, and Brigadier-General Agnew and Sir W. Erskine were commanders under him. When the enemy had landed and commenced their operations in their usual manner, by burning and destroying houses and other buildings, the country was alarmed, the militia collected, and were commanded by Major-General Wooster, Brigadier-Generals Arnold and Silliman. A smart action soon ensued, and continued about one hour, in which our militia and a small number of continentals conducted with distinguished bravery, but being overpowered by a superior force, they were obliged to retreat. The amount of stores destroyed by the enemy

MAJ. GEN. DAVID WOOSTER.

was very considerable, but the loss of valuable officers and men is infinitely more important. General Wooster was mortally wounded, and died soon after. Lieutenant-Colonel Gould and four or five other officers were killed, and about sixty men were killed and wounded. Among the slain is Dr. Atwater, a respectable character, whose death is greatly lamented. General Arnold had his horse shot under him when within ten yards of the enemy, and a soldier was advancing with fixed bayonet towards him, when, with great presence of mind, he drew his pistol from his holsters, and instantly shot him through the body. On the side of the royalists the loss, as stated by General Howe, is one hundred and seventy-two in killed, wounded and missing, but by other accounts it is much more considerable. Among their wounded is Brigadier-General Agnew and two other field-officers.

A Captain Roofa and his lieutenant, two noted tories, lately taken in arms as they were marching towards the enemy, were condemned by a court martial, and hanged at Esopus, in the state of New York, as a suitable reward, says a writer in the newspaper, for their treasonable practices, they having induced a number of others to enlist in the service of the enemy.

June.—Congress have appointed Major-General Schuyler to command in the northern department, including Albany, Ticonderoga, Fort Stanwix and their dependencies, and Major-General St. Clair has the immediate command of the posts of Ticonderoga and Mount Independence. It is also understood that the British government have appointed Lieutenant-General Burgoyne commander-in-chief of their army in Canada, consisting, it is said, of eight or ten thousand men. According to authentic reports, the plan of the British government for the present campaign is that General Burgoyne's army shall take possession of Ticonderoga, and force his way through the country to Albany; to facilitate this event, Colonel St. Leger is to march with a party of British, Germans, Canadians and Indians to the Mohawk river, and make a diversion in that quarter. The royal army at New York, under command of General Howe, is to pass up the Hudson river, and, calculating on success in all quarters, the three armies are to form a junction at Albany. Here, probably, the three commanders

are to congratulate each other on their mighty achievements, and the flattering prospect of crushing the rebellion.
This being accomplished, the communication between the
southern and eastern states will be interrupted, and New
England, as they suppose, may become an easy prey.
Judging from the foregoing detail, a very active campaign
is to be expected, and events of the greatest magnitude are
undoubtedly to be unfolded. The utmost exertions are
now making to strengthen our works at Ticonderoga, and,
if possible, to render the post invulnerable. Mount Independence, directly opposite to Ticonderoga, is strongly
fortified and well supplied with artillery. On the summit
of the mount, which is table-land, is erected a strong fort,
in the centre of which is a convenient square of barracks,
a part of which are occupied for our hospital. The communication between these two places is maintained by a
floating bridge; it is supported on twenty-two sunken piers
of very large timber, the spaces between these are filled
with separate floats, each about fifty feet long and twelve
wide, strongly fastened together with iron chains and rivets.
A boom composed of large pieces of timber, well secured
together by riveted bolts, is placed on the north side. of
the bridge, and by the side of this is placed a double iron
chain, the links of which are one and a half inch square.
The construction of this bridge, boom and chain, of four
hundred yards in length, has proved a most laborious
undertaking, and the expense must have been immense.
It is, however, supposed to be admirably adapted to the
double purpose of a communication, and an impenetrable
barrier to any vessels that might attempt to pass our works.
By way of amusement I went with three gentlemen of our
hospital to endeavor to explore a high mountain in this
vicinity. With much difficulty we clambered up and
reached the summit. From this commanding eminence
we had one of the most singularly romantic views which
imagination can paint. Northward we behold Lake
Champlain, a prodigious expanse of unruffled water, widen-
ing and straitening as the banks and clifts project into its
channel. This lake extends about one hundred miles
towards Quebec, and is from one to five miles wide. On
each side is a thick uninhabited wilderness, variegated by
hills and dales; here the majestic oak, chestnut and pine,

rear their lofty heads; there the diminutive shrub forms a thicket for the retreat of wild beasts. Looking southwest from our stand, we have a view of part of Lake George, emptying its waters into Lake Champlain, near Ticonderoga. Turning to the east, the prodigious heights called Green Mountains, ascending almost to the clouds, are exhibited to view, with the settlements in that tract of territory called New Hampshire grant. The ancient fortress at Crown Point is about twelve miles north of this place; it is by nature a very strong position, but it has been abandoned by both armies.

July 1st.—We are now assailed by a proclamation of a very extraordinary nature from General Burgoyne, enumerating a string of titles, which he has doubtless received from his royal master as a reward for his merit. From the pompous manner in which he has arrayed his titles, we are led to suppose that he considers them as more than a match for all the military force which we can bring against him. They stand thus: "*By John Burgoyne, Esquire, Lieutenant-General of his Majesty's forces in America, Colonel of the Queen's regiment of Light Dragoons, Governor of Fort William, in North Britain, one of the Commons of Great Britain in Parliament, and commanding an army and fleet employed on an expedition from Canada, &c. &c.*"

This sanguinary proclamation is to be viewed as the forerunner of his formidable army, and all the opposers of his authority are menaced with his avenging power. "I have," says the proclamation, "but to give stretch to the Indian forces under my direction, and they amount to thousands, to overtake the hardened enemies of Great Britain and America. I consider them the same wherever they may lurk." The British ministry, not satisfied with the disgraceful expedient of hiring foreign mercenaries, resort also to the savages of the wilderness for aid in the glorious cause of tyranny and of spreading the horrors of war by fire and sword throughout our country. The militia of New England are daily coming in to increase our strength; the number of our troops, and our ability to defend the works against the approaching enemy, are considerations which belong to our commanding officers; in their breasts let the important secret remain, and in their superior judgment our confidence must be reposed. One fact, however, is notorious, that when the troops are directed to man the lines, there is not a sufficient number to occupy their whole extent. It appears, nevertheless, so far as I can learn, to be the prevalent opinion, that we shall be able to repel the meditated attack, and defeat the views of the royal commander; both officers and men are in high spirits and prepared for the contest.

July 2d.—The British army is now approaching; some of their savage allies have been seen in the vicinity of our out works, which, with the block-house beyond the old French lines, has this day been abandoned. On the 3d and 4th, the enemy are making their approaches and gaining as is supposed some advantages. They have taken possession of Mount Hope, our batteries are now opened, and a cannonading has commenced. General St. Clair endeavors to animate the troops, and orders every man to repair to the alarm-posts at morning and evening roll-call, and to be particularly alert and vigilant. There seems to be a diversity of opinion whether General Burgoyne intends to besiege our garrison, or to attempt to possess himself of it by an assault on our lines.

5th.—It is with astonishment that we find the enemy have taken possession of an eminence called *Sugar-loaf Hill,* or *Mount Defiance,* which, from its height and proximity, completely overlooks and commands all our works at Ticonderoga and Mount Independence. This mount it is said ought long since to have been fortified by our army, but its extreme difficulty of access, and the want of a sufficient number of men, are the reasons assigned for its being neglected. The situation of our garrison is viewed as critical and alarming; a few days, it is expected, will decide our fate. We have reason to apprehend the most fatal effects from their battery on Sugar-loaf Hill.

14th.—By reason of an extraordinary and unexpected event, the course of my Journal has been interrupted for several days. At about twelve o'clock, in the night of the 5th instant, I was urgently called from sleep, and informed that our army was in motion, and was instantly to abandon Ticonderoga and Mount Independence. I could scarcely believe that my informant was in earnest, but the confusion and bustle soon convinced me that it was really true, and that the short time allowed demanded my utmost industry.

It was enjoined on me immediately to collect the sick and wounded, and as much of the hospital stores as possible, and assist in embarking them on board the batteaux and boats at the shore. Having with all possible despatch completed our embarkation, at three o'clock in the morning of the 6th, we commenced our voyage up the South bay to Skeensboro', about thirty miles. Our fleet consisted of five armed gallies and two hundred batteaux and boats deeply laden with cannon, tents, provisions, invalids and women. We were accompanied by a guard of six hundred men, commanded by Colonel Long, of New Hampshire. The night was moon-light and pleasant, the sun burst forth in the morning with uncommon lustre, the day was fine, the water's surface serene and unruffled. The shore on each side exhibited a variegated view of huge rocks, caverns and clefts, and the whole was bounded by a thick impenetrable wilderness. My pen would fail in the attempt to describe a scene so enchantingly sublime. The occasion was peculiarly interesting, and we could but look back with regret, and forward with apprehension. We availed ourselves, however, of the means of enlivening our spirits. The drum and fife afforded us a favorite music; among the hospital stores we found many dozen bottles of choice wine, and, breaking off their necks, we cheered our hearts with the nectareous contents. At three o'clock in the afternoon we reached our destined port at Skeensboro', being the head of navigation for our gallies. Here we were unsuspicious of danger; but, behold! Burgoyne himself was at our heels. In less than two hours we were struck with surprise and consternation by a discharge of cannon from the enemy's fleet, on our gallies and batteaux lying at the wharf. By uncommon efforts and industry they had broken through the bridge, boom and chain, which cost our people such immense labor, and had almost overtaken us on the lake, and horridly disastrous indeed would have been our fate. It was not long before it was perceived that a number of their troops and savages had landed, and were rapidly advancing towards our little party. The officers of our guard now attempted to rally the men and form them in battle array, but this was found impossible; every effort proved unavailing, and in the utmost panic they were seen to fly in

every direction for personal safety. In this desperate
condition, I perceived our officers scampering for their
baggage; I ran to the batteau, seized my chest, carried it
a short distance, took from it a few articles, and instantly
followed in the train of our retreating party. We took
the route to Fort Anne, through a narrow defile in the
woods, and were so closely pressed by the pursuing enemy,
that we frequently heard calls from the rear to "march on,
the Indians are at our heels." Having marched all night
we reached Fort Anne at five o'clock in the morning, where
we found provisions for our refreshment. A small rivulet
called Wood Creek is navigable for boats from Skeensboro'
to Fort Anne, by which means some of our invalids and
baggage made their escape; but all our cannon, provisions,
and the bulk of our baggage, with several invalids, fell
into the enemy's hands.

On the 7th instant, we received a small reïnforcement
from Fort Edward, by order of Major-General Schuyler,
and on discovering that a detachment of the enemy under
command of Colonel Hill had arrived in our vicinity, a
party from our fort was ordered to attack them in their
covert in the woods. The two parties were soon engaged
in a smart skirmish, which continued for several hours,
and resulted greatly to our honor and advantage; the
enemy, being almost surrounded, were on the point of
surrendering, when our ammunition being expended, and
a party of Indians arriving and setting up the war-whoop,
this being followed by three cheers from their friends the
English, the Americans were induced to give way and
retreat. One surgeon with a wounded captain and twelve
or fifteen privates, were taken and brought into our fort.
The surgeon informed me that he was in possession of
books, &c. taken from my chest at Skeensboro', and, singular to relate, some of the British prisoners obtained in
the same manner, and had in their pockets, a number, of
private letters which I had received from a friend in Massachusetts, and which were now returned to me. Fort
Anne being a small picket fort of no importance, orders
were given to set it on fire, and on the 8th we departed
for Fort Edward situated about thirty miles southward,
on the banks of Hudson river. General St. Clair, with
his main army from Ticonderoga, took a circuitous route

through the woods to Hubbardtown and Charlestown, in the New Hampshire grants, and being pursued by a strong detachment from Burgoyne's army, his rear guard, commanded by Colonel Francis, was overtaken, and on the 7th instant, a very close and severe engagement took place, in which bloody conflict, the brave Colonel Francis fell with other valuable officers, while fighting with distinguished gallantry. The Americans made an honorable defence, and finally a secure retreat. We lost in this action about three hundred, in killed, wounded and prisoners. The enemy, according to estimation, about two hundred. On the 12th, General St. Clair arrived here with the remains of his army, greatly distressed and worn down by fatigue. General Schuyler is commander at this post, he has a small army of continentals and militia, and is making every possible exertion, by taking up bridges, throwing obstructions in the roads and passes, by fallen trees, &c. to impede the march of Burgoyne's army towards Albany.

The abandonment of Ticonderoga and Mount Independence has occasioned the greatest surprise and alarm. No event could be more unexpected nor more severely felt throughout our army and country. This disaster has given to our cause a dark and gloomy aspect, but our affairs are not desperate, and our exertions ought to be in proportion to our misfortunes and our exigencies. The conduct of General St. Clair on this occasion has rendered him very unpopular, and subjected him to general censure and reproach; there are some, indeed, who even accuse him of treachery; but time and calm investigation must decide whether he can vindicate himself as a judicious and prudent commander. There is much reason to suppose that neither the strength of Burgoyne's army, nor the weakness of our garrison were properly considered or generally understood. It must be universally conceded, that when the enemy had effected their great object by hoisting cannon from tree to tree, till they reached the summit of *Sugar-loaf Hill*, the situation of our garrison had become perilous in the extreme. General Schuyler is not altogether free from public reprehension, alleging that he ought in duty to have been present at Ticonderoga during the critical period. It is predicted by some of our well-informed and respectable characters, that this event, apparently so calamitous, will ultimately prove advantageous, by drawing the British army into the heart of our country, and thereby place them more immediately within our power.

It may be deemed ludicrous that I should record a rumor so extravagantly ridiculous as the following, but it has received too much credence to be altogether omitted. It has been industriously reported, that Generals Schuyler and St. Clair acted the part of traitors to their country, and that they were paid for their treason by the enemy in *silver balls* shot from Burgoyne's guns into our camp, and that they were collected by order of General St. Clair, and divided between him and General Schuyler.

25*th*.—The sick soldiers under my care at this place have been accommodated in barracks and tents. I have now received orders to accompany them to the hospital at Albany, about fifty-five miles; boats being provided, we embarked about forty sick and invalids, and proceeded down the North river, and arrived on the third day at the place of our destination.

August 3*d*.—The pleasing information is received here that Lieutenant-Colonel Barton, of the Rhode Island militia, planned a bold exploit for the purpose of surprising and taking Major-General Prescott, the commanding officer of the royal army at Newport. Taking with him, in the night, about forty men in two boats with oars muffled, he had the address to elude the vigilance of the ships of war and guard boats, and having arrived undiscovered at the quarters of General Prescott, they were taken for the sentinels, and the general was not alarmed till his captors were at the door of his lodging chamber, which was fast closed. A negro man, named Prince, instantly thrust his beetle head through the pannel-door, and seized his victim while in bed. The general's aid-de-camp leaped from a window undressed, and attempted to escape, but was taken, and with the general brought off in safety. In repassing the water guards, General Prescott said to Colonel Barton, "Sir, I did not think it possible you could escape the vigilance of the water guards." This is the second time that General Prescott has been a prisoner in our hands within two years. This adventure is extremely honorable to the enterprising spirit of Colonel Barton, and is considered as ample retaliation for the capture of General Lee by Colonel Harcourt. The event occasions great joy and exultation, as it puts in our possession an officer of equal rank with General Lee, by which means an exchange may be obtained. Congress resolved that an elegant sword should be presented to Colonel Barton for his brave exploit. It has been ascertained that General Howe has relaxed in his rigid treatment of General Lee, and conducted towards him in a manner suitable to his rank. The Hessian officers, on whom retaliation had been inflicted, are also restored to their former condition as prisoners of war.

It appears by the papers, that Congress resolved, on the 14th of June last, that the flag of the thirteen United States be thirteen stripes, alternate red and white; that the union be thirteen stars, white in a blue field, representing a new constellation.

His Excellency General Washington, at his quarters in the Jerseys, has published a *manifesto* in answer to General Burgoyne's proclamation, from which I extract a few paragraphs. He observes, "The associated armies in America act from the noblest motives, and for the purest purposes: their common object is liberty. The same principles actuated the arms of Rome in the days of her glory, and the same object was the reward of Roman valor. When these sacred ideas are profaned, when the abominable mixture of mercenary, foreign and savage forces dare to mention *the love of country, and the general privileges of mankind,*" referring to Burgoyne's proclamation, "the freemen of America protest against such abuse of language and prostitution of sentiment." In another paragraph, "We beg leave to observe, if the power of his Britannic Majesty's fleets and armies have been driven from Boston, repulsed from Charleston, cut off at Trenton, expelled the Jerseys, and be now, after almost three campaigns, commencing its operation, that this is a power we do not dread." In the close, "Harassed as we are by unrelenting persecution, obliged by every tie to repel violence by force, urged by self-preservation to exert the strength which Providence has given us to defend our natural rights against the aggressor; we appeal to the hearts of all mankind for the justice of our cause; its event we submit to Him who speaks the fate of nations, in humble confidence that as his omniscient eye taketh note even of the sparrow that falleth to the ground, so He will not withdraw his countenance from a people who humbly array themselves under his banner in defence of the noblest principles with which he hath adorned humanity." It is a matter of pride to our country that our commander-in-chief has exhibited a production so far surpassing in dignity of sentiment and justness of observation the pompous proclamation to which this is a rejoinder. It is no less satisfactory to reflect, that the measure referred to has not been productive of those glorious advantages to the royal cause, or the dire consequences as respects our own, which the sanguine spirit of its author had contemplated. Though he threatened us with all the outrages of war, arrayed in terrific forms, aided by savages eager to be let loose on their prey, yet the proclamation has been viewed rather as a curious model of an ostentatious display of self-importance than a formidable weapon calculated to awe a free people into submission.

8th.—We have just been apprised, by express from the Mohawk country, that Colonel St. Leger and Sir John Johnson, with a body of Britons, Canadians, tories and Indians, had invested Fort Schuyler, one hundred and ten miles from Albany; that General Herkimer, with about eight hundred militia, was advancing to disperse this motley collection, and to relieve the garrison; but unfortunately he fell into an ambuscade and suffered a considerable loss. Being himself wounded in both legs, he was seen sitting on a stump, and courageously encouraging his men, by which they maintained their ground and did great execution among the enemy. Several of the Indian chiefs were slain by the first fire, which so disheartened the remainder, that they were thrown into the greatest confusion, and turning on the tories and other white people, a warm contention ensued between them, and many of the whites were killed. Colonel Gansevort, the commander of the fort, sent out Lieutenant-Colonel Willet with two hundred and fifty men, who bravely routed the Indians and tories, destroyed their provisions and took their kettles, blankets, muskets, tomahawks, deer-skins, &c. with five colors, and returned to the fort. The brave General Herkimer soon died of his wounds, and one hundred and sixty of his militia-men, having fought like lions, were killed, besides a great number wounded. St. Leger's victory over our militia was purchased at a dear price, more than seventy of his Indians were slain, and among them a large proportion of their most distinguished and favorite warriors, and the survivors were exceedingly dissatisfied. The object of the expedition was far from being accomplished; the commander did not, however, despair of getting possession of the fort; for this purpose he sent in a flag demanding a surrender. He greatly magnified his own strength, asserted that Burgoyne was at Albany; and threatened that on refusal his Indians would destroy all the inhabitants in the vicinity, and so soon as they could enter the fort every man would be sacrificed. Colonel Gansevort nobly replied in the negative, being determined to defend the fort at every hazard. Aware, however, of his perilous situation, he found means of sending to General Schuyler at Stillwater for assistance. General Arnold was now despatched with a brigade of troops to attack the besiegers; but finding their force greatly superior to his own, he sent back for a reinforcement of one thousand light troops.

An object which cannot be accomplished by force is often obtained by means of stratagem. Lieutenant-Colonel John Brooks, an intelligent officer from Massachusetts, being in advance with a small detachment, fortunately found one Major Butler, a noted officer among the Indians, endeavoring to influence the inhabitants in their favor, and he was immediately secured. A man also by the name of Cuyler, who was proprietor of a handsome estate in the vicinity, was taken up as a spy. Colonel Brooks proposed that he should be employed as a deceptive messenger to spread the alarm and induce the enemy to retreat. General Arnold soon after arrived, and approved the scheme of Colonel Brooks; it was accordingly agreed that Cuyler should be liberated and his estate secured to him on the condition that he would return to the enemy and make such exaggerated report of General Arnold's force as to alarm and put them to flight. Several friendly Indians being present, one of their head men advised that Cuyler's coat should be shot through in two or three places to add credibility to his story. Matters being thus adjusted, the impostor proceeded directly to the Indian camp, where

he was well known, and informed their warriors that
Major Butler was taken, and that himself narrowly escaped,
several shot having passed through his coat, and that
General Arnold with a vast force was advancing rapidly
toward them. In aid of the project, a friendly Indian followed, and arrived about an hour after with a confirmation
of Cuyler's report. This stratagem was successful: the
Indians instantly determined to quit their ground, and
make their escape, nor was it in the power of St. Leger
and Sir John, with all their art of persuasion, to prevent
it. When St. Leger remonstrated with them, the reply
of the chiefs was, "When we marched down, you told us
there would be no fighting for us Indians; we might go
down and smoke our pipes; but now a number of our
warriors have been killed, and you mean to sacrifice us."
The consequence was, that St. Leger, finding himself deserted by his Indians, to the number of seven or eight
hundred, deemed his situation so hazardous that he decamped in the greatest hurry and confusion, leaving his
tents with most of his artillery and stores in the field.
General Arnold with his detachment was now at liberty
to return to the main army at Stillwater; and thus have
we clipped the right wing of General Burgoyne. In the
evening, while on their retreat, St. Leger and Sir John
got into a warm altercation, criminating each other for
the ill success of the expedition. Two sachems, observing
this, resolved to have a laugh at their expense. In their
front was a bog of clay and mud; they directed a young
warrior to loiter in the rear, and then, of a sudden, run as
if alarmed, calling out, *They are coming, they are coming!*
On hearing this, the two commanders in a fright took to
their heels, rushing into the bog, frequently falling and
sticking in the mud, and the men threw away their packs
and hurried off. This and other jokes were several times
repeated during the night for many miles.

30th.—The city of Albany is situated on the west bank
of the Hudson, or North river, one hundred and sixty
miles north from New York, and the river admits of sloop
navigation between these two cities. It consists of about
three hundred houses, chiefly in the gothic style, the gable
ends to the street. There is an ancient Dutch church of
stone, a Congregational church, and a decent edifice called

MAJOR GENERAL PHILIP SCHUYLER.

City Hall, which accommodates occasionally their general assembly and courts of justice. The hospital was erected during the last French war; it is situated on an eminence overlooking the city. It is two stories high, having a wing at each end and a piazza in front above and below. It contains forty wards, capable of accommodating five hundred patients, besides the rooms appropriated to the use of surgeons and other officers, stores, &c.

Our army under General Schuyler have left their unimportant station at Fort Edward, and having made a stand for a few days at Saratoga, they fell back to Stillwater, twenty-five miles above Albany, where they have taken their station, and are daily receiving rëinforcements of militia and some continental troops. On the retreat of our army from Fort Edward, Major Hull commanded the rear guard, and being two miles in the rear, was attacked by a large body of the enemy, and after a severe contest, in which he lost thirty or forty of his men, he was compelled to retreat. He received the thanks of General Schuyler for his brave and judicious conduct. General Burgoyne, we learn, is extremely embarrassed, and his march greatly impeded by the obstructions in the roads effected by order of Gen. Schuyler; he has at length, however, surmounted numerous difficulties, and reached the vicinity of Saratoga. Finding himself in want of provisions, horses to mount his cavalry, and teams to transport his stores and baggage, he resorted to one of the most chimerical and romantic projects that could enter the imagination of man. Being informed that a large quantity of stores, corn, cattle, &c., were deposited at Bennington, in the New Hampshire grants, he planned an expedition for the purpose of possessing himself of this treasure. Presuming, probably, that his late success and his manifesto had produced such wonderful effects, that no more opposition would be made to his progress in the country, he despatched Col. Baum, a German officer, with five hundred Hessians and tories and one hundred Indians, with two field-pieces. The colonel was furnished with the following curious instructions, which fell into the hands of General Stark:

" *To proceed through the New Hampshire grants, cross the mountains, scour the country, with Peter's corps (tories) and the Indians, from Rockingham to Otter creek, to get horses, carriages, and cattle, and mount*
7

Reidesel's regiment of dragoons, to go down Connecticut river as far as Brattleborough, and return by the great road to Albany, there to meet General Burgoyne, to endeavor to make the country believe it was the advanced body of the General's army who was to cross Connecticut river and proceed to Boston; and that at Springfield they were to be joined by the troops from Rhode Island. All officers, civil and military, acting under the Congress, were to be made prisoners. To tax the towns where they halted, with such articles as they wanted, and take hostages for the performance, &c. You are to bring all horses fit to mount the dragoons or to serve as battalion horses for the troops, with as many saddles and bridles as can be found. The number of horses requisite besides those for the dragoons ought to be thirteen hundred, if you can bring more, so much the better. The horses must be tied in strings of ten each, in order that one man may lead ten horses."

This redoubtable commander surely must be one of the happiest men of the age, to imagine that such prodigious achievements were at his command; that such invaluable resources were within his grasp. But, alas! the wisest of men are liable to disappointment in their sanguine calculations, and to have their favorite projects frustrated by the casualties of war. This is remarkably verified in the present instance. Preceded by the manifesto, and having his commission in his pocket, Colonel Baum marched, on the 14th of August, at the head of his command, to execute the orders of his general; he proceeded about twelve or thirteen miles, where he halted, and secured himself by intrenchments. It was a providental circumstance that General Stark was at or near Bennington, with about eight hundred New England militia, part of whom being from the New Hampshire grants, are called Green Mountain Boys. He advanced towards the enemy to reconnoitre their position, and some skirmishing ensued, in which thirty of them with two Indian chiefs were killed and wounded, with little loss on our side. Colonel Baum, alarmed at his situation, despatched a messenger to Burgoyne for a reinforcement. The 15th being a very rainy day, there was only some skirmishing in small parties. On the 16th, General Stark, assisted by Colonel Warner, matured his arrangements for battle; he divided his troops into three divisions, and ordered Colonel Nichols, with two hundred and fifty men, to gain the rear of the left wing, of the enemy, and Colonel Hendrick the rear of their right wing, with three hundred men, while he attacked their front. The Indians, alarmed, at the appearance of being surrounded, endeavored to make their escape in a single file between the two parties, with their horrid yells and jingling of cow-bells. The flanking parties approaching each other in their rear, and General Stark making a bold and furious onset in front, a general and close conflict ensued, and continued with more or less severity for about two hours. Though Colonel Baum had nearly twice their numbers, and was defended by breastworks, the force opposed to them proved irresistible, forcing their breastworks at the muzzles of their guns, and obliging them to ground their arms and surrender at discretion, so that the victory on our part was complete. We took two pieces of brass cannon, and a number of prisoners, with baggage, &c. This was hardly accomplished, when Colonel Breyman, with one thousand German troops, arrived with two field-pieces, to reïnforce Colonel Baum, who had just been defeated. General Stark's troops were now scattered, some attending the wounded, some guarding the prisoners, and still more in pursuit of plunder; and all exhausted by extreme hunger and fatigue. At this critical moment, Colonel Warner's regiment arrived, and the other troops being rallied, the whole were ordered to advance. A field-piece had been taken from Baum in the forenoon, and Stark ordered it to be drawn to the scene of action, but his men having never seen a cannon, knew not how to load it; the general dismounted, and taught them by loading it himself. An action soon commenced, and proved warm and desperate, in which both sides displayed the most daring bravery, till night approached, when the enemy yielded a second time in one day to their Yankee conquerors. The German troops being totally routed, availed themselves of the darkness of night to effect their retreat. The whole number of killed, wounded and prisoners, was nine hundred and thirty-four, including one hundred and fifty-seven tories; of this number, six hundred and fifty-four are prisoners. Colonel Baum received a mortal wound, of which he soon after died. Besides the above, one thousand stand of arms, four brass field-pieces, two hundred and fifty dragoon swords, eight loads of baggage, and twenty horses, fell into our hands. The loss on our side is not more than one hundred in the whole. The officers and men engaged in this splendid enterprise merit all the praise which a grateful country can bestow; they fought

disciplined troops completely accoutred, while they wielded
their ordinary firelocks with scarce a bayonet, and at first
without cannon.   The consequences must be most auspicious as respects our affairs in the northern department.
Burgoyne must feel the clipping of another wing, and it
must diminish his confidence in his successful career.   The
event will also be productive of the happiest effects on the
spirits of our militia, by increasing their confidence in their
own prowess.   The following anecdote deserves to be
noticed for the honor of the person who is the subject of
it, though his name has not been ascertained.   A venerable
old man had five sons in the field of battle near Bennington, and being told that he had been unfortunate in one
of his sons, replied, "What! has he misbehaved? did he
desert his post, or shrink from the charge?"   "No, sir,"
says the informant, "worse than that: he is among the
slain; he fell contending mightily in the cause."   "Then
I am satisfied," replied the good old man; "bring him in,
and lay him before me, that I may behold and survey the
darling of my soul."   On which the corpse was brought
in and laid before him.   He then called for a bowl of
water and a napkin, and with his own hands washed the
gore and dirt from his son's corpse, and wiped his gaping
wounds, with a complacency, as he himself expressed it,
which before he had never felt or experienced.

Major-General Horatio Gates has superseded General
Schuyler as commander-in-chief of the northern department, and has passed through this city on his way to
Stillwater.   This appointment will be very satisfactory to
our army, as General Gates has the respect and confidence
of the New England troops.

September 2d.—General Gates has issued a proclamation
to counteract any influence which Burgoyne's sanguinary
manifesto might have produced, interdicting all communication with the royal army, and endeavoring to calm the
fears of the inhabitants, by promising them all the protection in his power.   Burgoyne's manifesto, however,
denouncing fire and sword, instead of alarming into submission, excites universal indignation and contempt; instead of conciliating, and increasing the number of his
friends, serves only to exasperate and augment our means
of resistance and opposition to his views.   It was not long

indeed before some innocent persons were made victims of savage barbarity, by means of the tomahawk and scalping-knife, in the hands of the barbarians under his command. Among the first of these victims, was Miss Jenny McCrea, who was murdered in a manner extremely shocking to the feelings of humanity. The father of Miss McCrea was friendly towards the royalists, and the young lady was engaged to marry a refugee officer in Burgoyne's army, by the name of Jones, and waited his arrival in order to have the marriage consummated. When our army retreated from Fort Edward, Miss McCrea had the indiscretion to remain behind, probably with the expectation of meeting her lover. The Indians, however, soon made her their prisoner, and on their return towards Burgoyne's camp, a quarrel arose to decide who should hold possession of the fair prize. During the controversy, one of the monsters struck his tomahawk into her skull, and immediately stripped off her scalp.

General Gates complains to General Burgoyne of this and other outrages in the following words: "A young lady, Miss McCrea, lovely to the sight, of virtuous character and amiable disposition, engaged to be married to an officer in your army, was, with other women and children, taken out of a house near Fort Edward, carried into the woods, and there scalped and mangled in a most shocking manner. Two parents with their six children, were all treated with the same inhumanity, while quietly residing in their own happy and peaceful dwellings. The miserable fate of Miss McCrea was peculiarly aggravated by her being dressed to receive her promised husband—but met her murderer, employed by you. Upwards of one hundred men, women and children, have perished by the hands of ruffians, to whom it is asserted you have paid the price of blood." This appears since to be rather an exaggerated charge. In General Burgoyne's reply, he says, "The fact was no premeditated barbarity: on the contrary, two chiefs who had brought Miss McCrea off, for the purpose of security, not of violence to her person, disputed which should be her guard, and in a fit of savage passion, in the one from whose hands she was snatched, the unhappy woman became the victim." He expressed sorrow and regret for the tragic scenes, and further stated

that he obliged the Indians to give up the murderer into
his hands, and he certainly should have suffered an ignominious death, had he not been convinced that a pardon
on his terms would be more efficacious than an execution,
to prevent further mischief. That he paid for scalps, he
denies; but the Indians were to receive compensation for
prisoners. This cruel conduct of the royalists is contemplated with horror and detestation by all ranks of people,
except their friends and adherents. It is impossible not to
detest that cause and that army which accepts the aid of savage auxiliaries, and encourages them in inhuman slaughter
and bloodshed. This measure was certainly countenanced
and recommended by his majesty and his ministers, and
General Burgoyne acknowledges that he allowed the Indians to take the scalps of the dead. . It must be most
painful for the impartial historian to record, and it will
require the strongest faith of the reader in future ages to
credit, the disgraceful story that Britons, who pride themselves on their civility and humanity, employed the wild
savages of the wilderness in a war against a people united
to them by the ties of consanguinity. That age, and the
helpless invalid, women, and children at the breast, are all
alike subjected to the merciless fury of barbarians. That
British generals should be so regardless of the dignity of
their station, and the voice of humanity, as to receive from
the hands of these ferocious wretches the scalps torn from
the skulls of innocent persons!

13th.—There is a constant intercourse kept up between
this city and our army near Stillwater, by which we are
regularly apprised of daily occurrences. It is now ascertained that Burgoyne has crossed the Hudson, and encamped at Saratoga, about thirty-six miles above Albany.

17th.—General Gates, reposing full confidence in the
courage and strength of his army, seems to have determined to march and confront his formidable enemy, and
endeavor to force him and his troops back to Canada,
which, in his orders, issued to inspire his troops with ardor,
he says, "has been successfully begun by General Stark
and Colonel Warner at the eastward; and by General
Herkimer and Colonel Gansevort at the westward; and
cannot, with the blessing of Heaven, fail to be equally
prosperous in the hands of the generals and soldiers ap

pointed to face the enemy's main army at the northward.
If the murder of aged parents, with their innocent children; if mangling the blooming virgin, and inoffensive
youth, are inducements to revenge—if the righteous cause
of freedom, and the happiness of posterity, are motives to
stimulate to conquer their mercenary and merciless foes,
the time is now come, when they are called on by their
country, by their general, and by every thing divine and
human, to vanquish the foe."

18th and 19th.—Our army is advancing towards the
enemy in three columns, under Generals Lincoln and
Arnold, General Gates in the centre. A terrible conflict
is daily expected; both parties appear to be determined to
commence the work of destruction.

20th.—By express arrived in this city last night, it is
announced that the two armies fought in the field, yesterday, a very sanguinary battle, the particulars of which
are not fully understood; but it is reported that from the
closeness and obstinacy of the combat, the carnage on both
sides was prodigious. It is with inexpressible satisfaction
that we learn our troops behaved with that undaunted
bravery which has secured to them the victory, and were
it not for the darkness of the evening when the battle
closed, it would have been more complete.

21st and 22d.—A considerable number of officers and
soldiers who were wounded in the late battle, have been
brought here to be accommodated in our hospital, or in
private houses in this city. Several of these unfortunate
but brave men have received wounds of a very formidable
and dangerous nature, and many of them must be subjected to capital operations.

23d.—From the officers who were engaged in the battle,
I have obtained the following particulars. Our army,
under the command of General Gates, was stationed in
the vicinity of Stillwater, when they advanced towards
the enemy and offered them battle. Colonel Morgan's
regiment of riflemen, and Major Dearborn's light infantry,
being in front, received the first fire about noon, on the
19th instant. General Burgoyne was at the head of his
army, and Generals Phillips, Reidesel and Frazer, with
their respective commands, were actively engaged. At
about three o'clock, both armies being formed in a line of

battle, the action became general, and the combatants on
both sides evinced that ardor and gallantry which shows
a determination to conquer or die. The firing for about
three hours was incessant, with continued tremendous roar
and blaze, filling the field with carnage and death. Few
battles have been more obstinate and unyielding—at one
point the British are overpowered; but being rëinforced,
the Americans are baffled; these, being supported and re-
newing their efforts, rēgain their advantages; the same
ground is occupied alternately, the dead and wounded of
both parties are mingled together. The British resort repeatedly to their bayonets without effect—the Americans
resist and foil their attempts. Captain Jones, of the British artillery, had the command of four pieces of cannon,
which he conducted with great skill and valor till he fell,
and thirty-six out of forty-eight of his artillery men were
killed or wounded; his cannon were repeatedly taken and
rētaken, but finally remained with the enemy for the want
of horses to bring them off. During the engagement, a
number of our soldiers placed themselves in the boughs
of high trees, in the rear and flanks, and took every opportunity of destroying the British officers by single shot;
in one instance, General Burgoyne was the object, but the
aid-de-camp of General Phillips received the ball through
his arm, while delivering a message to Burgoyne; the
mistake, it is said, was occasioned by having his saddle
furnished with rich lace, and was supposed by the marksman to be the British commander. In the dusk of evening the battle terminated, the British in one quarter silently
retreating, the Americans in another give way, and quit
the long-contested field. Lieutenant-Colonel Brooks, with
the eighth Massachusetts regiment, remained in the field
till about eleven o'clock, and was the last who retired.
Major Hull commanded a detachment of three hundred
men, who fought with such signal ardor, that more than
half of them were killed or wounded. The whole number
of Americans engaged in this action, was about two thousand five hundred; the remainder of the army, from its
unfavorable situation, took little or no part in the action.
The British have suffered a loss, as is supposed, of more
than five hundred in killed, wounded and prisoners. On
the side of the Americans, sixty-four were killed, two

hundred and seventeen wounded, and thirty-eight missing. Among the killed, are Colonels Adams and Colburn, two valuable officers, much regretted. The victory on this important occasion is claimed by the enemy, but the advantages are most decidedly on the side of the Americans; they were the assailants—they held their ground during the day, and at the close retired to their encampment without being pursued. The royal army lay all the ensuing night on their arms at some distance from the field of battle.

24th.—General Lincoln having the command of a body of New England militia, detached Colonel Brown with five hundred men to the landing at Lake George, about three miles from Ticonderoga, and more than forty miles in the rear of the British army. Two other detachments were also sent towards Mount Independence, Fort Anne and Fort Edward. These expeditions being faithfully executed, were attended with complete success. Colonel Brown had the address to surprise all the out-posts in the vicinity of Ticonderoga, and took immediate possession of Mount Defiance, Mount Hope, and a block-house, with two hundred batteaux, an armed sloop, and several gun-boats, about three hundred prisoners, with their small arms, and released one hundred American prisoners from their confinement.

October 1st.—The situation of the royal army under Burgoyne, is now considered extremely precarious; his march to Albany is deemed absolutely impracticable, and a retreat to Canada must be attended with insurmountable difficulties and dangers. It is well understood, that he calculates on the coöperation of Sir Henry Clinton, by sending from New York a force up the North river to endeavor to effect a passage to Albany, or at least to occasion such alarm, as to draw off a part of General Gates' army from before him. Messengers or persons in the character of spies, are frequently suspected of passing from one British commander to the other. A man, by name Nathan Palmer, was, a few days since, seized in General Putnam's camp, at Peekskill, under suspicious circumstances, and on trial was found to be a lieutenant in the tory new levies, and he was executed as a spy.[*]

---

[*] For General Putnam's letter to Governor Tryon, respecting Palmer, see life of Putnam in the Appendix.

4th.—By intelligence from camp, it appears that Burgoyne has thrown up a line of intrenchments in front of his camp, and is making every possible effort to strengthen his position and prepare for another conflict. The Canadians and his savage allies being greatly dissatisfied and discouraged, have deserted his standard since the last battle. The advantages obtained over the enemy on this occasion, excites the greatest exultation and rejoicing throughout our army and country. It is indeed a remarkable fact, which must animate the heart of every friend to the cause of America, that our troops, so little accustomed to encounter the prowess of European veterans, and the peculiar warfare of the savages, should face these enemies with such undaunted courage and intrepidity. Sanguine hopes are now entertained that we shall, by the help of Providence, be finally enabled to destroy or capture the whole British army. Our troops are panting for another opportunity of displaying their valor, and another dreadful conflict is daily expected; alternate hopes and fears continually agitate our minds, and create the greatest anxiety and solicitude. What can excite ideas more noble and sublime, than impending military events, on which depend the destiny of a nation?

6th.—An express passed through this city, on his way to General Gates' head-quarters, with the information that a detachment of troops from New York, supposed to be about four thousand, under command of Sir Henry Clinton and General Vaughan, have undertaken an expedition up the North river. Their object undoubtedly is, to possess themselves of Fort Montgomery and Fort Clinton, in the highlands, and to make a diversion in favor of Burgoyne. General Putnam was stationed at Peekskill with a small force, but being totally unable to cope with the enemy, has retired to some distance. Should this expedition be crowned with success, it will be in the power of Sir Henry Clinton to convey his army to this city, and even to our camp at Stillwater, which will place our army between two fires. Should General Gates detach a part of his troops to oppose the march of General Clinton, it will liberate Burgoyne, and he would probably force his way to this city. In either event, the consequences must be exceedingly disastrous to our country. We tremble with apprehensions.

8th.—The anticipated important intelligence has just reached us, that a most severe engagement took place yesterday, between the two armies, at a place between Stillwater and Saratoga, called Bemis' Heights. It is supposed to be the hardest fought battle, and the most honorable to our army, of any since the commencement of hostilities. The enemy was completely repulsed in every quarter, and his defeat was attended with irreparable loss of officers, men, artillery, tents and baggage. Our officers and men acquired the highest honor; they fought like heroes, and their loss is very inconsiderable. General Arnold has received a wound in his leg. I am impatient to receive the particular details of this capital event.

9th and 10th.—I am fortunate enough to obtain from our officers, a particular account of the glorious event of the 7th instant. The advanced parties of the two armies came into contact, about three o'clock on Tuesday afternoon, and immediately displayed their hostile attitude. The Americans soon approached the royal army, and each party in defiance awaited the deadly blow. The gallant Colonel Morgan, at the head of his famous rifle corps, and Major Dearborn, leading a detachment, of infantry, commenced the action, and rushed courageously on the British grenadiers, commanded by Major Ackland; and the furious attack was most firmly resisted. In all parts of the field, the conflict became extremely arduous and obstinate; an unconquerable spirit on each side disdaining to yield the palm of victory. Death appeared to have lost his terrors; breaches in the ranks were no sooner made than supplied by fresh combatants awaiting a similar fate. At length the Americans press forward with renewed strength and ardor, and compel the whole British line, commanded by Burgoyne himself, to yield to their deadly fire, and they retreat in disorder. The German troops remain firmly posted at their lines; these were now boldly assaulted by Brigadier-General Learned and Lieutenant-Colonel Brooks, at the head of their respective commands, with such intrepidity, that the works were carried, and their brave commander, Lieutenant-Colonel Breyman, was slain. The Germans were pursued to their encampment, which, with all the equipage of the brigade, fell into our hands. Colonel Cilley, of General Poor's brigade, having acquitted himself honorably, was seen astride on a brass field-piece, exulting in the capture. Major Hull, of the Massachusetts line, was among those who so bravely stormed the enemy's intrenchment and acted a conspicuous part. General Arnold, in consequence of a serious misunderstanding with General Gates, was not vested with any command, by which he was exceedingly chagrined and irritated. He entered the field, however, and his conduct was marked with intemperate rashness; flourishing his sword and animating the troops, he struck an officer on the head without cause, and gave him a considerable wound. He exposed himself to every danger, and with a small party of riflemen, rushed into the rear of the enemy, where he received a ball which fractured his leg, and his horse was killed under him. Nightfall put a stop to our brilliant career, though the victory was most decisive, and it is with pride and exultation that we recount the triumph of American bravery. Besides Lieutenant-Colonel Breyman slain, General Frazer, one of the most valuable officers in the British service, was mortally wounded, and survived but a few hours.*   Sir Francis Clark, aid-de-camp to General Burgoyne, was brought into our camp with a mortal wound, and Major Ackland, who commanded the British grenadiers, was wounded through both legs, and is our prisoner. Several other officers and about two hundred privates are prisoners in our hands, with nine pieces of cannon and a considerable supply of ammunition, which was much wanted for our troops. The loss on our side is supposed not to exceed thirty killed and one hundred wounded, in obtaining this signal victory.

11th.—The night after the battle, Burgoyne silently

* The death of General Frazer, from Professor Silliman's Travels. "In the action of 7th October, 1777, Frazer was the soul of the British army, and was just changing the disposition of a part of the troops to repel a strong impression which the Americans had made, and were still making, on the British right, when Morgan called together two or three of his best marksmen, and pointing to Frazer, said, 'Do you see that gallant officer?—that is General Frazer—I respect and honor him; but it is necessary he should die.' This was enough. Frazer immediately received his mortal wound, and was carried off the field." See the Appendix.

moved from his position, and on the 8th there was considerable skirmishing through the day, with some loss on both sides. We have to lament the misfortune of Major-General Lincoln, who, while reconnoitring the enemy, advanced so near, that a whole volley of musketry was discharged at him, and he received a dangerous wound in his leg. It is reported that, the day after the battle, upwards of one hundred of the enemy's dead were found unburied in the field. General Gates having detached a body of troops to get into the rear of the British army, Burgoyne took the alarm, and resolved to retreat immediately to Saratoga; accordingly in the night of the 9th instant, he silently moved off, leaving in our possession his hospital, containing three hundred sick and wounded, with medicinal stores, and two hundred barrels of flour, &c. It is a fact, both unaccountable and disgraceful, that on their retreat they committed the most wanton devastations, burning and destroying almost every house within their reach; the elegant and valuable country seat of General Schuyler, near Saratoga, did not escape their fury. The situation of the royal army is now extremely deplorable, and there is scarcely a possibility of their final escape. General Gates has so arranged his forces as to cut off their retreat, and is endeavoring to surround them on every quarter. May the Almighty Ruler grant that our efforts may be crowned with still more glorious success!

12th.—The wounded officers and soldiers of our army, and those of the enemy who have fallen into our hands, are crowding into our hospital, and require our constant attention. The last night I watched with the celebrated General Arnold, whose leg was badly fractured by a musket-ball while in the engagement with the enemy on the 7th instant. He is very peevish, and impatient under his misfortunes, and required all my attention during the night, but I devoted an hour in writing a letter to a friend in Boston, detailing the particulars of the late battle.

In the severe battle of the 7th, General Burgoyne himself, it is now ascertained, had a hair breadth escape, having one bullet pass through his hat and another tore his waistcoat.*

* The following anecdote shows the imminent danger to which a part General Gates' army was at one time exposed. General Gates had

We have the most flattering accounts from camp. Our army is now posted within musket-shot of the enemy at Saratoga, and are forming a circle round them. Some skirmishing takes place every day, in which we have taken one hundred and twenty prisoners, and have received one hundred and sixty deserters. A party of our men have taken fifty batteaux loaded with provisions, stores, and medicines, among which are one thousand barrels of pork and beef. This must be to the enemy an irreparable loss, and a blow which must hasten the destruction or surrender of their whole army.

14*th*.—We have now a confirmation of the intelligence that Sir Henry Clinton and General Vaughan have pushed up the North river, and made a successful attack on our forts at the highlands. Fort Montgomery and Fort Clinton are near to each other, on the western bank of the Hudson. They have been considered of great importance as defensive posts, against the passage of the enemy up the river. In addition to these forts, a strong boom and an iron chain of immense size were stretched across the river, and a frigate and two gallies were stationed above

received what he supposed to be certain intelligence that the main body of Burgoyne's army had marched off for Fort Edward, and that a rear guard only was left in the camp, who after a while were to push off as fast as possible, leaving the heavy baggage behind. On this it was concluded to advance and attack the camp in half an hour. General Nixon's being the eldest brigade, crossed the Saratoga Creek first: unknown to the Americans, Burgoyne had a line formed behind a parcel of brushwood to support the post of artillery where the attack was to be made. General Glover with his brigade was on the point of following Nixon. Just as he entered the water, he saw a British soldier crossing, whom he called and examined. This soldier was a deserter, and communicated the very important fact, that the whole British army were in their encampment. Nixon was immediately stopped, and the intelligence conveyed to Gates, who countermanded his orders for the assault, and called back his troops, not without sustaining some loss from the British artillery.—*Gordon and Marshal.*

N. B. General Wilkinson, who acted as General Gates' adjutant-general, asserts in his memoirs, that he first discovered the British at their post, through a thick fog while his horse halted to drink in fording the creek, and that he instantly arrested the march of our troops, and thereby saved them from destruction. He makes no mention of the deserter. It is known that Burgoyne has frequently expressed his extreme disappointment that he was baffled in this stratagem; and Americans ought never to forget the remarkable Providential escape.

them. By these means it was always supposed that the position was invulnerable, provided a proper number of troops were posted in the forts; but it unfortunately happened that most of the continenial troops were necessarily called off to join General Gates' army. The forts were defended by Governor George Clinton and his brother, General James Clinton, of New York, having about six hundred militia-men—a force greatly inadequate to the defence of the works. The enemy came up the river, landed, and appeared unexpectedly, and demanded a surrender of the forts, which being resolutely refused, were taken by assault, though not without a firm and brave resistance. General James Clinton received a bayonet wound in his thigh, but he and the governor with a part of the garrison made their escape, leaving about two hundred and fifty men killed, wounded and prisoners. The enemy suffered a severe loss of three field-officers killed, and their dead and wounded is estimated at about three hundred. General Putnam, who commanded at Peekskill in the vicinity, having a small force only to guard the deposit of stores, was obliged to retire, and the barracks, stores and provisions, to a very considerable amount, fell into the hands of the enemy and were destroyed. With wanton cruelty they set fire to the houses and buildings of every description, and spread ruin and devastation to the extent of their power. To consummate their destructive scheme, General Vaughan destroyed by conflagration the beautiful town of Esopus, with the church, and every other building it contained. Thus we experience the horrid effects of malice and revenge; where they cannot conquer, they wantonly exterminate and destroy. They are well apprised of the disastrous and desperate situation of their boastful General Burgoyne, and if they dare not march to his relief, they can cowardly retaliate by conflagration with impunity. It is the prevalent opinion here, that by taking advantage of wind and tide, it is in the power of Sir Henry Clinton to convey his forces to this city within the space of five or six hours, and having arrived here, a march of about twenty miles will carry him without opposition to Stillwater, which must involve General Gates in inexpressible embarrassment and difficulty, by placing him between two armies, and thereby extricating Burgoyne from his perilous situation. We have been tremblingly alive to this menacing prospect, but our fears are in a measure allayed by the following singular incident. After the capture of Fort Montgomery, Sir Henry Clinton despatched a messenger, by the name of Daniel Taylor, to Burgoyne with the intelligence; fortunately he was taken on his way as a spy, and finding himself in danger, he was seen to turn aside and take something from his pocket and swallow it. General George Clinton, into whose hands he had fallen, ordered a severe dose of emetic tartar to be administered; this produced the happiest effect as respects the prescriber; but it proved fatal to the patient. He discharged a small silver bullet, which, being unscrewed, was found to inclose a letter from Sir Henry Clinton to Burgoyne. "Out of thine own mouth thou shalt be condemned." The spy was tried, convicted and executed. The following is an exact copy of the letter inclosed:

Fort Montgomery, October 8th, 1777.

Nous voici—and nothing between us but *Gates.* I sincerely hope this *little* success of ours may facilitate your operations. In answer to your letter of the 28th of September by C. C. I shall only say, I cannot presume to order, or even advise, for reasons obvious. I heartily wish you success.   Faithfully yours,   H. CLINTON.
To General Burgoyne.

14*th.*—An express from camp. Burgoyne has this day made proposals to General Gates to enter into a treaty for the surrender of his army. He desires a cessation of arms till the preliminary terms can be settled, to which General Gates has assented. The glorious event is about to be consummated.

15*th and* 16*th.*—Burgoyne's message to General Gates by the hands of Major Kingston is as follows:

" *October* 14*th,* 1777.

"After having fought you twice, Lieutenant-General Burgoyne has waited some days, in his present position, determined to try a third conflict against any force you could bring to attack him.

"He is apprised of the superiority of your numbers, and the disposition of your troops to impede his supplies and render his retreat a scene of carnage on both sides. In this situation he is impelled by humanity, and thinks himself justified by established principles and precedents of state and of war, to spare the lives of brave men on honorable terms: should Major-General Gates be inclined to treat on this idea, General

LIEUTENANT GENERAL JOHN BURGOYNE.

Burgoyne would propose a cessation of arms during the time necessary to communicate the preliminary terms, by which, in any extremity, he and his army mean to abide."

A convention was in consequence opened, and two days were spent in a discussion and interchange of articles between the two commanders. It was agreed that the articles should be mutually signed and exchanged to-morrow morning the 17th instant, at nine o'clock; and the troops under Lieutenant-General Burgoyne are to march out of their intrenchments at three o'clock in the afternoon.

The substance of the treaty is, that the troops under the command of General Burgoyne shall march out of their camp with the honors of war and their field-artillery, to the place assigned, where their arms and artillery shall be piled at the command of their own officers.

That the troops be allowed to return to England, on condition that they shall not serve again in America during the present war. That the officers be allowed to wear their side-arms, and be treated according to their rank. That the European troops march immediately for Boston, to be in readiness to embark when transports shall be sent for them, and that the Canadians be permitted to return home immediately, on the sole condition of their not arming again against the United States.

18th.—At the appointed hour yesterday morning the Americans marched into the lines of the British to the tune of Yankee Doodle, where they continued till the royal army had marched to the place appointed and deposited their arms according to the treaty.

It is a circumstance characteristic of the amiable and benevolent disposition of General Gates, that, unwilling to aggravate the painful feelings of the royal troops, he would not permit the American soldiery to witness the degrading act of piling their arms. This instance of delicacy and politeness, at the moment of triumph, towards an enemy who had committed the most unprecedented outrages, is a mark of true magnanimity, and deserves the highest praise, though it deprives our army of the satisfaction to which they are justly entitled.*

The preliminaries having been acceded to by the two

---

* For the first interview between the royal general officers and their conqueror, see Life of General Gates, in the Appendix.

commanders, Lieutenant-Colonel Wilkinson, deputy adjutant-general, and Brigadier-General Whipple, of the militia, on our part, and Lieutenant-Colonel Sutherland, Major Kingston, and Captain Craig, on the part of the British, were appointed to stipulate and arrange the particular articles of capitulation. So very tenacious were the British of the trivial points of military honor, that, after they had signed the "treaty of *capitulation*," as it was termed, they required that the term should be altered to "treaty of *convention*," in which they were indulged by General Gates, as being of little consequence on our part. During the pending negotiation, several hundred of the New York militia, whose term of service had expired, marched off the ground without permission from General Gates; and the same night Burgoyne received intelligence by a spy that Sir H. Clinton, having taken Fort Montgomery, would attempt to force his way to Albany. Though the articles of convention were fully adjusted, signed and exchanged, by those appointed for the purpose, and the hour stipulated by the parties for Burgoyne to affix his signature, he addressed a note to General Gates, purporting that he should recede from the treaty, on the ground that a part of the American force had been detached from the army during the negotiation; and with a bold effrontery, required that he might be permitted to send *two officers to our camp* to ascertain the fact. This dishonorable conduct, as may be supposed, raised the ire of our spirited commander, who sent Lieutenant-Colonel Wilkinson to have a personal interview with Burgoyne, and to insist that hostilities should recommence, if the treaty was not immediately ratified. This, after much hesitation on the part of Burgoyne and his officers, produced the desired effect. His contemplated alternative was, to abandon his camp, artillery, heavy baggage and sick, and, by a desperate effort in the night, to force his way through our army, and make a rapid march to Albany with the hope of meeting General Sir H. Clinton. It is considered singular that it was not demanded of the captured general to deliver up his military chest, colors, and soldiers' accoutrements; but the success of General Clinton in reducing Fort Montgomery, and the serious apprehensions of General Gates that he would force his way to Albany, and the desire of the latter to spare the effusion of blood, are the substantial causes which procured for Burgoyne the favorable terms which he enjoys. It is satisfactory to learn that the British officers, in general, candidly acknowledged that the American troops conducted on all occasions with the greatest bravery, and when, after their surrender, they visited and took a view of our camp, expressed much surprise at the military order and economy which were conspicuous in every part, and said that they never had seen, even in Germany, an encampment more systematically and properly disposed. The trophies which we have achieved by this great event, are, officers and soldiers, five thousand seven hundred and ninety-one. It has been estimated that Burgoyne's army, at the commencement of the campaign, was full ten thousand strong; the deficiency now, must be accounted for by the killed, loss by sickness, prisoners and deserters. Among the officers taken, are six members of the British Parliament. The train of brass artillery and other ordnance are immensely valuable, consisting of forty-two pieces of brass ordnance, besides seven thousand muskets, with six thousand dozen cartridges and an ample supply of shot, shells, &c. To these are added, clothing for seven thousand men, a large number of tents and other military stores. Thus we witness the incalculable reverse of fortune, and the extraordinary vicissitudes of military events, as ordained by Divine Providence. The same haughty commander, who but a few weeks since, flushed with victory, was harassing our retreating army in every direction; that proud, assuming foe, who so often threatened to lay waste our cities and country, and who said in his orders, early in the campaign, "this army must not retreat," is now reduced to the mortifying alternative of suing for terms of surrender, to those powers whom he affected to treat with sovereign contempt. It must be doubly mortifying to contrast his present humble condition with that when he published his pompous and bombastic proclamation, calling on towns and people to send delegates to supplicate his favor and clemency, and threatening vengeance against all those who should dare to disobey his commands, or oppose his authority. There are perhaps few examples in the annals of warfare, of a whole army under a celebrated general, and officers of the first character; gentlemen of noble families, and military merit, being reduced to the mortifying condition of captives, led through a country which it was designed should have been devoted to their all-conquering power. The intelligence of these events to the British government, must affect them like the shock of a thunderbolt, and demonstrate to them the invincibility of a people united in the noble cause of liberty and the rights of man. This event will make one of the most brilliant pages of American history. General Gates has crowned himself with unfading laurels and immortal honor; he has vanquished a commander of established military fame, at the head of a veteran army. He has displayed the qualities of a general, the magnanimity of a philanthropist, and the amiable and polite civilities of a gentleman. No less dignified and brave as a commander, than beneficent and generous as a conqueror, he is remarkable for his humanity to prisoners, and a desire to mitigate the sufferings of the unfortunate. Among the objects in distress, which claimed his attention, was the lady of Major Ackland, commander of the British grenadiers, who was dangerously wounded and captured during the battle of the 7th of October. This heroic lady, from conjugal affection, was induced to follow the fortune of her husband during the whole campaign through the wilderness. Having been habituated to a mode of life with which those of rank and fortune are peculiarly favored, her delicate frame is ill-calculated to sustain the indescribable privations and hardships to which she was unavoidably exposed during an active campaign. Her vehicle of conveyance was, part of the time, a small two-wheeled tumbril, drawn by a single horse, over roads almost impassable. Soon after she received the affecting intelligence that her husband had received a wound, and was a prisoner, she manifested the greatest tenderness and affection, and resolved to visit him in our camp to console and alleviate his sufferings. With this view she obtained a letter from Burgoyne to General Gates, and not permitting the prospect of being out in the night, and drenched in rain, to repress her zeal, she proceeded in an open boat, with a few attendants, and arrived at our out-post in the night, in a suffering condition, from extreme wet and cold. The sentinel, faithful to his duty, detained them in the boat till Major Dearborn, the officer of the guard, could arrive. He permitted them to land, and afforded Lady Ackland the best accommodations in his power, and treated her with a cup of tea in his guard-house. When General Gates, in the morning, was informed of the unhappy situation of Lady Ackland, he immediately ordered her a safe escort, and treated her himself with the tenderness of a parent, directing that every attention should be bestowed which her rank, or sex, character and circumstances required. She was soon conveyed to Albany, where she found her wounded husband. For further particulars respecting this highly respectable and interesting lady, the reader is referred to the Appendix.

In the military transactions in the northern department, the labors and efforts of Major-General Schuyler are acknowledged to be eminently important and useful. He is undoubtedly entitled to the character of an intelligent and meritorious officer. As a private gentleman he is dignified, but courteous, his manners are urbane, and his hospitality is unbounded. He is justly considered as one of our most distinguished champions of liberty, and his noble mind has soared above despair, even at a period when he experienced injustice from the public, and when darkness and gloom overspread our land. Though he was not invested with any active command, he was present at the surrender of the British army, which was near the spot where his elegant country-seat had been demolished. Here he sought an interview with the Baroness Reidesel, who with her three children, for she was entrusted with this charge during the campaign, he politely accommodated in his own tent, and invited her to become his guest at his residence at Albany. On the day of the surrender, all the captive generals dined with General Gates, and received from him the kindest civilities and attention.

We have now brought to a glorious termination a military campaign, pregnant with remarkable vicissitudes and momentous events; the result of which, seemed for a time to poise on a pinnacle of sanguine hopes and expectations on the one side, and the most appalling apprehensions on the other. All gratitude and praise be ascribed to Him who alone limits the extent of human power, and decrees the destiny of nations!

21*st.*—The captive Generals Burgoyne, Phillips, Reide-sel, &c. with a number of ladies of high rank, arrived last evening at the hospitable mansion of General Schuyler in this city. His seat is about one mile out of town, and I have frequently made it a walk for amusement. It is a house of two stories, in elegant ancient style, and fancifully ornamented. I am informed that it has for several generations been celebrated for the great respectability and generous hospitality of its inhabitants. During the last French war, it was almost a general resort for British officers, as well as strangers and travellers of note.

22*d.*—The magnanimous General Schuyler, with his lady and daughters, have given their unfortunate guests a friendly and polite reception, characteristic of this noble spirited family. Notwithstanding General Burgoyne destroyed their beautiful villa at Saratoga, they appear disposed to console them in their misfortune by all the civilities and attention in their power.

23*d.*—General Burgoyne gratefully acknowledged the generous treatment received from General Schuyler, and observed to him, "You show me great kindness, sir, though I have done you much injury." To which he magnanimously replied, "*That was the fate of war!* let us say no more about it."

24*th.*—This hospital is now crowded with officers and soldiers from the field of battle; those belonging to the British and Hessian troops, are accommodated in the same hospital with our own men, and receive equal care and attention. The foreigners are under the care and management of their own surgeons. I have been present at some of their capital operations, and remarked that the English surgeons perform with skill and dexterity, but the Germans, with a few exceptions, do no credit to their profession; some of them are the most uncouth and clumsy operators I ever witnessed, and appear to be destitute of all sympathy and tenderness towards the suffering patient. Not less than one thousand wounded and sick are now in this city; the Dutch church, and several private houses are occupied as hospitals. We have about thirty surgeons, and mates; and all are constantly employed. I am obliged to devote the whole of my time, from eight o'clock in the morning to a late hour in the evening, to the care of our patients. Here is a fine field for professional improvement. Amputating limbs, trepanning fractured skulls, and dressing the most formidable wounds, have familiarized my mind to scenes of woe. A military hospital is peculiarly calculated to afford examples for profitable contemplation, and to interest our sympathy and commiseration. If I turn from beholding mutilated bodies, mangled limbs and bleeding, incurable wounds, a spectacle no less revolting is presented, of miserable objects, languishing under afflicting diseases of every description—here, are those in a mournful state of despair, exhibiting the awful harbingers of approaching dissolution—there, are those with emaciated bodies and ghastly visage, who begin to triumph over grim disease and just lift their feeble heads from the pillow of sorrow. No parent, wife or sister, to wipe the tear of anguish from their eyes, or to soothe the pillow of death, they look up to the physician as their only earthly friend and comforter, and trust the hands of a stranger to perform the last mournful duties. Frequently have I remarked their confidence in my friendship, as though I was endeared to them by brotherly ties. Viewing these unfortunate men as the faithful defenders of the liberties of our country, far separated from their dearest friends, who would be so lost to the duties of humanity, patriotism, and benevolence, as not to minister to their comfort, and pour into their wounds the healing balm of consolation? It is my lot to have twenty wounded men committed to my care, by Dr. Potts, our surgeon-general; one of whom, a young man, received a musket-ball through his cheeks, cutting its way through the teeth on each side, and the substance of the tongue; his sufferings have been great, but he now begins to articulate tolerably well. Another had the whole side of his face torn off by a cannon-ball, laying his mouth and throat open to view. A brave soldier received a musket-ball in his forehead, observing that it did not penetrate deep, it was imagined that the ball rebounded and fell out; but after several days, on examination, I detected the ball laying flat on the bone, and spread under the skin, which I removed. No one can doubt but he received his wound while facing the enemy, and it is fortunate for the brave fellow that his skull proved too thick for the ball to penetrate. But in another instance, a sol-

dier's wound was not so honorable; he received a ball in
the bottom of his foot, which could not have happened
unless when in the act of running from the enemy. This
poor fellow is held in derision by his comrades, and is
made a subject of their wit for having the mark of a *coward.* Among the most remarkable occurrences which
came under my observation, the following is deserving of
particular notice. Captain Greg, of one of the New York
regiments, while stationed at Fort Stanwix, on the Mohawk
river, went with two of his soldiers into the woods a short
distance to shoot pigeons; a party of Indians started suddenly from concealment in the bushes, shot them all down,
tomahawked and scalped them, and left them for dead.
The captain, after some time, revived, and perceiving his
men were killed, himself robbed of his scalp, and suffering
extreme agony from his numerous wounds, made an effort
to move, and lay his bleeding head on one of the dead
bodies, expecting soon to expire. A faithful dog who
accompanied him, manifested great agitation, and in the
tenderest manner licked his wounds, which afforded him
great relief from exquisite distress. He then directed the
dog, as if a human being, to go in search of some person
to come to his relief. The animal, with every appearance
of anxiety, ran about a mile, when he met with two men
fishing in the river, and endeavored in the most moving
manner, by whining and piteous cries, to prevail on them
to follow him into the woods; struck with the singular
conduct of the dog, they were induced to follow him part
of the way, but fearing some decoy or danger, they were
about to return, when the dog, fixing his eyes on them,
renewed his entreaties by his cries, and taking hold of
their clothes with his teeth, prevailed on them to follow
him to the fatal spot. Such was the remarkable fidelity
and sagacity of this animal. Captain Greg was immediately carried to the fort, where his wounds were dressed;
he was afterwards removed to our hospital, and put under
my care. He was a most frightful spectacle, the whole
of his scalp was removed; in two places on the fore part
of his head, the tomahawk had penetrated through the
skull; there was a wound on his back with the same instrument, besides a wound in his side and another through
his arm by a musket-ball. This unfortunate man, after

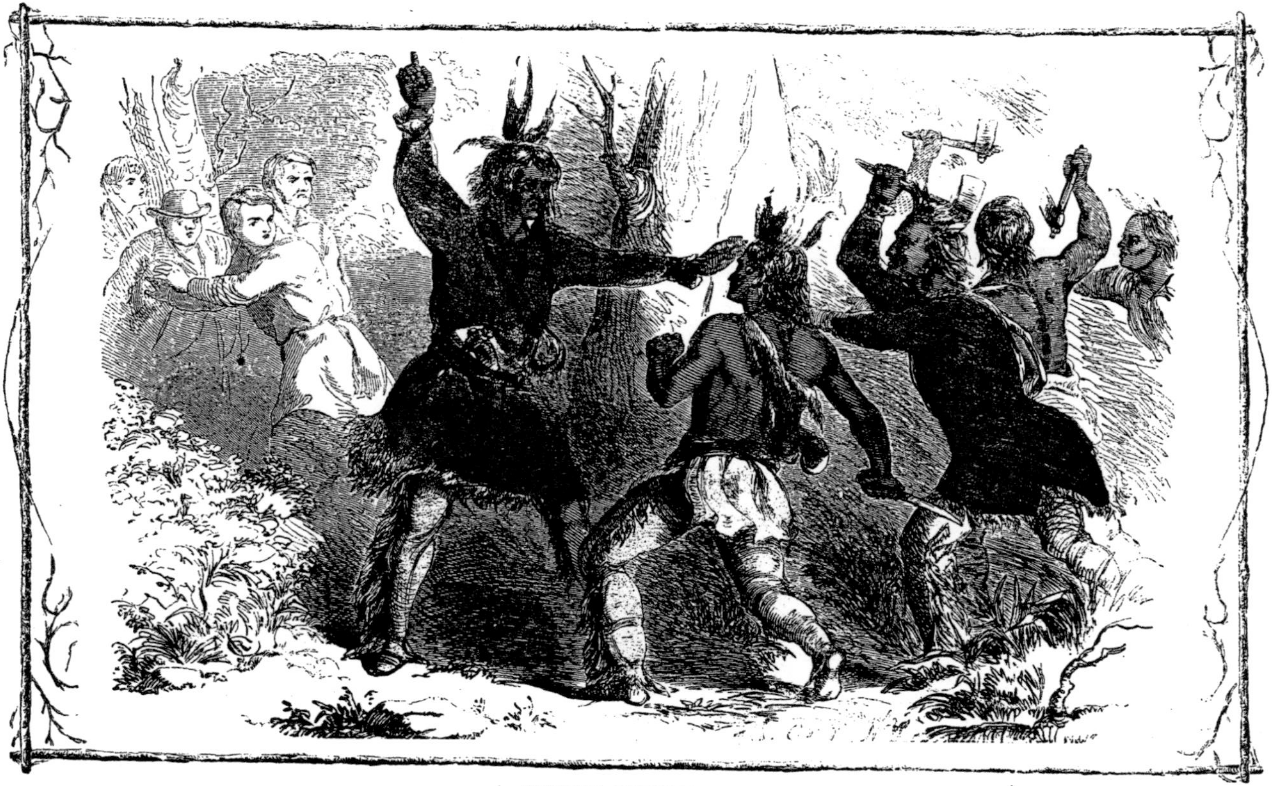

INDIAN CUSTOMS.

suffering extremely for a long time, finally recovered, and appeared to be well satisfied in having his scalp restored to him, though uncovered with hair. The Indian mode of scalping their victims is this—with a knife they make a circular cut from the forehead, quite round, just above the ears, then taking hold of the skin with their teeth, they tear off the whole hairy scalp in an instant, with wonderful dexterity. This they carefully dry and preserve as a trophy, showing the number of their victims, and they have a method of painting on the dried scalp, different figures and colors, to designate the sex and age of the victim, and also the manner and circumstances of the murder.

November 10*th.*—I witnessed yesterday the singular ceremony performed at a treaty with the Six Nations of Indians. General Schuyler, and two other gentlemen, were the commissioners on our part. Of the Indians, about two hundred men and women attended. In the morning, I walked into the woods near this city, and was amused to see them occupied in dressing and ornamenting themselves for the ceremony; painting their faces, adjusting their hair, putting jewels into their ears, noses, &c. The face was painted of various colors; in general red, spotted with black and white in a fanciful manner. The men had their hair cut close to the skin, except a lock on the top of the head. The women wore long hair, ornamented with beads and other trinkets. The bodies and limbs of both sexes were decently covered in the Indian style, and some displayed large silver rings round the arm, and a profusion of party-colored beads, fancifully arranged about the legs and feet. Several of the young men and girls were furnished with little bells about their feet, to make a jingling when dancing. About eleven o'clock, the ceremony commenced on the common; the Indians arranged themselves, by sitting on the ground in a circle, the men on one side, the women on the other, leaving a vacancy for our commissioners, who were seated in chairs. In the centre of the circle was a fire, over which a large pot containing meat broth, or soup, was placed. The speakers were three elderly chiefs; their speeches or talks were short, and at the close of each, the speaker delivered to the commissioners a belt or string of wampum, curiously worked with porcupine quills, and handsomely painted, as a pledge of sincerity. The interpreter explained in English. In the intervals between the talks, the whole of the Indians and squaws threw their bodies into odd motions, and at the same time a noise came from their throats very similar to the grunting of swine, which, I suppose, was a token of approbation. They next commenced dancing, by uniting hands two or three at a time, and jumping merrily round the pot over the fire, animated by the music of a small drum resembling a keg covered with a skin, and the jingling of the bells attached to their legs and feet. The interpreter, by desire of the chiefs, requested that our commissioners would not be offended at the liberty which they were about to take. One of the chiefs then took the commissioners, one at a time, by the hand, and danced them round the circle; then rubbing his hand about the grease and blacking of the pot, he blackened the face, first of General Schuyler, and then the other gentlemen, which excited much laughter. Whether this was a trick to excite a laugh, or a part of their national ceremony, I was unable to ascertain. The Indians continued dancing round the fire, drinking the soup from the pot, and regaling themselves with rum all night, and many of them were found drunk in the morning.

My professional duties have been so pressing as to preclude the possibility of journalizing to the full extent of my wishes. The numerous important events which have occurred to our main army under General Washington, in the Jerseys and Pennsylvania, have been from time to time announced in the public papers, and in our general orders. A very brief retrospect of the most interesting occurrences during the campaign in that quarter must suffice me.

General Washington, having ascertained that it was the great object of Sir William Howe to possess himself of the city of Philadelphia, put in requisition every effort in his power to counteract his measures for this purpose. His force during the whole campaign was considerably inferior to that of the enemy. Battles and skirmishing of more or less importance were frequent, but not decisive, though attended by no inconsiderable loss of human lives. On the 11th of September the two armies approached each other in the order of battle, and a general action took place at Brandywine, in which the officers and soldiers of both armies displayed a spirit of intrepidity and heroism, scarcely ever exceeded. The British claim the victory; but it was only a partial one, and, besides a prodigious sacrifice of lives, they failed in their main object, that of forcing their way to Philadelphia. It is stated, that from particular circumstances, little more than one-half of General Washington's force was opposed to nearly the whole strength of the enemy. Our loss is mentioned in round numbers at one thousand. The Marquis de la Fayette and General Woodford were slightly wounded. The loss of the royalists, according to accounts published, greatly exceeds that of the Americans.

On the 16th of September, Monsieur de Condry, an officer of rank and distinction in the French service, and acting as a volunteer in our army, having occasion to cross the Schuylkill ferry, rode a high-spirited horse into the boat, which, taking fright, leaped into the river, and the rider was unfortunately drowned. Congress resolved that the corpse of Monsieur de Condry be interred at the expense of the United States, and with the honors of war.

Sir William Howe, on the 26th of September, after much manœuvring and skirmishing, accomplished his great enterprise, and made his triumphal entry into the city of Philadelphia, where he met with a cordial welcome from the Quakers, and a considerable number of the inhabitants, who have long been known to be in favor of the royalists.

On the 4th of October, General Washington planned an attack on the main body of the enemy stationed at Germantown, near Philadelphia. The enterprise was planned with such judgment and skill, as to afford promise of a complete victory. The execution of it was conducted by his excellency, who attacks like a hero and retreats like a general, and whose presence infuses into the ranks the spirit of heroism and enthusiasm. Were it not for some unfortunate incidents, and the faulty conduct of a few individuals, his most sanguine hopes would have been realized. The enemy was actually taken by surprise, and in one point a party was routed, and one hundred and ten made prisoners, but were afterwards retaken. Almost the whole force of both armies was involved in the tremendous contest, in which British and American bravery were equally conspicuous, and sealed the fate of many valiant officers and men. "The morning," says General Washington's letter to Congress, "was extremely foggy, which prevented our improving the advantage we had gained, so well as we otherwise should have done. This circumstance, by concealing from us the true situation of the enemy, obliged us to act with more caution and less expedition than we could have wished, and gave the enemy time to recover from the effects of our first impression; and what was still more unfortunate, it served to keep our different parties in ignorance of each other's movements, and hindered their acting in concert; it also occasioned them to mistake one another for the enemy, which I believe more than any thing else, contributed to the misfortunes which ensued. In the midst of the most promising appearances, when every thing gave the most flattering hopes of victory, the troops began suddenly to retreat, and entirely left the field, in spite of every effort that could be made to rally them. On the whole, it may be said, this day was rather unfortunate than injurious. The principal impediment to our success was, that at the moment of victory, the enemy threw a party into Mr. Chew's stone house, who were in a situation not easily to be forced; and had it in their power, from the windows, to give us considerable annoyance, and in a measnre to obstruct our advance."

A general officer who was engaged in the battle says: "Fortune smiled on our arms for hours. The enemy were broken, dispersed and flying on all quarters: we were in possession of their whole encampment, together with their artillery park, &c. But confusion at last ensued, and we ran away from the arms of victory ready to receive us." It is not to be concealed, however, that our army suffered a very considerable loss, the whole number is not ascertained. General Nash, of North Carolina, received a mortal wound, and General Sullivan's two aids were killed. On the side of the royalists, General Agnew, General de Heister's son, and several other officers were killed. General Kniphausen was wounded, and a great number of rank and file were wounded and slain.

The Americans have erected several forts and redoubts

BATTLE OF BRANDYWINE

on the banks of the Delaware river, and on Mud Island, to guard against the passage of the British fleet up this river to Philadelphia. In one of these forts at Red Bank, Colonel Greene, of Rhode Island, was posted with about four hundred men. General Howe, perceiving the great importance of reducing these works, detached Count Donop, an officer held in high estimation in the royal army, with twelve or fifteen hundred Hessian troops, well supplied with artillery, to take possession of it. Having arrived near the redoubts, he summoned the commander to surrender, to which he resolutely replied, he would defend the place to the last extremity. This fort being originally constructed on a large scale, it was found necessary to run a line across the middle, and divide it into two, so that the external part was left without defence. The Hessian commander ordered his troops to advance under cover of the smoke of his cannon and storm the redoubt; they soon gained the unoccupied part with loud huzzas on their supposed victory; but on approaching the new lines within, where our troops were stationed, the brave garrison poured on them such hot and well-directed fire for about forty minutes, that they were completely overpowered, and fled in every direction. Colonel Donop, their commander, was mortally wounded and taken, and more than one hundred were killed on the spot, and a greater number wounded and prisoners. The enemy retreated with great precipitation, leaving many of their wounded on the road, and returned to Philadelphia with the loss of one-half their party. Colonel Greene, and his brave troops, acquired great honor for their gallant defence of the fort, which is a key to other posts on the river. Congress have rewarded the colonel with an elegant sword. The British army found it difficult to procure the necessary supplies in Philadelphia, and the continental galleys and strong *chevaux de frize* in the Delaware, rendered a passage of their ships up to the city almost impossible. Admiral Lord Howe determined to attempt the removal of these formidable obstructions, and he ordered six of his ships to engage in this service. They were so unmercifully handled by our galleys, and from Fort Mifflin, at Mud Island, that two of them, one of sixty-four guns, run aground and were set on fire by the crews, who deserted them, and soon after they blew up.

December.—Fort Mifflin, on Mud Island, has been evacuated by the continental garrison, after having been bravely defended against the prodigious force of the enemy's shipping. Our troops secured all their stores, destroyed the block-houses, and demolished the bank, to let in the water, by which the island is entirely inundated. The fort at Red Bank is also abandoned, and the continental fleet has been burned, to prevent its falling into the hands of the enemy. The British are now in full possession of the city of Philadelphia, and their fleet has obtained access to it by way of the Delaware river. The continental army, since the close of the campaign, has retired for winter-quarters to a place called *Valley Forge*, about twenty miles from Philadelphia. Here they are subjected to the fatigue and labor of clearing the woods and constructing log huts for their accommodation during the winter.

An occurrence of a very singular complexion has lately been published in a Pennsylvania newspaper, which occasions much indignant speculation. The Reverend Jacob Duche, a popular Episcopal minister in Philadelphia, was the first chaplain appointed by Congress. He performed his official duties to general acceptance, frequently and fervently imploring Heaven to succeed the American cause. Whether from alarm at the success of the royalists, or from any change in his sentiments respecting the justice of our cause, is uncertain, but after having officiated about three months, he gave in his resignation. He left Philadelphia, and "took shelter under the arm of that power which from the sacred pulpit he had exhorted his hearers to oppose." But it is no less extraordinary, that this apostate addressed a letter to his Excellency General Washington, with whom he was on terms of friendship, in which, to use the author's own words, "*he has spoken freely of Congress, and of the army.*" He enjoins it on his excellency to abandon the American cause, and resign his command of the army; or at the head of it, to force Congress immediately to desist from hostilities and to rescind their declaration of Independence. If this is not done, he says, "You have an infallible resource still left, *negotiate for America at the head of your army.*" He represents the Congress in the most despicable point of view, as consising of weak, obscure persons, not fit associates for his excellency, and the very dregs of the first Congress. The New England delegates he treats with the greatest indelicacy. The officers and men which compose our army, he describes as destitute of principle and courage; undisciplined, taken from the lowest of the people, unfit for a seat at his excellency's table, &c., &c. Thus has this vile calumniator disgraced his profession, and involved his own character in that ignominy which he designed for his superiors. His excellency in noticing this transaction in a letter of October the 16th, observes, "To Mr. Duche's ridiculous, illiberal performance, I made a very short reply, by desiring the bearer, Mrs. Ferguson, if she should hereafter, by any accident meet with Mr. Duche, to tell him I should have returned his letter unopened if I had had any idea of its contents.*

20th.—The wounded soldiers committed to my care in

* The following is the form of prayer made use of by the Reverend Mr. Duche in the Congress after Independence was declared:

"O Lord! our heavenly Father, high and mighty, King of kings, and Lord of lords, who dost from thy throne behold all the dwellers on earth, and reignest with power supreme and uncontroled over all kingdoms, empires and governments. Look down in mercy, we beseech thee, on these our American states, who have fled to thee from the rod of the oppressor, and thrown themselves on thy gracious protection, desiring to be henceforth dependent only on thee; to thee have they appealed for the righteousness of their cause; to thee do they now look up for that countenance and support, which thou alone canst give; take them, therefore, heavenly Father, under thy nurturing care; give them wisdom in council, and valor in the field; defeat the malicious designs of our cruel adversaries; convince *them* of the unrighteousness of their cause, and if they still persist in their sanguinary purposes, O! let the voice of thine own unerring justice, sounding in their hearts, constrain them to drop the weapons of war from their unnerved hands in the day of battle. Be thou present, O God of wisdom, and direct the councils of this honorable assembly; enable them to settle things on the best and surest foundation, that the scene of blood may be speedily closed, that order, harmony and peace may be effectually restored, and truth and justice, religion and piety, prevail and flourish amongst thy people; preserve the health of their bodies and the vigor of their minds; shower down on *them*, and the *millions* they here represent, such temporal blessings, as thou seest expedient for them in this world, and crown them with everlasting glory in the world to come. All this we ask in the name, and through the merits of Jesus Christ thy Son and our Saviour. AMEN."

October last, have all recovered, and as a compliment for my assiduity, and attention to my patients, I have received from Dr. Potts, our surgeon-general, a generous and handsome present. The duties of our hospital being now greatly diminished, I have obtained a furlough for forty days, and shall to-morrow commence my journey to visit my friends in New England.

February 4th, 1778.—Having performed a journey on horseback to Boston and Barnstable, in Massachusetts, I returned here two days before the expiration of my furlough, and resumed my duties in the hospital. Several gentlemen belonging to the hospital being desirous of improving in the accomplishment of dancing, Mr. John Trotter has agreed to open a special school for our accommodation and we are to attend every afternoon. Master Trotter has for many years been in the practice of teaching the art in the city of New York, and has acquired great fame as a man of knowledge and experience in his profession. He is about fifty-eight years of age, a small, genteel, well-proportioned man, every limb and joint proclaiming that he is formed for his profession; and the ease and grace with which he moves on the floor, evince that he is an accomplished master, and that he has lost none of his agility by age. Under the tuition of such a master, we flatter ourselves that in due time, if we improve our advantages, we shall be able to figure in a ball-room.

10th.—I have now obtained a particular description of the American Torpedo, and other ingenious submarine machinery, invented by Mr. David Bushnell, for the purpose of destroying shipping while at anchor, some account of which may be found in this Journal, page 62. The external appearance of the torpedo bears some resemblance to two upper tortoise shells, of equal size, placed in contact, leaving, at that part which represents the head of the animal, a flue or opening, sufficiently capacious to contain the operator, and air to support him thirty minutes. At the bottom, opposite to the entrance, is placed a quantity of lead for ballast. The operator sits upright, and holds an oar for rowing forward or backward, and is furnished with a rudder for steering. An aperture at the bottom, with its valve, admits water for the purpose of descending, and two brass forcing pumps serve to eject the water withın, when necessary for ascending. The vessel is made completely water-tight, furnished with glass windows for the admission of light, with ventilators and air-pipes, and is so ballasted, with lead fixed at the bottom, as to render it solid, and obviate all danger of oversetting. Behind the submarine vessel, is a place above the rudder for carrying a large powder magazine; this is made of two pieces of oak timber, large enough, when hollowed out, to contain one hundred and fifty pounds of powder, with the apparatus used for firing it, and is secured in its place by a screw turned by the operator. It is lighter than water, that it may rise against the object to which it is intended to be fastened. Within the magazine, is an apparatus constructed to run any proposed length of time under twelve hours; when it has run out its time, it unpinions a strong lock, resembling a gun-lock, which gives fire to the powder. This apparatus is so pinioned, that it cannot possibly move, till, by casting off the magazine from the vessel, it is set in motion. The skilful operator can swim so low on the surface of the water, as to approach very near a ship in the night, without fear of being discovered; and may, if he choose, approach the stern or stem, above water, with very little danger. He can sink very quickly, keep at any necessary depth, and row a great distance in any direction he desires without coming to the surface. When he rises to the surface, he can soon obtain a fresh supply of air, and, if necessary, he may then descend again and pursue his course. Mr. Bushnell found that it required many trials and considerable instruction to make a man of common ingenuity a skilful operator. The first person, his brother, whom he employed, was very ingenious, and made himself master of the business, but was taken sick before he had an opportunity to make use of his skill. Having procured a substitute, and given him such instruction as time would allow, he was directed to try an experiment on the Eagle, a sixty-four-gun ship, on board of which Lord Howe commanded, lying in the harbor of New York. He went under the ship, and attempted to fix the wooden screw into her bottom, but struck, as he supposes, a bar of iron which passes from the rudder hinge, and is spiked under the ship's quarter Had he moved a few inches, which he might have done

9

without rowing, there is no doubt he would have found wood where he might have fixed the screw; or if the ship had been sheathed with copper, he might easily have pierced it. But not being well skilled in the management of the vessel, in attempting to move to another place, he lost the ship. After seeking her in vain, for some time, he rowed some distance, and rose to the surface of the water, but found day-light had advanced so far, that he durst not renew the attempt. He says that he could easily have fastened the magazine under the stern of the ship, above water, as he rowed up to the stern and touched it before he descended. Had he fastened it there, the explosion of one hundred and fifty pounds of powder, the quantity contained in the magazine, must have been fatal to the ship. In his return from the ship to New York, he passed near Governor's Island, and thought he was discovered by the enemy on the island. Being in haste, to avoid the danger he feared, he cast off the magazine, as he imagined it retarded him in the swell, which was very considerable. After the magazine had been cast off one hour, the time the internal apparatus was set to run, it blew up with great violence, throwing a vast column of water to an amazing height in the air, and leaving the enemy to conjecture whether the stupendous noise was produced by a bomb, a meteor, a water-spout, or an earthquake. Some other attempts were made in Hudson's river, in one of which the operator, in going towards the ship, lost sight of her and went a great distance beyond her, and the tide ran so strong as to baffle all his efforts. Mr. Bushnell being in ill health, and destitute of resources, was obliged to abandon his pursuit at that time, and wait for a more favorable opportunity, which never occurred. In the year 1777, Mr. Bushnell made an attempt from a whale-boat, against the Cerberus frigate lying at anchor, by drawing a machine against her side, by means of a line. The machine was loaded with powder, to be exploded by a gun-lock, which was to be unpinioned by an apparatus to be turned by being brought alongside of the frigate. This machine fell in with a schooner at anchor astern of the frigate, and concealed from his sight. By some means it became fixed, and exploding, demolished the schooner. Commodore Simmons, being on board the Cerberus, addressed an official letter to Sir Peter Parker, describing this singular disaster. Being at anchor to the westward of New London, with a schooner which he had taken, discovered about eleven o'clock in the evening a line towing astern from the bows. He believed that some person had veered away by it, and immediately began to haul in. A sailor, belonging to the schooner, taking it for a fishing-line, laid hold of it, and drew in about fifteen fathoms. It was buoyed up by small pieces of wood tied to it at stated distances. At the end of the rope a machine was fastened, too heavy for one man to pull up, for it exceeded one hundred pounds in weight. The other people of the schooner coming to his assistance, they drew it on deck. While the men were examining the machine, about five minutes from the time the wheel had been put in motion, it exploded, blew the vessel into pieces, and set her on fire. Three men were killed, and the fourth blown into the water, much injured. On examining round the ship, after this accident, the other part of the line was discovered, buoyed up in the same manner. This the commodore ordered to be instantly cut away, for fear of hauling up another of the *infernals*, as he termed it. These machines were constructed with wheels, furnished with irons sharpened at the end, and projecting about an inch, in order to strike the sides of the vessel when hauling them up, thereby setting the wheels in motion, which in the space of five minutes causes the explosion. Had the whole apparatus been brought to operate on a ship at the same time, it must have occasioned prodigious destruction. Mr. Bushnell contrived another ingenious expedient to effect his favorite object. He fixed a large number of kegs under water, charged with powder, to explode on coming in contact with any thing while floating along with the tide. He set his squadron of kegs afloat in the Delaware, above the English shipping, in December, 1777. The kegs were in the night set adrift, to fall with the ebb, on the shipping; but the proper distance could not be well ascertained, and they were set adrift at too great a distance from the vessels, by which means they were obstructed and dispersed by the ice. They approached, however, in the day time, and one of them blew up a boat, and others exploded, which occasioned among the British seamen the greatest alarm and consternation. They actually manned the wharves and shipping at Philadelphia, and discharged their small arms and cannon at every thing they could see floating in the river, during the ebb tide. This incident has received the name of the *Battle of the Kegs*, and furnished a subject for an excellent and humorous song by the Honorable Francis Hopkinson, which is inserted in the Appendix.

April.—Major-General Lee, captured by the enemy in December, 1776, has been exchanged for Major-General Prescott, who was taken at Rhode Island, by Colonel Barton.

The glorious intelligence being announced, that Congress have negotiated a *treaty of alliance with the Court of France*, General Washington has issued the following orders for the army to celebrate the momentous event:

"*Head Quarters, Camp, Valley Forge, May 5th*, 1778.

"It having pleased the Almighty Ruler of the Universe propitiously to defend the cause of the United American States, and finally, by raising us up a powerful friend among the princes of the earth, to establish our liberty and independence on a lasting foundation; it becomes us to set apart a day for gratefully acknowledging the Divine goodness, and celebrating the important event which we owe to His benign interposition.

"The several brigades are to be assembled for this purpose at nine o'clock to-morrow morning, when their chaplains will communicate the intelligence contained in the Postscript to the Pennsylvania Gazette of the second instant, and offer up a Thanksgiving, and deliver a discourse suitable to the occasion.

"At half-past ten o'clock a cannon will be fired, which is to be a signal for the men to be under arms. The brigade inspectors will then inspect their dress and arms, form the battalions according to the instructions given them, and announce to the commanding officers of brigades that the battalions are formed. The brigadiers and commandants will then appoint the field-officers to command the battalions; after which, each battalion will be ordered to load and ground their arms.—At half-past eleven, another cannon will be fired as a signal for the march; on which the several brigades will begin their march by wheeling to the right by platoons, and proceed by the nearest way to the left of their ground, in the new position that will be pointed out by the brigade inspectors.—A third signal will be given, on which there will be a discharge of thirteen cannon: when the thirteenth has fired, a running fire of the infantry will begin on the right of Woodford's, and continue throughout the whole front line; it will then be taken up on the left of the second line, and continue to the right—on a signal given, the whole army will huzza—*Long live the King of France!*

"The artillery will then begin again, and fire thirteen rounds. This will be succeeded by a second general discharge of the musketry in a running fire—*Huzza! long live the Friendly European Powers!* Then the last discharge of thirteen pieces of artillery will be given, followed by a general running fire—*Huzza for the American States!*"

Agreebly to the above orders, his Excellency General Washington, his lady and suite, Lord Stirling, the Countess of Stirling, with other general officers and ladies, attended at nine o'clock at the Jersey brigade, when the Postscript mentioned above, was read, and after prayer a suitable discourse delivered to Lord Stirling's division by the Rev. Mr. Hunter.

On the signal at half-after eleven, the whole army repaired to their alarm-posts; on which General Washington, accompanied by the general officers, reviewed the whole army at their respective posts; and after the firing of the cannon and musketry, and the huzzas were given agreeably to the orders, the army returned to their respective brigade parades, and were dismissed.

All the officers of the army then assembled, and partook of a collation provided by the general, at which several patriotic toasts were given, accompanied with three cheers. His excellency took leave of the officers at five o'clock, on which there was universal huzzaing—*Long live General Washington!*—and clapping of hands till the general rode some distance. The non-commissioned officers and privates followed the example of their officers as the general passed their brigades. Approbation indeed was conspicuous in every countenance, and universal joy reigned throughout the camp.

My friend, Major Minnis, from head-quarters at Valley Forge, has detailed to me the particular circumstances of the distress and privations which our army suffered, while in winter-quarters at that place, the last winter. In the month of December, the troops were employed in erecting log huts for winter-quarters, when about one-half of the men were destitute of small-clothes, shoes, and stockings; some thousands were without blankets, and were obliged to warm themselves over fires all night, after the fatigues of the day, instead of reposing in comfortable lodgings. At one time nearly three thousand men were returned unfit for duty, from the want of clothing, and it was not uncommon to track the march of the men over ice and frozen ground, by the blood from their naked feet. Several times during the winter, they experienced little less than a famine in camp; and more than once our general officers were alarmed by the fear of a total dissolution of the army from the want of provisions. For two or three weeks in succession, the men were on half-allowance, and for four or five days without bread, and again as many without beef or pork. It was with great difficulty that men enough could be found in a condition fit to discharge the military camp duties from day to day, and for this purpose those who were naked, borrowed from those who had clothes. It cannot be deemed strange that sickness and mortality were the consequence of such privations, in the midst of an inclement season. Under these unexampled sufferings, the soldiers exercised a degree of patience and fortitude, which reflects on them the highest honor, and which ought ever to entitle them to the gratitude of their country. The army indeed was not without consolation, for his excellency the commander-in-chief, whom every soldier venerates and loves, manifested a fatherly concern and fellow-feeling for their sufferings, and made every exertion in his power to remedy the evil, and to administer the much-desired relief. Being authorized by Congress, he reluctantly resorted to the unpopular expedient of taking provisions from the inhabitants by force, and thus procured a small supply for immediate necessity.* This was the unhappy condition of that army, on whom General Washington had to rely for the defence of every thing held most dear by Americans, and this, too, while situated within sixteen miles of a powerful adversary, with a greatly superior army of veterans, watching with a vigilant eye for an opportunity to effect its destruction. But a fact which excites the greatest indignation and astonish-

---

* It was on this occasion that a foreign officer of distinction said to a friend of mine, that he despaired of our Independence, for while walking with General Washington, along the soldiers' huts, he heard from many voices echoing through the open crevices between the logs, "*No pay, no clothes, no provisions, no rum,*" and when a miserable being was seen flitting from one hut to another, his nakednesss was only covered by a dirty blanket. It will be difficult to form a just conception of the emotions of grief and sorrow which must have harrowed up the soul of our illustrious patriot and philanthropist. In this darkening hour of adversity, any man who possesses less firmness than Washington, would despair of our Independence.

ment is, that, at the critical period above mentioned, a party in Congress, in concert with General Conway, was endeavoring to remove General Washington from the supreme command. If the American army is to be annihilated, and the cause of our country sacrificed to gratify individual ambition, then is there a faction ripe for the execution of the object. No man, perhaps, ever had a greater combination of vexatious evils and uncontrollable obstacles to encounter, than this incomparable patriot and warrior; and no one surely ever possessed in a more eminent degree the peculiar talents and qualities requisite for the discharge of the important duties assigned him in his elevated station. He has acquired the full confidence of every faithful officer and soldier under his command, and his wisdom and judgment are considered adequate to the most trying exigencies. He rises in the midst of distress, and gains strength by misfortunes. The Assembly of Pennsylvania, and a certain party in our Congress, entertain an idea that the royal army was permitted to take possession of Philadelphia by the timidity, or by the excessive caution, of our commander-in-chief. It is well known, that from necessity he has evinced himself more the disciple of Fabius Maximus, than of Marcellus. He temporizes, and acts on the defensive, when a superior force and the peculiar circumstances of his army compel him to adopt such conduct. But no one will deny that he has displayed the greatest courage in opposing danger, and the greatest presence of mind in retreating from it. He has perplexed the enemy by his judicious manœuvres, and braved him frequently in his camp; and it is by his superior generalship, and the unfailing resources of his mind, that the enemy was not sooner in possession of Philadelphia, and that our feeble, half-starved, naked army, has not been entirely destroyed. The candidates who have been named to supersede his excellency in the supreme command, are Generals Lee, Mifflin, Gates and Conway. Lee has many advocates in his favor. Mifflin has no claim, and it is believed no desire, to be elevated to this highly responsible station. The splendid achievement of General Gates at Saratoga is auspicious to his preferment, but even the officers and soldiers who served under him in the northern army, would not willingly yield their attachment to their beloved Washington, in whose wisdom and judgment they repose such unbounded confidence. It is most unfortunate that Congress appears to be split into factions at this eventful period, when the salvation of our country depends on the harmony and unanimity in our councils. A strong party exists in this body, who are exerting every nerve to effect their favorite scheme of elevating General Gates to the supreme command. This gentleman is made the object of their applause and caresses, though he has been deficient in duty and respect in his official station, in not communicating to the commander-in-chief the important intelligence of the capture of General Burgoyne and his army. General Conway, a French gentleman, has been appointed by Congress inspector-general, with the rank of major-general, over a number of brigadiers of regular standing, and this, even when it was notorious that he was inimical to the commander-in-chief, and the author of letters in which his excellency's character is basely aspersed and calumniated. These unhappy dissensions and jealousies occcasion the greatest solicitude in our army, and consequences of a fatal tendency are seriously apprehended. The brigadiers and a number of colonels have remonstrated in strong terms to Congress respecting the preferment of General Conway. The machinations of this insolent foreigner have at length recoiled on his own head. Having, by his vile intrigue and insufferable effrontery, rendered himself an object of disgust in his station, he has been induced to resign his commission, and has withdrawn himself from the army.* On this serious occasion, the character of Washington was found unassailable, and it shines with redoubled lustre. His excellency displays a noble magnanimity in overlooking a want of confidence in his skill and judgment in his profession. Envy and malice are ever attendant on exalted station and superior merit.

* General Conway, after his resignation, was challenged by General Cadwallader, for his conduct, and in the combat he received a wound which he supposed to be a mortal one; and conceiving death to be near at hand, he conducted honorably in addressing to General Washington a letter of apology. Further particulars relative to this unpleasant business may be found in the characters of Lee, Gates and Conway, in the Appendix.

May 16*th.*—In various parts of this state the inhabitants are constantly infested with a banditti of tories and other villains, following the practice of robbing and plundering, stealing horses and cattle, and often committing murder on those who oppose them; and even on innocent persons. A number of these vile wretches have been apprehended and condemned; two of them were executed yesterday. They had been convicted of robbing the house of Mr. Van Ness, whose son, being a captain in our militia, was taken by them and cruelly murdered. The criminals were conducted to the gallows by a guard of soldiers, and were attended by a prodigious number of spectators. They manifested, at the gallows, the most agonizing horrors. One of them held in his hand a Bible till the halter deprived him of the power of holding it. Had this sacred volume been his companion in early life, it might have been the means of averting this awful and untimely death.

20*th.*—I attended the judicial court at the City Hall for the trial of a number of criminals accused of house robbery, horse stealing, and murder, among the defenceless inhabitants on our frontiers. No less than ten of these miscreants were arraigned at the bar. The jury brought in a verdict of guilty against the whole number. Judge John Jay, who officiated on the bench, pronounced the awful sentence of death, and addressed them in a very solemn and affecting manner, calculated to rouse them to a sense of their dreadful condition, and in a moving and pathetic strain, enjoined it on them to prepare to meet their God. This scene was rendered the more melancholy, by observing among the criminals a grey-headed man of seventy years, and his son about twenty. The criminality of the son admits of some extenuation from his ignorance and the example of his father. The youth was afterwards pardoned; but the old man, with several others, expiated their crimes by a public execution on the gallows.

In the town of Schoharie, about thirty miles from this city, a company of our troops, under the command of Captain Patrick, has been for some time stationed for the purpose of guarding the inhabitants against the incursions and cruel ravages of the Indians and tories. We have just received the melancholy intelligence, that about two hundred Indians and their tory allies, fell on our party by surprise, killed the captain and all but fifteen men, and most of the inhabitants shared the same miserable fate. The bodies were cut and mangled in a savage manner, and some of them were scalped.

June 1st.—Orders have been received for the removal of our hospital from this city to the highlands, on the Hudson river, where our whole army, it is said, is about to assemble. During my residence in this city, I have contracted but a limited acquaintance with the inhabitants. They are chiefly Low Dutch, and not much inclined to associate with strangers. There are, however, several families of respectability and fashion, who have taken refuge here from New York, among whom are some amiable and accomplished ladies, in whose society I have been permitted to enjoy a social intercourse. The charming Miss M. H. has captivated the heart, and is destined to receive the hand of my excellent friend Dr. W. P. S., an auspicious union of congenial souls. But in military life our associates must be chiefly those of a military character. In a society of about thirty professional gentlemen, harmonizing in similar pursuits and inclinations, our sympathies and mutual pleasures are mingled, and raised to a state of the purest enjoyment. We are now to be separated, and subjected to vicissitudes and incidents beyond our calculation. Three of our number are to continue with the sick in this place, and the remainder are destined to a new situation.

5th.—We embarked with our hospital stores and baggage on board of a sloop, and proceeded with a fair wind down the Hudson. In the evening we landed at Kinderhook, a small town on the bank of the river.

7th.—Arrived at Fishkill, where we replenished our stock of provisions.

10th.—Proceeded on our voyage, took in a pilot at New Windsor, lodged on board, and on the 11th reached the place of our destination, landed our stores and baggage, and took possession of the house which we are to occupy for a hospital. This house was erected by Colonel Beverly Robinson, a respectable gentleman from Scotland, for his summer residence, but being induced to adhere to the British interest, he has, with his excellent family, removed to New York, and thereby forfeited his large estate. This is a spacious and very convenient building, situated on the eastern bank of the Hudson, about two miles from West Point, which is on the opposite shore. Robinson's house, with the out-buildings, is found very convenient for a hospital; the farm and gardens are very extensive, affording excellent pasturing for horses and cows, and containing three or four large orchards, abounding in fruit of various descriptions. In the location of a country-seat, the judgment of Colonel Robinson is not much to be admired, unless he was guided altogether by a taste for romantic singularity and novelty. It is surrounded on two sides by hideous mountains and dreary forests, not a house in view, and but one within a mile. The Hudson, which washes the borders of this farm, affords a facility of communication with New York and with Albany; and the excursion up or down the river is truly romantic; nature exhibits a diversified scenery of wild mountains, craggy precipices, and noble lofty cliffs, on each side the river, which at this place is about one mile wide. The bank on the west side is formed by a large mountain called Butterhill, and that on the east by another named Brecknock. At a small distance south of Robinson's is a remarkable bluff, whose rocky cliffs ascend almost perpendicularly from the water's edge to the height of about twelve or fifteen hundred feet. This, from its singular form and appearance, is known by the name of *Anthony's Nose.* Not far from Robinson's house is Sugar-loaf mountain, covered with various kinds of forest trees.

12*th.*—A little party, consisting of three gentlemen of the hospital and myself, resolved on the attempt to ascend to the summit of Sugar-loaf mountain, which from its rude acclivity is deemed almost inaccessible. It was with great difficulty and fatigue that we effected our purpose, holding by the limbs and bushes, while the decayed wood and loose stones, sliding from under our feet, kept us in continual fear of a fatal fall. Having reached the summit, we contemplated with amazement the sublime scene which opened to our view. Looking down as from a cloud, we beheld the Hudson, resembling a vast canal cut through mountains of stupendous magnitude; a few boats playing on its surface were scarcely visible. But to the pen of the poet, and the pencil of the painter, be consigned the

task of describing the wonders of nature there exhibited
in the form of huge mountains, rocky cliffs, and venerable
forests, in one confused mass. From this summit, too, we
have a most interesting view of the fortress and garrison
of West Point. Fort Putnam, on its most elevated part,
the several redoubts beneath, and the barracks on the
plain below, with numerous armed soldiers in active motion, all defended by the most formidable machinery of
war, combine to form a picturesque scenery of peculiar
interest, which can be heightened only when from the
cannon's mouth issue fire and smoke, and the earth trembles with its roar and thunder. While musing on the
rich scenery, we observed a number of large rocks, which
seemed to have but a slender hold at their basis, we conceived that it would not be difficult to undermine and
precipitate them down the steep precipice. Having a
consultation to decide on the most eligible mode of effecting our purpose, we resolutely commenced the laborious
enterprise; destitute of every kind of utensil, we procured each one a limb of a sapling, with which we bur-
rowed away the earth, and soon perceived the happy
effects of our industry; the rock began to totter. Among
other curiosities, we viewed the path made by the descent
of Putnam's rock. Colonel Rufus Putnam ascended this
mountain with forty men, who were, for amusement, employed about two days in precipitating from its summit a
rock of many tons weight into the river. Such was the
force of this ponderous body, that in its passage it cut
down trees of a large size, and nothing could impede its
course till it fell with a tremendous crash into the river.
The rock was of such size, that a part of it remained
above water, and Colonel Putnam, standing on its top,
holding in his hand a bottle of spirits, gave to it the name
of *Putnam's Rock*.

July 2d.—By Dr. Brown, surgeon-general, just arrived
from Philadelphia, we are favored with the intelligence
that commissioners have arrived from the British government with new proposals for the purpose of a reconciliation between the two countries. It appears that in
consequence of the capture of General Burgoyne and his
army, the Parliament had manifested great mortification
and alarm, and have been induced to pass some acts, with

a view of reconciliation, more consistent with the just claims of America than those formerly declared. The royal commissioners have presented to our Congress their proposals for a mutual adjustment of existing difficulties, couched in such plausible, and apparently conciliatory language, as to excite serious apprehensions that it may occasion considerable disaffection among the people, if not division in our public councils. Fears are entertained by many, in and out of Congress, that the expedient now adopted by Parliament may be productive of the consequences which the authors probably intended, that of relaxation and delay in our military preparations. There is, however, a very important and radical defect in the terms proposed by the commissioners: they are not authorized to treat with Congress on the principles of independency, but still adhere to the idea of a reunion of the states, as colonies, under the government of Great Britain. Firm in their determination never to relinquish this fundamental principle, the Congress unanimously rejected the proffered conditions, and it is morally certain that no terms short of an explicit acknowledgment of our Independence, will ever be accepted. A very animated address has been published by Congress to their constituents, respecting the terms proposed by the commissioners, in which they observe, that "the haughty prince who spurned us from his feet with contumely and disdain, and the Parliament who proscribed us, now descend to offer terms of accommodation. While in the full career of victory, they pulled off the mask, and avowed despotism. But having lavished in vain the blood and treasure of their subjects, in pursuit of this execrable purpose, they now endeavor to ensnare us with the insidious offers of peace. They would seduce us into a *dependence* which necessarily and inevitably leads to the most humiliating slavery. And do they believe you will accept these fatal terms because you have suffered the distresses of war? Do they suppose that you will basely lick the dust before the feet of your destroyers? Can there be a man so lost to the feelings that adorn human nature, to the generous pride, the elevation, the dignity of freedom? Is there a man who would not abhor a dependence on those who have deluged his country in the blood of its inhabitants? We cannot suppose this,

neither can we suppose that they themselves expect to
make many converts. What then is their intention? Is
it not to lull you with the fallacious hopes of peace, till
they can assemble new armies to prosecute their nefarious
designs? If this is not the case, why do they meanly
court each little tyrant of Europe to sell them his unhappy
slaves? Why do they continue to embitter the minds of
the savages against you? Surely, this is not the way to
conciliate the affections of America. *Be not deceived.*"
The address then proceeds to encourage the people with
the fairest prospect of success in the full establishment of
their liberty and independence. The most powerful incentives to *perseverance* and *exertion* are held forth as the
means of vanquishing the foes of our country. "Above
all, bring forward your armies into the field. Trust not
to appearances of peace or safety. Be assured that, unless
you persevere, you will be exposed to every species of
barbarity; but if you exert the means of defence which
God and nature have given you, the time will soon arrive
when every man shall sit under his own vine and under his
own fig-tree, and there shall be none to make him afraid."

3d.—A great degree of dissatisfaction has prevailed for
some time among the officers of our army. At the commencement of the war, a considerable proportion of our
officers, it is presumed, engaged in the service from the
purest motives of patriotism; some doubtless were actuated
by pecuniary views, or influenced by the novelty of the
employment, and with the expectation that the contest
would be of short continuance. These incentives appear
in a great measure to have vanished. The active spirit
of patriotism is not to be considered as inexhaustible;
when it has made the most liberal personal sacrifice, it is
disposed to languish, and to resign its duties to others who
hold an equal stake in the public weal. The military
commission, which in other armies is eagerly sought for,
and prized, as entitling the bearer to the post of honor
and profit, is in ours held in little estimation, and in some
instances it is scarcely considered as reputable. The paper
money in which our army is paid, has greatly depreciated,
and an officer can with difficulty realize an adequate support while in camp, and those who have families dependent on them, are reduced to the greatest embarrassments.

Many officers, when commissioned, relinquished lucrative professions or employments, and are devoting the most precious portion of life to the service of their country. When we contemplate the destitute condition which may be his lot at the close of the war, or the wretched circumstances in which he may be called to leave his family in case he should not survive this period, no one can be surprised that he is dissatisfied in his present situation, and that he claims from the public a more ample remuneration. These considerations will account for the numerous resignations which have taken place, and which has occasioned the commander-in-chief much anxiety and concern. Apprehending that he should be deprived of the services of many meritorious officers, his Excellency General Washington made a feeling representation to Congress relative to the subject. A committee of that honorable body has been appointed to confer with the general, and in concert with him to make and recommend such new arrangements as should appear eligible. His excellency strongly recommended a half-pay establishment, which he conceived was indispensably necessary, to induce the officers to continue in the service, and cheerfully discharge their respective duties; as many have already resigned, and application for it is frequently made by others. Besides adopting some method to make the provision to officers equal to their present exigencies, a due regard should be paid to futurity. "Nothing, in my opinion," says his excellency, "would serve more powerfully to reanimate their languishing zeal, and interest them thoroughly in the service, than a half-pay establishment." This conference and representation produced the desired effect. Congress, being convinced of the propriety and necessity of making further provision for the encouragement of their army, resolved, unanimously, that all military officers, commissioned by Congress, who now are, or hereafter may be, in the service of the United States, and shall continue therein during the war, shall, after the conclusion of it, be entitled to receive annually for the term of seven years, if they live so long, one-half of the present pay of such officers. They further resolved, unanimously, that every non-commissioned military officer or soldier who has enlisted or shall enlist in the service of these states during the war, and shall continue therein to the end thereof, shall be entitled to receive a further reward of eighty dollars at the expiration of the war.

4th.—Intelligence has reached us that the royal army, under the command of General Sir Henry Clinton, has evacuated Philadelphia, and while marching through Jersey to New York, General Washington attacked them near Monmouth court-house, on the 28th of June, and a warm engagement ensued. This contest was conducted with military ardor and spirit on the side of both armies; but was not on so broad a scale as to prove very decisive in its consequences. The intense heat of the weather, great fatigue, and drinking cold water, proved fatal to about sixty or eighty men of each party.

Molly Pitcher, wife of one of the officers, was engaged in bringing water from a spring for the men at the guns, when she saw her husband struck down, and instantly killed;—at the same time she heard the commandant order his piece to be withdrawn as he had no one to fill his place.

Maddened at her loss, Molly rushed forward, and with great activity and courage, continued to work the gun until it was withdrawn. This so strongly enlisted the feelings of the soldiers, that they obtained for her an interview with Washington, and her enrollment on the list of half-pay officers, for life. She was ever afterward called Capt. Molly. General Washington commanded in person on this memorable day. He was exposed to every danger while encouraging and animating his troops, and his presence and example were of the utmost importance during the day. After the action, at night, he laid down in his cloak under a tree, with the expectation of recommencing the battle in the morning, but the royal army silently retreated during the night without being pursued.

One unfortunate circumstance occurred on this occasion, which created considerable embarrassment, and deranged the plan of operations. Major-General Lee was ordered, by the commander-in-chief, to advance and attack the enemy's rear, so soon as a proper opportunity should offer. Having approached very near, instead of engaging, he suffered his troops to retreat in some confusion. On learn-

MOLLY PITCHER

ing this, his excellency was exceedingly mortified and astonished. Coming up to General Lee, and meeting part of his corps in their flight, he with some warmth inquired the cause of his retreat, and addressed General Lee in language which implied censure. The high-spirited Lee could not brook the slightest appearance of disapprobation, and replied with an air of disrespect. He, however, requested of his excellency fresh orders for the conduct of his corps, and these he promptly obeyed, and discovered no want of bravery in the field. But, unable to quell the rankling of a turbulent temper, he addressed, after the battle, two letters to the commander-in-chief, containing improper and disrespectful expressions. As if in defiance of superior authority, he demanded a trial by a court-martial, that he might have an opportunity of vindicating his conduct, in consequence of which his excellency has put him under arrest to await his trial.

5th.—Congress have passed a vote of thanks to General Washington and his army for their brave conduct at the battle of Monmouth.

8th.—I accompanied Dr. Woodruff to Fishkill village, about fourteen miles. Dined at the hospital with our old friends Drs. Adams and Eustis. They are pleasantly situated in a secure retreat for the accommodation of our sick and wounded soldiers.

It is expected the French government will lend us their assistance and coöperation against our English adversaries. It is asserted that a powerful French fleet will soon arrive on our coast.

16th.—His excellency the commander-in-chief visited West Point, to take a view of the works which are constructing there. His arrival was announced by the discharge of thirteen cannon, the number of the United States.

20th.—Having a number of sheep running at large in the woods belonging to our hospital, and being in want of mutton, I was induced to assist the slaughterers with my gun against these harmless animals. In pursuit of this game, I devoted most of the day, and a single sheep only was the reward of my labor and fatigue. On my return, I was accused of want of skill as a marksman, and Dr. Prescott challenged me to decide our superiority by firing at a mark; the challenge accepted, we placed an

10

object at the end of our garden.   After the third fire, we were checked by an unpleasant incident.   Several horses were grazing in a field directly in our range, and one of them, a valuable animal, received a ball through his body. The wound on examination was found to be fatal, the skill of the surgeon could avail nothing, and, to add to our chagrin, we were informed that the animal was the property of Brigadier-General Glover, and was by him highly prized.   We soon received a billet from the general, and on waiting on him at West Point, to adjust the terms of settlement, he demanded the cost of the horse, which was one hundred and fifty dollars.   Justice and honor required that we should promptly comply with his demand.   A soldier who had the charge of the horses informed us that one of the balls struck the ground within a yard of his feet; had the poor fellow been the victim, the catastrophe would have been much more melancholy; but the event is sufficiently unfortunate to deter us from again sporting with our guns at random shot.

27th.—Colonel Malcome, from West Point, with his much-admired lady, and several other officers, favored us with their company to dine; we treated our polite guests with all the civilities and all the comforts in our power, and the cheering glass was not removed till evening, when we accompanied them to the river side, and finished two bottles of port on board their barge.

28th.—Agreeably to invitation, the gentlemen of our hospital returned the visit to Colonel Malcome, at West Point, and were entertained in the most genteel manner.

The public mind is now in a state of excitement, occasioned by the improper proceedings of the royal commissioners for restoring peace.   They have made a second communication to Congress, but still without any intimation of a recognition of the Independence of the United States; but address them on the supposition that the people of America are still the subjects of the crown of Britain.   This last communication is drafted with much art and address, calculated to excite jealousies and division among the people.   Not content with their public declarations, and proposals addressed to Congress, they have actually descended to the dishonorable act of insidious offers to corrupt some distinguished individuals.   Governor

Johnstone, one of the commissioners, with inexcusable effrontery, offered a bribe to Mr. Reed, a member of Congress. In an interview with Mrs. Ferguson at Philadelphia, whose husband is a royalist, he desired she would mention to Mr. Reed that if he would engage his interest to promote the object of their commission, he might have any *office in the colonies, in the gift of his Britannic majesty, and ten thousand pounds in hand.* Having solicited an interview with Mr. Reed, Mrs. Ferguson made her communication. Spurning the idea of being purchased, he replied, "that he was not worth purchasing, but such as he was, the king of Great Britain was not rich enough to do it." Congress declined all further intercourse with the commissioners, and terminated their attempts at negotiation, unless their royal master would first withdraw his fleets and armies, or expressly acknowledge the independence of the United States. In order to demonstrate their most pointed indignation against such daring attempts to corrupt their integrity, they resolved that it was incompatible with their honor to hold any further intercourse with George Johnstone, Esquire, more especially to negotiate with him on affairs in which the cause of liberty and virtue are interested.

We are just informed of a new order of fanatics, who have recently introduced themselves into our country, pretending to be a religious sect; but, if reports be true, they are a disgrace both to religion and to human nature. They are called Shaking Quakers, or dancing quakers, though they have no affinity either in principle or character to the established order of Quakers. Their leader is a female by the name of Ann Lee, niece of General Lee, of our army. She is lately from England, and has brought over with her a few followers, and has had the address to seduce several individuals of our country to her party. She is known by the appellation of Mother Ann, and pretends to have received a revelation from heaven. The method which they practice under the idea of religious worship, is so obviously impious, as to exceed the bounds of credibility; but we have the particulars from eye-witnesses, who have been admitted to their midnight orgies. They spend whole nights in their revels, and exhibit the most unbecoming scenes, violating all

rules of propriety and decency. Both sexes, nearly divested of clothing, fall to dancing in extravagant postures,
and frequently whirl themselves round on one leg with
inconceivable rapidity, till they fall apparently lifeless on
the floor. A spectator asserts that the fantastic contor-
tions of body in which their pretended religious exercises
consist, bear the semblance of supernatural impulse, and
that no imagination can form an adequate idea of the
extravagant conduct of these infatuated people—a burlesque on all moral and religious principle.*

August 3d.—I am now to notice one of the most dreadful instances of perfidious savage cruelty that can perhaps
be found on the records of history. However incredible
the particulars may appear, they are found in various
publications, and received as indubitable facts. Nor
would I tarnish a page with the diabolical transaction,
till the detailed account has been incontrovertibly established. At a place on the eastern branch of the Susquehannah river, was a flourishing settlement called Wyoming.
It consisted of eight townships, containing one thousand
families; and such was the zeal with which they espoused
the cause of America, that they voluntarily raised about
one thousand soldiers for the continental army. The
climate and soil of this territory are admirably adapted to
the production of grain, hemp, fruit and stock of all kinds.
The inhabitants of this secluded spot might have lived in
the enjoyment of all the happiness which results from
harmony and the purest natural affection. But unfortunately they suffered themselves to be divided by the
turbulent spirit of party, distinguished by the epithet of
whig and tory. When this rancorous spirit was permitted to disclose itself, animosities arose to such an astonishing height, as to sever the tenderest ties of family
friendship and the dearest connexions. Many of the
active inhabitants, influenced by malice and revenge,
abandoned their plantations, forsook their neighbors and
friends, and allied themselves with the savages, whom
they instigated and assisted in the barbarous work of

---

* The sect now denominated Shaking Quakers, are an orderly and
civil people; they have rendered themselves remarkable for industry
and ingenuity, and for their particular attention to agriculture and the
mechanic arts.

COL. BUTLER AND THE INEBRIATE.

slaughter and death among their friends. The inhabitants, on receiving intelligence that an enterprise was preparing against them, and sensible of their perilous situation, threw up intrenchments and redoubts, to defend themselves against the gathering storm. About the 1st of July last, the ferocious enemy, consisting of one thousand six hundred tories, Indians and half-blooded Englishmen, approached the settlement, and were perceived lurking about their borders. This motley combination was commanded by a Colonel John Butler, a tory refugee, and others no less inhuman and cruel than their savage allies. In order to lull the inhabitants into security, the enemy several times sent messages to the settlers that they had no hostile designs against them, and the treacherous Butler himself declared that he should not molest them the present season. The inhabitants, however, had reason to distrust their professions, and those capable of bearing arms were immediately embodied under the command of Colonel Zeb. Butler, cousin to the commander of the savages.

Finding his efforts to rally the retreating Americans unavailing, and hoping to be able to collect a sufficient number to defend the fort until assistance could arrive, he turned his horse's head in the direction of the garrison and hastened forward. As he was speeding along the road, he overtook an Indian warrior in pursuit of one of his men, who, almost exhausted, would in a few moments have yielded, from utter exhaustion, his scalp to the knife of the pursuer. Having either lost his sword, or there being not time to use it, Butler was compelled to pass the Indian without attacking him.

The danger was too imminent to allow him to stop for the man, and he was obliged to pass him also.

Despair gave momentary strength and renewed activity, however, to the latter, and springing forward, he seized the long tail of the colonel's horse, and held on with the tenacity of death. The Indian still continued to pursue, hoping probably that something would "turn up" to his advantage. Something did turn up, but not as he anticipated.

As Butler proceeded, he beheld a man, lying under a tree, evidently intoxicated, rubbing his eyes, as if to clear up the mist which enshrouded his faculties. Perceiving at a glance the state of the case, Col. Butler, as he passed the spot, leaned forward and shouted to the man to kill the Indian. With a coolness which would have won him laurels in the battle, the inebriate, resting his elbow upon the trunk of the fallen tree, took deliberate aim at the breast of the pursuer, and a moment after he was in the dust—dead. Then, as if he had just discovered the state of affairs, he took to his heels, and pushed forward at his utmost speed after the colonel.

Butler was betrayed by his relative, and the tragical scenes which followed, would not be recited here, were it not that they have been already promulgated from authentic sources.

Human ingenuity seemed tasked to its utmost to devise new methods of cruelty, to be exercised upon poor, defenseless victims, and scenes were enacted inconceivably dreadful. Barracks, in which women and children were confined, were set on fire and the whole consumed together. One of the prisoners, a Captain Badlock, was committed to torture, by having his body stuck full of splinters of pine knots, and a fire of dry wood made around him, when his two companions, Captains Ranson and Durkee, were thrown into the same fire, and held down with pitch-forks till consumed. One Partial Terry, the son of a man of respectable character, having joined the Indian party, several times sent his father word that he hoped to wash his hands in his *heart's blood; the monster with his own hands murdered his father, mother, brothers and sisters, stripped off their scalps, and cut off his father's head!!* Thomas Terry *with his own hands butchered his own mother, his father-in-law, his sisters and their infant children, and exterminated the whole family!* A few individuals, mostly women and children, made their escape during the carnage of the day, and dispersed themselves, wandering in the woods destitute of provision or covering, shuddering with terror and distress; their sufferings must be extreme, and their fate uncertain. It is only in the infernal regions that we can look for a parallel instance of unnatural wickedness. The cries of widows and orphans call for the avenging hand of Heaven. The name of *Colonel John Butler* ought to be consigned to eternal infamy, for the base treachery and cruelty with which he betrayed his kinsman, Colonel Zeb. Butler, a respectable American officer, while under the sanction of a flag.

4th.—In company with Mr. Governeur Morris and Dr. Brown, our surgeon-general, I rode to camp near White Plains; waited on Colonel Scammel, adjutant-general, to inquire whether any regiment is destitute of a surgeon, as I am desirous of exchanging my present station for the office of regimental surgeon. This object I might have effected, but Dr. Brown prevailed on me not to dissolve my connexion with the General Hospital at present. From camp I performed a journey to Branford, and from thence to Danbury, in Connecticut. Dined with Drs. Eustis and Adams, at their quarters at Branford, and reached Danbury in the evening. On my return, the 5th, dined at a tavern at Crompond, and in the afternoon I missed my road, and my horse tired. I was directed into an obscure path through a thick forest, and arrived at the hospital late in the evening. Riding through a thick wood, my attention was arrested by a novel spectacle: On a branch of a large oak, about thirty feet high, I observed a monstrous black-snake, suspended by a coil of its tail, his head and about half his length inclining downwards, basking in the sun. It appeared about two yards in length, and the size of a man's arm. Its skin was of a jet black, and its prominent sparkling black eyes were very beautiful. He viewed me as I passed with the fierceness of a tiger; but discovering none of those fascinating charms by which our credulous mother Eve was so wofully beguiled, and disdaining the whole progeny of deceivers, I passed on without viewing him as an object of my civilities.

7th.—An unusual number of patients have been brought into our hospital within a few days. Their diseases are putrid fever and dysentery; many of the cases appear so malignant, that it is feared they will baffle all the skill of the physician.

10th.—A friend from Albany informs me that three men and two girls have lately been sentenced to suffer death for murder and robbery. The two girls are sisters, and one of the men is their brother. Another brother was executed last autumn, and their mother is now in prison, awaiting her trial for the same crime. The women had disguised themselves in men's apparel, and united with the tories and Indians in perpetrating the most inhuman cruelties and savage barbarities among the defenceless and innocent inhabitants. It is time this notorious family should be exterminated from the earth, as an awful example to those wretches who are still in the practice of similar crimes. One of the British ships in the harbor of New York took fire by lightning, and blew up; the explosion shook the whole city like an earthquake, and excited great consternation among the inhabitants.

September 4th.—A large French fleet has arrived on our coast, under the command of Count D'Estaign, and has blocked up the harbor of Newport. An army, chiefly of militia and volunteers, from the New England states, with two brigades of continental troops, under command of Major-General Sullivan, laid siege to the royal army on the island. From this land force, with the cöoperation of the French fleet, very sanguine expectations were formed that the enterprise would have been crowned with success. But the English fleet appeared, and Count D'Estaign was induced to pursue them and to offer battle, when unfortunately a violent storm arose, by which his fleet suffered so considerably that the count was obliged to quit the expedition, and proceed to Boston to repair his ships. General Sullivan's army continued several days on the island, besieging the enemy, and finally a smart engagement ensued, in which both our regular troops and the militia, emulous of fame and glory, combatted the enemy during the day. The result of the contest was a repulse of the royal forces; they retired from the field with considerable loss, and employed themselves in fortifying their camp. In the absence of the French fleet, Sir Henry Clinton sent from New York large reïnforcements, in consequence of which it was unanimously agreed in a council of war to retire from the island. The retreat was conducted by General Sullivan with great judgment and discretion, without loss of men or baggage, though in the face of an enemy of superior force. This exploit reflects great honor both on the general and the brave troops under his command. In the honors of this expedition, and retreat, Major General Greene, and the Marquis de la Fayette participated conspicuously, but were greatly disappointed in the final result.

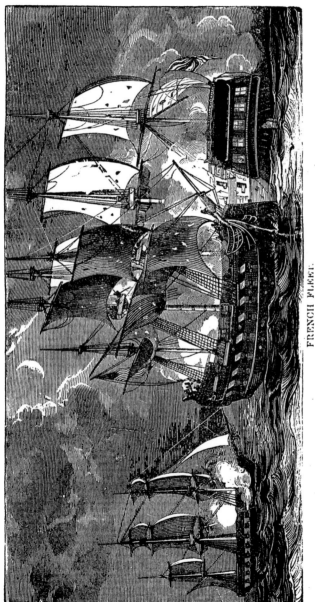

FRENCH FLEET.

5th.—Major-General Lee has gone through his trial before a court martial appointed for the purpose. The charges exhibited against him were—1st, Disobedience of orders, in not attacking the enemy on the 28th of June, agreeably to repeated instructions. 2, For misbehavior before the enemy on the same day, in making an unnecessary, disorderly and shameful retreat. 3d, For disrespect to the commander-in-chief, in two letters, dated June 28th and July 1st. To these several charges the general made a very able and excellent defence, particularizing all the circumstances attending the unhappy affair, and to the utmost of his ability extenuating and vindicating his conduct. The court, nevertheless, pronounced him guilty, and their sentence was, "that Major-General Lee be suspended from his command in the armies of the United States for the space of one year." This sentence is like a mortal wound to the lofty, aspiring spirit of General Lee; few men are less calculated to sustain such a rebuff to pride and ambitious views.*

6th.—A duel was fought a few days since between General G. and Colonel W. Two shots were exchanged without bloodshed, and a reconciliation was effected. The gentlemen, it is said, displayed a firmness and bravery becoming their rank and character, and have established their claim to the title of gentlemen of *honor.* As their courage has never been called in question, the present rencontre was unnecessary, unless it be to evince that they possess malice enough in their hearts to commit a murderous deed. The example of superior officers will have great influence with those of inferior rank, whether contending with the *dogs of war,* or in adjusting the minor points of *honor.*

8th.—Major-General Putnam has arrived in this vicinity, with the division of Virginia and Maryland troops under his command, and they have encamped on the borders of the river. Brigadiers Woodford and Muhlenburg have taken up quarters in apartments in our hospital. This is my first interview with this celebrated hero. In his person he is corpulent and clumsy, but carries a bold, undaunted front. He exhibits little of the refinements of

* See Appendix, for General Lee's character and abuse of General Washington.

the well-educated gentleman, but much of the character of the veteran soldier. He appears to be advanced to the age of about sixty years, and it is famed of him that he has, in many instances, proved himself as brave as Cæsar. He visited our hospital, and inquired with much solicitude into the condition of our patients; observing a considerable number of men who were infected with the *ground itch*, generated by lying on the ground, he inquired why they were not cured. I answered, "Because we have no hog's-lard to make ointment." "Did you never," says the general, "cure the itch with tar and brimstone?" "No, sir." "Then," replied he, good-humoredly, "you are not fit for a doctor."*

Dr. Ferguson, secretary to the British commissioners, forwarded to Congress a declaration signed George Johnstone, respecting the resolve of Congress relative to his attempt on the fidelity of one of their members, which resolve he thinks to be calculated by Congress to delude the people of America, and to defeat the design of the commissioners in effecting an accommodation, which he says he would not prevent, and therefore declines acting any more as a commissioner. Another declaration, signed by the three commissioners, (Carlisle, Clinton, and Eden,) in which they disclaim all knowledge of the conduct of Governor Johnstone, in tampering with a member of Congress, till they read it in the newspapers. This paper contains ungenerous reflections on France, and intimates their astonishment that the Americans should prefer an alliance with France to a submission to the government of England. This, their last manifesto, has been published, and by permission of Congress circulated through the United States. It was addressed to the members of Congress, the members of the general assemblies or conventions of the several colonies, plantations, and provinces, and was to be in force forty days from the date. It offers a general or separate peace to the colonies, with the revival of their ancient government, secured against future infringements, and protected for ever from taxation by Great Britain, if they will *relinquish their independence, break their faith with France, Congress having formed a treaty of alliance with that nation, and submit to the British yoke.* These, if not the

* See Appendix for his character.

positive, are the implied terms on which they offer peace. But if their terms are not complied with, then are we to expect more severe expressions of British vengeance than we have hitherto experienced. Hostilities are, they say, to be conducted in a more rigorous and terrific form, that the United States may be rendered of *less importance* to the *French king*, their inveterate enemy, and our new ally. We are, therefore, if we persevere in our obstinacy, threatened with the cruel extremes of war, and a desolation of our country. This last manifesto contains a recital of what the commissioners term the blessings they are empowered to confer, and a warning of the continued train of evils to which the colonies are at present blindly and obstinately exposing themselves, &c., &c. The commissioners explicitly declared that they had *neither authority nor inclination* to acknowledge the colonies to be independent—and Congress having informed them "that they would treat with Great Britain on no other terms," it put an end to the negotiation, and the commissioners, it is understood, are preparing to depart from the continent. The British government manifests extreme chagrin and disappointment on account of the prosperous career of the United States, and are very indignant that their conceited omnipotent authority should be so presumptuously called in question by those whom they still affect to consider in the light of dependent colonies.

In their reply to the declarations of the commissioners, our Congress mention the causes which induced the people of America to array themselves in arms, that it was the oppressive and tyrannical measures of the British ministry; and after briefly reciting the cruelties that had hitherto been exercised by their troops and navy, acting against us, they add, "that since their incorrigible dispositions cannot be touched by kindness and compassion, it becomes the duty of Congress, by other means, to vindicate the rights of humanity," and they conclude by saying, "that if our enemies presume to execute their threats, and persist in their present mode of barbarity, we will take such exemplary vengeance as shall deter others from a like conduct." They appeal to that God who searches the hearts of all men for the rectitude of their intentions, and in his holy presence declare, "that as they are not moved by any light or hasty suggestions of anger or revenge, so through every possible change of fortune they shall adhere to this their determination."

October.—The regiment of cavalry, commanded by Colonel Baylor, being posted on our lines near Tappan, their situation was betrayed by some tories, and a party of the enemy surprised them while in a barn, in the night, and massacred a part of them with circumstances of savage cruelty. The commander of the party who disgraced themselves by this foul deed, was the English General Grey. Colonel Baylor's detachment consisted of one hundred and four horsemen; the attack was so sudden, that they were entirely defenceless, and the enemy immediately commenced the horrid work of slaughter; their entreaties and cries for mercy were totally disregarded by their savage foes. It has been well ascertained that the British soldiers were ordered by their inhuman officers to bayonet every man they could find, and to give no quarter. Major-General Lord Stirling, having by request ascertained the particulars respecting this execrable transaction, makes the following statement: "On its being intimated to me," says his lordship, "that Congress were desirous to know the particulars of the massacre of Colonel Baylor's regiment, I desired Dr. Griffith, surgeon and chaplain to General Woodford's brigade, and who attended Colonel Baylor and the other wounded persons, to collect all the evidence he could of this barbarous affair. I have just now received collections on this subject." The collection contains the affidavits and depositions of a number of soldiers belonging to that unfortunate regiment, who solemnly declare that after they had surrendered and asked for quarter, it was refused. *Thomas Hutchinson,* sergeant of the third troop, escaped unhurt; but heard the British soldiers cry out, "Sliver him!" repeatedly. *Cullency,* of the first troop, who received twelve wounds, says, "that when the enemy entered the barn where his troops lay, he and the men asked for quarter, and were refused; that the British captain, Bull, after inquiring how many of the rebels were dead, on being told the number, ordered all the rest to be knocked on the head, and that his orders were executed on five or six of the wounded." *Benson,* of the second troop, received also twelve wounds; he declared he heard the men in the barn with him ask for quarter, which was returned with wounds and abusive language; he thought it in vain to ask for quarter himself, as he heard the soldiers reply to others that begged it, "that their captain had ordered them to stab all, and make no prisoners." *Thomas Talley,* of the sixth troop, received six wounds; he declared, "that after the enemy had taken him and partly stripped him, the soldiers inquiring of their captain what should be done with him, he ordered him to be killed, and after that he received six wounds in his breast with their bayonets at different times." *Southward,* of the fifth troop, says, that five men out of thirteen of their regiment, in the barn with him, were killed outright, and the rest, excepting himself, bayoneted; that he heard the British officer order his men to put all to death, and afterwards ask if they had finished all; that they offered quarters to some, who on surrendering themselves, they bayoneted." The depositions of seven others, attested by Governor Livingston of New Jersey, confirm the above declarations. *Mr. Morris,* lieutenant and adjutant in Baylor's regiment, received seven wounds; he declared that, on begging his life after he had surrendered, they replied, "Yes, d—n you, we will give you quarters!" and then rushed on and stabbed him with their bayonets, and stripped him of all his clothes. It is a melancholy and awful consideration, that any unnecessary severity should be put in practice to aggravate the common horrors of war. Britain, who boasts of her bravery, her progress in the polite arts, and generosity of temper, has, in her manner of conducting the war in America, most infamously outraged all the laws of humanity, and set an example of savage brutality, detestable to every civilized people, and to every friend of human kind. They are destroying the character of their nation in the eyes of all the world. Witness their fatal prison-ships, their murders in cold blood, their wanton burning and devastations, their licentious abuses, which exhibit a picture of barbarity scarcely to be credited among civilized nations. What then must be our situation, should our country ever be reduced to an absolute subjection to such a mean-spirited people? These considerations should awaken every motive that can animate a manly bosom, to despise every danger in repelling from our shores such barbarous invaders, and in humbling such unprincipled foes to our freedom.

His excellency the commander-in-chief made a visit to our hospital; his arrival was scarcely announced, before he presented himself at our doors. Dr. Williams and myself had the honor to wait on this great and truly good man through the different wards, and to reply to his inquiries relative to the condition of our patients. He appeared to take a deep interest in the situation of the sick and wounded soldiers, and inquired particularly as to their treatment and comfortable accommodations. Not being apprised of his intended visit in time to make preparation for his reception, we were not entirely free from embarrassment, but we had the inexpressible satisfaction of receiving his excellency's approbation of our conduct, as respects the duties of our department. The personal appearance of our commander-in-chief, is that of the perfect gentleman and accomplished warrior. He is remarkably tall, full six feet, erect and well proportioned. The strength and proportion of his joints and muscles appear to be commensurate with the preeminent powers of his mind. The serenity of his countenance, and majestic gracefulness of his deportment, impart a strong impression of that dignity and grandeur which are his peculiar characteristics, and no one can stand in his presence without feeling the ascendancy of his mind, and associating with his countenance the idea of wisdom, philanthropy, magnanimity, and patriotism. There is a fine symmetry in the features of his face, indicative of a benign and dignified spirit.

His nose is strait, and his eyes inclined to blue. He wears his hair in a becoming cue, and from his forehead it is turned back and powdered in a manner which adds to the military air of his appearance. He displays a native gravity, but devoid of all appearance of ostentation. His uniform dress is a blue coat, with two brilliant epaulettes, buff-colored under-clothes, and a three-cornered hat, with a black cockade. He is constantly equipped with an elegant small-sword, boots and spurs, in readiness to mount his noble charger. There is not in the present age, perhaps, another man so eminently qualified to discharge the arduous duties of the exalted station he is called to sustain, amidst difficulties which to others would appear insurmountable, nor could any man have more at command the veneration and regard of the officers and soldiers of our army, even after defeat and misfortune. This is the illustrious chief whom a kind Providence has decreed as the instrument to conduct our country to peace and to independence.

Major-General Schuyler, having for more than a year been suspended from military command, in consequence of his concurrent responsibility respecting the evacuation of Ticonderoga, in July, 1777, has at length undergone his trial by a court-martial, of which Major-General Lincoln was president, and is acquitted, with the highest honor, of the charge exhibited against him. This excellent officer has finally obtained that justice which, from undue prejudice, has so long been denied him.

Major-General Arthur St. Clair has also by the same court been acquitted with the highest honor of the charge exhibited against him, of evacuating the post at Ticonderoga. His masterly defence before the court is admired for the display of superior intellect, sound principle, pure integrity, and correctness of judgment. General St. Clair, it is presumed, will never receive an adequate compensation for the unmerited contumely which he has experienced from Congress and the public. It is the height of injustice to subject a man of established character to suffer in reputation and in sensibility, merely from surmise and suspicion; and the injury is greatly aggravated when the accused is long held up to public odium, and not permitted to adduce evidence in his own vindication. General St. Clair has frequently been heard to express a consciousness of the uprightness and propriety of his conduct, and to despise the vague censure of an uninformed populace; and when Burgoyne was advancing into the country, he said he had the most sanguine hope that the progress of the enemy would be checked, and that he should have the satisfaction to experience that, *though he had lost a post, he had eventually saved the state.* This hope he has realized in its fullest extent, by the event that the British commander and army, to whom he surrendered a post, has since been compelled to submit as captives to our army. General St. Clair was an officer in the army of General Wolfe, and was in the battle in which that celebrated com-

mander was slain on the Plains of Abraham. He was
estimated as a young officer of merit, capable of obtaining
a high grade of military reputation. Soon after the commencement of hostilities, in 1775, he was, without his
solicitation, appointed to the office of colonel, and he
marched with his regiment into Canada, where he rendered very important services. He was subsequently promoted to the rank of major-general, and on all occasions
supported an honorable distinction, and shared largely in
the confidence and friendship of the commander-in-chief.

November 3d.—Having made a visit to Fishkill, I returned in company with Dr. Treat, our physician-general,
and found a large number of gentlemen collecting to partake of an entertainment, by invitation of Brigadier-General Muhlenburg, who occupies a room in our hospital.
The guests consisted of forty-one respectable officers, and
our tables were furnished with fourteen different dishes,
arranged in fashionable style. After dinner, Major-General Putnam was requested to preside, and he displayed
no less urbanity at the head of the table than bravery at
the head of his division. A number of toasts were pronounced, accompanied with humorous and merry songs.
In the evening we were cheered with military music and
dancing, which continued till a late hour in the night.
General Muhlenburg was a minister of a parish in Virginia, but participating in the spirit of the times, exchanged
his clerical profession for that of a soldier. Having in his
pulpit inculcated the principles of liberty and the cause
of his country, he found no difficulty in enlisting a regiment of soldiers, and he was appointed their commander.
He entered his pulpit with his sword and cockade, preached his farewell sermon, and the next day marched at the
head of his regiment to join the army, and he does honor
to the military profession.

10th.—Having for a long time served in the hospital
department, and having no claim to promotion there, I
resolved to relinquish that station, and accept the appointment of surgeon to the first Virginia state regiment, commanded by Colonel George Gibson. Being introduced to
the officers of the regiment, I received a polite invitation
to take my quarters in the marquee with Colonel Gibson

CORNWALLIS.

and his lieutenant-colonel, William Brent. Thomas Meriweather is his major.

18th.—Rode to the village of Fishkill, breakfasted with Dr. Treat and Colonel Hayes, and waited on Dr. John Cochran, who is now in close attendance on the Marquis de la Fayette, who is dangerously sick with a fever.

23d.—We have now had a long respite from battles and skirmishes, the season for the campaign is about expiring, and no one can boast of having achieved deeds of much fame and glory. As we are stationed at a considerable distance from the enemy at New York, we feel secure from the annoyance of the dogs of war; and military duty not being very urgent, our officers appear disposed to relax in their discipline, and contract a habit approaching to dissipation. They have adopted the practice of giving suppers alternately, with music and dancing through half the night. These are the favorite amusements of the Virginia and Maryland officers, but they do not accord precisely with my own views of time well spent, though I am frequently enticed to a participation in their banqueting revels.

24th.—I accepted an invitation to dine with Captain Carter, at West Point. He is a gentleman of independent fortune, and lives in splendid style. His guests were numerous and highly respectable, and the entertainment rich and arranged with taste.

25th.—Dined with General Muhlenburg, in company with several Virginia officers, and, as usual, closed the day with music and dancing.

27th.—Visited my friends at Fishkill, and by the request of Colonel Gibson I waited on the Marquis de la Fayette. The colonel furnished me with a letter of introduction and his compliments, with inquiries respecting the marquis's health. I was received by this nobleman in a polite and affable manner. He is just recovering from a fever, and was in his chair of convalescence. He is nearly six feet high, large, but not corpulent, being not more than twenty-one years of age. He is not very elegant in his form, his shoulders being broad and high, nor is there a perfect symmetry in his features; his forehead is remarkably high, his nose large and long, eyebrows prominent, and projecting over a fine animated hazel eye.

11

His countenance is interesting and impressive. He converses in broken English, and displays the manners and address of an accomplished gentleman. Considering him a French nobleman of distinguished character, and a great favorite of General Washington, I felt myself highly honored by this interview.*

December 15*th*.—At a settlement called Cherry Valley, about sixty miles above Albany, Colonel Alden, of Duxbury, Massachusetts, was stationed with about two hundred and fifty continental troops, to protect the inhabitants from the incursions of the frontier enemy. It is now announced that a body consisting of about seven hundred Indians, tories and soldiers assaulted our party, massacred Colonel Alden, several of the inhabitants, men, women and children, and made prisoners of the lieutenant-colonel and many of the inhabitants. The account states that one hundred and eighty of the surviving inhabitants had neither house nor provisions, were almost naked, and destitute of money to provide necessaries.

Our division, commanded by General Putnam, marched according to general orders from our encampment near Robinson's house, 28th November; arrived at King's ferry, twelve miles, and encamped; 29th, crossed the North river in batteaux, and pitched our camp on the Jersey shore; 30th, marched twelve miles only, in a severe storm of snow and sleet, encamped near the small town of Kakiat. December 1st and 2d, passed through Paramus and Aquackanock, twenty-six miles. These towns are inhabited chiefly by Dutch people; their churches and dwelling-houses are built mostly of rough stone, one story high. There is a peculiar neatness in the appearance of their dwellings, having an airy piazza supported by pillars in front, and their kitchens connected at the ends in the form of wings. The land is remarkably level, and the soil fertile; and being generally advantageously cultivated, the people appear to enjoy ease and happy competency. The furniture in their houses is of the most ordinary kind, and such as might be supposed to accord with the fashion of the days of Queen Anne. They despise the superfluities of life, and are ambitious to

---

* For the character of the marquis, see Appendix.

appear always neat and cleanly, and never to complain of an empty purse.

Pursued our route on the 3d, passed through Westfield, and part of Newark, a handsome village situated on a river of that name, which is navigable to New York, distance eight miles. In this village there is a public academy and several handsome churches. This is the garden of New Jersey, it is a most delightful country, uniformly level, and every acre abundantly productive. 4th, marched through Springfield, a small but handsome English town. Encamped near the village of Scotch Plains. Here we received orders by express from head-quarters to halt, in consequence of some movement of the enemy in New York. 9th, ordered to resume our march; passed through Quibbletown and the village of Middle-brook. In this vicinity we are erecting log huts for our winter-quarters.

I called at a house with Colonel Gibson and other officers to view a phenomenon in the human form—a child that has grown to an enormous size at the age of seven years; he measures three feet six inches round his breast, and three feet nine inches round his belly, his limbs and joints are proportionably large, and he weighs one hundred and thirty pounds. I was informed by the boy's mother that she discovered in him an extraordinary growth when two years old, since which he has increased very rapidly. He enjoys good health, and is not deficient in capacity.

30th.—Our officers have not permitted the Christmas days to pass unnoticed, not a day without receiving invitations to dine, nor a night without amusement and dancing. I dine to-day with General Muhlenburg. Our soldiers are constantly employed in cutting down trees and building log huts for our winter's accommodation, and we are obliged to live in our uncomfortable tents till they can be completed. This is appropriated as a day of Thanksgiving throughout the state. Our brigade was paraded in the field to attend divine service. Dr. Belmain, our chaplain, delivered a judicious sermon, well adapted to the occasion, adverting to the great cause in which we are engaged, and enjoining a grateful reverence to the Almighty Ruler of the universe, and a faithful discharge of the duties incumbent on us in our several stations.

January 1st, 1779.—Colonel Gibson made an entertainment, and invited all the officers of his regiment to dine at his quarters in the country a short distance from camp. The table was amply furnished, and the guests did not separate till evening, when we were requested to resort to General Muhlenburg's quarters. Here we were introduced to a number of ladies assembled to unite with the gentlemen in the ball-room; a very elegant supper was provided, and not one of the company was permitted to retire till three o'clock in the morning. Thus have the gallant Virginians commenced the new year.

February.—Having continued to live under cover of canvas-tents most of the winter, we have suffered extremely from exposure to cold and storms. Our soldiers have been employed six or eight weeks in constructing log huts, which at length are completed, and both officers and soldiers are now under comfortable covering for the remainder of the winter. Log houses are constructed with the trunks of trees cut into various lengths, according to the size intended, and are firmly connected by notches cut at their extremities in the manner of dovetailing. The vacancies between the logs are filled in with plastering consisting of mud and clay. The roof is formed of similar pieces of timber, and covered with hewn slabs. The chimney, situated at one end of the house, is made of similar but smaller timber, and both the inner and the outer side are covered with clay plaster, to defend the wood against the fire. The door and windows are formed by sawing away a part of the logs of a proper size, and move on wooden hinges. In this manner have our soldiers, without nails, and almost without tools, except the axe and saw, provided for their officers and for themselves comfortable and convenient quarters, with little or no expense to the public. The huts are arranged in strait lines, forming a regular, uniform, compact village. The officers' huts are situated in front of the line, according to their rank, the kitchens in the rear, and the whole is similar in form to a tent encampment. The ground for a considerable distance in front of the soldiers' line of huts is cleared of wood, stumps and rubbish, and is every morning swept clean for the purpose of a parade-ground and roll-call for the respective regiments. The officers' huts are in general

divided into two apartments, and are occupied by three
or four officers, who compose one mess. Those for the
soldiers have but one room, and contain ten or twelve
men, with their cabins placed one above another against
the walls, and filled with straw, and one blanket for each
man. I now occupy a hut with our field-officers, Colonel
Gibson, Lieutenant-Colonel Brent, and Major Meriweather.

4th.—A duel has lately been fought between a surgeon
and an adjutant in General Scott's brigade; the former
received a bad wound, and the latter escaped with *honor.*
"Who will hesitate," says one, "to exchange a few shots
with a friend to obtain the appellation of a gentleman of
honor? If I kill my antagonist I have the satisfaction of
settling a point of *honor!* If I receive a ball through my
own heart, I die in the glorious cause of *honor!* 'You
have offended me in a delicate point,' says an officer to his
friend, 'and I now demand of you the satisfaction of a
gentleman: I have settled my affairs, and prepared myself
to die, if that shall be my fate.'—'Then,' replied the
other, 'we cannot fight on equal terms, for I have not
had time to do either.'"

The anniversary of our alliance with France was celebrated in proper style a few days since near head-quarters,
at Pluckemin. A splendid entertainment was given by
General Knox and the officers of artillery. General
Washington and his lady, with the principal officers of
the army and their ladies, and a considerable number of
respectable ladies and gentlemen of the state of New Jersey, formed the brilliant assembly. About four o'clock
sixteen cannon were discharged, and the company collected in a large public building to partake of an elegant
dinner. In the evening a very beautiful set of fire-works
was exhibited, and the celebration was concluded by a
splendid ball, opened by his Excellency General Washington, having for his partner the lady of General Knox.

26th.—A party of the enemy made an attempt yesterday to surprise our troops stationed at Elizabethtown,
under the command of General Maxwell, but the vigilance
of the general prevented their success. They sent a party
to capture Governor Livingston, of New Jersey, but in this
attempt they were also frustrated. After burning and
plundering a few houses, they returned to Staten Island,

but were pursued by General Maxwell's brigade, which occasioned the loss of a few men on each side.

His excellency the commander-in-chief has long been in the practice of inviting a certain number of officers to dine at his table every day. It is not to be supposed that his excellency can be made acquainted with every officer by name, but the invitations are given through the medium of general orders, in which is mentioned the brigade from which the officer is expected. Yesterday I accompanied Major Cavil to head-quarters, and had the honor of being numbered among the guests at the table of his excellency, with his lady, two young ladies from Virginia, the gentlemen who compose his family, and several other officers.

It is natural to view with keen attention the countenance of an illustrious man, with a secret hope of discovering in his features some peculiar traces of excellence, which distinguishes him from and elevates him above his fellow-mortals. These expectations are realized in a peculiar manner in viewing the person of General Washington. His tall and noble stature and just proportions—his fine, cheerful, open countenance—simple and modest deportment—are all calculated to interest every beholder in his favor, and to command veneration and respect. He is feared even when silent, and beloved even while we are unconscious of the motive. The table was elegantly furnished, and the provisions ample, but not abounding in superfluities. The civilities of the table were performed by Colonel Hamilton and the other gentlemen of the family, the general and lady being seated at the side of the table. In conversation, his excellency's expressive countenance is peculiarly interesting and pleasing; a placid smile is frequently observed on his lips, but a loud laugh, it is said, seldom, if ever, escapes him. He is polite and attentive to each individual at table, and retires after the compliments of a few glasses. Mrs. Washington combines in an uncommon degree great dignity of manner with the most pleasing affability, but possesses no striking marks of beauty. I learn from the Virginia officers that Mrs. Washington has ever been honored as a lady of distinguished goodness, possessing all the virtues which adorn her sex, amiable in her temper and deportment, full of benignity, benevolence and charity, seeking for objects of

affliction and poverty, that she may extend to the sufferers the hand of kindness and relief. These surely are
the attributes which reveal a heart replete with those
virtues which are so appropriate and estimable in the
female character.

April 13*th.*—We have passed a winter remarkably mild
and moderate; since the 10th of January, we have scarcely
had a fall of snow, or a frost, and no severe weather. At
the beginning of this month the weather was so mild that
vegetation began to appear; the fruit-trees were budded
on the 1st, and in full blossom on the 10th. In Virginia
the peach-trees were in blossom on the 14th of February,
but a small frost since has, it is feared, proved fatal to
the fruit.

14*th.*—I accompanied several gentlemen to the village
of Middle-brook, where a number of horses were offered
for sale; I purchased a handsome young bay for six hundred dollars. This shows the depreciated value of the
paper money, which we receive for pay; the horse could
not be valued at more than eighty dollars in silver.

16*th.*—The officers of our regiment provided a genteel
entertainment, and invited Generals Woodford, Smallwood, and Muhlenburg, with all the officers of the Virginia
line, as our guests. Our table was furnished with an
ample variety of dishes, and the choicest liquors that could
be procured.

20*th.*—Five soldiers were conducted to the gallows, according to their sentence, for the crimes of desertion and
robbing the inhabitants. A detachment of troops and a
concourse of people formed a circle round the gallows,
and the criminals were brought in a cart, sitting on their
coffins, and halters about their necks. While in this
awful situation, trembling on the verge of eternity, three
of them received a pardon from the commander-in-chief,
who is always tenderly disposed to spare the lives of his
soldiers. They acknowledged the justice of their sentence,
and expressed the warmest thankfulness and gratitude for
their merciful pardon. The two others were obliged to
submit to their fate; one of them was accompanied to the
fatal spot by an affectionate and sympathizing brother,
which rendered the scene uncommonly distressing, and
forced tears of compassion from the eyes of numerous

spectators. They repeatedly embraced and kissed each other, with all the fervor of brotherly love, and would not be separated till the executioner was obliged to perform his duty, when, with a flood of tears, and mournful lamentations, they bade each other an eternal adieu—the criminal, trembling under the horrors of an untimely and disgraceful death—and the brother, overwhelmed with sorrow and anguish for one whom he held most dear.

May 1st.—Thirteen cannon have just announced the arrival of M. Gerard, the French minister, and a gentleman of distinction from Spain, by the name of Don Juan de Mirrilliars; and preparations are making to afford these foreign gentlemen an opportunity of reviewing our army.

_2d._—The whole of our army in this quarter was paraded in martial array in a spacious field, and a stage was erected for the accommodation of the ladies and gentlemen spectators. At the signal of thirteen cannon, the great and splendid cavalcade approached in martial pomp and style. A very beautiful troop of light-horse, commanded by Major Lee, a Virginian, marched in front, then followed his excellency the commander-in-chief and his aids-de-camp, next the foreign ministers and their retinue, and the general officers of our army and their aids, closed the procession. Having arrived on the field of parade, the commander-in-chief, with the foreign ministers and general officers, passed in front of the line of the army, from right to left, in review, and received the military honors due to their rank; after which, the gentlemen dismounted and retired to the stage, and took seats with Mrs. Washington, Mrs. Greene, Mrs. Knox, and a number of other ladies, who had arrived in their carriages. The army then performed the field manœuvres and evolutions, with firing of cannon and musketry. The business of the day was closed by the troops deploying, and marching in front of the stage, and paying the marching salute to their excellencies. The whole performance was conducted with such marked regularity and precision, as to reflect great honor on the character of our army, and afford the commander-in-chief and the spectators the highest degree of satisfaction. On this occasion we cannot but pride ourselves on the conspicuous figure exhibited by our commander-in-chief. While mounted on his noble bay charger, his stature appears remarkable; and being a good horseman, he displays a lofty carriage, and benign dignity of demeanor, and I hope not to incur the charge of undue partiality, when I say, his appearance was incomparably more majestic and dignified than either of his illustrious visitors.

14th.—Our brigade was paraded for the purpose of being reviewed by General Washington and a number of Indian chiefs. His excellency, with his usual dignity, followed by his mulatto servant Bill, riding a beautiful gray steed, passed in front of the line, and received the salute. He was accompanied by a singular group of savages, whose appearance was beyond description ludicrous. Their horses were of the meanest kind, some of them destitute of saddles, and old lines were used for bridles. Their personal decorations were equally farcical, having their faces painted of various colors, jewels suspended from their ears and nose, their heads without covering, except tufts of hair on the crown, and some of them wore dirty blankets over their shoulders waving in the wind. In short, they exhibited a novel and truly disgusting spectacle. But his excellency deems it good policy to pay some attention to this tribe of the wilderness, and to convince them of the strength and discipline of our army, that they may be encouraged, if disposed to be friendly, or deterred from aggression, if they should become hostile to our country.

28th.—The Baron Steuben reviewed and inspected our brigade. The troops were paraded in a single line with shouldered arms, every officer in his particular station. The baron first reviewed the line in this position, passing in front with a scrutinizing eye; after which, he took into his hand the muskets and accoutrements of every soldier, examining them with particular accuracy and precision, applauding or condemning, according to the condition in which he found them. He required that the musket and bayonet should exhibit the brightest polish; not a spot of rust or defect in any part could elude his vigilance. He inquired also into the conduct of the officers towards their men, censuring every fault and applauding every meritorious action. Next he required of me, as surgeon, a list of the sick, with a particular statement of their accommodations and mode of treatment, and even visited some of the sick in their cabins. The baron has sustained the office of aid-de-camp to his Majesty the King of Prussia, and is now inspector-general with the rank of major-general in our army. He appears to be about fifty years of age, and is venerable and dignified in his deportment, rich and elegant in dress, having a splendid medal of gold and diamonds, designating the order of *fidelity*, suspended at his breast. He is held in universal respect, and considered as a valuable acquisition to our country. He is distinguished for his profound knowledge of tactics, his ability to reform and discipline an army—for his affectionate attachment to a good and faithful soldier, and his utter aversion to every appearance of insubordination and neglect of duty. The continental army has improved with great rapidity under his inspection and review.

30th.—Dined with Major Storer, at his quarters in the country. Spent a few hours at General St. Clair's quarters, with Dr. McKenzie and Major Dunn, and called on Colonel Scammel at the adjutant-general's office.

June 10th.—Smith's Clove is a fine level plain of rich land, situated at the foot of the high mountains on the west side of Hudson river. It is about fourteen miles in the rear of the garrison at West Point, and surrounded on all sides by the highlands. The few families who reside here find a profitable employment in cultivating the fertile soil. Our brigade marched from quarters at Middle-brook on the 2d instant, and arrived at Morristown, where we received orders to leave all our heavy baggage, and proceed with all possible expedition, as the enemy was advancing towards West Point. Marched rapidly through Troy, Pompton and Ringwood, and on the 7th instant, encamped in the Clove. By a number of deserters from the enemy, information has been received that the greater part of the British army is advancing, and is now near King's ferry, only thirteen miles below West Point; and that part of their fleet is proceeding up the river: their object is supposed to be the garrison at West Point. For the security of this very important post, General Washington has arranged his army as follows: Three divisions, consisting of the Virginia, Maryland, and Pennsylvania troops, commanded by Major-Generals Lord Stirling,

Baron de Kalb, and Major-General St. Clair, form the right wing, and is commanded by General Putnam as the senior major-general, and posted at Smith's Clove. All the New England troops, including the militia, compose the left wing, and are so distributed at West Point and its vicinity, on the east side of the river, as to guard all the passes leading to the garrison. Our army thus posted is supposed to be adequate to the defence of the garrison against all the force which the enemy can bring in array against it; and such is the confidence among our officers, that many of them express a strong desire that the royal troops would afford an opportunity to try our strength and courage. Should this be the event, the struggle must indeed be violent, and the slaughter immense. The British commander, however, not deeming it prudent to hazard a battle, after a few days retired to New York.

12th.—Two officers of our regiment have just had occasion to adjust an affair of honor. Captain E. had given offence to Captain H., and a challenge ensued. Captain E. was well apprised that if the ball from the pistol of his antagonist should pass through his heart, it would produce immediate death: of course it was most prudent to decline the hazardous combat. But the consequence is, he subjected himself to a contest of a less *honorable* nature. His antagonist inflicted the chastisement of the horse-whip. This he supported with wonderful fortitude and magnanimity; apprehending, probably, that powder and ball might prove more disastrous than the chastisement which he had received. But his brother-officers treated him with contempt, and threatened to hoot him out of camp. There is a kind of mechanical courage excited by the necessity of the occasion, which may push a coward to venture on an act of heroism. This fact was now exemplified; for Captain E., reduced to the alternative of retrieving his character in a spirited manner, or of quitting the army in disgrace, came to the desperate resolution of deciding his fate by facing his bold antagonist in single combat. The usual arrangements being made, my services as surgeon were held in requisition. The parties took their stand at ten paces, and each discharged his pistol. But behold, a *harmless explosion!* no blood shed, not even a hair of their heads injured. But the combatants conducted like gentlemen of *honor:* of course, harmony and mutual friendship were restored. Captain E. has the best cause of triumph, for he has res- cued his character from the stigma of poltroon, to an hon- orable standing among the gentlemen officers.

14*th.*—I rode with Major Meriweather to West Point; took our route through the woods, over abrupt and rocky mountains, almost impassable for our horses. Spent an hour at General Parsons's head-quarters, then crossed the North river to Fishkill. The next day we recrossed at Fishkill-landing, and rode to New Windsor, thence we visited my friend Colonel Malcolm at his seat fourteen miles in the country. This gentleman, having resigned his office in the army, is beautifully situated on a farm west of the Hudson, retired from the bustle of war, and devoted to domestic affairs and rural enjoyments. We spent the night with this agreeable family, and Mrs. Mal- colm received in the evening the visits of a number of ladies and gentlemen. We returned to our camp the next morning, and found the brigade under marching orders.

16*th.*—We marched from Smith's Clove through a thick wilderness, and over the prodigious highland mountains. My curiosity was excited by a vast number of huge rocks, marked with fissures and cavities, occasioned by some stupendous power beyond our comprehension. These, with various brooks, winding in every direction, among rude clefts and precipices, afford a singular and romantic landscape. Our path was narrow and rugged, and proba- bly will not again be traversed but by savages and wild beasts. We arrived here in the evening, without our baggage, and were obliged to seek lodgings among our friends. The next day dined with Dr. I. Thomas, and accompanied him to General Patterson's quarters, where we spent the evening, and I was introduced to Major Has- kill, aid-de-camp to General Patterson. He is a native of Rochester, and Dr. Thomas of Plymouth, Massachusetts.

20*th.*—I have lately been favored with a letter from my friend Dr. D. Townsend, who is a surgeon in the military hospital at Providence, state of Rhode Island. He invites me to accept of the office of surgeon to the Massachusetts regiment, commanded by Colonel Henry Jackson, which is now stationed at that place. My principal inducement to exchange my present station for the proposed new appointment is, that Colonel Jackson and all his officers are from my native state, and there is a prospect of receiving some compensation in clothing and other articles to which 1 could have no claim while serving in the Virginia line. It is proper, and on many accounts convenient, that officers should serve in the line of their own state; and though I have enjoyed the most friendly intercourse, and numerous kind favors from the Virginians, yet I cannot but prefer the manners and habits of the New Englanders.

21st.—The officers of our regiment invited a select number of officers of the Pennsylvania line to dine on sturgeon, a large fish which Major Meriweather caught in the North river. This fish is a favorite with the Dutch, at Albany, and is on that account by some called Albany beef; but in my view it is worse than horse beef, and it was merely an auxiliary to our table.

24th.—I have just had the satisfaction, with a number of gentlemen, of viewing a remarkably large fat ox, which has been presented by some gentlemen in Connecticut to his Excellency General Washington. He is six feet seven inches high, and weighs on the hoof three thousand five hundred pounds, the largest animal I ever beheld.

Having resolved to resign my commission in Colonel Gibson's regiment, I shall in a few days commence my journey to Providence, and join the regiment commanded by Colonel H. Jackson. Colonel Gibson has favored me with a complimentary certificate of my services. It is with sincere regret that I bid adieu to those associates, for whom I have a strong attachment.

July 1st.—Engaged to spend this evening with General Patterson and Dr. Crowell, and to breakfast with the Rev. Mr. Avery and Mr. Hitchcock, and shall immediately set off for Providence, in company with Dr. Skinner.

I left West Point, in company with Dr. Skinner, on the 2d instant, and on the 3d arrived at Crompond, where my favorite young horse was seized with the horse distemper, and I was put to the cruel necessity of disposing of him for not one-half his real value. Pursued our journey through Litchfield and Farmington, in Connecticut, and the next day reached Hartford, a well-built, handsome town on Connecticut river, and the capital of that state.

Having crossed over to East Hartford, we found the whole country in a state of alarm in consequence of the enemy's having landed at New Haven, and there committing depredations among the inhabitants. A spirit of revenge seemed to pervade the whole country, and the militia were marching from all quarters to encounter and arrest the progress of the invading foe. We passed through Windham, and arrived at this place on the 8th instant. Here I had an interview with my old friends Drs. Brown and Townsend, surgeons of the hospital. I was by Dr. Townsend introduced to Colonel Jackson and his officers, and I commenced my duty by visiting the sick soldiers of the regiment. The field-officers of this regiment are Colonel Henry Jackson, Lieutenant-Colonel David Cobb, and Major Lemuel Trescott. It is now learned that the party of the enemy that landed at New Haven was commanded by Governor Tryon, and consisted of three thousand men. They met with a powerful resistance from the militia, which occasioned skirmishing, and a considerable loss on each side. After plundering the inhabitants of Fairfield and Norwalk, they maliciously destroyed both these flourishing towns, with their houses of religious worship, by a general conflagration.

13th.—Dined with Colonel Jackson, and in the afternoon rode with Major Trescott to Pawtuxet, a very pleasant ride of about five miles.

21st.—By express from General Washington to General Gates, we are informed of a glorious victory, which a detachment of our army, commanded by the intrepid General Wayne, obtained over the enemy at Stony Point, situated on the banks of the North river. In consequence of this intelligence, thirteen cannon have been fired at the several posts in this department. Extract from General Gates' orders:

"Providence, *July* 21*st*, 1779.

"The general congratulates the army on the glorious success of Brigadier-General Wayne, and the gallant troops under his command, in taking by assault the enemy's fortified post at Stony Point, and, with the point of the bayonet alone, forcing the garrison to surrender at discretion, not one man escaping. This signal and brilliant victory was gained with the loss of but fifteen men killed, and the general and eighty-three wounded, while, on the part of the enemy, five hundred soldiers and twenty officers were killed, wounded and taken prisoners, with all their cannon, arms, military-stores and provisions."

30th.—Dined at head-quarters with a number of gentlemen; was introduced to General Gates by Dr. Brown. General Gates is the commander-in-chief in this department; his capture of General Burgoyne at Saratoga, in 1777, has given him *eclat* and popularity as a brave and skillful warrior. He displays the complaisant manners of a gentleman; in conversation he is affable and interesting, but appears better versed in military tactics than in subjects appertaining to general science. He adopted the profession of arms in his early days, and his prowess and valor, as well as his zeal and partiality for our country, are incontestably established.

Congress have recently passed the following resolve in favor of an American heroine: "That Margaret Corbin, who was wounded and disabled at the attack of Fort Washington, while she heroically filled the post of her husband, who was killed by her side, serving a piece of artillery, do receive during her natural life, or the continuance of the said disability, the one-half of the monthly pay drawn by a soldier in the service of these states; and that she now receive, out of the public stores, one complete suit of clothes, or the value thereof in money."

Mr. T., an ensign in our regiment, has for some time discovered symptoms of mental derangement. He is frequently strolling abroad, and amusing people with his wit and humor, or arresting attention by his solemn appeals to the Deity. Yesterday he intruded himself at General Gates' head-quarters, and after some amusing conversation, he put himself in the attitude of devotion, and prayed that God would pardon General Gates for endeavoring to supersede that god-like man Washington. The general appeared to be much disturbed, and directed Mr. Pierce, his aid-de-camp, to take him away. Whether this address provoked in the general a consciousness of the fact is uncertain, but the subject is of such a delicate nature that no man in his sober senses would have broached it to him.

August.—The British a few weeks since detached a force from Halifax, and established a post on Penobscot river, in the Province of Maine. Their force is supposed to consist of about one thousand men, under command of Brigadier-General Maclean, with several armed vessels, which occupy the river. This invasion of our territory has excited the greatest indignation, and all classes of people are burning with an ardent desire of revenge. The General Court of Massachusetts have planned an expedition, for the purpose of driving the invading foe from our shores. Such was their zeal and confidence of success, that it is said the General Court neither consulted any experienced military character, nor desired the assistance of any continental troops on this important enterprise— thus taking on themselves the undivided responsibility, and reserving for their own heads all the laurels to be derived from the anticipated conquest. They drafted one thousand five hundred militia, and appointed General Lovell, who acquired some reputation in Rhode Island, under General Sullivan, the last year, to command the expedition. They obtained of Congress the loan of the United States frigate Warren, of thirty-two guns, and with an unprecedented spirit of enterprise and industry, no less than nineteen continental, state, and private ships, and more than twenty transports, were specially equipped, and prepared to cöoperate with the land forces destined for this service. With a laudable spirit of patriotism, and animated by the flattering prospect of success, thirty masters of merchant vessels in Newburyport honorably volunteered their services as common seamen. Captain Saltonstall was appointed commodore of the fleet, and took his station on board the Warren frigate. This combined force sailed about the 20th of July on their destined service, but having some reason to apprehend a failure of their enterprise, the General Court have applied to General Gates for permission for Colonel Jackson's regiment to rëinforce General Lovell, to which he has assented, and we are accordingly under marching orders.

Colonel Henry Jackson, who commands our regiment, is a native of Boston; he is very respectable as a commander, is gentlemanly in his manners, strongly attached to military affairs, and takes a peculiar pride in the discipline and martial appearance of his regiment. Many of his officers are from Boston and its vicinity; they appear in handsome style, and are ambitious to display their taste for military life and their zeal to contend with the enemies of their country. Colonel Jackson, with his regiment, acquired reputation by their gallantry in the battle on

GENERAL JOHN SULLIVAN, LL. D.

Rhode Island, under General Sullivan. Our regiment consists of about four hundred men, in complete uniform, well disciplined, and not inferior to any in the continental army. We commenced a forced march from Providence on the 10th, and completed the forty miles in twenty-four hours. A severe rain all night did not much impede our march, but the troops were broken down with fatigue. We reached Boston-neck at sun-rising, and near the entrance of the neck is a tavern having for its sign a representation of a globe, with a man in the act of struggling to get through it; his head and shoulders were out, his arms extended, and the rest of his body inclosed in the globe. On a label from his mouth was written, "Oh! how shall I get through this world?" This was read by the soldiers, and one of them exclaimed, "List, d—n you, list, and you will soon get through this world! Our regiment will all be through it in an hour or two, if we don't halt by the way."

We are treated by the gentlemen of this town with great attention and respect. They have generously presented to Colonel Jackson and the officers of his regiment a hogshead of Jamaica spirits and a cask of wine. For the soldiers they have collected a liberal sum of money, which is distributed among them. A public dinner is to be provided at the Bunch of Grapes tavern for the officers, before our departure. The transports are in preparation to receive our troops on board.

On the 14th, our regiment marched through the town to the Long wharf, and embarked on board the transports, receiving as we passed through King-street the cheers of the inhabitants. After the regiment had embarked, the officers, according to previous arrangement, returned to the Bunch of Grapes tavern, where a liberal and elegant entertainment had been provided, and where we were politely received by a number of respectable gentlemen of the town. Having dined and enjoyed a number of songs over the cheering glass, wishing success to the Penobscot expedition, we repaired on board our respective transports, awaiting a fair wind for our voyage. Our transports are the Rising Empire, a brig carrying eight guns, two sloops, and one schooner. Our convoy is the ship Renown, of fourteen guns, and a brig of sixteen guns. About four o'clock on the 15th instant, the Renown, our convoy, fired her signal-guns for sailing, on which our little fleet weighed anchor, and after giving three cheers, which were returned by a concourse of people on the wharves, and by a French ship in the harbor, we sailed after our convoy, but dropped anchor near Castle William, by reason of contrary winds.

17*th*.—In the evening we obeyed the signal-guns, and were beating against contrary wind off Cape Anne till the 19th, when we fell in with a small boat off the Isle of Shoals, which had been despatched with the unwelcome intelligence that our fleet at Penobscot had been attacked by the British, and was totally defeated and destroyed, and that our land forces, under General Lovell, were also entirely defeated and dispersed. Orders were received for our fleet to put into Portsmouth harbor for safety, as several British ships were supposed to be in pursuit of us.

21*st*.—Our regiment disembarked and encamped at Kittery; being Sunday, I accompanied several of our officers to the Reverend Mr. Hemmenway's church; he is a sensible and animating preacher, displaying considerable eloquence and much *orthodoxy*. In his fervent prayers, he was not forgetful of the calamities of war, and the righteous cause in which we are engaged. Here we have a confirmation of the unfortunate failure of the Penobscot expedition, which is a source not only of universal regret, but of infinite chagrin and mortification among all who had been concerned in the plan.

August.—Having received orders to march to Falmouth, (now Portland,) left Kittery on the 23d instant, and on the 27th entered this town in martial order, and were received with marks of the greatest joy and satisfaction, as the inhabitants were under serious apprehensions of a visit from the British. We behold here only the relics of a town, which a few years since was very respectable and flourishing. It was the capital of the province of Maine, and enjoyed the happy prospect of becoming one of the most important seaports in New England. But in October, 1775, the inhabitants opposed the lading of a British vessel with ship timber, which so enraged Admiral Graves, that he sent Captain *Mowat* with several ships of war, demanding of the inhabitants to deliver up all their artillery and small arms. On refusal to comply with this demand, the enemy opened a severe cannonade, which soon set fire to the town, and no less than four hundred and eight houses, stores and other buildings, were consumed to ashes. A large number of seamen and mariners were landed, but the people having collected in considerable force, compelled the enemy to retreat to their boats, with the loss of several men.

By several gentlemen just returned from Penobscot, I have obtained the following particulars respecting the failure of the expedition. On the arrival of General Lovell, instead of one thousand five hundred militia, nine hundred only could be collected; it was resolved, however, in a council of war, to make an attempt to achieve the object of the expedition; accordingly, on the 28th of July, the militia, with about three hundred marines, were disembarked, and soon effected a landing under a height which rose almost perpendicularly from the banks of the river, on the summit of which the enemy's advanced guard was posted under cover of a wood. Our militia were opposed by about an equal number of the enemy, whom they bravely encountered and drove within their works; but we suffered a loss of several officers of merit, and about one hundred of the militia and marines were killed and wounded. It now became a subject of consideration whether it was expedient to storm the enemy's principal works, but in a council it was decided that our force was inadequate to the object. It was at this juncture supposed that by a vigorous coöperation of our navy, a complete victory might have been obtained, and the most urgent and pressing entreaties were made to Commodore Saltonstall for the purpose, but he declined, and continued in a state of pusillanimous inactivity, thereby proclaiming himself totally incompetent to the important trust with which, most unfortunately, he had been invested.

On the 14th instant, Sir George Collier, with a sixty-four-gun ship and five frigates, arrived from New York. General Lovell, on receiving this intelligence, ordered all his troops, with the artillery and baggage, to be embarked on board the transports, which, with our whole fleet, moved up the Penobscot river, pursued by the British. On the near approach of the enemy, our vessels were abandoned; two of them fell into the hands of the enemy, the remainder were burned and blown up. General Lovell and General Peleg Wadsworth, the second in command, both of whom have the reputation of brave men, now dispensed with all command of the troops, as did Saltonstall of the seamen. The soldiers separated from their officers, and every individual was seeking his own safety, wandering in the wilderness, suffering fatigue, hunger, and vexation, till after much difficulty they reached the settlements on the Kennebec; a few of their number indeed actually perished in the wilderness. Thus disgracefully has ended the famous Penobscot expedition, which, had a competent force been provided, might have terminated to the glory of Massachusetts. Those concerned in the plan or its execution, a few individuals excepted, were publicly execrated. The expense attending the expedition is immense. The fleet was invaluable, and its loss is altogether irreparable. It was extremely fortunate for our regiment that we were detained two or three days on our passage by contrary winds; had there been no impediment to our voyage, we must inevitably have fallen into the hands of the enemy.

September 3d.—Two armed vessels, accompanied by two others, being perceived approaching this harbor, excited a great degree of consternation among the inhabitants, but it was soon ascertained to be our two continental frigates, the Boston and the Dean, returning from a cruise with two prizes of very considerable value, and having on board two hundred soldiers for the British army, and stores and goods to a large amount.

The inhabitants of this town have shown us numerous marks of respect and generous hospitality. A respectable committee of the town have invited our officers to a tavern to partake of a treat of punch and wine, in company with a number of respectable inhabitants, and we experience many other polite civilities, indicating a disposition to contribute to the comfort and happiness of those who are serving the great cause of our common country. Orders are now received from General Gates for our regiment to return immediately to Boston.

Commenced our march from Falmouth on the 7th instant; passed through Scarborough, Kennebunk and York, to Portsmouth, in New Hampshire. At York, all the officers of our regiment were politely invited to an elegant breakfast, with the genteel and hospitable family of Mr. Sewall. Having crossed the ferry at Portsmouth on the 10th, we encamped on the common. A number of gentlemen of this town treated us with buckets of punch at the ferry-way, and as we passed through the streets. This attention was extremely grateful during the heat and fatigue of the day. We had the satisfaction of visiting the seventy-four-gun ship on the stocks near this town; she will be ready for sea in June next. This is the first seventy-four ever built in America. On the 12th, crossed the ferry at Newbury, and marched to Ipswich Hamlet, passing through Salem; we reached Cambridge on the 14th, and encamped on the common. Accompanied a number of ladies and gentlemen to view the colleges, and were admitted to the library-room and museum. From Cambridge we marched to Dorchester Point, where we embarked in boats, crossed over to the castle, and encamped. On the 18th, went with Colonel Jackson to Boston to attend the funeral of a Mr. Deshon, a brother-mason. A procession of one hundred and twenty of the brethren preceded the corpse, and added greatly to the solemnity of the occasion.

Walking in the street, I met with James Otis, Esq. He has for some time labored under an unhappy mental derangement. I had no expectation that I should be recognized by him, but he accosted me in a very familiar manner by my Christian name, and inquired about my connexions. He was inquisitive respecting the affairs of the army, and wished to be informed whether I had on any occasion been exposed to personal danger, and whether my courage had failed me. A friend related to me the following anecdote, which he received from O. W. Esq., who was present on the occasion: Mr. Otis invited several respectable gentlemen to dinner; in carving at table, he observed a fish not sufficiently boiled, which drew from him some expressions of disapprobation. His lady retorted with an air of ill-humor. Mr. Otis, wishing to avoid altercation, waived his rebuke till dinner was finished, when he rendered thanks to God that, among other favors, the guests had escaped the danger of having their noses snapped off at table.

A particular account of the brilliant achievement in the capture of the fortress at Stony Point, by General Wayne, has been obtained. Stony Point is a strongly-fortified post on the west bank of the Hudson, near King's ferry. The possession of this post is of vast importance to either army, as it completely commands the great road, and the ferry-way which affords communication between the middle and eastern states. This fortress has lately been visited by Sir Henry Clinton in person, and by his orders strengthened, and rendered, as supposed, entirely defensible. General Washington was extremely desirous to dislodge the enemy from this position, and to Brigadier-General Wayne he intrusted the hazardous enterprise. At the head of his detachment of light-infantry, consisting of one thousand two hundred, he marched about fourteen miles, reached the vicinity of the fort at eleven o'clock in the evening of July the 16th, and instantly prepared for the assault. He peremptorily ordered that every man should advance in silence with unloaded muskets and fixed bayonets. A soldier disobeyed his order, and began to load his piece; the order was repeated, and he persisted in the resolution to load, on which an officer instantly run him through the body with his sword. On no occasion is a strict obedience to orders more indispensable than at this critical moment; had a single gun been fired, the victory might have been lost, or the slaughter been immense. The plan being adjusted, one hundred and fifty volunteers under Lieutenant-Colonel Fleury, a French gentleman, formed the van of the right column, and one hundred volunteers, under Major Stuart, composed the van of the left column, each of which was preceded by a forlorn hope of twenty picked men, commanded by Lieutenants Gibbon and Knox, for the express purpose of removing the abatis and other obstructions. At about twenty minutes after twelve, the columns advanced to the assault, and such was the impetuosity of the troops, that in the face of a most tremendous and incessant fire of musketry and cannon loaded with grape-shot, they forced their way at the point of the bayonet, surmounted every obstacle, and both columns met in the centre of the enemy's works nearly at the same instant. Colonel Fleury first entered the fort, and struck their standard with his own hand. Major Posey was the first to give the watch-word, "The fort's our own." General Wayne, in his letter to the commander-in-chief, extols highly the brave conduct of his officers and men, and particularizes Lieutenant-Colonel Fleury, Major Stuart, Colonels Butler, Hull, Meigs and Febiger, for their exemplary valor and intrepidity. Lieutenant-Colonel Hay was wounded in the thigh, while fighting with firmness in the heat of the action. General Wayne himself received a slight wound in his head, but, supported by his aids, he entered the fort with the troops. The truly brave are ever ambitious of distinguishing themselves by a nice observance of the laws of humanity and generosity towards the conquered foe. It is highly creditable to our troops, that they conducted towards the prisoners with a humane forbearance, which is directly the reverse of the conduct of the British on too many similar occasions; they disdained to take the lives of those who were in their power, and calling for mercy; not an individual suffered after their surrender, and this will account for the few of the enemy killed on this occasion; being about one hundred killed and wounded. The continentals had fifteen killed and eighty-three wounded. The number of prisoners was five hundred and forty-three. Colonel Johnson, commander of the fort, and several other officers, were among the number. It is remarkable that out of the twenty men who formed the *forlorn hope*, under Lieutenant Gibbon, seventeen were killed or wounded.

General Washington's letter to Congress applauds the conduct of all the officers and men; but he names particular officers, whose situation placed them foremost in danger, which rendered their conduct more conspicuous. Lieutenants Gibbon and Knox, he observes, who commanded the advanced parties, or *forlorn hope*, acquitted themselves as well as it was possible. With respect to *General Wayne*, he observes, "that his conduct throughout the whole of this arduous enterprise, merits the warmest approbation of Congress; he improved on the plan recommended by me, and executed it in a manner that does signal honor to his judgment and to his bravery. In a critical moment of the assault, he received a flesh-wound in the head, with a musket-ball, but continued leading on his men with unshaken firmness." His excellency informed Congress that two flags and two standards were taken, the former belonging to the garrison, the latter to the 17th regiment. Lieutenant-Colonel Hull, at the head of four hundred light-infantry, displayed a noble gallantry, for which he received the thanks of General Wayne and of Washington.

As distinguishing marks of approbation, Congress directed that a *gold* medal, emblematical of the action, be presented to Brigadier-General Wayne, and a *silver* one to Lieutenant-Colonel Fleury and Major Stuart, and brevets of captain given to Lieutenants Gibbon and Knox, and that the value of the military stores taken, should be divided among the gallant troops who reduced Stony Point, in such a manner as the commander-in-chief should prescribe.

The fortifications at Paulus Hook, on the west side of North river, opposite New York city, was taken by Major Lee of the horse. The garrison made a faint resistance and surrendered. Major Southerland and about fifteen of his men escaped to a small block-house. The approach of day, and the vicinity of the main body of the enemy, made it impossible to bring off any stores. The continentals had possession of all the artillery and magazine; the prisoners were one hundred and thirty-four, rank and file, and seven officers; about forty were killed. Major Lee's loss is said to be very few in killed and wounded; four only is the number mentioned.

According to orders from General Gates, our regiment left Castle William on the 26th, and arrived at Providence on the 28th instant, and encamped at Fox's Point. Sunday I rode with several officers to Pawtuxet, to attend the religious services of the celebrated Mr. Murray, whose professed doctrine is the universal salvation of mankind. Mr. Murray is not admitted into the pulpits of the orthodox clergy; his peculiar sentiments are revolting to the consciences, and repugnant to the belief of a large proportion of the people of New England. In this village the people are destitute of an ordained minister. The audience was numerous, and the preacher peculiarly eloquent; freely and solemnly declaring the sentiments which he has adopted, and quoting various portions of Scripture to enforce a belief in the opinion which his own conscience and judgment approve.

General Prescott, who was taken at Rhode Island by Colonel Barton, on his route through Connecticut, called at a tavern to dine; the landlady brought on the table a dish of succotash (boiled corn and beans). The general, unaccustomed to such kind of food, with much warmth exclaimed, "What! do you treat us with the food of hogs?" and taking the dish from the table, emptied the contents over the floor. The landlord, being informed of this, soon entered with his horsewhip, and gave the general a severe chastisement. After the general was exchanged, and he resumed his command on the island, the inhabitants of Nantucket deputed Dr. Gilston to negotiate some concerns with General Prescott, in behalf of the town. Prescott treated the doctor very cavalierly, and gave as the cause, that the doctor looked so like that d—d landlord who horsewhipped him in Connecticut, that he could not treat him with civility.

When the Count D'Estaing's fleet appeared near the British batteries, in the harbor of Rhode Island, a severe cannonade was commenced, and several shot passed through the houses in town, and occasioned great consternation among the inhabitants. A shot passed through the door of Mrs. Mason's house, just above the floor. The family were alarmed, not knowing where to flee for safety. A negro man ran and sat himself down very composedly, with his back against the shot-hole in the door, and being asked by young Mr. Mason why he chose that situation, he replied, "Massa, you never know two bullet go in one place."

October.—Information is received that the enemy are preparing to evacuate the town of Newport. They have burned the light-house, blown up some of their works, and embarked their heavy baggage.

16th.—It is ascertained that the British have abandoned the town of Newport, and that some of our troops have taken possession of the town. It is but justice to remark, that the enemy left the town in good condition, and that they treated the inhabitants with civility. They left a large quantity of hay, wood, and military stores. Our regiment is under marching orders.

November.—In obedience to orders, we marched from Providence on the 8th instant, passing through the towns of Coventry, Windham, Bolton, Hartford, Woodbury, and Newtown, and arrived at Danbury, (Conn.,) on the 23d. Our regiment is united with General Stark's brigade, the whole of which is now billeted in private houses. Danbury was formerly a flourishing town, but the principal part of it has been destroyed by the enemy. A soldier having anointed himself for the itch, with mercurial ointment, last night, was found dead this morning; and another suffered the same fate, in consequence of drinking six gills of rum. Our troops have suffered greatly by snow and rain, and excessively bad travelling, since we left Providence.

December.—Our brigade left Danbury on the 5th instant. It snowed all the afternoon, and we took shelter in the woods at Cortland's manor. Having no other shelter than bushes thrown together, we passed a very cold, uncomfortable night. Marched the next day through a deep snow, and took lodgings at night in private houses at Crompond; marched again early, crossed the Hudson at King's ferry, and proceeded twenty miles, it being late at night before our men could all find accommodations in the scattering houses and barns on the road. I visited my friend Doctor S. Findley, of General Glover's brigade, and being invited to breakfast, the only food he could furnish was coffee, without milk or sugar, and meagre beef-steaks, without bread or even salt. Such has been for some time the unaccountable scarcity of provisions in the main army. We marched to Pompton on the 9th, and on the 14th reached this wilderness, about three miles from Morristown, where we are to build log-huts for winter-quarters. Our baggage is left in the rear, for want of wagons to transport it. The snow on the ground is about two feet deep, and the weather extremely cold; the soldiers are destitute of both tents and blankets, and some of them are actually barefooted and almost naked. Our only defence against the inclemency of the weather, consists of brush-wood thrown together. Our lodging the last night was on the frozen ground. Those officers who have the privilege of a horse, can always have a blanket at hand. Having removed the snow, we wrapped ourselves in great-coats, spread our blankets on the ground, and lay down by the side of each other five or six together, with large fires at our feet, leaving orders with the waiters to keep it well supplied with fuel during the night. We could procure neither shelter nor forage for our horses, and the poor animals were tied to trees in the woods for twenty-four hours without food, except the bark which they peeled from the trees. Lieutenant W. and myself rode to Morristown, where we dined, and fed our starving horses at a tavern. General Washington has taken his head-quarters at Morristown, and the whole army in this department are to be employed in building log huts for winter-quarters. The ground is marked out, and the soldiers have commenced cutting down the timber of oak and walnut, of which we have a great abundance. Our baggage has at length arrived, the men find it very difficult to pitch their tents on the frozen ground, and notwith. standing large fires, we can scarcely keep from freezing. In addition to other sufferings, the whole army has been for seven or eight days entirely destitute of the staff of life; our only food is miserable fresh beef, without bread, salt, or vegetables.

It is a circumstance greatly to be deprecated, that the army, who are devoting their lives and every thing dear to the defence of our country's freedom, should be subjected to such unparalleled privations, while in the midst of a country abounding in every kind of provisions. The time has before occurred when the army was on the point of dissolution for the want of provisions, and it is to be ascribed to their patriotism, and to a sense of honor and duty, that they have not long since abandoned the cause of their country. The heroic fortitude with which our officers and soldiers support their distresses, proclaims their fidelity and intrinsic merit. Besides the evils above mentioned, we experience another, in the rapid depreciation of the continental money, which we receive for our pay; it is now estimated at about thirty for one. It is from this cause, according to report, that our commissary-general is unable to furnish the army with a proper supply of provisions. The people in the country are unwilling to sell the produce of their farms for this depreciated currency, and both the resources and the credit of our Con-

gress appear to be almost exhausted. The year is now
closed, and with it expires the term of enlistment of a
considerable number of our soldiers; new conditions are
offered them to encourage their reënlistment during the
war; but such are the numerous evils which they have
hitherto experienced, that it is feared but a small proportion of them will reënlist. Should these apprehensions be
realized, the fate of our country, and the destiny of its
present rulers and friends, will soon be decided.

It has hitherto been our grievous misfortune, that the
several states have attempted to supply their quota of the
army by short enlistments. No fact is more susceptible
of demonstration, than that enlisting or draughting men
for nine months or one year never fails of being attended
with disappointment and a train of pernicious consequences. General Washington has, from the beginning of the
contest, most pointedly protested against it, and labored
with unwearied assiduity to induce the states to adopt a
more just and permanent system. By the present mode,
the strength of the army is continually precarious and
fluctuating; the recruits have scarcely time to learn the
discipline and police of a camp, before they are at liberty
to return to their farms, and their places are supplied by
others who require the same course of instruction. The
consequence is, that but a small proportion of our troops
are inured to actual service, they are continually liable to
camp diseases, and are undeserving of confidence in the
most critical moments of the campaign. Another discouraging circumstance attending this mode of recruiting the
army is, the great inequality of the bounties given to the
soldiers at different times, and the disparity in the provision made by the several states, which occasions murmurs
and discontent among their respective troops. It is consistency and stability that give character and efficiency to
an army, and this has ever been the great desideratum in
the view of our commander-in-chief. The state of Massachusetts, in order to fill up their regiments, have offered
a bounty of three hundred dollars, in addition to the continental bounty of two hundred dollars, to induce men to
enlist for three years, or during the war.

Intelligence has been received from Savannah, Georgia,
which city has for some time been in the possession of the

enemy, under command of General Prevost. Major-General Lincoln is commander-in-chief of our army in that department. The Count D'Estaing had arrived there with a French fleet and a body of troops. With these forces, combined with the Americans, the two commanders, after having besieged the city for some time, resolved on the almost desperate resolution of possessing it by assault. The allied force consisted of between four and five thousand men. General Lincoln and Count D'Estaing led their respective troops to the lines of the enemy, with the most signal firmness and intrepidity, and faced their fire for about fifty-five minutes, when they were repulsed with considerable loss. Count D'Estaing received two slight wounds; more than six hundred of his brave troops, and about one hundred and seventy continentals were killed or wounded. Count Pulaski, a brigadier-general in our service, at the head of two hundred horsemen, was in full gallop, with the intention of charging the enemy in the rear, when he received a mortal wound. This gentleman was a Polander, of distinguished rank and character; having viewed the American cause in a favorable light, he offered his services to our Congress, who appointed him to the rank of brigadier-general. He has by his active and enterprising spirit rendered essential service to our army, and his death is universally lamented.

During the siege of Savannah, an event occured, singularly honorable to an enterprising individual, which should never be forgotten. A captain of Colonel Delany's battalion of refugee troops, with about one hundred American royal regulars, was posted near a river twenty-five miles from Savannah, where were four armed British vessels, manned with about forty sailors. Colonel John White, of the Georgia line, was desirous of the honor of capturing this party; his whole force, however, consisted of no more than *six volunteers*, including his own servant; it was only by a well-concerted stratagem, therefore, that he could hope for success. In the night, he kindled a number of fires, in different places, and exhibited the appearance of a large encampment, and having arranged his plan, he summoned the captain to surrender, threatening his entire destruction, by a superior force, in case of a refusal. Intimidated, and deceived by appearances, the captain immediately signified his readiness to comply with the demand, and made no further defence. The American captain, White, had now the satisfaction, by his peculiar address, to see the whole of the prisoners, amounting to one hundred and forty, divest themselves of their arms, and submit to himself and his six volunteers. The prisoners were afterwards safely conducted by three of the captors for twenty-five miles through the country, to an American post. During the present month, one Hessian lieutenant and seven Hessian soldiers, and four British, deserted from the enemy at New York. The lieutenant pretended to desire to enter our service as a volunteer, but deserters are generally suspicious or worthless characters, undeserving of attention. One of the British deserters pretended to be a prophet, but probably a disguised spy.

January 1st, 1780.—A new year commences, but brings no relief to the sufferings and privations of our army. Our canvas covering affords but a miserable security from storms of rain and snow, and a great scarcity of provisions still prevails, and its effects are felt even at headquarters, as appears by the following anecdote: "We have nothing but the rations to cook, sir," said Mrs. Thomson, a very worthy Irish woman and house-keeper to General Washington.—"Well, Mrs. Thomson, you must then cook the rations, for I have not a farthing to give you."— "If you please, sir, let one of the gentlemen give me an order for six bushels of salt."—"Six bushels of salt! for what?"—To preserve the fresh beef, sir." One of the aids gave the order, and the next day his excellency's table was amply provided. Mrs. Thomson was sent for, and told that she had done very wrong to expend her own money, for it was not known when she could be repaid. "I owe you," said his excellency, "too much already to permit the debt being increased, and our situation is not at this moment such as to induce very sanguine hope."—"Dear sir," said the good old lady, "it is always darkest just before day-light, and I hope your excellency will forgive me for bartering the salt for other necessaries which are now on the table." Salt was eight dollars a bushel, and it might always be exchanged with the country people for articles of provision.

The weather for several days has been remarkably cold

and stormy. On the 3d instant, we experienced one of the most tremendous snow-storms ever remembered; no man could endure its violence many minutes without danger of his life. Several marquees were torn asunder and blown down over the officers' heads in the night, and some of the soldiers were actually covered while in their tents, and buried like sheep under the snow. My comrades and myself were roused from sleep by the calls of some officers for assistance; their marquee had blown down, and they were almost smothered in the storm, before they could reach our marquee, only a few yards, and their blankets and baggage were nearly buried in the snow. We are greatly favored in having a supply of straw for bedding; over this we spread all our blankets, and with our clothes and large fires at our feet, while four or five are crowded together, preserve ourselves from freezing. But the sufferings of the poor soldiers can scarcely be described, while on duty they are unavoidably exposed to all the inclemency of storms and severe cold; at night they now have a bed of straw on the ground, and a single blanket to each man; they are badly clad, and some are destitute of shoes. We have contrived a kind of stone chimney outside, and an opening at one end of our tents gives us the benefit of the fire within. The snow is now from four to six feet deep, which so obstructs the roads as to prevent our receiving a supply of provisions. For the last ten days we have received but two pounds of meat a man, and we are frequently for six or eight days entirely destitute of meat, and then as long without bread. The consequence is, the soldiers are so enfeebled from hunger and cold, as to be almost unable to perform their military duty, or labor in constructing their huts. It is well known that General Washington experiences the greatest solicitude for the sufferings of his army, and is sensible that they in general conduct with heroic patience and fortitude. His excellency, it is understood, despairing of supplies from the commissary-general, has made application to the magistrates of the state of New Jersey for assistance in procuring provisions. This expedient has been attended with the happiest success. It is honorable to the magistrates and people of Jersey, that they have cheerfully complied with the requisition, and furnished for the present an ample supply, and have thus probably saved the army from destruction.

As if to make up the full measure of grief and embarrassment to the commander-in-chief, repeated complaints have been made to him that some of the soldiers are in the practice of pilfering and plundering the inhabitants of their poultry, sheep, pigs, and even their cattle, from their farms. This marauding practice has often been prohibited in general orders, under the severest penalties, and some exemplary punishments have been inflicted. General Washington possesses an inflexible firmness of purpose, and is determined that discipline and subordination in camp shall be rigidly enforced and maintained. The whole army has been sufficiently warned, and cautioned against robbing the inhabitants on any pretence whatever, and no soldier is subjected to punishment without a fair trial, and conviction by a court-martial. Death has been inflicted in a few instances of an atrocious nature; but in general, the punishment consists in a public whipping, and the number of stripes is proportioned to the degree of offence. The law of Moses prescribes forty stripes save one, but this number has often been exceeded in our camp. In aggravated cases, and with old offenders, the culprit is sentenced to receive one hundred lashes, or more. It is always the duty of the drummers and fifers to inflict the chastisement, and the drum-major must attend and see that the duty is faithfully performed. The culprit being securely tied to a tree, or post, receives on his naked back the number of lashes assigned him, by a whip formed of several small knotted cords, which sometimes cut through the skin at every stroke. However strange it may appear, a soldier will often receive the severest stripes without uttering a groan, or once shrinking from the lash, even while the blood flows freely from his lacerated wounds. This must be ascribed to stubbornness or pride. They have, however, adopted a method which they say mitigates the anguish in some measure: it is by putting between the teeth a leaden bullet, on which they chew while under the lash, till it is made quite flat and jagged. In some instances of incorrigible villains, it is adjudged by the court that the culprit receive his punishment at several different times, a certain number of stripes repeated

MARQUIS DE LA FAYETTE.

at intervals of two or three days, in which case the wounds are in a state of inflammation, and the skin rendered more sensibly tender; and the terror of the punishment is greatly aggravated. Another mode of punishment is that of running the *gauntlet:* this is done by a company of soldiers standing in two lines, each one furnished with a switch, and the criminal is made to run between them and receive the scourge from their hands on his naked back; but the delinquent runs so rapidly, and the soldiers are so apt to favor a comrade, that it often happens in this way that the punishment is very trivial; but on some occasions, a soldier is ordered to hold a bayonet at his breast to impede his steps. If a non-commissioned officer is sentenced to corporeal punishment, he is always degraded to the soldier's rank. The practice of corporeal punishment in an army has become a subject of animadversion, and both the policy and propriety of the measure have been called in question. It may be observed that the object of punishment is to exhibit examples, to deter others from committing crimes; that corporeal punishment may be made sufficiently severe as a commutation for the punishment of death in ordinary cases; it is more humane, and by saving the life of a soldier, we prevent the loss of his services to the public. In justification of the practice, it is alleged, also, that in the British army it has long been established in their military code, and it is not uncommon to sentence a criminal to receive a thousand lashes, and that they aggravate its horrors in the most cruel manner, by repeating the stripes from day to day, before the wounds are healed; and instances are not wanting of its having been attended with fatal consequences. On the other hand, it is objected that corporeal punishment is disreputable to an army; it will never reclaim the unprincipled villain, and it has a tendency to repress the spirit of ambition and enterprise in the young soldier; and the individual thus ignominiously treated, can never, in case of promotion for meritorious services, be received with complacency as a companion for other officers; These objections will apply to most other modes of punishment, and it remains to be decided, which is the most eligible for the purpose of maintaining that subordination so indispensable in all armies.

13

Notwithstanding the numerous difficulties and discouragements with which our army have been compelled to struggle, we are happy to find that a considerable proportion of those soldiers whose terms of enlistment have lately expired, have reënlisted during the continuance of the war. It may seem extraordinary that those who have experienced such accumulated distress and privations, should voluntarily engage again in the same service. But amid all the toils and hardships, there are charms in a military life: it is here that we witness heroic actions and deeds of military glory. The power of habit and the spirit of ambition, pervade the soldiers' ranks, and those who have been accustomed to active scenes, and formed their social attachments, cannot without reluctance quit the tumult and the bustle of a camp, for the calm and quiet of domestic pursuits. There is to be found, however, in the bosom of our soldiers the purest principles of patriotism: they glory in the noble cause of their country, and pride themselves in contributing to its successful termination. It is hoped they will not again be subjected to a starving condition.

17th.—A detachment, consisting of about two thousand five hundred men, under the command of Major-General Lord Stirling, was a few days since sent off in about five hundred sleighs on a secret expedition. The sleighs were procured, and preparations made, under the pretence of going into the country after provisions. It is now ascertained that the object of the expedition was to attack the enemy in their works on Staten Island, by surprise. Our party passed over on the ice from Elizabethtown in the night, but the enemy having received intelligence of their design, retired into their strong works for safety, and the object of the enterprise was unfortunately defeated; they, however, brought off a quantity of blankets and stores. The snow was three or four feet deep, and the weather extremely cold, and our troops continued on the island twenty-four hours without covering, and about five hundred were slightly frozen, and six were killed by a party of horse, who pursued our rear-guard. A number of tents, arms, and a quantity of baggage, with several casks of wine and spirits, were brought off, with sevnteen prisoners.

27th.—A party of the enemy made an excursion from Staten Island in the night, surprised our picket-guard, and succeeded in taking off a major and forty men. Our officers were censured for their conduct in not being sufficiently alert to guard against a surprise. We are now rejoicing in having a plentiful supply of provisions and a favorable prospect of a full supply in future. Our log huts are almost completed, and we promise ourselves very comfortable quarters for the remainder of the winter.

A detachment of eighty men, levies and volunteers, under command of Captains Keeler and Lockwood, marched to Morrissania in the night, and made an attack on Colonel Hatfield. The colonel and his men took to the chambers, and fired out of the windows and down stairs at those who entered the house. Our party found it almost impossible to dislodge them till they set fire to the house by putting a straw bed into a closet while in blaze, which compelled them to jump out at the chamber-windows to avoid the flames. Colonel Hatfield, one captain, one lieutenant, and one quarter-master, and eleven private soldiers were taken and brought off.

We are just informed that on the first of this month about two hundred soldiers of the Massachusetts line, who were stationed at West Point, pretending that their term of enlistment had expired, marched off with the intention of going home. A party of troops were despatched after them, and they were brought back. Several soldiers from other posts followed their example. The subject being investigated by the proper officers, it was found that many of them had several months to serve: some of these were punished, and the remainder returned to their duty. Those whose term had actually expired were discharged. During the present month a considerable number of deserters, both British and Hessians, have come from the enemy.

February.—Lieutenant-Colonel Thompson had the command of about two hundred and fifty men, as an advanced party, on our lines. He was instructed to be constantly alert and in motion, that the enemy might not be able to take advantage, and form a plan for his destruction. It happened, however, that a detachment of British, Hessians, and mounted refugees, were discovered advancing towards him, but on account of a very deep snow obstructing the road, they marched slowly, and Colonel Thompson resolved to defend his ground. The enemy's horse first advanced, and commenced skirmishing till their infantry approached, when a sharp conflict ensued, which continued about fifteen minutes; some of our troops manifested symptoms of cowardice, and gave way. The enemy secured the advantage, and rushed on with a general shout, which soon decided the contest. The Americans lost thirteen men killed, and Captain Roberts, being mortally wounded, soon expired; seventeen others were wounded. Lieutenant-Colonel Thompson and six other officers, with with eighty-nine rank and file, were made prisoners. Of the enemy, two officers and eighteen men were wounded, and five men killed. One of our men, by the name of Mayhew, of Massachusetts, was pursued by two of the enemy's horse, the snow being almost up to his hips: they gained fast on him; he inquired if they would give him quarter; they replied, "Yes, you dog! we will quarter you," and this was again repeated. Mayhew, in despair, resolving to give them a shot before he submitted to his fate, turned and fired at the first horseman, who cried out, "The rascal has broken my leg!" when both of them wheeled round and rode off, leaving Mayhew to rejoice at his fortunate escape.

14th.—Having continued to this late season in our tents, experiencing the greatest inconvenience, we have now the satisfaction of taking possession of the log huts, just completed by our soldiers, where we shall have more comfortable accommodations. Major Trescott, Lieutenant Williams, our pay-master, and myself, occupy a hut with one room, furnished with our lodging cabins, and crowded with our baggage.

20th.—Two soldiers were brought to the gallows for the crime of robbery. One of them was pardoned under the gallows, and the other executed. The poor criminal was so dreadfully tortured by the horror of an untimely death, that he was scarcely able to sustain himself, and the scene excited the compassion of every spectator. It is hoped that this example will make such an impression as to deter others from committing similar crimes.

March.—The present winter is the most severe and distressing which we have ever experienced. An immense body of snow remains on the ground. Our soldiers are in a wretched condition for the want of clothes, blankets and shoes; and these calamitous circumstances are accompanied by a want of provisions. It has several times happened that the troops were reduced to one-half, or to one-quarter allowance, and some days have passed without any meat or bread being delivered out. The causes assigned for these extraordinary deficiencies, are the very low state of the public finances, in consequence of the rapid depreciation of the continental currency, and some irregularity in the commissary's department. Our soldiers, in general, support their sufferings with commendable firmness, but it is feared that their patience will be exhausted, and very serious consequences ensue.

April.—A party of our troops being stationed on the line, under the command of Major Boyles, of the Pennsylvania line, was unfortunately surprised by the enemy in the night. The major defended himself in a house till he was mortally wounded, when he and his guard surrendered. The enemy set fire to several houses, and carried off about fifty of our men, and five or six officers, among whom is Ensign Thacher, of our regiment. The militia pursued, and rētook a number of horses and a quantity of valuable goods, which they had plundered from the inhabitants.

19th.—The Chevalier de la Luzerne, minister of France, with another French gentleman, and Don Juan de Miralles, a gentleman of distinction from Spain, arrived at headquarters, from Philadelphia, in company with his Excellency General Washington. Major Trescott was ordered out with two hundred men, to meet and escort them to head-quarters, where two battalions were paraded to receive them with the usual military honors. Several of our general officers rode about five miles to meet the gentlemen, and their arrival was announced by the discharge of thirteen cannon. The foreign gentlemen and their suites, having left their carriages, were mounted on elegant horses, which, with General Washington, the general officers of our army, with their aids and servants, formed a most splendid cavalcade, which attracted the attention of a vast concourse of spectators. General Washington accompanied his illustrious visitors to take a distant view of the enemy's position and works, on York and Staten Island, and of the different posts of our army, while preparations were making for a grand field review of our troops.

24th.—A field of parade being prepared under the direction of the Baron Steuben, four battalions of our army were presented for review, by the French minister, attended by his excellency and our general officers. Thirteen cannon, as usual, announced their arrival in the field, and they received from the officers and soldiers the military honors due to their exalted rank. A large stage was erected in the field, which was crowded by officers, ladies, and gentlemen of distinction from the country, among whom were Governor Livingston, of New Jersey, and his lady. Our troops exhibited a truly military appearance, and performed the manœuvres and evolutions in a manner which afforded much satisfaction to our commander-in-chief, and they were honored with the approbation of the French minister, and by all present. After the gentlemen had received the standing salute in review, they dismounted and retired to the stage with the ladies, and the troops performed several evolutions, and paid the marching salute as they passed the stage. The minister of France was highly gratified, and expressed to General Washington his admiration at the precision of their movements, and the exactness of their fires, as well as the spirit and alacrity which seemed to pervade all ranks in the army. In the evening, General Washington and the French minister attended a ball, provided by our principal officers, at which were present a numerous collection of ladies and gentlemen of distinguished character. Fire-works were also exhibited by the officers of the artillery. It is much regretted that M. de Miralles is confined at head-quarters by indisposition. On the 25th, the whole army was paraded under arms, to afford M. de la Luzerne another opportunity of reviewing the troops; after which, he was escorted part of the way to Philadelphia. The Spanish gentleman remained dangerously sick of a pulmonic fever at head-quarters, and on the 28th he expired.

29th.—I accompanied Doctor Schuyler to head-quarters, to attend the funeral of M. de Miralles. The deceased was a gentleman of high rank in Spain, and had been

about one year a resident with our Congress, from the
Spanish court. The corpse was dressed in rich state, and
exposed to public view, as is customary in Europe. The
coffin was most splendid and stately, lined throughout
with fine cambric, and covered on the outside with rich
black velvet, and ornamented in a superb manner. The
top of the coffin was removed, to display the pomp and
grandeur with which the body was decorated. It was in
a splendid full dress, consisting of a scarlet suit, embroid-
ered with rich gold-lace, a three-cornered gold-laced hat,
and a genteel cued wig, white silk stockings, large diamond
shoe and knee-buckles, a profusion of diamond rings decorated the fingers, and from a superb gold watch set with
diamonds, several rich seals were suspended. His Excellency General Washington, with several other general
officers and members of Congress, attended the funeral
solemnities, and walked as chief mourners. The other
officers of the army, and numerous respectable citizens,
formed a splendid procession, extending about one mile.
The pall-bearers were six field officers, and the coffin was
borne on the shoulders of four officers of the artillery in
full uniform. Minute-guns were fired during the procession, which greatly increased the solemnity of the occasion. A Spanish priest performed service at the grave,
in the Roman Catholic form. The coffin was inclosed in
a box of plank, and all the profusion of pomp and grandeur were deposited in the silent grave, in the common
burying-ground, near the church at Morristown. A guard
is placed at the grave, lest our soldiers should be tempted
to dig for hidden treasure. It is understood that the
corpse is to be removed to Philadelphia. This gentleman
is said to have been in possession of an immense fortune,
and has left to his three daughters in Spain one hundred
thousand pounds sterling each. Here we behold the end
of all earthly riches, pomp, and dignity. The ashes of
Don Miralles mingle with the remains of those who are
clothed in humble shrouds, and whose career in life was
marked with sordid poverty and wretchedness.

May.—The officers of our army have long been dissatisfied with their situation, conceiving that we are devoting
our lives to the public service without an adequate remuneration. Our sacrifices are incalculably great, and far

exceed the bounds of duty, which the public can of right claim from any one class of men. Our wages are not punctually paid, we are frequently five or six months in arrears, and the continental money which we receive is depreciated to the lowest ebb. Congress have established a scale of depreciation, by which the continental bills are valued at forty for one of silver, and at this rate they have resolved that all their bills shall be called in and a new emission shall be issued, and received at the rate of one for forty of the old emission. But the public confidence in paper money is greatly diminished, and it is with extreme difficulty that proper supplies can be procured to serve the pressing exigencies of our army. I have just seen in the newspaper an advertisement offering for an article forty dollars a pound, or three shillings in silver. This is the trash which is tendered to requite us for our sacrifices, for our sufferings and privations, while in the service of our country. It is but a sordid pittance even for our common purposes while in camp, but those who have families dependent on them at home, are reduced to a deplorable condition. In consequence of this state of things, a considerable number of officers have been compelled to resign their commissions. His Excellency General Washington, is perplexed with an apprehension that he shall lose many of his most experienced and valuable officers; and knowing the injustice which they suffer, he has taken a warm interest in their cause, and repeatedly represented to Congress the absolute necessity of making such provision as will encourage the officers to continue in service to the end of the war. This subject he has pressed with such earnestness and solicitude, as at length to effect the desired purpose. Congress have resolved that all officers of the line of the army who shall continue in service till the close of the war, shall be entitled to half-pay during *life*, and the depreciation of their pay shall be made good; and also that they shall receive a number of acres of land, in proportion to their rank, at the close of the war. This measure meets the approbation, and is satisfactory to those who are to be entitled to the provision; but it includes the officers of the line of the army only; it is not extended to the medical staff, and they consider themselves pointedly neglected. Why are the officers

of the line allowed this exclusive act of justice—a compensation for the depreciation of the currency? If it is
just for the line, what reasons can be assigned why the
staff-officers should not be included, when the depreciation
is known to be common to both? Equal justice should
be the motto of every government. The officers on the
staff have a right to think themselves treated with the
most flagrant injustice.

A committee have arrived in camp from Congress, for
the purpose of investigating the circumstances and condition of the army, and of redressing our grievances, if in
their power. The regimental surgeons and mates have
convened, and chosen a committee of three, to wait on the
committee of Congress, and to present for their consideration our complaints and grievances, and to inquire
whether we are to be included in the resolve making provision for regimental officers, and entitled to the emoluments granted to the line of the army? The committee
replied, that they could not give a decisive answer, that
the subject of our complaints did not come under their
cognizance, but that they would make the proper representation to Congress.

Our brigade was paraded for inspection and review by
Baron Steuben, in the presence of his Excellency General
Washington. The troops appeared to much advantage,
and the officers received the thanks of the baron for the
military and soldierly appearance of the men.

10th.—Dined with Colonel Jackson, who entertained a
party of gentlemen. Our table was not ornamented with
numerous covers, our fare was frugal, but decent. Colonel
Jackson possesses a liberal and generous spirit, and entertains his friends in the kindest manner. We sat at table
till evening, enjoying the conversation of the learned
Doctor Shippin, director-general of the hospital department, accompanied by Colonel Proctor and Major Eustis.
The Marquis de la Fayette has just arrived at head-quarters, lately from France. The safe return of this respectable personage is matter of joy and congratulation.

26th.—Eleven soldiers are condemned to suffer death
for various crimes, three of whom are sentenced to be
shot; the whole number were prepared for execution this
day, but pardons were granted by the commander-in-chief

to those who were to have been shot, and the seven others, while under the gallows. This was a most solemn and affecting scene, capable of torturing the feelings even of the most callous breast. The wretched criminals were brought in carts to the place of execution. Mr. Rogers, the chaplain, attended them to the gallows, addressed them in a very pathetic manner, impressing on their minds the heinousness of their crimes, the justice of their sentence, and the high importance of a preparation for death. The criminals were placed side by side, on the scaffold, with halters round their necks, their coffins before their eyes, their graves open to their view, and thousands of spectators bemoaning their awful doom. The moment approaches when every eye is fixed in expectation of beholding the agonies of death—the eyes of the victims are already closed from the light of this world. At this awful moment, while their fervent prayers are ascending to Heaven, an officer comes forward and reads a reprieve for seven of them, by the commander-in-chief. The trembling criminals are now divested of the habiliments of death, and their bleeding hearts leap for joy. How exquisitely rapturous must be the transition when snatched from the agonizing horrors of a cruel death, and mercifully restored to the enjoyment of a life that had been forfeited! No pen can describe the emotions which must have agitated their souls. They were scarcely able to remove from the scaffold without assistance. The chaplain reminded them of the gratitude they owed the commander-in-chief for his clemency towards them, and that the only return in their power to make, was a life devoted to the faithful discharge of their duty. The criminal who was executed had been guilty of forging a number of discharges, by which he and more than a hundred soldiers had left the army. He appeared to be penitent, and behaved with uncommon fortitude and resolution. He addressed the soldiers, desired them to be faithful to their country and obedient to their officers, and advised the officers to be punctual in all their engagements to the soldiers, and give them no cause to desert. He examined the halter, and told the hangman the knot was not made right, and that the rope was not strong enough, as he was a heavy man. Having adjusted the knot and fixed it round his own neck, he was swung off instantly. The rope broke, and he fell to the ground, by which he was very much bruised. He calmly rëascended the ladder, and said, "I told you the rope was not strong enough: do get a stronger one." Another being procured, he was launched into eternity.

29*th*.—Four battalions of our troops were paraded for review by the committee of Congress, in the presence of General Washington; they were duly honored with the military salute.

We are again visited with the calamity of which we have so often complained, a great scarcity of provisions of every kind. Our poor soldiers are reduced to the very verge of famine; their patience is exhausted by complicated sufferings, and their spirits are almost broken. It is with extreme pain that we perceive in the ranks of the soldiers a sensible diminution of that enthusiastic patriotism, and that ardent attachment to our cause, by which they were formerly distinguished. Much praise is due to the officers of every grade, who make all possible exertions to encourage, to satisfy and to soothe the desponding spirits of the soldiery. Under the most trying circumstances, however, both officers and soldiers retain their full confidence in the wisdom and goodness of our illustrious commander-in-chief, whom they almost adore, looking up to him as children to an affectionate father, participating in the same sufferings. Another source of dissatisfaction is the great inequality subsisting among the soldiers respecting their pecuniary compensation. Those who enlisted at an early period, for a small bounty, now find in the ranks with themselves others who have recently enlisted for a bounty of more than ten times the nominal value. This, as may be supposed, excites the most poignant chagrin and disgust, and, with other causes of discontent, has produced a considerable degree of relaxation in discipline, and an unusual number of desertions from our ranks. An event still more alarming occurred on the 25th instant. Two regiments of the Connecticut line took the liberty to parade without their officers, and in the spirit of mutiny, resolved to march into the country to relieve themselves from present difficulties, and to furnish themselves with provisions at all hazards. Colonel Meigs, in attempting to restore order, received a blow from one of the mutineers. A brigade of Pennsylvanians was ordered to arrest their progress. The leaders were secured, and the two regiments were returned to their duty. Their complaints are, that they have too long served the public without any present, or prospect of future recompense; that their sufferings are insupportable, that their pay is five months in arrear, and that it is of no value when received. These circumstances are known to be substantially true, and in justice they ought, and undoubtedly will, be admitted in extenuation of the crime which they have committed. It is nevertheless indispensably important that every symptom of insubordination should be crushed as soon as discovered, lest the example become contagious, and involve the whole army in ruin.

June.—In consequence of some movements of the enemy, our brigade was ordered to Chatham. A party of the enemy, about five thousand strong, came out of New York on the 7th instant, to a place called Connecticut Farms, where they burned a few houses and plundered the inhabitants; but being opposed by General Maxwell's brigade of Jersey troops, and the militia, who turned out with spirit, they soon retreated to Elizabethtown Point with some loss, and were pursued by our troops. In this little skirmish, the British General Stirling received a wound which it is supposed will prove mortal. A number of other officers and soldiers, on the side of the British, were killed and wounded, and twenty prisoners taken by our militia. Our loss does not exceed ten or twelve killed, and twenty or thirty wounded.

Among the horrid and barbarous deeds of the enemy, one has just been perpetrated, which will be an everlasting stigma on the British character. In the vicinity of the Connecticut Farms, state of New Jersey, resided the Rev. James Caldwell, a Presbyterian minister. This gentleman had uniformly taken an active part with his parishioners on the side of the Americans, in consequence of which he was marked for British vengeance. On the approach of the enemy, he retired into the country, leaving his lady with the care of the family, supposing that the customary respect for the female character would be a pledge for her safety. Mrs. Caldwell, soon after the approach of the royal troops to the house, and a young woman, having Mrs. Caldwell's infant in her arms, seated themselves on the bed, when a British soldier came to the house, and putting his gun to the window of the room, shot her through the breast, and she instantly expired. Soon after, an officer with two Hessian soldiers came and ordered a hole to be dug, the body to be thrown in, and the house to be set on fire. Thus was murdered an amiable and excellent lady, and the worthy husband left with nine children, destitute of even a change of clothes, or any thing to render them comfortable. The house and every article belonging to this respectable family were consumed, together with the church and thirteen dwelling-houses. The British, during their excursion, took the opportunity of distributing a number of hand-bills, containing a pompous account of the capture of Charleston, South Carolina, by Sir Henry Clinton, with the garrison, commanded by Major-General Lincoln. This unfortunate event is now confirmed by Generals Arnold and Wayne, who have just arrived from Philadelphia. General Lincoln was posted in the town of Charleston, with a force consisting of between two and three thousand men, including militia and seamen. General Clinton, invested the town with a powerful fleet and an army of thirteen thousand strong. He proceeded with regular approaches, till he advanced within twenty-five yards of the American lines, and repeatedly demanded the surrender of the garrison. Through the very judicious management of General Lincoln, the siege was protracted from the 13th of April to the 12th of May; and during fifteen days of this time his troops were reduced to an allowance of six ounces of pork a man, and for the last six days to one and a half-pint of rice and three ounces of sugar a day. General Lincoln had to consult the interest and opinions of the inhabitants, which greatly increased his embarrassments. At length the lines of defence being almost entirely demolished, by an incessant bombardment and cannonade, the besieged were reduced to the last extremity; and being in hourly expectation of an assault, it was agreed between General Lincoln and the principal inhabitants that the town and garrison should be surrendered by capitulation. General Lincoln, in this most important transaction of his life, manifested a cool intrepidity, a zealous perseverance, and a presence of mind which proclaim him prëeminently qualified to encounter the extreme difficulties and dangers, in which he was involved; and the terms of surrender were as honorable as could have been expected.

15th.—Major Lee, from Virginia, has just arrived in camp, with a beautiful corps of light-horse, the men in complete uniform, and the horses very elegant and finely disciplined. Major Lee is said to be a man of great spirit and enterprise, and much important service is expected from him. By a gentleman just from New York, we are informed that General Stirling died a few days ago of the wounds which he received in the skirmish with our troops on the 7th instant.

16th.—A soldier of the Jersey line was hanged for attempting to desert to the enemy. This is one of those hardened villains who were pardoned under the gallows about three weeks since.

19th.—Four emissaries from the enemy, were found concealed in a barn, belonging to a tory, in the vicinity of our lines; one of them, their leader, refused to surrender, and was killed on the spot. The other three were tried by court-martial, and being convicted as spies, were sentenced to be hanged. These unfortunate young men came to the gallows overwhelmed with the horrors of death. Their whole frames were thrown into a tremor, and they were tortured at the sight of the gallows and halters. They had flattered themselves that mercy would be extended to them, and that they would either be pardoned, or their lives be prolonged for a few days; but when they found that the executioner was about to perform his office, their mournful cries and lamentations were distressing beyond description. It has some where been noted, that a girl walked seven miles, in a torrent of rain, to see a man hanged, and returned in tears, because the criminal was reprieved; on the present occasion, a heart so full of depravity might have enjoyed an indulgence even to satiety.

The enemy in New York are reported to be in motion, and we shall probably very soon be called to engage in battle. General orders are issued for the whole army to be in readiness to march at a moment's warning. At six o'clock in the morning of the 23d, the alarm guns were fired, and the drums throughout our camp beat to arms, announcing the approach of the enemy; the whole army is instantly in motion, the scene to my contemplation is awfully sublime, yet animation and composure seem to pervade every countenance. The present hour is undoubtedly pregnant with death and carnage; every arm is nerved for defence, and every heart, it is presumed, fortified to abide its destiny. Soon after the alarm, our advanced party, consisting of General Maxwell's brigade and a few militia, discovered the enemy advancing towards the village of Springfield. A close engagement with the enemy's advance immediately ensued; but being pressed by four times our number, General Maxwell, after an obstinate resistance, was obliged to retreat, till a reïnforcement could arrive. Our brigade, commanded by General Stark, soon joined Maxwell, on the high ground near the village of Springfield. Colonel Angel's regiment, of Rhode Island, with several small parties, were posted at a bridge over which the enemy were to pass, and their whole force, of five or six thousand men, was actually held in check by these brave soldiers for more than forty minutes, amidst the severest firing of cannon and musketry. The enemy, however, with their superior force, advanced into the village, and wantonly set fire to the buildings. We had the mortification of beholding the church, and twenty or thirty dwelling-houses and other buildings, in a blaze, and they were soon consumed to ashes. Having thus completed their great enterprise, and acquired to themselves the honor of burning a village, they made a precipitate retreat to Elizabeth Point, and the ensuing night crossed over to Staten Island. Our brigade was ordered to pursue the retreating enemy, but we could not overtake them; we discovered several fresh graves, and found fifteen dead bodies, which they left in the field, and which we buried. We were informed by the inhabitants, that they carried off eight or ten wagon-loads of dead and wounded. Our militia took fifteen prisoners. General Knyphausen was the commander, and his force consisted of five or six thousand men; the particular object of the expedition is not ascertained; if it was to force their way to Morristown, to destroy our magazines and stores, they were disappointed; if to burn the village of Springfield, they are welcome to the honor of the exploit. Our troops were commanded by Major-General Greene; not more than one thousand were brought into action at any one time; their conduct was marked with the commendable coolness and intrepidity of veteran troops. Colonel Angel's regiment, in a special manner, acquired immortal honor, by its unexampled bravery. In the heat of the action, some soldiers brought to me in a blanket Captain-Lieutenant Thompson of the artillery, who had received a most formidable wound, a cannon-ball having passed through both his thighs near the knee-joint. With painful anxiety, the poor man inquired if I would amputate both his thighs. Sparing his feelings, I evaded his inquiry, and directed him to be carried to the hospital tent in the rear, where he would receive the attention of the surgeons. "All that a man hath will he give for his life." He expired in a few hours. While advancing against the enemy, my attention was directed to a wounded soldier in the field. I dismounted, and left my horse at a rail-fence. It was not long before a cannon-ball shattered a rail within a few feet of my horse, and some soldiers were sent to take charge of the wounded man, and to tell me it was time to retire. I now perceived that our party had retreated, and our regiment had passed me. I immediately mounted, and applied spurs to my horse, that I might gain the front of our regiment. Colonel Jackson being in the rear, smiled as I passed him; but as my duty did not require my exposure, I felt at liberty to seek a place of safety. It may be considered a singular circumstance, that the soldier above mentioned was wounded by the wind of a cannonball. His arm was fractured above the elbow, without the smallest perceptible injury to his clothes, or contusion or discoloration of the skin. He made no complaint, but I observed he was feeble and a little confused in his mind. He received proper attention, but expired the next day. The idea of injury by the wind of a ball, I learn, is not new—instances of the kind have, it is said, occurred in naval battles, and are almost constantly attended with fatal effects.

Our troops in camp are in general healthy, but we are troubled with many perplexing instances of indisposition, occasioned by absence from home, called by Dr. Cullen *nostalgia*, or home-sickness. This complaint is frequent

MAJOR GENERAL BENJAMIN LINCOLN.

among the militia and recruits from New England. They become dull and melancholy, with loss of appetite, restless nights, and great weakness. In some instances they become so hypochondriacal as to be proper subjects for the hospital. This disease is in many instances cured by the raillery of the old soldiers, but is generally suspended by a constant and active engagement of the mind, as by the drill exercise, camp discipline, and by uncommon anxiety, occasioned by the prospect of a battle.

July.—Our brigade marched from Short hills on the 25th of June, and arrived at Prackanes, Jersey, the 1st of July. I rode with Dr. Tenney and Captain Hughes about five miles, to take a view of the Passaic falls, called by some Totowa falls, which are represented as a great natural curiosity. The Passaic river runs over large rocky mountains covered with fir-trees. At this place an immense body of rock would totally interrupt its passage, had it not been by some stupendous power rent in several places from top to bottom, forming huge clefts, some of which are twenty or thirty feet wide, others not more than two or three, and from fifty to seventy feet deep. The depth of one of them, it is said, has never been ascertained. It is here that the whole torrent of the river falls perpendicularly, with amazing violence and rapidity, down a rocky precipice of seventy feet, with a tremendous roar and foaming. But being interrupted in its course, by craggy rocks, it turns abruptly to the right, and again to the left, and falling into huge cavities below, the whole torrent vanishes from our sight; but stepping to another precipice a few yards distant, we behold the same torrent emerging from its subterraneous course, and rushing into a large basin, or cavern, formed in the rock. This basin contains forty fathoms of water, and is never full, but its rocky walls on all sides ascend sixty feet above the surface of the water. Such is the astonishing depth of this receptacle, that the water neither foams nor forms whirlpools by the rushing current, but is calm and undisturbed. From this basin the water rushes through its outlet, reassumes the form of a river, and in majestic silence pursues its course towards the sea.

In the afternoon we were invited to visit another curiosity in the neighborhood. This is a monster in the human

14

form. He is twenty-seven years of age; his face, from the
upper part of his forehead to the end of his chin, measures
twenty inches, and round the upper part of his head is
twenty-one inches; his eyes and nose are remarkably
large and prominent, chin long and pointed. His features
are coarse, irregular, and disgusting, and his voice is rough
and sonorous. His body is only twenty-seven inches in
length, his limbs are small and much deformed, and he
has the use of one hand only. He has never been able to
stand or sit up, as he cannot support the enormous weight
of his head; but lies constantly in a large cradle, with his
head supported on pillows. He is visited by great numbers of people, and is peculiarly fond of the company of
clergymen, always inquiring for them among his visitors,
and taking great pleasure in receiving religious instruction. General Washington made him a visit, and asked,
"whether he was a whig or tory?" He replied, that "he
had never taken an *active* part on either side."

5*th*.—I took an excursion a few miles into the country,
to visit the surgeons of the flying hospital; took tea at
their quarters, with a wealthy Dutch family, and was
treated with great civility. They live in a style superior
to the Low Dutch in general; the table was amply furnished with cherries, raspberries and other fruits, which
abound in this country.

10*th*.—The officers of our regiment and those of Colonel
Webb's united in providing an entertainment, and invited
a respectable number of gentlemen of our brigade to dine;
Dr. West and myself were appointed caterers and super-
intendents. We erected a large arbor, with the boughs
of trees, under which we enjoyed an elegant dinner, and
spent the afternoon in social glee, with some of the wine
which was taken from the enemy when they retreated
from Elizabethtown. Our drums and fifes afforded us a
favorite music till evening, when we were delighted with
the song composed by Mr. Hopkinson, called the "*Battle of
the Kegs*," sung in the best style by a number of gentlemen.

14*th*.—An express has arrived at head-quarters, from
Rhode Island, with the pleasing information of the arrival
there of a French fleet, accompanied by an army of six
thousand regular French troops, who are to coöperate
with our army as allies in our cause. They are com-

manded by Count Rochambeau, a distinguished general
in the French service.

20th.—In general orders, the commander-in-chief congratulates the army on the arrival of a large land and
naval armament at Rhode Island, sent by his Most Christian Majesty, to cöoperate with us against the common
enemy. The lively concern which our allies manifest for
our safety and independence, has a claim to the affection
of every virtuous citizen. The general with confidence
assures the army, that the officers and men of the French
forces come to our aid animated with a zeal founded in
sentiment for us, as well as in duty to their prince, and
that they will do every thing in their power to promote
harmony and cultivate friendship; he is equally persuaded,
on our part, that we shall vie with them in their good
disposition, to which we are excited by gratitude as well
as by common interest; and that the only contention between the two armies will be to excel each other in good
offices, and in the display of every military virtue. This
will be a pledge of the most solid advantage to the common cause, and a glorious issue to the campaign. The
commander-in-chief has recommended to the officers of
our army to wear cockades of black and white, inter-
mixed, as a symbol of friendship for our French allies,
who wear white cockades.

22d.—The officers of our regiment received an invitation
to dine with Major-General Lord Stirling. We were introduced to his lordship by Colonel Jackson, and were
received with great civility and politeness. Colonel Bid-
dle and his lady were of the guests. Our entertainment
was sumptuous and elegant. After the covers were removed, the servants brought in pails filled with cherries
and strawberries, which were strewed over the long table;
with these, and excellent wine, accompanied by martial
music, we regaled ourselves till evening. This gentleman's proper name is William Alexander, and he is a
native of the state of New York. He visited Scotland in
pursuit of the title and estate of an earldom, which he
claimed as the rightful heir of his ancestor, who had this
title, and a grant of Nova Scotia, anno. 1621. In this
pursuit, he expended a large proportion of his fortune,
but failed in obtaining an acknowledgment of his claim

by the government; yet, by courtesy, he bears the title of Lord Stirling. He is considered as a brave, intelligent and judicious officer. In the battle on Long Island in August, 1776, he unfortunately fell into the hands of the enemy; but it occasioned no impeachment of his character and conduct. He possesses the genuine principles of patriotism, and is strongly attached to General Washington. He disclosed to the commander-in-chief the intrigue of General Conway, when in 1777 he attempted to supersede his excellency, saying in his letter, "such wicked duplicity of conduct, I shall always think it my duty to detect." In his personal appearance, his lordship is venerable and dignified; in his deportment, gentlemanly and graceful; in conversation, pleasing and interesting.* He is said to be ambitious of the title of lordship. Being present at the execution of a soldier for desertion, the criminal at the gallows repeatedly cried out, "the Lord have mercy on me!" his lordship with warmth exclaimed, "I won't, you rascal, I won't have mercy on you."

23d.—Sunday I attended a sermon preached by Mr. Blair, chaplain of the artillery. The troops were paraded in the open field, the sermon was well calculated to inculcate religious principles and the moral virtues. His Excellency General Washington, Major-Generals Greene and Knox, with a number of other officers, were present.

August.—Orders are given for the army to be in readiness for a movement.

According to orders, our brigade marched from Prackanes on the 29th of July, and encamped at Paramus at night, fifteen miles. The men were exceedingly affected with the heat and fatigue. We marched on the succeeding day at two o'clock in the morning; at this early hour, the drums beat the reveille, which summons us from our hard beds and slumbers, in haste we roll up our travelling bed furniture, strike our tents, order them thrown into the wagons, mount our horses, and with a slow pace follow the march of our soldiers, bending under the weight of the burden on their backs. We arrived at the North river and crossed the ferry, August 1st, where we found the whole of our main army collecting to a point. All the troops from West Point that can be spared, and de-

* His lordship died at Albany, January 15th, 1783, aged fifty-seven years.

tachments from different stations, have formed a junction
in this vicinity. Two brigades have been selected from
the different regiments in the main army, to form a corps
of light infantry, to be commanded by the Marquis de la
Fayette. They have been reviewed by the commander-
in-chief and other general officers, on the grand parade,
and are pronounced to be as excellent a corps as can be
produced in any army. The marquis is delighted with
his command, and is at his own expense providing for
them some extra equipments. It is understood that General Clinton has despatched a part of the British fleet and
army on an expedition against our allies, the French fleet
and army at Rhode Island. The whole of our army having crossed to the east side of the Hudson, it is conjectured
that his excellency contemplates some important enterprise
against the enemy at New York, or at least to compel
General Clinton to recall his expedition from Rhode Isl-
and, for his own safety. Our commander-in-chief has
ordered that the army disencumber itself of all heavy
baggage, which, with the women and children, are to be
immediately sent to West Point, and that the troops have
constantly two days' provisions cooked on hand, and hold
themselves in readiness to march at a moment's warning.
Such is our condition for order and regularity, that the
whole army, which occupies an extent of several miles,
can be put in motion, and take up a line of march in less
than one hour. The horses belonging to our baggage-
wagons and to the artillery are constantly in harness, and
those belonging to the officers are kept in readiness; every
man and every horse are taught to know their place and
their duty. Marching orders, so soon as issued, are communicated to each brigade and regiment. The whole line
of encampment resounds with martial music; all is bustle
and activity, but free from confusion. The drums and
fifes beating a march, the tents are instantly struck and
thrown into wagons, the line of march commences, every
subordinate officer and soldier follows his commander, and
whether to rush into battle and encounter the dogs of war,
or only to manœuvre in the field, it is no man's business
to know or inquire. The secret is where it ought to be,
in the breast of him who directs our destiny, and whom
it is our pride to obey. Such is the state and condition

of a well-regulated and disciplined army, and such only can
attain to military fame and glory. It is now ascertained,
August 4th, that the formidable manœuvre of our army
has effected the object intended. The enemy's expedition
to Rhode Island has returned to New York, in consequence probably of the alarm excited for the safety of that
city. Orders are now received for our army to recross the
Hudson to the Jersey shore. Our brigade crossed the
ferry in the night of the 5th, and encamped in a field about
five miles from the ferry. The crossing of the whole
army, occupied three days and nights, during which a
vast number of large boats and floats were continually in
motion. On the 6th, marched to Greenbush, and on the
7th and 8th, the whole army arrived and encamped at
Orangetown. The light infantry, under the marquis, is
constantly advanced three miles in front of the army.
The fatigue and extreme heat during this march, have produced very unfavorable effects on our troops, and they are
now becoming sickly. Cholera-morbus, dysentery and
remittent fevers, are the prevailing complaints, which demand all my attention.

9th.—Dined with Baron Steuben, and spent the afternoon with the guests. The baron keeps a splendid table,
and treats his visitors with polite attention. Captain
William North, of our regiment, is one of the aids-de-camp
of the baron, and has ingratiated himself so highly in his
favor, that he treats him with all the affection of a son.

A committee from Congress have again arrived in our
camp, with the view of investigating the affairs of the
army, to attend to complaints, and to redress grievances,
so far as may be in their power; and they will find that
their task and duty are not to be envied. The regimental
surgeons and mates have deputed a committee to present
a list of our grievances for their honors' consideration.
We claim of Congress the same emoluments and remuneration which are promised to the officers of the line
of the army.

14th.—Visited Dr. Cochran, our surgeon-general, at his
quarters in the country, and thence proceeding to the light
infantry encampment, took tea with Major Trescott and
Captain Cushing. I accompanied a number of officers to
Dobbs' ferry, where our troops are engaged in erecting a

block-house and batteries, to defend the passage at the ferry-way. The Hudson at this place is about three miles wide, so that no battery can prevent the enemy's shipping from passing up the river from New York.

20th.—Sunday, attended a sermon preached by Mr. Enos Hitchcock, chaplain of General Patterson's brigade; the troops were assembled in the open field. Mr. Hitchcock is respected as a sensible and learned divine, of pure morals and correct principles. His patriotic zeal and ardent attachment to his country's freedom, induced him to quit his people and domestic enjoyments at Beverly, Massachusetts, for the turmoil and fatigue of camp. I dined with my friends Dr. Skinner and Major Winslow. We are again visited with the alarming apprehension of a famine; no meat has been drawn for two days past; no money, no rum, and no contentment among our soldiers —great dissatisfaction prevails.

25th.—The whole army in this quarter has decamped, the object and destination a secret; the conjectural object is to procure a supply of provisions and forage from the inhabitants between the lines, which otherwise would go to supply the wants of the enemy. All the sick and disabled are left in camp, and I am directed to take charge of those belonging to our brigade; but with this charge I am left entirely destitute of provisions. Feeling myself authorized to take a small supply from the inhabitants for immediate necessity, I required from a Dutchman four sheep from his farm; as he was offended and made some opposition, I was obliged to force them from him, giving a receipt, that he might recover a compensation from the public.

28th.—Our army has returned from below, with a large quantity of forage, and provisions of various kinds, taken from the disaffected inhabitants on the lines. This affords us an important relief, when almost in a starving condition. A small party of the enemy was discovered near the lines, a slight skirmish ensued, and they soon disappeared.

29th.—I accompanied Captain W. to the village of Charlestown, met Major-General Schuyler and other gentlemen at a tavern, with whom we dined. Here I learned that a duel had just been fought between Lieutenant O. and Mr. P., both of Colonel Mayland's regiment of dragoons, and both of whom were yesterday on the most intimate terms of friendship. Mr. O. killed his antagonist on the spot, and received a dangerous wound in his thigh. When I visited him, his wound had been dressed, and I was astonished at the calmness and composure with which he related all the particulars of this melancholy and murderous catastrophe, and the agonizing state of mind of his late friend in his dying moments. The duel originated in a trivial misunderstanding, which excited these close friends to assume the character of assassins, and to hazard life for life. Nor did O. discover the least sorrow or remorse of conscience for having sacrificed the life of a friend and valuable officer to the mistaken points of honor!

30th.—Another dreadful appeal has this day been made to the deadly combat on a point of honor. The parties were Lieutenant S. and Mr. L. a volunteer in the army; the latter gentleman fell, and instantly expired; his murderer escaped uninjured. Thus have two valuable lives been sacrificed within two days, to what is termed principles of honor, or rather to the vindictive spirit of malice and revenge. Is there no remedy for this fashionable folly, this awful blindness and perversion of mind, this barbarous and infernal practice, this foul stain on the history of man! The following anecdote is in point: The practice of duelling had become alarming in the Prussian army, and the great Frederic was desirous of checking its progress. Two officers of high rank had engaged to meet in personal combat. The king commanded that they should fight in his presence, and at a time and place which he appointed. When the parties appeared, they were astonished to find the whole army paraded to witness the combat, a gallows erected, and a halter and coffins prepared. The king now commanded that they should decide their fate in his presence, and that the survivor should be instantly hung on the gallows. The two champions were appalled, and glad to implore his majesty's forgiveness; and this example proved an effectual remedy against duelling in the Prussian army.

September.—Intelligence of an unpleasant and distressing nature, has just reached us from South Carolina. Our southern army, under the command of Major-General Gates, has been totally defeated, in a general action with

Lord Cornwallis, on the 19th of August. General Gates, as is reported, retreated with precipitation to the distance of eighty miles, to escape the pursuit of the enemy. This mortifying disaster gives a severe shock to our army, as it must be productive of the most important and serious consequences as it respects the welfare of the Southern states. In his letter to the President of Congress, General Gates says: "In the deepest distress and anxiety of mind, I am obliged to acquaint your excellency with the defeat of the troops under my command." The letter states that the continental troops displayed their usual courage and bravery, but at the first onset of the enemy, the whole body of militia became panic-struck, were completely routed, and ran like a torrent, bearing all before them, and leaving the continentals to oppose the whole force of the enemy. This victory was not obtained without loss on the part of the foe, they having upwards of five hundred men, with officers in proportion, killed and wounded. The whole number of continental officers killed, wounded and missing, is forty-eight. Among the killed, is Baron de Kalb, a major-general; while leading on the Maryland and Delaware troops, he was pierced with eleven wounds, and soon after expired. He was a German by birth, a brave and meritorious officer, a knight of the order of military merit, and a brigadier-general in the armies of France. He had served three years, with high reputation, in the American army. General Gates' command in this army is said to consist of three thousand, of which number were only nine hundred continental regulars. The royalists, under Lord Cornwallis, were upwards of three thousand two hundred, and a great part of them regular troops. This very unfortunate event has given an impression universally unfavorable to the character and conduct of General Gates, as he has disappointed the high expectations of the public. He is indeed a painful example of the vicissitudes of the fortune of war; but it ought not to be expected that an officer should be held accountable for the strokes of fortune; nor for the effects of superior force or address in the enemy. Considering the former high character and meritorious services of the general, we cannot justly suspect him to be chargeable with any deficiency in point of integrity or

conduct, and time and investigation must decide how far
he has been guilty of any culpable error.

5th.—Our army marched from Orangetown, and encamped at Steenrapie, yesterday. It is mortifying that
our stock of provisions is again exhausted; the soldiers
have for several days drawn nothing but one pound of
flour a man.

8th.—I had again the honor of dining at the table of
Baron Steuben, in company with a number of officers.
Notwithstanding the scarcity of provisions in camp, the
baron's table continues to be well supplied; his generosity is unbounded.

10th.—We are now lamenting the loss of Brigadier-
General Poor, who died last night of putrid fever. His
funeral solemnities have been attended this afternoon.
The corpse was brought this morning from Paramus, and
left at a house about a mile from the burying-yard at
Hackensack, whence it was attended to the place of inter-
ment by the following procession: a regiment of light-
infantry, in uniform, with arms reversed; four field-pieces;
Major Lee's regiment of light-horse; General Hand and
his brigade; the major on horseback; two chaplains; the
horse of the deceased, with his boots and spurs suspended
from the saddle, led by a servant; the corpse borne by
four serjeants, and the pall supported by six general officers. The coffin was of mahogany, and a pair of pistols
and two swords, crossing each other and tied with black
crape, were placed on the top. The corpse was followed
by the officers of the New Hampshire brigade; the officers
of the brigade of light-infantry, which the deceased had
lately commanded. Other officers fell in promiscuously,
and were followed by his Excellency General Washington,
and other general officers. Having arrived at the burying-yard, the troops opened to the right and left, resting
on their arms reversed, and the procession passed to the
grave, where a short eulogy was delivered by the Rev.
Mr. Evans. A band of music, with a number of drums
and fifes, played a funeral dirge, the drums were muffled
with black crape, and the officers in the procession wore
crape round the left arm. The regiment of light-infantry
were in handsome uniform, and wore in their caps long
feathers of black and red. The elegant regiment of horse,

commanded by Major Lee, being in complete uniform and well disciplined, exhibited a martial and noble appearance. No scene can exceed in grandeur and solemnity a military funeral. The weapons of war reversed, and embellished with the badges of mourning, the slow and regular step of the procession, the mournful sound of the unbraced drum and deep-toned instruments, playing the melancholy dirge, the majestic mien and solemn march of the war-horse, all conspire to impress the mind with emotions which no language can describe, and which nothing but the reality can paint to the liveliest imagination. General Poor was from the state of New Hampshire. He was a true patriot, who took an early part in the cause of his country, and during his military career was respected for his talents and his bravery, and beloved for the amiable qualities of his heart. But it is a sufficient eulogy to say, that he enjoyed the confidence and esteem of Washington.

11*th*.—We had a most violent shower of rain, accompanied with tremendous peals of thunder and lightning; we were obliged to quit our beds in the night, but no part of our marquee could shield us from the drenching rains—not a blanket about us remained dry.

12*th*.—A soldier was executed for robbery; he was one of five who broke into a house with their arms, and robbed the inhabitants of a sum of money and many valuable articles. He conducted with fortitude at the gallows.

13*th*.—The army was paraded to be reviewed by General Washington, accompanied by a number of Indian chiefs. His excellency, mounted on his noble bay charger, rode in front of the line of the army, and received the usual salute. Six Indian chiefs followed in his train, appearing as the most disgusting and contemptible of the human race; their faces painted of various colors, their hair twisted into bunches on the top of their heads, and dressed in a miserable Indian habit, some with a dirty blanket over the shoulders, and others almost naked. They were mounted on horses of the poorest kind, with undressed sheep skins, instead of saddles, and old ropes for bridles. These bipeds could not refrain from the indulgence of their appetites for rum on this occasion, and some of them fell from their horses on their return to headquarters. This tribe of Indians is friendly to America, and it is good policy to show them some attention, and give them an idea of the strength of our army.

20*th*.—The army decamped from Steenrapie this morning, and encamped at Orangetown, or Tappan. His Excellency General Washington, with the Marquis de la Fayette and General Knox, with a splendid retinue, left the camp on the 17th instant, bound to Hartford in Connecticut, to have an interview with the commanding officers of the French fleet and army, which have lately arrived at Rhode Island.

I have just been introduced to three young clergymen, from Connecticut, Mr. Lockwood, Mr. Ely, and Mr. Joel Barlow; the latter is a chaplain in the Connecticut line, and is said to possess a poetical genius. Being present when he made a prayer in public, it was remarked that his performance was very ordinary, and it was replied that the gentleman had not been much accustomed to public performances, and that he was more calculated to attain to eminence in the art of poetry than in the clerical profession.

21*st*.—Major-General Greene succeeds to the command of our army, in the absence of his Excellency General Washington. This gentleman is a native of the state of Rhode Island. His father was an anchor-smith, and his business in that line was very extensive. He was a member of the Society of Friends, and when about to engage in a military station, they remonstrated with him, as war was a violation of the established principles of their sect. But his patriotism and ardent zeal for the cause of liberty were irresistible, and he was, at the age of thirty, appointed a brigadier-general by his government in the year 1775. After the battle of Lexington, actuated by a native martial ardor, he repaired to Cambridge, and, with the troops under his command, joined the continental army under General Washington. General Greene has conducted in a manner to meet the expectations and full approbation of the public, and has been promoted to the rank of major-general. By his military talents, skill and judgment, he has acquired a character of the highest order, and is held in respect and estimation throughout the army, as second only to the commander-in-chief. It is the prevailing sentiment, that if in any event of Providence we should be deprived of our chief commander, General

Greene is of all others the most suitable character to be his successor, and in this sentiment there is the greatest reason to believe that the illustrious Washington himself would readily coincide.

26th.—At three o'clock this morning an alarm was spread throughout our camp. Two regiments from the Pennsylvania line were ordered to march immediately to West Point, and the whole army to be held in readiness to march at a moment's warning. It was soon ascertained that this sudden movement was in consequence of the discovery of one of the most extraordinary events in modern history, and in which the interposition of Divine Providence is remarkably conspicuous. It is the treacherous conspiracy of Major-General Arnold, and the capture of Major John Andre, adjutant-general to the British army. The army being paraded this morning, the following communication in the orders of General Greene was read by the adjutants to their respective regiments:

"Treason, of the blackest dye, was yesterday discovered. General Arnold, who commanded at West Point, lost to every sentiment of honor, of private and public obligation, was about to deliver up that important post into the hands of the enemy. Such an event must have given the American cause a dangerous, if not a fatal wound; happily the treason has been timely discovered, to prevent the fatal misfortune. The providential train of circumstances which led to it, affords the most convincing proofs that the liberties of America are the object of Divine protection. At the same time that the treason is to be regretted, the general cannot help congratulating the army on the happy discovery. Our enemies, despairing of carrying their point by force, are practising every base art to effect by bribery and corruption what they cannot accomplish in a manly way. Great honor is due to the American army, that this is the first instance of treason of the kind, where many were to be expected from the nature of our dispute; the brightest ornament in the character of the American soldiers is, their having been proof against all the arts and seductions of an insidious enemy. Arnold has made his escape to the enemy, but Major Andre, the adjutant-general in the British army, who came out as a spy to negotiate the business, is our prisoner."

West Point is situated in the midst of the highlands, on the west side of the Hudson, sixty miles above New York, and seven below Fishkill. It is a strongly-fortified castle, which, with its dependencies, is considered by General Washington as the key which locks the communication between the Eastern and Southern states; and of all the posts in the United States, this is the most important.

The position is remarkably well calculated by nature for a defensive post, being on a bend of the river, with rocky ridges rising one above another, and the lofty summit is covered with a range of redoubts and batteries, planned by the most skillful engineers. The most elevated and formidable fortress is erected on a natural platform of rocks, very steep, and almost inaccessible on every side; this is called "Fort Putnam," from the general who had the principal share in its plan and construction. It overlooks the whole plain below, and commands a landscape-view thirty miles in extent, the Hudson having the appearance of a vast canal, cut through huge mountains. As additional security, an iron chain of immense strength is thrown across at the short bend of the river, and fixed to huge blocks on each shore, and under the fire of batteries on both sides the river. The links of this chain are about twelve inches wide, and eighteen long, the bars about two inches square. It is buoyed up by very large logs, of about sixteen feet long, pointed at the ends to lessen their opposition to the force of the current at flood and ebb tide. The logs are placed at short distances from each other, the chain carried over them and made fast to each by staples. There are also a number of anchors dropped at proper distances, with cables made fast to the chain to give it a greater stability. Such is the formidable state and strength of this post, that it has received the appellation of the American Gibraltar, and when properly guarded, may bid defiance to an army of twenty thousand men. General Arnold was well apprised of the great importance of this fortress; no position in America could afford the British greater advantages. It commands the whole extent of country on the Hudson, from New York to Canada, and secures a communication between the Eastern and Southern states.

From the commencement of the American war, General Arnold has been viewed in the light of a brave and heroic officer, having exhibited abundant proof of his military ardor and invincible temper. He has fought in various battles, with an intrepid gallantry which cannot be exceeded, and it is from his bravery in the field, more than any intrinsic merit, that his character and fame have been established. His meritorious services have been amply rewarded by his promotion to the rank of major-general, but his name will now be transmitted to posterity with marks of infamy, and the pages of our history will be tarnished by the record of crimes of the most atrocious character by a native of our land. After the evacuation of Philadelphia by the British, Arnold was appointed to the command in that city, and such was his conduct, as respects both his official station and individual concerns, that his former standing and important services could no longer shield him from public odium and the just censure of the government.* Being afterward, by his own solicitation, intrusted with the command of the post at West Point, he engaged in a secret correspondence with Sir Henry Clinton, and actually agreed to put him in possession of this very important garrison. The British general, ever ready to avail himself of treachery to accomplish an object which he could not achieve by the strength of his arms, selected Major John Andre, his adjutant-general and aid-de-camp, to have a personal interview with the traitor, to mature the plan, and make arrangements for the surrender of the post. A British sloop-of-war, called the Vulture, came up the North river, and anchored near King's ferry, about twelve miles below West Point. On board of this vessel were a Colonel Robinson, and Major Andre, under the assumed name of John Anderson. A communication was now maintained between Arnold and the persons on board the Vulture, without exciting the least suspicion of treasonable designs. But a personal interview was found necessary, and the place chosen for this purpose was the beach near the house of Joshua Smith, Esquire, who has long been suspected of a predilection for the British interest. In the night of the 21st instant, Smith, by the desire of Arnold, went with a boat, rowed by some men employed on his farm, and brought Major Andre, *alias* John Anderson, on shore, where he was received by Arnold, and conducted to the house of Smith, within our lines. Andre remained concealed at Smith's house till the following night, when he became extremely anxious to return on board the Vulture; but the boatmen, whom Arnold and Smith had seduced to bring him on shore the preceding night, could not be

* See Life of Arnold in the Appendix.

prevailed on to reconduct him on board, as the Vulture
had been driven from her station by a cannon on shore.
Finding it impossible to procure a boat and men for the
purpose, it was resolved that Andre should return to New
York by land, to which he reluctantly submitted, as the
only alternative, to escape the danger into which he had
been betrayed. For this hazardous attempt Arnold and
Smith furnished him with a horse, and with clothes, in
exchange for his military uniform; and Arnold gave him
a passport under the fictitious name of John Anderson, as
being on public business. Thus prepared, and accompanied by Smith part of the way, he proceeded on his
journey. The passport served his purpose till he got beyond all our out-posts and guards without suspicion.
They lodged together at Crompond that night, and Smith
having given him directions about the road, left him the
next morning, within about thirty miles of New York.
Having arrived at Tarrytown, however, near the lines of
the royal army, Andre was arrested by one of three men,
who were patrolling between the out-posts of the two
armies. He held his horse by the bridle, till his two
companions came from their concealment to his assistance.
This was the moment which was to decide the fate of the
adjutant-general of the royal army. Alarmed and disconcerted, instead of producing his passport, he asked where
they belonged? They replied, "To below," alluding to
New York. "And so do I," said Andre; "I am a British
officer, on urgent business, and must not be detained."
He was soon, however, undeceived, and confounded on
being obliged to yield himself a prisoner, and finding his
passport, though having the authority of Arnold's signature, availed him nothing. His captors, suspecting that
they had taken a valuable prize, resolved to hold him in
durance, and realize his worth. The unfortunate prisoner
now produced his gold watch, and said, "This will convince you that I am a gentleman. and if you will suffer
me to pass, I will send to New York, and give you *any
amount you shall name,* in cash, or in dry goods;"* and,

---

* English goods were, at that time, more valuable than gold or silver.
It has in general been understood, that Andre offered his captors his
horse, his purse, and a valuable watch, but Dr. Eustis assures me that
the above are the facts, as stated to him by Isaac Van Vert, who first
stopped Andre.

MAJOR JOHN ANDRE.

pointing to an adjacent wood, "you may keep me in that wood till it shall be delivered to you." All his offers, however, were rejected with disdain, and they declared that ten thousand guineas, or any other sum, would be no temptation. It is to *their virtue, no less glorious to America,* than Arnold's apostacy is disgraceful, that his detestable crimes are discovered. Their names are John Paulding, David Williams, and Isaac Van Vert.* Taking their prisoner into the bushes, to undergo a search and examination, they found, concealed in his boots, the important papers, containing exact returns of the state of the forces, ordnance and defences at West Point and its dependencies, with critical remarks on the works, with a return of the number of troops at West Point, and their distribution; copies of confidential letters from General Washington, &c., &c., all in the hand-writing of General Arnold. Besides which, it is ascertained that the traitor carried with him to the interview a general plan of West Point and its vicinity, and all the works, and also particular plans of each work on a large scale, elegantly drawn by the engineer at that post. But these were not given up to Major Andre; it is supposed they were to be delivered at a future time. The captors now very properly delivered their prisoner, with the papers found on him, into the hands of Lieutenant-Colonel Jameson, the commanding officer on our lines. Andre, with the view, no doubt, of giving Arnold an opportunity to escape, had the address to induce Colonel Jameson to inform the traitor, by letter, that John Anderson was taken on his way to New York. It is probable that Colonel Jameson had not examined the papers in his possession, or it may well be supposed that, having such ample evidence before him, he would have

---

* Congress resolved "That they have a high sense of the virtuous and patriotic conduct of *John Paulding, David Williams,* and *Isaac Van Vert,* In testimony whereof, ordered, that each of them receive annually, two hundred dollars in specie, or an equivalent in the current money of these states, during life, and that the Board of War be directed to procure each of them a silver medal, on one side of which shall be a shield with this inscription, *Fidelity,* and on the other, the following motto, *Vincit amor Patriæ,* and forward them to the commander-in-chief, who is requested to present the same with a copy of this resolution, and the thanks of Congress for their fidelity, and the eminent service they have rendered their country."

15

hesitated before complying with this request; but, unsuspicious of treachery, and under the embarrassment of the
moment, as though his mind was bewildered, or devoid of
reason, he immediately despatched an express to Arnold,
at Robinson's house, with the intelligence.

After sufficient time had elapsed for Arnold to receive
the information and make his escape, Major Andre declared himself to Colonel Jameson to be the adjutant-general of the British army. Sensible of the *finesse* which
had been practised on him, Colonel Jameson now despatched an express to meet General Washington, on his
return from Hartford to Arnold's quarters, with an account
of the capture of Major Andre, and the papers which were
found on him, and this was accompanied by a letter from
the prisoner, disclosing to his excellency his real character and condition, and relating the manner of his capture,
&c. It unfortunately happened that the express took a
different road, and missed of meeting the commander-in-
chief, and Arnold first received the information about ten
o'clock on the morning of the 15th instant. At this moment Major Shaw and Dr. McHenry, two of his excellency's aids, had arrived, and were at breakfast at Arnold's
table. His confusion was visible, but no one could devise
the cause. Struck with the pressing danger of his situation, expecting General Washington would soon arrive,
the guilty traitor called instantly for a "*horse, any one, even
if a wagon horse*"—bid a hasty adieu to his wife, and enjoined a positive order on the messenger not to inform
that he was the bearer of a letter from Colonel Jameson,
and having repaired to his barge, he ordered the cock-
swain with eight oarsmen to proceed down the river, and
he was soon on board the Vulture, which Andre had left
two nights before, and which immediately sailed with her
prize for New York. General Washington arrived about
twelve o'clock, and was informed that Arnold had ab-
sented himself, saying he was going to West Point, and
should soon return. His excellency passed over the river
to view the works there; but, not finding Arnold at his
post, he returned, in the hope of meeting him at his quarters. But here he was again disappointed, for no person
could account for his absence. Mrs. Arnold was now in
her chamber, in great agitation and distress, deprived of

her reason, and Dr. Eustis in attendance. At a lucid interval she inquired of the doctor if General Washington was in the house, desiring to see him. Believing that she intended to say something which would explain the secret of Arnold's unaccountable absence, he hastened below, and conducted the general to her chamber, who remained no longer than to hear her deny that he was General Washington, and to witness the return of her distraction. His excellency sat down to dine, but soon rose from table with apparent agitation, called out Colonel Lamb, the commander of artillery at West Point, and expressed to him his suspicion that Arnold had deserted to the enemy. In less than two hours it was ascertained that the conjecture was too well founded, for the despatches arrived from Colonel Jameson, with an account of the capture of Major Andre, accompanied by his own letter of confession. Major Andre was conducted to West Point, and thence to head-quarters at Tappan; and a board, consisting of fourteen general officers, is constituted and directed to sit on the 29th instant, for his trial. It was to be expected that Sir Henry Clinton would make every possible overture and exertion, with the hope of rescuing his friend, and the adjutant-general of his army, from an ignominious death. Accordingly he addressed General Washington, claimed the release of Major Andre, alleging that he ought not to be considered in the character of a spy, as he had a passport from, and was transacting business under the sanction of General Arnold; but arguments so obviously absurd and futile could have no influence, and the prisoner was ordered before the military tribunal for trial, and the following are the particulars of their proceedings.

Major Andre, adjutant-general to the British army, was brought before the board, and the following letter from General Washington to the board, dated "Head-Quarters, Tappan, September 29th, 1780," was laid before them and read:

"GENTLEMEN: Major Andre, adjutant-general to the British army, will be brought before you, for your examination. He came within our lines in the night, on an interview with Major-General Arnold, and in an assumed character; and was taken within our lines, in a disguised habit, with a pass under a feigned name, and with the inclosed papers concealed on him. After a careful examination, you will be pleased as speedily as possible to report a precise state of his case, together with your opinion of the light in which he ought to be considered, and the punishment that ought to be inflicted. The judge-advocate will attend to assist in the examination, who has sundry other papers relative to this matter, which he will lay before the board.

"I have the honor to be, gentlemen, your
most obedient and humble servant,
"G. WASHINGTON.
" *To the Board of General Officers, convened at Tappan.*"

The names of the officers composing the board were read to Major Andre, with the following letter of his to General Washington—namely:

"SALEM, 24*th September*, 1780.

"SIR: What I have as yet said, concerning myself, was in the justifiable attempt to be extricated; I am too little accustomed to duplicity to have succeeded.

"I beg your excellency will be persuaded, that no alteration in the temper of my mind, or apprehension for my safety, induces me to take the step of addressing you, but that it is to secure myself from an imputation of having assumed a mean character for treacherous purposes or self-interest—a conduct incompatible with the principles that actuated me, as well as with my condition in life.

"It is to vindicate my fame, that I speak, and not to solicit security.

"The person in your possession is Major John Andre, adjutant-general to the British army.

"The influence of one commander in the army of his adversary is an advantage taken in war. I agreed to meet, on ground not within the posts of either army, a person who was to give me intelligence; I came up in the Vulture man-of-war, for this effect, and was fetched by a boat from the shore to the beach: being there, I was told that the approach of day would prevent my return, and that I must be concealed till the next night. I was in my regimentals, and had fairly risked my person.

"Against my stipulation, my intention, and without my knowledge beforehand, I was conducted within one of your posts. Your excellency may conceive my sensation on this occasion, and will imagine how much more I must have been affected by a refusal to reconduct me back the next night, as I had been brought. Thus become a prisoner, I had to concert my escape. *I quitted my uniform*, and was passed another way in the night, without the American posts to neutral ground, and informed I was beyond all armed parties, and left to press for New York. I was taken at Tarrytown by some volunteers.

"Thus, as I have had the honor to relate, was I betrayed into the vile condition of an enemy in disguise within your posts.

"Having avowed myself a British officer, I have nothing to reveal but what relates to myself, which is true, on the honor of an officer and a gentleman.

"The request I have to make your excellency, and I am conscious I address myself well, is that in any rigor which policy may dictate, a decency of conduct towards me may evince that, though unfortunate, I am branded with nothing dishonorable, as no motive could be mine but the service of my king, and as I was involuntarily an impostor.

"Another request is, that I may be permitted to write an open letter to Sir Henry Clinton, and another to a friend for clothes and linen.

"I take the liberty to mention the condition of some gentlemen at Charleston, who, being either on parole or under protection, were engaged in a conspiracy against us. Though their situation is not similar they are objects who may be set in exchange for me, or are persons whom the treatment I receive might affect.

"It is no less, sir, in a confidence in the generosity of your mind, than on account of your superior station, that I have chosen to importune you with this letter. I have the honor to be, with great respect, sir your excellency's most obedient and most humble servant,

"JOHN ANDRE, Adjutant-General.

"*His Excellency General Washington, &c., &c., &c.*"

And on being asked whether he confessed or denied the matters contained in this letter, he acknowledged the letter, and in addition stated, that he came on shore from the Vulture sloop-of-war in *the night* of the 21st of September, instant, somewhere under the Haverstraw mountain. That the boat he came on shore in, carried *no flag*, and that he had on a surtout-coat over his regimentals, and that he wore his surtout-coat when he was taken. That he met General Arnold on the shore, and had an interview with him there. He also said, that when he left the Vulture sloop-of-war, it was understood he was to return that night; but it was then doubted, and if he could not return, he was promised to be *concealed on* shore in a place of safety till the next *night*, when he was to return in the same manner he came on shore; and when the next day came, he was solicitous to get back, and made inquiries in the course of the day how he should return; he was informed he could not return that way, and he must take the route he did afterwards. He also said, that the first notice he had of his being within *any of our posts*, was his being challenged by the sentry, which was the first night he was on shore. He also said, that in the evening of the 22d of September, instant, he passed *King's ferry, between our posts of Stony and Verplank's Points,* in the *dress he is at present in, and which he said was not his regimentals,* and which dress he procured after he landed from the Vulture, and when he was within *our post,* and that he was proceeding to New York, but was arrested at Tarrytown, as he has mentioned in his letter, on Saturday, the 23d of September, instant, about nine o'clock in the morning.

The board having interrogated Major Andre, about his

conception of his coming on shore under the sanction of a flag, *he said, that it was impossible for him to suppose he came on shore under that sanction*, and added, that if he came on shore under that sanction, he certainly might have returned under it.

Major Andre having acknowledged the preceding facts, and being asked whether he had any thing to say respecting them, answered, he left them to operate with the board.

The examination of Major Andre being concluded, he was remanded into custody.

"The board having considered the letter from his Excellency General Washington, respecting Major Andre, adjutant-general to the British army, the confession of Major Andre, and the papers produced to them, report to his excellency the commander-in-chief the following facts, which appear to them relative to Major Andre. First, that he came on-shore from the Vulture sloop-of-war, in the night of the 21st of September, instant, on an interview with General Arnold, in a private and secret manner. Secondly, that he changed his dress within our lines, and under a feigned name, and disguised habit, passed our works at Stony and Verplank's Points, in the evening of the 22d of September, instant, and was taken the morning of the 23d of September, at Tarrytown, in a disguised habit, being then on his way to New York; and when taken he had in his possession several papers which contained intelligence for the enemy. The board having maturely considered these facts, do also report to his Excellency General Washington, that Major Andre, adjutant-general to the British army, ought to be considered as a spy from the enemy, and that agreeably to the law and usage of nations it is their opinion he ought to suffer death.

[SIGNED]   ' NATHANIEL GREENE, *Major-General and President.*
            STIRLING,   "   "
            ST. CLAIR,   "   "
            LA FAYETTE,   "   "
            R. HOWE,   "   "
            STEUBEN,   "   "
            SAMUEL H. PARSONS, *Brigadier-General.*
            JAMES CLINTON,   "   "
            HENRY KNOX,   "   "   *Artillery.*
            JOHN GLOVER,   "   "
            JOHN PATTERSON,   "   "
            EDWARD HAND,   "   "
            JOHN HUNTINGTON,   "   "
            JOHN STARK,   "   "
            JOHN LAWRENCE, *Judge Advocate General.*"

"HEAD-QUARTERS, *September 30th*, 1780.
"The commander-in-chief approves of the opinion of the Board of General officers, respecting Major Andre, and orders that the execution of Major Andre take place to-morrow, at five o'clock P. M."

During the trial of this unfortunate officer, he conducted
with unexampled magnanimity and dignity of character.
He very freely and candidly confessed all the circumstances
relative to himself, and carefully avoided every expression
that might have a tendency to implicate any other person.
So firm and dignified was he in his manners, and so honorable in all his proceedings on this most trying occasion,
that he excited universal interest in his favor.   He requested only to die the death of a soldier, and not on a
gibbet.   The following is a copy of a very pathetic letter
from Major Andre to General Washington, dated

"TAPPAN, *October 1st,* 1780.
"SIR: Buoyed above the terrors of death by the consciousness of a
life devoted to honorable pursuits, and stained with no action that can
give me remorse, I trust that the request I make to your excellency at
this serious period, and which is to soften my last moments, will not be
rejected.   Sympathy towards a soldier will surely induce your excellency and a military tribunal to adapt the mode of my death to the feelings of a man of honor.   Let me hope, sir, if aught in my character
impresses you with esteem towards me—if aught in my misfortunes
marks me as the victim of policy, and not of resentment—I shall experience the operation of these feelings in your breast by being informed
that I am not to die on a gibbet.
"I have the honor to be your excellency's most
obedient and most humble servant,
"JOHN ANDRE,
"*Adjutant-General to the British army.*"

This moving letter, as may be supposed, affected the
mind of General Washington with the tenderest sympathy,
and it is reported that he submitted it to a council of general officers, who decided that as Major Andre was condemned as a spy, the circumstances of the case would not
admit of the request being granted, and his excellency,
from a desire to spare the feelings of the unfortunate man,
declined making a reply to the letter.

October 1st.—I went this afternoon to witness the execution of Major Andre: a large concourse of people had
assembled, the gallows was erected, and the grave and
coffin prepared to receive the remains of this celebrated
but unfortunate officer; but a flag of truce arrived with a
communication from Sir Henry Clinton, making another
and further proposals for the release of Major Andre, in
consequence of which the execution is postponed till to-
morrow, at twelve o'clock.

The flag which came out this morning brought General Robertson, Andrew Eliot, and William Smith, Esquires, for the purpose of pleading for the release of Major Andre, the royal army being in the greatest affliction on the occasion. The two latter gentlemen, not being military officers, were not permitted to land, but General Greene was appointed by his excellency to meet General Robertson at Dobbs' ferry, and to receive his communications. He had nothing material to urge, but that Andre had come on shore under the sanction of a flag, and therefore could not be considered as a spy. But this is not true; he came on shore in the night, and had no flag, on business totally incompatible with the nature of a flag. Besides, Andre himself, candidly confessed on his trial that he did not consider himself under the sanction of a flag. General Robertson, having failed in his point, requested that the opinion of disinterested persons might be taken, and proposed Generals Knyphausen and Rochambeau as proper persons. After this he had recourse to threats of retaliation on some people in New York and Charleston, but he was told that such conversation could neither be heard nor understood. He next urged the release of Andre on motives of humanity, saying, he wished an intercourse of such civilities as might lessen the horrors of war, and cited instances of General Clinton's merciful disposition; adding that Andre possessed a great share of that gentleman's affection and esteem, and that he would be infinitely obliged if he was spared. He offered that, if his earnest wishes were complied with, to engage that any prisoner in their possession, whom General Washington might name, should immediately be set at liberty. But it must be viewed as the height of absurdity that General Robertson should, on this occasion, suffer himself to be the bearer of a letter which the vile traitor had the consummate effrontery to write to General Washington. This insolent letter is filled with threats of retaliation, and the accountability of his excellency for the torrents of blood that might be spilled if he should order the execution of Major Andre. It should seem impossible that General Robertson could suppose that such insolence would receive any other treatment than utter contempt.

October 2d.—Major Andre is no more among the living.

I have just witnessed his exit. It was a tragical scene of the deepest interest. During his confinement and trial, he exhibited those proud and elevated sensibilities which designate greatness and dignity of mind. Not a murmur or a sigh ever escaped him, and the civilities and attentions bestowed on him were politely acknowledged. Having left a mother and two sisters in England, he was heard to mention them in terms of the tenderest affection, and in his letter to Sir Henry Clinton, he recommended them to his particular attention.

The principal guard officer, who was constantly in the room with the prisoner, relates that when the hour of his execution was announced to him in the morning, he received it without emotion, and while all present were affected with silent gloom, he retained a firm countenance, with calmness and composure of mind. Observing his servant enter the room in tears, he exclaimed, "Leave me till you can show yourself more manly!" His breakfast being sent to him from the table of General Washington, which had been done every day of his confinement, he partook of it as usual, and having shaved and dressed himself, he placed his hat on the table, and cheerfully said to the guard officers, "I am ready at any moment, gentlemen, to wait on you." The fatal hour having arrived, a large detachment of troops was paraded, and an immense concourse of people assembled; almost all our general and field officers, excepting his excellency and his staff, were present on horseback; melancholy and gloom pervaded all ranks, and the scene was affectingly awful. I was so near during the solemn march to the fatal spot, as to observe every movement, and participate in every emotion which the melancholy scene was calculated to produce. Major Andre walked from the stone house, in which he had been confined, between two of our subaltern officers, arm in arm; the eyes of the immense multitude were fixed on him, who, rising superior to the fears of death, appeared as if conscious of the dignified deportment which he displayed. He betrayed no want of fortitude, but retained a complacent smile on his countenance, and politely bowed to several gentlemen whom he knew, which was respectfully returned. It was his earnest desire to be shot, as being the mode of death most conformable to the feelings

of a military man, and he had indulged the hope that his
request would be granted. At the moment, therefore,
when suddenly he came in view of the gallows, he involuntarily started backward, and made a pause. "Why this
emotion, sir?" said an officer by his side. Instantly recovering his composure, he said, "I am reconciled to my
death, but I detest the mode." While waiting and standing near the gallows, I observed some degree of trepidation; placing his foot on a stone, and rolling it over and
choking in his throat, as if attempting to swallow. So
soon, however, as he perceived that things were in readiness, he stepped quickly into the wagon, and at this moment he appeared to shrink, but instantly elevating his
head with firmness, he said, "It will be but a momentary
pang," and taking from his pocket two white handkerchiefs,
the provost-marshal, with one, loosely pinioned his arms,
and with the other, the victim, after taking off his hat and
stock, bandaged his own eyes with perfect firmness, which
melted the hearts and moistened the cheeks, not only of
his servant, but of the throng of spectators. The rope
being appended to the gallows, he slipped the noose over
his head and adjusted it to his neck, without the assistance
of the awkward executioner. Colonel Scammel now informed him that he had an opportunity to speak, if he
desired it; he raised the handkerchief from his eyes, and
said, "I pray you to bear me witness that I meet my fate
like a brave man." The wagon being now removed from
under him, he was suspended, and instantly expired; it
proved indeed "but a momentary pang." He was dressed
in his royal regimentals and boots, and his remains, in
the same dress, were placed in an ordinary coffin, and interred at the foot of the gallows; and the spot was consecrated by the tears of thousands.

Thus died, in the bloom of life, the accomplished Major
Andre, the pride of the royal army, and the valued friend
of Sir Henry Clinton. He was about twenty-nine years
of age, in his person well proportioned, tall, genteel and
graceful. His mien respectable and dignified. His countenance mild, expressive and prepossessing, indicative of an
intelligent and amiable mind. His talents are said to have
been of a superior cast, and, being cultivated in early life,
he had made very considerable proficiency in literary attain-

ments. Colonel Hamilton, aid-de-camp to General Washington, having had an interview with him, entertains an exalted opinion of his character. In the line of his profession, Major Andre, was considered as a skilful, brave and enterprising officer, and he is reported to have been benevolent and humane to our people who have been prisoners in New York. Military glory was the mainspring of his actions, and the sole object of his pursuits, and he was advancing rapidly in the gratification of his ambitious views, till by a misguided zeal he became a devoted victim. He enjoyed the confidence and friendship of Sir Henry Clinton, being consulted in his councils and admitted to the secrets of his cabinet. The heart of sensibility mourns when a life of so much worth is sacrificed on a gibbet. General Washington was called to discharge a duty from which his soul revolted; and it is asserted that his hand could scarcely command his pen, when signing the warrant for the execution of Major Andre. But, however abhorrent in the view of humanity, the laws and usages of war must be obeyed, and in all armies it is decreed that the gallows shall be the fate of spies from the enemy. It was universally desired that Major Andre should experience every possible favor and indulgence, consistent with his peculiar circumstances, but it was well considered that, should he be indulged in his request to be shot, it would imply that his case admitted of extenuation, and it might be doubted whether in justice he ought to be convicted as a spy. The British general himself has not hesitated to execute several persons of the same description sent from our army into New York.* Could Arnold

* It is with the highest degree of satisfaction, that I am enabled to copy the following interesting narrative, vouched by Major-General Hull, of Newton, from Hannah Adams' History of New England. Let the reader draw the striking contrast between the conduct of the royalists and the Americans, on an occasion where the duties of humanity and benevolence, were equally and imperiously demanded.

"The retreat of General Washington left the British in complete possession of Long Island. What would be their future operations, remained uncertain. To obtain information of their situation, their strength and future movements, was of high importance. For this purpose, General Washington applied to Colonel Knowlton, who commanded a regiment of light infantry, which formed the van of the American army, and desired him to adopt some mode of gaining the necessary information. Colonel Knowlton communicated this request to Captain have been suspended on the gibbet erected for Andre, not a tear or a sigh would have been produced, but exultation

Hale, of Connecticut, who was then a captain in his regiment. This young officer, animated by a sense of duty, and considering that an opportunity presented itself by which he might be useful to his country, at once offered himself a volunteer for this hazardous service. He passed in disguise to Long Island, examined every part of the British army, and obtained the best possible information respecting their situation and future operations.

"In his attempt to return, he was apprehended, carried before Sir William Howe, and the proof of his object was so clear, that he frankly acknowledged who he was, and what were his views.

"Sir William Howe at once gave an order to the provost-marshal to execute him the next morning.

"The order was accordingly executed in a most unfeeling manner, and by as great a savage as ever disgraced humanity. A clergyman, whose attendance he desired, was refused him; a Bible for a moment's devotion was not procured, though he requested it. Letters which, on the morning of his execution, he wrote to his mother and other friends, were destroyed; and this very extraordinary reason given by the provost-marshal, 'that the rebels should not know that they had a man in their army who could die with so much firmness.'

"Unknown to all around him, without a single friend to offer him the least consolation, thus fell as amiable and as worthy a young man as America could boast, with this as his dying observation, 'that he only lamented he had but one life to lose for his country.' How superior to the dying words of Andre! Though the manner of his execution will ever be abhorred by every friend to humanity and religion, yet there cannot be a question but that the sentence was conformable to the rules of war, and the practice of nations in similar cases.

"It is, however, a justice due to the character of Captain Hale, to observe, that his motives for engaging in this service were entirely different from those which generally influence others in similar circumstances. 'Neither expectation of promotion nor pecuniary reward induced him to this attempt. A sense of duty, a hope that he might in this way be useful to his country, and an opinion which he had adopted, that every kind of service necessary to the public good became honorable by being necessary, were the great motives which induced him to engage in an enterprise by which his connexions lost a most amiable friend and his country one of its most promising supporters.'

"The fate of this unfortunate young man excites the most interesting reflections. To see such a character, in the flower of youth, cheerfully treading in the most hazardous paths, influenced by the purest intentions, and only emulous to do good to his country, without the imputation of a crime, fall a victim to policy, must have been wounding to the feelings even of his enemies.

"Should a comparison be drawn between Major Andre and Captain Hale, injustice would be done to the latter, should he not be placed on an equal ground with the former. Whilst almost every historian of the American Revolution has celebrated the virtues and lamented the fate and joy would have been visible on every countenance. But General Clinton suffers the vile and infamous traitor to elude the hand of justice, and even bestows on him a reward for his crime. It may perhaps be suggested, that in this last act of his life Major Andre derogated from his character and station. That the laurels to adorn the brow of a soldier, can only be acquired in the field of battle, and not by encouraging acts of treason, by bribery and corruption. Surprise and stratagem, it is well known, constitute a valuable part of the art of war, by which many important objects are effected, and by some it is said that when acts of treason are practised, the infamy devolves on the head of the traitors alone. In the present instance, it is supposed that Arnold made the first overture. It is well understood that Sir Henry Clinton enjoined it on Andre to transact the business on board the Vulture, and it was his own determination not to land on our shore; but such was the management of Arnold and his confederate, Smith, that he was actually compelled, contrary to his own judgment and intention, to come within our lines, and this circumstance alone placed him in the character of a common spy. The commander-in-chief was generously disposed to compassionate his unhappy condition, and to soothe and mitigate his sorrow, and every officer in the army was actuated by feelings of sympathy and tenderness towards him. The base and perfidious Arnold is held in the utmost abhorrence and detestation throughout our army, and his person, with the garrison at West Point into the bargain, would have been a dear purchase to Sir Henry for the life of his valuable friend and adjutant-general.

West Point is now become a very celebrated and memorable spot, by the attempt of the royal general to obtain possession of it through the defection and treachery of one of our officers, and the defeat of the conspiracy. Arnold

of Andre, *Hale has remained unnoticed, and it is scarcely known that such a character ever existed.*

"To the memory of Andre, his country has erected the most magnificent monuments, and bestowed on his family the highest honors and most liberal rewards. To the memory of Hale not a stone has been erected, nor an inscription to preserve his ashes from insult."[*]

[*] In the autumn of 1821, the remains of Major Andre were disinterred, and transported to England.

was well apprised of its importance, and it was obviously his design to strike a fatal blow to the cause of his native country, and it was his intention that it should cost the British nothing more than the price of his own villany and treason.   He had actually removed a New York regiment from the point to the plain on the east side of the river, and sent off a number of soldiers from the garrison to cut wood at a distance, and disposed and arranged the remaining troops in such manner that little or no opposition could have been made, and an immediate surrender would have been inevitable, or our troops must have fallen a sacrifice.   Deplorable indeed would have been the event, the loss of this highly important garrison with some of our best officers and men, the immense quantity of ordnance and military stores, together with the prodigious panic and gloom which at this critical period must have pervaded the whole people, could scarcely have failed of being productive of consequences overwhelming the physical powers and energies of our country.   But we are saved by a *miracle*, and we are confounded in awful astonishment. In a private letter, General Washington thus expresses himself respecting this transaction:

"In no instance since the commencement of the war has the interposition of Providence appeared more remarkably conspicuous than in the rescue of the post and garrison at West Point.   How far Arnold meant to involve me in the catastrophe of this place, does not appear by any indubitable evidence, and I am rather inclined to think he did not wish to hazard the more important object, by attempting to combine two events, the lesser of which might have marred the greater.   A combination of extraordinary circumstances, and unaccountable deprivation of presence of mind in a man of the first abilities, and the virtue of three militia-men, threw the adjutant-general of the British forces, with full proof of Arnold's intention, into our hands, and but for the egregious folly or the bewildered conception of Lieutenant-Colonel Jameson, who seemed lost in astonishment, and not to have known what he was doing, I should undoubtedly have gotten Arnold.   Andre has met his fate, and with that fortitude which was to be expected from an accomplished man and a gallant officer; but I mistake if Arnold is suffering at this time the torments of a mental hell.   He wants feeling.   From some traits of his character which have lately come to my knowledge, ne seems to have been so hacknied in crime, so lost to all sense of nonor and shame, that while his faculties still enable him to continue his sordid pursuits, there will be no time for remorse."

For the sake of human nature, it were to be wished that a veil could be for ever thrown over so vile an example of depravity and wickedness. Traitor! you never can know the precious enjoyment of a quiet conscience! While you sleep, your heart must be awake, and the voice of Andre must thrill through your very soul. Though you may console yourself that you have escaped the gallows, a consciousness of your crimes and the infamy and contempt which will for ever await you, must incessantly harrow and torment your spirit, rendering you of all villains the most wretched and miserable. The only atonement in your power to alleviate your poignant mental misery, is a humble and hearty confession, and to implore in sincerity the forgiveness of Heaven!*

Our brigade and three others decamped from Orangetown on the 7th instant. Our tents and baggage were sent up the Hudson in boats, and we took our route through the highlands. The road was almost impassable through a thick wood and over high mountains, constantly intersected by prodigious rocks, running brooks and deep vallies. We arrived at West Point on the evening of the 8th, distance thirty-two miles; the troops much fatigued, and our tents not arrived, took our sleep for the night on the ground in the woods and on the 9th, encamped on the plain, near the banks of the river. General Greene is now the commander of this garrison, and good order takes place of the confusion occasioned by Arnold's elopement.

Joshua Smith, Esquire, the confederate of Arnold, has been tried by a court-martial, of which Colonel Henry Jackson was president; the evidence against him and his own confession go to prove that he went on board the Vulture, in the night, and brought on shore a gentleman who was called John Anderson, to have an interview with General Arnold; that he secreted him in his house, furnished him with a horse and change of clothes, and that he accompanied him through our out-posts, and directed him into the proper road to New York. All this, he pleads in his defence, was by the express desire of General Arnold, who assured him that his object was to obtain some important intelligence from New York, which would be highly advantageous to the public interest. He considered himself, therefore, in the character of a confidental agent in

* See the character of Arnold, in the Appendix.

the employment of Arnold, without suspicion of treasonable conduct in this officer.   This pretence is plausible,
and it is his good fortune that no positive evidence could
be produced to countervail his assertions.   Though his
actions appear criminal, yet it is possible his motives and
views may have been laudable.   The want of positive
evidence, therefore, of his criminality, prevented his conviction; but so strong was the circumstantial proof of his
guilt, that it was deemed proper that he should be kept in
confinement.   Being seized with indisposition, from apprehension and anxiety of mind, I was requested to visit him
in his prison.   I found him very conversable, and he immediately entertained me with a relation of the particular
circumstances of his case, which agreed substantially with
the above statement.   He promised to show me his written defence, produced at his trial, but no future opportunity
occurred.   He pretended that it was unjust and cruel that
he should be deprived of his liberty, when no evidence
of guilt could be produced against him.   He was soon
removed to some prison in the country;* after which, his
lady arrived, expecting to find him here.   I received a
polite billet, requesting I would wait on her at the house
of my friend Major Bowman, where I was introduced to
her and to Mrs. B. and her daughter, with whom I took
tea and spent the evening.   Mrs. Smith was grievously
disappointed that her husband was removed; she was very
solicitous to be informed of the particular circumstances
which attended him in his illness, and whether he was
dejected in spirits, and politely thanked me for my attention to him.   She appears to be an accomplished and interesting woman, but is in much distress for the fate of her
husband.   She could not conceal her natural partiality
and bias in his favor, and would willingly have left the
impression which Arnold wished to make, when in his
letter to General Washington, he says of his wife, "she is
as good and as innocent as an angel, and is incapable of
doing wrong."

15th.—I have just returned from Orangetown, in company with Captain Hunt, of our regiment, where I was

* Smith was for several months in confinement; but either from a
want of vigilance in his keeper, or the indifference of the proper authority, he was at length allowed to escape to New York.

BENEDICT ARNOLD.

called to visit his brother, who was left sick when we marched from that place. We dined with Doctors Eustis and Townsend at the hospital on our way, and with Captain Livingston, a respectable officer, commanding at Stony Point, on our return.

20th.—Major-General Greene has been ordered to the southward, to take command of the American army in the Carolinas, and Major-General Heath succeeds to the command of this post.

We have the mortifying intelligence that the enemy has laid waste a great part of the fertile country above Saratoga, and likewise the vicinity of Schenectady. The party consisted of Indians, tories, and Canadians, commanded by Sir John Johnston. General Van Rensselaer, with the militia and some new levies, engaged the enemy at Fox's mills, Tryon county, and after a very severe action of three-quarters of an hour, forced them to give way and cross the river, leaving their plunder, baggage and prisoners, which they had taken, behind them. One hour of day-light would have given us the whole party. The action was general and vigorous; we have to lament the loss of Colonel Brown, who was killed in skirmishing with the enemy. The devastation committed by this savage party is found to be very important, as it respects the inhabitants of the north. It is estimated at two hundred dwellings, one hundred and fifty thousand bushels of wheat, with a proportion of other grain and forage. The same party destroyed also the town of Schoharie, but the inhabitants fortunately secured themselves in the fort.

Official intelligence is received of a very brilliant exploit of our militia in North Carolina. The famous royal partizan, Major Ferguson, was at the head of about one thousand four hundred British troops and tories. Colonels Campbell, Cleveland, Williams, Shelby and Sevier, brave and enterprising officers, had collected detached parties of militia, and by agreement the whole were united, and formed a body amounting to near three thousand. Colonel Campbell was appointed their commander. They immediately marched in pursuit of Major Ferguson, and came up with him advantageously posted, at a place called King's mountains. No time was lost in making a vigorous attack, and giving the enemy a total defeat, in which

16

Major Ferguson and one hundred and fifty of his men were killed, eight hundred made prisoners, and fifteen hundred stand of arms taken, with a trifling loss on our side, excepting the brave Colonel Williams, who received a mortal wound after being crowned with honor.

Congress have resolved that the regular army of the United States, from and after the first day of January, 1781, shall consist of four regiments of artillery, forty-nine regiments of infantry, exclusive of Colonel Hazen's, called "the Congress' own regiment," and one regiment of artificers. The respective states are to furnish their quotas as proportioned by Congress. And as, by the foregoing arrangement, many deserving officers may become supernumerary, Congress resolved that, after the reform of the army takes place, the officers shall be entitled to half-pay for seven years, in specie or other current money equivalent, and to have grants of land at the close of the war, agreeably to the resolution of the 16th September, 1776.

A scarcity of provisions is again complained of in camp.

It has long been the desire of General Washington to make some arrangement with General Clinton for an exchange of prisoners; but many difficulties have attended to prevent the accomplishment of the object. A partial exchange has now been effected; Major-General Lincoln, who was taken at Charleston, has been exchanged for Major-General Phillips, captured at Saratoga. General Thompson and a number of other American officers, who have long been prisoners, are also liberated by exchange.

November 1st.—A most tremendous storm of wind, snow and hail has continued almost incessantly for two days. Many of our tents were levelled with the ground, and officers and men exposed without a shelter.

2d.—This is a day of public Thanksgiving throughout the state of New York, on occasion of the discovery of Arnold's conspiracy.

3d.—A soldier has been executed to-day for desertion and persuading others to follow his example.

A large detachment of troops has been ordered by General Heath to be in readiness, with two days' provisions cooked, to march on a foraging expedition, under command of Brigadier-General Stark. The detachment crossed the Hudson on the 21st instant, and paraded on

Nelson's point, where they were reviewed by the Marquis de Chastellux, one of the generals of the French army at Newport. It is understood that the object of the expedition is to procure a quantity of forage from the farms on the neutral ground, between the two armies, towards King's-bridge. After the review, the marquis crossed over to West Point, where his arrival was announced by the discharge of thirteen cannon. The detachment marched about ten miles, and took lodgings on the ground in the woods, beside large fires. In the night a severe storm of rain came on, that drenched our troops, and becoming more violent the next day, rendered the roads extremely bad, and our march very uncomfortable; we reached North Castle, seventeen miles, and lodged in the woods, where our fires did not secure us from suffering much by wet and cold.

23d.—Marched to West Farms, near West Chester, within eight miles of the enemy's works at King's-bridge. Here we kindled numerous fires in open view of the enemy, and in the evening the troops were ordered to leave the fires and retire back about two miles, and remain under arms prepared for battle; but the enemy made no advances.

24th.—Another severe storm of rain, which continued through the day; we, however, began to march at sun-rise, on our return, but soon halted, and took shelter under the bushes near White Plains. In this comfortless situation, we continued through the day and night. The next day, the storm continuing, I was so fortunate as to crowd into a house with some officers for shelter. 26th and 27th, marched twenty miles each day, and reached our former station at this place before night.

The country which we lately traversed, about fifty miles in extent, is called neutral ground, but the miserable inhabitants who remain, are not much favored with the privileges which their neutrality ought to secure to them. They are continually exposed to the ravages and insults of infamous banditti, composed of royal refugees and tories. The country is rich and fertile, and the farms appear to have been advantageously cultivated, but it now has the marks of a country in ruins. A large proportion of the proprietors having abandoned their farms, the few that remain find it impossible to harvest the produce. The meadows and pastures are covered with grass of a summer's growth, and thousands of bushels of apples and other fruit are rotting in the orchards. We brought off about two hundred loads of hay and grain, and ten times the amount might have been procured, had teams enough been provided. Those of the inhabitants of the neutral ground who were tories, have joined their friends in New York, and the whigs have retired into the interior of our country. Some of each side have taken up arms, and become the most cruel and deadly foes. There are within the British lines banditti consisting of lawless villains, who devote themselves to the most cruel pillage and robbery among the defenceless inhabitants between the lines, many of whom they carry off to New York, after plundering their houses and farms. These shameless marauders have received the names of *Cow-boys* and *Skinners*. By their atrocious deeds they have become a scourge and terror to the people. Numerous instances have been related of these miscreants subjecting defenceless persons to cruel torture, to compel them to deliver up their money, or to disclose the places where it has been secreted. It is not uncommon for them to hang a man by his neck till apparently dead, then restore him, and repeat the experiment, and leave him for dead. One of these unhappy persons informed me that when suffering this cruel treatment, the last sensation which he recollects, when suspended by his neck, was a flashing heat over him, like that which would be occasioned by boiling water poured over his body; he was, however, cut down, and how long he remained on the ground insensible, he knows not. A peaceable, unresisting Quaker, of considerable respectability, by the name of Quimby, was visited by several of these vile ruffians; they first demanded his money, and after it was delivered, they suspected he had more concealed, and inflicted on him the most savage cruelties, in order to extort it from him. They began with what they call *scorching*, covering his naked body with hot ashes, and repeating the application till the skin was covered with blisters; after this, they resorted to the halter, and hung the poor man on a tree by his neck; then took him down, and repeated it a second, and even a third time, and finally left him almost lifeless.

30*th*.—It is now well understood that our detachment, under the pretext of a foraging expedition, was intended by the commander-in-chief' to coöperate with the main army in an attempt against the enemy's post on York island. Boats, mounted on travelling carriages, have been kept with the army all the campaign. The Marquis de la Fayette, at the head of his beautiful corps of light-infantry, constantly advancing in front, was to have commenced the attack in the night, and the whole army was prepared to make a general attack on the enemy's works. By some movement of the British vessels, or other cause, known only to the commander-in-chief and his confidential officers, this noble enterprise was unfortunately defeated. The campaign is now brought to a close, without effecting any very important object. We have several times offered the enemy battle, but they refuse to accept the challenge. The marquis suffers on this occasion the most painful disappointment. He had spared no pains or expense to render his corps of infantry as fine a body of troops as can be produced in any country; every officer under his command received from him a present of an elegant sword, and the soldiers were put in uniform mostly at his expense. The officers cheerfully seconded his endeavors to perfect the men in discipline, and a noble spirit of emulation universally prevailed among them. The marquis viewed this corps as one formed and modelled according to his own wishes, and as meriting his highest confidence. They were the pride of his heart, and he was the idol of their regard, who were constantly panting for an opportunity of accomplishing some signal achievement, worthy of his and their character. This brilliant corps is now dissolved, and the men have rejoined their respective regiments, and we are soon to retire into the wilderness to prepare for winter-quarters.

Intelligence is received from Boston that his Excellency John Hancock has been elected by the people of the state of Massachusetts the first governor under their new constitution. This event affords universal satisfaction, and has been announced in Boston by public rejoicing, firing of thirteen cannon, military parade, *feu de joie*, and elegant entertainments.

It is with inexpressible satisfaction that we learn, the

patriotic ladies of Philadelphia and its vicinity have distinguished themselves by a generous and liberal regard to the sufferings of our soldiery, and have engaged in the benevolent work of raising contributions among themselves, and stimulating others, for the purpose of affording a temporary relief for the soldiers on service in that vicinity. I extract from the newspapers the sentiments of an "*American Woman*," addressed to American ladies relative to the subject, which should be recorded for the honor of the sex:

"On the commencement of actual war, the women of America manifested a firm resolution to contribute as much as could depend on them to the deliverance of their country. Animated by the purest patriotism, they are full of sorrow at this day in not offering more than barren wishes for the success of so glorious a revolution. They aspire to render themselves more really useful; and this sentiment is universal, from the north to the south of the Thirteen United States. Our ambition is kindled by the fame of those heroines of antiquity, who have rendered their sex illustrious, and have proved to the world that, if the weakness of our constitution, if opinion and manners did not forbid us to march to glory by the same path as the men, we should at least equal, and sometimes surpass them in our love for the public good. I glory in all that my sex have done that is great and commendable. I call to mind with enthusiasm and with admiration all those acts of courage, of constancy and patriotism, which history has transmitted to us: the people favored by Heaven, preserved from destruction by the virtues, the zeal and the resolution of Deborah, of Judith, of Esther—the fortitude of the mother of the Maccabees, in giving up her sons to die before her eyes—Rome saved from the fury of a victorious enemy by the efforts of Volumnia and other Roman ladies—so many famous sieges where the women have been seen forgetting the weakness of their sex, building new walls, digging trenches with their feeble hands, furnishing arms to their defenders, they themselves darting the missile-weapons on the enemy, resigning the ornaments of their apparel, and their fortune, to fill the public treasury, and to hasten the deliverance of their country; burying themselves under its ruins; throwing themselves into the flames, rather than submit to the disgrace of humiliation before a proud enemy.

"We are certain that he cannot be a good citizen, who will not applaud our efforts for the relief of the armies, which defend our lives, our possessions, our liberty. The situation of our soldiery has been represented to me; the evils inseparable from war, and the firm and generous spirit which has enabled them to support these. But it has been said that they may apprehend that, in the course of a long war, the view of their distresses may be lost, and their services be forgotten. Forgotten! never; I can answer in the name of all my sex. Brave Americans, your disinterestedness, your courage, and your constancy, will always be dear to America, so long as she shall preserve her virtue.

"We know that at a distance from the theatre of war, if we enjoy any tranquillity, it is the fruit of your watchings, your labors, your dangers. If I live happy in the midst of my family; if my husband cultivates his field, and reaps his harvest in peace; if, surrounded with my children, I myself nourish the youngest, and press it to my bosom, without being afraid of seeing myself separated from it by a ferocious enemy; if the house in which we dwell, if our barns, our orchards, are safe at the present time from the hands of the incendiary; it is to you that we owe it. And shall we hesitate to evidence to you our gratitude? shall we hesitate to wear a clothing more simple; hair dressed less elegantly, while, at the price of this small privation, we shall deserve your benedictions? Who among us will not renounce with the highest pleasure those vain ornaments, when she shall consider that the valiant defenders of America will be able to draw some advantage from the money which she may have laid out in these?—that they will be better defended from the rigors of the seasons; that after their painful toils they will receive some extraordinary and unexpected relief; that these presents will perhaps be valued by them at a greater price, when they will have it in their power to say, *This is the offering of the ladies!* The time is arrived to display the same sentiments which animated us at the beginning of the revolution, when we renounced the use of teas, however agreeable to our taste, rather than receive them from our persecutors; when we made it appear to them that we placed former necessaries in the rank of superfluities, when our liberty was interested; when our republican and laborious hands spun the flax and prepared the linen intended for the use of our soldiers; when, exiles and fugitives, we supported with courage all the evils which are the concomitants of war. Let us not lose a moment: let us be engaged to offer the homage of our gratitude at the altar of military valor; and you, our brave deliverers, while mercenary slaves combat to cause you to share with them the irons with which they are loaded, receive with a free hand our offering, the purest which can be presented to your virtue."

After this publication, the ladies divided the city of Philadelphia into districts, and a select number visited every house, and received the contribution. The method proposed of distributing their bounty to the troops, was through the medium of Mrs. Washington, but in her absence, through that of her husband, the father and friend of the soldiery. From the kind and generous exertions of these ladies, the soldiers received at one time two thousand one hundred and seven shirts, made by their own hands; and in another paper it is mentioned that the sum total of the donations received by the ladies of Philadelphia, in their several districts, for the American army, amounts to three hundred thousand seven hundred and sixty-six dollars in paper currency. Such free-will offerings are *examples truly worthy of imitation*, and are to be considered as expressions of kindness and benevolence, which ought to be recorded to the honor of American ladies.

December 1st.—Our brigade is now ordered into the woods, in the highlands, in the rear of West Point, where we are to build log-huts for winter cantonments. We are again subjected to numerous privations and difficulties, to support which requires all our patience and fortitude. The soldiers, though very miserably clad, have been for some time obliged to bring all the wood for themselves and officers on their backs, from a. place a mile distant, and almost half the time are kept on half-allowance of bread, and entirely without rum. Twelve or fourteen months' pay are now due to us, and we are destitute of clothing and the necessaries of life. The weather is remarkably cold, and our tents are comfortless.

10th.—For three days I have not been able to procure food enough to appease my appetite; we are threatened with starvation. That a part of our army, charged with the defence of a post so highly important to America, should be left in such an unprovided and destitute condition, is truly a matter of astonishment; and unless a remedy can be found, our soldiers will abandon the cause of their country, and we must submit to the yoke of Great Britain, which we so much abhor.

20th.—During the last ten days we have experienced almost continued storms of rain, high winds, and disagreeable fogs. Our canvas dwellings afford us but little protection against such powerful assailants; they are frequently rent asunder, and we are almost overwhelmed with inundation.

A very spirited and honorable enterprise has lately been planned and executed by Major Talmadge, of Colonel Sheldon's regiment of dragoons. The enemy having large magazines of forage and stores in the vicinity of fort St. George, on Long Island, he resolved to hazard the attempt to seize them by surprise. Fort St. George was stockaded, and covered a large spot of ground, having a square redoubt, with a ditch and abatis. With about eighty dismounted dragoons, under Captain Edgar, and eight or ten on horseback, Major Talmadge passed the Sound, where it was about twenty miles from shore to shore, marched across the island in the night with such facility and address, that his enterprise was crowned with complete success. The enemy were not alarmed till too late to make much resistance; seven, however, were killed and wounded, and the remainder, amounting to fifty-four, among whom were one lieutenant-colonel, one captain and a subaltern, were made prisoners. The fort was demolished, two armed vessels were burned, and a large magazine of hay, said to be three hundred tons, with stores to a large amount, shared the same fate. Major Talmadge recrossed the Sound with his brave party without the loss of a man. The commander-in-chief was so well pleased with this exploit, that he recommended Major Talmadge to the notice of Congress, and they voted him their thanks for his brave and spirited conduct.

The extraordinary patience and fortitude which have hitherto been so honorably displayed by our officers and soldiers under their complicated distresses, appear now to be exhausted. From repeated disappointments of our hopes and expectations, the confidence of the army in public justice and public promises is greatly diminished, and we are reduced almost to despair.

The present crisis is alarming. Regimental officers are continually resigning their commissions, and a large proportion of those who remain have pledged themselves to follow their example, unless a redress of grievances can soon be obtained. Nothing short of what we conceive to be justly our due, a comfortable and permanent support, will retain our officers, however ardent their desire to serve their country. They exclaim, "Let others come and take their turn! we have served years longer than we expected, and have acquitted ourselves of duty." All the general officers belonging to New England have united in a memorial to their respective state governments, complaining of our grievances, and requesting immediate relief and security for the future. This memorial, being put into the mail, was taken from the Fishkill post-rider by some emissary from the enemy, and has been published in the New York papers, by which our forlorn situation has been exposed, and much exultation occasioned among those who are watching for our destruction.

The resolution of Congress for a new arrangement of the army was not conformable to the expectations of the officers, and caused uneasiness among them. The commander-in-chief saw that a storm was gathering, and thought it prudent on this occasion to communicate his opinion to Congress on the best means to avert it. On the 11th of October, he informed Congress, "that the general topic of declamation in the army is, that it is as hard as dishonorable for men who had made every sacrifice to the service, to be turned out of it, at the pleasure of those in power, without an adequate compensation. Too many of the officers wish to get rid of their commissions, but they are not willing to be forced to it."

The commander-in-chief, in his communication to Congress, suggests the policy of making ample provision, both for the officers who stay and for those who are reduced. He recommended what he thought would be the most economical, the most politic, and the most effectual provision, *half-pay* for life. "Supported," the general says, "by a prospect of a permanent dependence, the officers would be tied to the service, and would submit to many momentary privations, and to the inconveniences which the situation of the public service make unavoidable. If the objection drawn from the principle that this measure is incompatible with the genius of our government, be thought insurmountable, I would propose a substitute, less eligible in my opinion, but which may answer the purpose: it is to make the present *half-pay*, for seven years, *whole pay* for the same period, to be advanced at two different payments, one half in a year after the conclusion of peace, the other half in two years after."

His excellency also takes notice of the injuries and inconveniences which attend a continual change of officers, and consequent promotions in the army.

Soon after Congress were possessed of the sentiments of General Washington, they resolved, "that the commander-in-chief and commanding officer in the northern department, direct the officers of each state to meet and agree on the officers for the regiments to be raised by their respective states, from those who incline to continue in service, and where it cannot be done by agreement, to be determined by seniority; and make return of those who are to remain, which is to be transmitted to Congress, together with the names of the officers reduced, who are

to be allowed half-pay for life. That the officers who shall
continue in service to the end of the war, shall also be
entitled to half-pay during life, to commence from the time
of their reduction."

January 1st, 1781.—On this, the first day of the new
year, an arrangement of our army takes place, according
to a late resolve of Congress. The supernumerary regiments are to be incorporated with those which continue
on the new establishment, and the supernumerary officers
are to retire from service on the establishment fixed by
Congress, and are to be entitled to the same privileges and
emoluments which are to be allowed to those who continue to the end of the war. It being optional with me
either to retire or to continue in service, I shall retain my
commission as surgeon to Colonel H. Jackson's regiment.
We are encouraged to anticipate more favorable circumstances and more liberal compensation—Congress having
at length passed several resolves, entitling all officers who
shall continue in service till the end of the war, or shall
be reduced before that time, as supernumeraries, to receive
half-pay during life, and a certain number of acres of land,
in proportion to their rank. Besides these pecuniary considerations, we are actuated by the purest principles of
patriotism; having engaged in the mighty struggle, we
are ambitious to persevere to the end. To be instrumental
in the achievement of a glorious independence for our
country and posterity, will be a source of infinite satisfaction, and of most grateful recollection, during the remainder
of our days. Notwithstanding the unparalleled sufferings
and hardships which have hitherto attended our military
career, scarcely an officer retires without the deepest regret
and reluctance. So strong is the attachment, and so fascinating the idea of participating with our illustrious
commander in military glory, that a separation is like a
relinquishment of principle, and abandonment of the great
interest of our native country.

3d.—Our brigade took possession of our huts for the
winter, in the woods about two miles in the rear of the
works at West Point. Our situation is singularly romantic, on a highly-elevated spot, surrounded by mountains
and craggy rocks of a prodigious size, lofty broken clefts,
and the banks of the beautifully meandering Hudson,

affording a view of the country for many miles in all
directions. We have now no longer reason to complain
of our accommodations; the huts are warm and comfortable, wood in abundance at our doors, and a tolerable supply of provisions. Our only complaint is want of money.

4th.—Reports of a very serious and alarming nature
have this day reached us from the Jerseys. The Pennsylvania line of troops, consisting of about two thousand
men, in winter-quarters in the vicinity of Morristown,
have come to the desperate resolution of revolting from
their officers. Though the Pennsylvania troops have been
subjected to all the discouragements and difficulties felt
by the rest of the army, some particular circumstances
peculiar to themselves have contributed to produce the
revolt. When the soldiers first enlisted, the recruiting
officers were provided with enlisting-rolls for the term of
three years, or during the continuance of the war, and as
the officers indulged the opinion that the war would not
continue more than three years, they were perhaps indifferent in which column the soldier's name was inserted,
leaving it liable to an ambiguity of construction. It is
clear, however, that a part enlisted for three years, and
others for the more indefinite term "during the war."
The soldiers now contend that they enlisted for three
years at furthest, and were to have been discharged sooner,
in case the war terminated before the expiration of this
term. The war being protracted beyond the time expected, and the officers, knowing the value of soldiers who
have been trained by three years' service, are accused of
putting a different construction on the original agreement,
and claiming their services during the war. The soldiers,
even those who actually enlisted for the war, having received very small bounties, complain of imposition and
deception, and their case is extremely aggravated by the
fact, that three half-joes have now been offered as a bounty
to others who will enlist for the remainder of the war,
when these veteran soldiers have served three years for a
mere shadow of compensation! It was scarcely necessary
to add to their trying circumstances a total want of pay
for twelve months, and a state of nakedness and famine, to
excite in a soldier the spirit of insurrection. The officers
themselves, also feeling aggrieved, and in a destitute con-

dition, relaxed in their system of camp-discipline, and the soldiers occasionally overheard their murmurs and complaints. Having appointed a sergeant-major for their commander, styling him major-general, and having concerted their arrangements, on the first day of the new year they put their mutinous scheme into execution. On a preconcerted signal, the whole line, except a part of three regiments, paraded under arms without their officers, marched to the magazines, and supplied themselves with provisions and ammunition, and, seizing six field-pieces, took horses from General Wayne's stable to transport them. The officers of the line collected those who had not yet joined the insurgents, and endeavored to restore order; but the revolters fired, and killed a Captain Billing, and wounded several other officers, and a few men were killed on each side. The mutineers commanded the party who opposed them to come over to them instantly, or they should be bayoneted, and the order was obeyed. General Wayne, who commanded the Pennsylvania troops, endeavored to interpose his influence and authority, urging them to return to their duty till their grievances could be inquired into and redressed. But all was to no purpose, and on cocking his pistol, they instantly presented their bayonets to his breast, saying, "We respect and love you; often have you led us into the field of battle, but we are no longer under your command; we warn you to be on your guard; if you fire your pistols, or attempt to enforce your commands, we shall put you instantly to death." General Wayne next expostulated with them, expressing his apprehension that they were about to sacrifice the glorious cause of their country, and that the enemy would avail themselves of the opportunity to advance and improve so favorable an occasion. They assured him that they still retained an attachment and respect for the cause which they had embraced, and that, so far from a disposition to abandon it, if the enemy should dare to come out of New York, they would, under his and his officers' orders, face them in the field, and oppose them to the utmost in their power. They complained that they had been imposed on and deceived respecting the term of their enlistment; that they had received no wages for more than a year; and that they were destitute of clothing, and had often been deprived of their rations. These were their grievances, and they were determined to march to Philadelphia, and demand of Congress that justice which had so long been denied them. They commenced their march in regular military order, and when encamped at night, they posted out piquets, guards, and sentinels. General Wayne, to prevent their depredations on private property, supplied them with provisions, and he, with Colonels Stewart and Butler, officers whom the soldiers respected and loved, followed and mixed with them, to watch their motions and views, and they received from them respectful and civil treatment. On the third day, the insurgent troops reached Princeton, and, by request of General Wayne, they deputed a committee of sergeants, who stated to him formally in writing their claims, as follows: 1st, A discharge for all those, without exception, who had served three years under their original engagements, and had not received the increased bounty and reenlisted for the war. 2d, An immediate payment of all their arrears of pay and clothing, both to those who should be discharged and those who should be retained. 3d, The residue of their bounty, to put them on an equal footing with those recently enlisted, and future substantial pay to those who should remain in the service.—To these demands, in their full extent, General Wayne could not feel himself authorized to answer in the affirmative, and a further negotiation was referred to the civil authority of the state of Pennsylvania. General Washington, whose head-quarters are at New Windsor, on the west side of the Hudson, received the intelligence on the 3d instant, and summoned a council of war, consisting of the general and field officers, to devise the most proper measures to be pursued on this alarming occasion. Great apprehension was entertained that other troops, who have equal cause of discontent, would be excited to adopt a similar course. It is ordered that five battalions be formed by detachments from the several lines, to be held in perfect readiness to march on the shortest notice, with four days' provision cooked; and measures, it is understood, are taken to bring the militia into immediate service, if required. Intelligence of the revolt having reached Sir Henry Clinton, he cherished the hope that, by encouraging a rebellion, and turning the swords of our own soldiers against their country and brethren, he should have it in his power to effect an object, which by his own arms he could not accomplish. He immediately despatched two emissaries— a British sergeant, and one Ogden, of New Jersey—to the dissatisfied troops, with written instructions that, by laying down their arms and marching to New York, they should receive their arrearages and depreciation in hard cash, and should be well clothed, have a free pardon for all past offences, and be taken under the protection of the British government, and no military service should be required of them, unless voluntarily offered. They were requested to send persons to meet agents, who would be appointed by Sir Henry, to adjust the terms of a treaty, and the British general himself passed over to Staten Island, having a large body of troops in readiness to act as circumstances might require. The proposals from the enemy were rejected with disdain, and the mutineers delivered the papers to General Wayne, but refused to give up the emissaries, preferring to keep them in durance till their difficulties could be discussed and settled. A committee of Congress was appointed, who conferred with the executive council of the state of Pennsylvania, and by the latter authority an accommodation of the affairs with the revolters has been effected, by giving an interpretation favorable to the soldiers of the enlistments which were for three years or during the war, declaring them to expire at the end of three years. The insurgents now surrendered the two emissaries into the hands of General Wayne, on the stipulated condition that they should not be executed till their affairs should be compromised; or, in case of failure, the prisoners should be redelivered when demanded. They were eventually, however, tried as spies, convicted, and immediately executed. A board of commissioners was now appointed, of whom three were deputed from the revolters, authorized to determine what description of soldiers should be discharged. The result is, that the soldiers have accomplished their views, the committee, from prudential motives, without waiting for the enlisting papers, complied with their demands, and discharged from service a majority of the line, on their making oath, that they enlisted for three years only. The enlisting rolls having since been produced, it is found that by far the largest number of those liberated, had actually enlisted for the whole war. Thus has terminated a most unfortunate transaction, which might have been prevented, had the just complaints of the army received proper attention in due season. General Wayne is a native of Pennsylvania, and has acquired the affection of the soldiery of that state. He possesses a commanding presence, genteel and pleasing address, a daring bravery, is excellent in discipline, aspiring and unrivalled in enterprise, and is held in high respect by his compatriots in arms.

A detachment, under the command of Lieutenant-Colonel Hull, has returned from a successful expedition, having attacked by surprise the royal refugee corps, under the command of the noted Colonel Delancy, posted at Morrisania. Colonel Hull has for several months past sustained the command of a detachment of our troops posted in advance of our army, a situation requiring the most active vigilance and precaution, to guard against surprise and stratagem. In this station, as in many others, this officer has evinced his military skill and judgment. He has executed an enterprise with such address and gallantry, as to merit for himself and his detachment the highest honor. He bravely forced a narrow passage to the enemy, and besides a number being killed, he took upwards of fifty prisoners, cut away the bridge, burned their huts and a considerable quantity of forage, and brought off a number of horses and cattle. Colonel Hull possesses in a high degree the confidence of the commander-in-chief, and for his judicious arrangements in the plan, and intrepidity and valor in the execution of the enterprise, he received the thanks of his excellency, and afterwards of Congress. The enemy pursued our troops, and fell in with a covering party, under command of Colonel Hazen, and in a skirmish which ensued, they suffered an additional loss of about thirty-five men. Of Colonel Hull's detachment, one ensign and twenty-five rank and file were killed and wounded. This successful exploit is calculated to raise the spirits of our troops, and to divert their minds from the unhappy occurrence which has recently taken place in camp, and at the same time it may convince the enemy that the affairs of our army are not altogether desperate.

MAJOR GENERAL ANTHONY WAYNE.

We are again afflicted with alarming intelligence. That part of the Jersey line of troops, which are cantoned at Pompton, in the state of New Jersey, have followed the example of the Pennsylvanians, having revolted, and abandoned their officers. General Washington is resolutely determined that this instance of mutiny shall not pass with impunity. Instead of temporizing, he has ordered a detachment of five hundred men, properly officered, to march for the purpose of reducing them to a proper sense of duty. It falls to my lot to accompany the detachment. Major-General Robert Howe commands on this expedition, and Lieutenant-Colonel Sprout is second in command, and the other field-officers are Lieutenant-Colonel Mellen and Major Oliver. We marched on the 23d as far as the forest of Dean, and at night crowded into houses and barns. A body of snow, about two feet deep, without any track, rendered the march extremely difficult. Having no horse, I experienced inexpressible fatigue, and was obliged several times to sit down on the snow. 24th, Marched over the mountains, and reached Carle's tavern, in Smith's Clove; halted for two hours, then proceeded thirteen miles, and quartered our men in the scattering houses and barns. 25th, Marched nine miles, and reached Ringwood. General Howe and all the field-officers took lodgings at the house of Mrs. Erskine, the amiable widow of the late respectable geographer of our army. We were entertained with an elegant supper and excellent wine. Mrs. Erskine is a sensible and accomplished woman, lives in a style of affluence and fashion; every thing indicates wealth, taste and splendor; and she takes pleasure in entertaining the friends of her late husband with generous hospitality.

Marched on the 27th, at one o'clock A. M. eight miles, which brought us in view of the huts of the insurgent soldiers by dawn of day. Here we halted for an hour, to make the necessary preparations. Some of our officers suffered much anxiety, lest the soldiers would not prove faithful on this trying occasion. Orders were given to load their arms: it was obeyed with alacrity, and indications were given that they were to be relied on. Being paraded in a line, General Howe harangued them, representing the heinousness of the crime of mutiny, and the absolute necessity of military subordination; adding that

17

the mutineers must be brought to an unconditional submission: no temporizing, no listening to terms of compro-
mise, while in a state of resistance. Two field-pieces were
now ordered to be placed in view of the insurgents, and
the troops were directed to surround the huts on all sides.
General Howe next ordered his aid-de-camp to command
the mutineers to appear on parade in front of their huts
unarmed, within five minutes; observing them to hesitate,
a second messenger was sent, and they instantly obeyed
the command, and paraded in a line without arms, being
in number between two and three hundred. Finding
themselves closely encircled and unable to resist, they
quietly submitted to the fate which awaited them. General Howe ordered that three of the ringleaders should be
selected as victims for condign punishment. These unfortunate culprits were tried on the spot, Colonel Sprout
being president of the court-martial, standing on the snow,
and they were sentenced to be immediately shot. Twelve
of the most guilty mutineers were next selected to be
their executioners. This was a most painful task; being
themselves guilty, they were greatly distressed with the
duty imposed on them, and when ordered to load, some
of them shed tears. The wretched victims, overwhelmed
by the terrors of death, had neither time nor power to
implore the mercy and forgiveness of their God, and such
was their agonizing condition, that no heart could refrain
from emotions of sympathy and compassion. The first
that suffered was a sergeant, and an old offender; he was
led a few yards' distance, and placed on his knees; six of
the executioners, at the signal given by an officer, fired,
three aiming at the head and three at the breast, the other
six reserving their fire in order to despatch the victim,
should the first fire fail; it so happened in this instance;
the remaining six then fired, and life was instantly extinguished. The second criminal was, by the first fire, sent
into eternity in an instant. The third being less criminal,
by the recommendation of his officers, to his unspeakable
joy, received a pardon. This tragical scene produced a
dreadful shock, and a salutary effect on the minds of the
guilty soldiers. Never were men more completely humbled and penitent; tears of sorrow and of joy rushed from
their eyes, and each one appeared to congratulate himself

that his forfeited life had been spared. The executions being finished, General Howe ordered the former officers to take their stations, and resume their respective commands; he then, in a very pathetic and affecting manner, addressed the whole line by platoons, endeavoring to impress their minds with a sense of the enormity of their crime, and the dreadful consequences that might have resulted. He then commanded them to ask pardon of their officers, and promise to devote themselves to the faithful discharge of their duty as soldiers in future. It is most painful to reflect that circumstances should imperiously demand the infliction of capital punishment on soldiers who have more than a shadow of plea to extenuate their crime. These unfortunate men have long suffered many serious grievances, which they have sustained with commendable patience; but have at length lost their confidence in public justice. The success of the Pennsylvania insurgents undoubtedly encouraged them to hope for exemption from punishment. But the very existence of an army depends on proper discipline and subordination. The arm of authority must be exerted, and public examples be exhibited, to deter from the commission of crimes. The spirit of revolt must be effectually repressed, or a total annihilation of the army is inevitable. Sir Henry Clinton on this occasion had his hopes again excited; ever ready to profit by treachery or revolt, he despatched an emissary to encourage the insurrection, and to make the most tempting offers to induce the mutineers to desert, and join the British standard; but the messenger himself frustrated his hopes by delivering the papers to our own officers.

Having completed the object of our expedition, we returned to our cantonments on the 31st instant.

February.—Major-General Greene has transmitted to Congress an account of a brilliant action of General Sumpter, of the southern army, a few weeks since. General Sumpter engaged with a body of three hundred cavalry, of Tarleton's legion, and about two hundred and fifty British infantry. The conflict was warm and close, in which the enemy were repulsed. They rallied, and on the second charge were repulsed again. They made a third effort, but a fire from an eminence, occupied by the continentals, gave them an effectual check; they quitted the field and retired, leaving ninety dead and one hundred wounded. Only three were killed and four wounded on the part of the Americans; among the latter is General Sumpter. A party of tories from the outposts of the British, advanced to intercept the wagons, and avail themselves of the supplies. General Smallwood despatched Brigadier-General Morgan and Lieutenant-Colonel Washington to attack them. Lieutenant-Colonel Washington, being destitute of artillery, made use of the following stratagem: He mounted on a carriage a pine log, cut into the form of a cannon, and holding out the appearance of an attack with field-pieces, gained his point by sending a flag, and demanding the immediate surrender of Colonel Rugely and his party, consisting of one hundred and twelve men, who, on the approach of Lieutenant-Colonel Washington, had retired to a log barn on Rugely's plantation. They surrendered without firing a gun.

10th.—Accounts have been received that an action has been fought at a place called the Cowpens, in Carolina, between a body of the enemy, under the celebrated Colonel Tarleton, with one thousand one hundred men, and a party of about eight hundred Americans, under the command of the equally celebrated General Morgan; the enemy were totally routed, and pursued upwards of twenty miles. Of Tarleton's party, ten officers and one hundred rank and file were killed, and two hundred wounded, twenty-nine officers and five hundred rank and file were taken prisoners, with two field-pieces, two standards, eight hundred muskets, thirty-five wagons, seventy negroes, one hundred dragoon horses, one travelling forge, and all their music. The loss on Morgan's side was not more than twelve killed and sixty wounded. Morgan and his party have acquired immortal honor, and in this action Lieutenant-Colonel Washington and Lieutenant-Colonel Howard were most highly distinguished for their brave and gallant conduct.

14th.—General Warner and Colonel Ashley, of Massachusetts, have arrived at West Point, to distribute to the soldiers of the Massachusetts line, engaged for a small bounty to serve during the war, twenty-four dollars in specie each, as a gratuity from the state. This very generous act serves to dissipate the gloom on the countenances of our brave soldiers; it enlivens their dejected spirits, and convinces them that they are yet the objects of a friendly recollection.

The advance-guard of our army, consisting of about two hundred men, is posted at Crompond, about twenty miles below West Point, and is relieved every two or three weeks. A surgeon constantly attends, and I am now ordered to repair to that post to relieve Dr. Thomas.

March.—I have taken my quarters at Crompond, in a house with Major Trescott, who commands at this post. This vicinity is constantly harassed by small parties of volunteers on our side, and parties of royalists and tories on the other, who are making every effort to effect mutual destruction; seeking every opportunity to beat up each others' quarters, and to kill or capture all who are found in arms. This is to be considered as a very hazardous situation; it requires the utmost vigilance to guard against a surprise. Major Trescott is an excellent disciplinarian, an active, vigilant officer, and well acquainted with his duty. A party of volunteers collected here on horseback, for a secret expedition, and by their earnest request Major Trescott marched in the night with a party to cover their retreat, and to take any advantage which might offer. The party returned the next day with six tory prisoners, three of whom were wounded by the broad-sword. One of our volunteers, named Hunt, received a dangerous wound through his shoulder and lungs, the air escaped from the wound at every breath. Dr. Eustis came to the lines, and dilated the wound in the breast, and as the patient is athletic and has not sustained a very copious loss of blood, he recommended repeated and liberal blood letting, observing that, in order to cure a wound through the lungs, you must bleed your patient to *death.*. He eventually recovered, which is to be ascribed principally to the free use of the lancet and such abstemious living as to reduce him to the greatest extremity. A considerable number of wounded prisoners receive my daily attention.

A gentleman volunteer, by name Requaw, received a dangerous wound, and was carried into the British lines; I was requested by his brother to visit him, under the sanction of a flag of truce, in company with Dr. White, who resides in this vicinity. This invitation I cheerfully

accepted, and Mr. Requaw having obtained a flag from
the proper authority, and procured horses, we set off in
the morning, arrived at West Chester before evening, and
dressed the wounded man. We passed the night at Mrs.
Barstow's, mother-in-law of Dr. W. She has remained
at her farm between the lines during the war, and being
friendly to our interest, has received much abusive treatment from the royalists. We are treated in the most
friendly manner, and her daughter, a sensible, well-educated girl, entertained us in conversation till one o'clock
in the morning, relating numerous occurrences and incidents of an interesting nature respecting the royal party.
The next day we visited our patient again, paid the necessary attention, and repaired to a tavern, where I was gratified with an interview with the much-famed Colonel
Delancy, who commands the refugee corps. He conducted
with much civility, and having a public dinner prepared
at the tavern, he invited us to dine with him and his
officers. After dinner, Colonel Delancy furnished us with
a permit to return with our flag; we rode ten miles, and
took lodgings in a private house. Here we were informed
that six of our men, having taken from the refugees thirty
head of cattle, were overtaken by forty of Delancy's corps,
and were all killed but one, and the cattle rētaken. In
the morning, breakfasted with a friendly Quaker family,
in whose house was one of our men, who had been wounded when four others were killed; we dressed his wounds,
which were numerous and dangerous. In another house,
we saw four dead bodies, mangled ·in a most inhuman
manner by the refugees, and among them one groaning
under five wounds on his head, two of them quite through
his skull-bone with a broad sword. · This man was capable
of giving us an account of the murderer of his four companions. They surrendered, and begged for life; but their
entreaties were disregarded, and the swords of their cruel
foes were plunged into their bodies so long as signs of life
remained. We found many friends to our cause, who
reside on their farms between the lines of the two armies,
whose situation is truly deplorable, being continually exposed to the ravages of the tories, horse-thieves, and Cow-
boys, who rob and plunder them without mercy, and the
personal abuse and punishments which they inflict, is

almost incredible—the particulars of which have been already noticed, page 238.

On the 4th of this month, the grand confederation and perpetual union of the Thirteen American States, from New Hampshire to Georgia, inclusive, was signed and ratified by all the delegates in Congress. This instrument has long been a subject of discussion and consideration by the several states, and by some, considerable opposition has been maintained against it, which has impeded its ratification. It consists of thirteen articles, entitled "*Articles of Confederation and Perpetual Union between the Thirteen American States.*" By this instrument, each state retains its sovereignty, freedom and independence, and the states severally enter into a firm league of friendship with each other for their common defence, the security of their liberties, and their mutual and general welfare, &c., &c.

April.—I received orders to return to the highlands near West Point, to inoculate the troops with the small-pox. Dined with Colonel Scammel, on my route, with a number of gentlemen.

12*th.*—Crossed the Hudson, to the hospital at Robinson's house, and passed the night with Dr. Eustis; the next day accompanied him to Peekskill to visit the family of Colonel Laurence, who are under inoculation with the small-pox, thence to the quarters of Colonel Scammel and Dr. Findlay, returned to the hospital at night, and the next day crossed with Dr. Eustis to West Point, and dined at General Heath's quarters.

20*th.*—A soldier was hanged to-day for desertion, and another was pardoned under the gallows with a rope round his neck.

All the soldiers, with the women and children, who have not had the small-pox, are now under inoculation. Of our regiment, one hundred and eighty-seven were subjects of the disease. The old practice of previous preparation by a course of mercury and low diet, has not been adopted on this occasion; a single dose of jalap and calomel, or of the extract of butternut, *juglans cinerea*, is in general administered previous to the appearance of the symptoms. As to diet, we are so unfortunate as to be destitute of the necessary comfortable articles of food, and they subsist principally on their common rations of beef, bread and salt pork. A small quantity of rice, sugar, or molasses, and tea are procured for those who are dangerously sick. Some instances have occurred of putrid fever supervening, either at the first onset or at the approach of the secondary stage, and a few cases have terminated fatally. Many of our patients were improper subjects for the disease, but we were under the necessity of inoculating all, without exception, whatever might be their condition as to health. Of five hundred who have been inoculated, four only have died, but in other instances the proportion of deaths is much more considerable. The extract of butternut is made by boiling down the inner bark of the tree; the discovery of this article is highly important, and it may be considered as a valuable acquisition to our materia medica. The country people have for some time been in the practice of using it, and Dr. Rush, who was for a short period at the head of our hospital department, has recommended the employment of it among our patients, as a mild yet sufficiently active cathartic, and a valuable and economical substitute for jalap. It operates without creating heat or irritation, and is found to be efficacious in cases of dysentery and bilious complaints. As the butternut-tree abounds in our country, we may obtain at a very little expense a valuable domestic article of medicine. Though there is much reason to suppose that our own soil is prolific in remedies adapted to the diseases of our country, the butternut is the only cathartic deserving of confidence which we have yet discovered.

30th.—Dined at West Point with Dr. Thomas, and accompanied him to General Patterson's quarters: the general humorously apologized, that he could afford us nothing better than a miserable glass of whiskey grog. Passed the river to the hospital. Dr. Eustis being indisposed, he requested me to bleed him, and I passed the night at the Point.

Intelligence has reached us that Brigadier-General Peleg Wadsworth, who commanded a detachment of militia at a place called Camden, in the province of Maine, has been surprised and taken prisoner, in the night, by a party of British soldiers, sent for this purpose from their post at Penobscot. It is added, that the general defended himself in the most daring and spirited manner till he received a wound, and was entirely overpowered. See particulars of this extraordinary affair in the Appendix.

I accompanied Dr. John Hart to New Windsor, to pay our respects to Dr. John Cochran, who is lately promoted to the office of director-general of the hospitals of the United States, as successor to Dr. Shippen, resigned. We dined with Dr. Cochran, in company with Drs. Eustis and S. Adams. Dr. Cochran, is a native of Pennsylvania. He served in the office of surgeon's-mate in the hospital department during the war between the English and French, which commenced in America in 1775, and left the service with the reputation of an able and experienced practitioner. From that time to this, he has devoted himself to his professional pursuits in New Jersey, and has been eminently distinguished as a practitioner in medicine and surgery. Finding his native country involved in a war with Great Britain, his zeal and attachment to her interest impelled him to the theatre of action, and he proffered his services as a volunteer in the hospital department. General Washington, justly appreciating his merit and character, recommended him to Congress, by whom he was in April, 1777, appointed physician and surgeon-general in the middle department He is now promoted to the office of director-general of the hospitals of the United States.* Dr James Craig, who now succeeds Dr. Cochran, as surgeon and physician-general, was also employed in the French war of 1759, with General Washington, who

* Not long after the close of the war, Dr. Cochran removed with his family to New York, where he attended to the duties of his profession, till the adoption of the new constitution, when his friend, President Washington, retaining, to use his own words, "a cheerful recollection of his past services," nominated him to the office of commissioner of loans for the state of New York. This office he held till a paralytic stroke disabled him in some measure from the discharge of its duties, on which he gave in his resignation, and retired to Palatine, in the county of Montgomery, where he terminated a long and useful life, on the 6th of April, 1807, in the 77th year of his age.

"He united a vigorous mind and correct judgment with information derived and improved from long experience, and faithful habits of attention to the duties of his profession." He possessed the pure and inflexible principles of patriotism, and his integrity was unimpeachable. It is gratifying to have this opportunity of expressing a respectful recollection of his urbanity and civilities, and of affording this small tribute to his cherished memory.

held the office of major, and when a mutual attachment was formed between them.

By intelligence from our army of the south, under command of Major-General Greene, affairs in that quarter are exceedingly unpropitious and discouraging. The troops are so destitute of clothing, that their footsteps are marked with blood for want of shoes; their food consists, part of the time, of rice, with frogs from ponds and ditches, and sometimes of peaches and berries. When they obtain a small supply of beef, it is so miserably poor as scarcely to be eatable. The army is continually harassed in marching through the country, sometimes executing successful and honorable exploits, and again compelled to retreat before a victorious enemy with hair-breadth escapes. Never perhaps were opposing commanders more equally matched than General Greene and Lord Cornwallis, though the former is almost constantly laboring under the disadvantage of inferiority of numbers and of physical force. General Greene communicates to Congress an account of a very obstinate and bloody battle fought by the two armies at Guilford court-house, North Carolina, a few weeks since. Our commander was compelled to yield to his adversary, but it is a victory purchased at a ruinous price. Seven days after the action, General Greene writes that Cornwallis' troops were too much galled to improve their success, that he had been preparing for another action, expecting the enemy to advance, but of a sudden they took their departure, and left behind them evident marks of distress. All the wounded at Guilford who had fallen into their hands, and seventy of their own, too ill to be moved, were left behind. Most of their officers suffered; Lord Cornwallis had his horse shot under him. Colonel Stuart, of the guards, was killed. General O'Hara and Colonels Tarleton and Webster wounded. Their whole loss is reported to be six hundred and sixty-three, exclusive of officers. General Greene returned three hundred and twenty-nine killed, wounded and missing; many of the latter went to their homes after the action. General Stevens and Huger were wounded.

A large detachment of British troops and refugees embarked at New York some time since, bound on an expedition to Virginia, under the command of the infamous traitor Arnold. He took possession of Portsmouth, on James river, where they are employed in ravaging and rifling the plantations, and destroying public and private property. Another body of royalists has lately been sent from New York, under Major-General Phillips, who, now having the chief command of the British in Virginia, united with Arnold in a predatory warfare. General Phillips died soon after, and Arnold again resumed the command. The Marquis de la Fayette, with a command of about one thousand five hundred light-infantry, detached from our main army, is on his march to Virginia, where he is to join a body of continentals and militia under Baron Steuben and General Muhlenburg, for the purpose of protecting that country from the depredations of the enemy.

The continental army in Carolina, were successful after the action of Guilford, and gained the ascendency in that quarter over the British. On the 10th of May, Lord Rawdon evacuated Camden with precipitation, leaving behind three of his officers and fifty privates, who had been dangerously wounded, and were unable to be removed. He burned the stores, baggage, &c., and left the town a heap of ruins. The next day the strong post of Orangeburg surrendered to General Sumpter. One colonel, several other officers, and eighty rank and file were made prisoners. Next followed, on the 12th, Fort Motte, the garrison consisting of nineteen officers and one hundred and sixty men, who surrendered to General Marion, as did also Fort Granby, on the 14th, to Lieutenant-Colonel Lee, when one lieutenant-colonel, two majors, six captains, six lieutenants, three ensigns, one surgeon, and three hundred and thirty-three rank and file, became his prisoners. Large quantities of provisions and some military stores were found in several of the forts, and in the baggage belonging to the nineteenth regiment were found seven hundred guineas, which it is said General Greene distributed among his troops, as a reward for their bravery and sufferings.

May.—The spirit of desertion appears to prevail to a considerable degree among both the British and Hessians at New York. Instances have been frequent for several months past of two or three coming out together. Some of them offer to engage in our service, but they are rejected and sent into the country, where they cannot effect any mischievous purpose. Deserters are always to be suspected, as they are not unfrequently employed as spies, who desert back again with intelligence for the enemy. Not long since, a Captain Simmons, of Delancy's corps, came over to our lines, and was sent up to West Point. He asserted that, being disaffected with the enemy on some pretences, he had resigned his commission and deserted from them; he was delivered over to the governor of the state. A few days since a groom belonging to an officer in the British service deserted with a valuable horse from his master, which he sold for one hundred dollars in specie.

A party of continental troops, commanded by Colonel Christopher Greene, of Rhode Island, being stationed on our lines, near Croton river, were surprised by a party of the enemy, about sunrise on the 13th instant. They first attacked Colonel Greene's and Major Flagg's quarters, and killed the major while in bed. The colonel being badly wounded in the house, was carried into the woods and barbarously murdered. Two subalterns and twenty-seven privates were also killed, and a lieutenant and surgeon, with about twenty men, taken prisoners. This melancholy event is most deeply regretted; Colonel Greene bravely distinguished himself in defence of Fort Mercer, at Red Bank, in October, 1777, and has ever been considered as a valiant and vigilant officer. He had taken post in a situation to guard a certain fording-place at Croton river, and had practised the greatest vigilance in the night time, calling off his guards at sunrise, on the idea that the enemy would not presume to cross in the day-time; but the enemy having learned his mode of performing duty, effected their purpose by crossing the ford immediately after the guard had been withdrawn, and the surprise was so complete that no practicable defence could avail them. It will not be denied that an enemy may be justified in availing himself of every opportunity of gaining an advantage over his antagonist, or that in some instances slaughter is unavoidable; but a wanton and unnecessary sacrifice of life is on all occasions to be deprecated as a disgraceful violation of the dictates of humanity.

General Washington has performed a journey to Connecticut, for the purpose of an interview with the Count de Rochambeau, chief commander of the French troops, now at Rhode Island. The object of this interview is supposed to be the concerting of a system of measures to be pursued by the allied army in the ensuing campaign.

Private intelligence from a confidential source we understand has been received at head-quarters, that a plan has been concerted in New York, to send out four parties —one to assassinate or take General Washington; another, Governor Livingston, of New Jersey; a third, Governor Clinton, of the state of New York; and the object of the fourth is unknown. Measures will undoubtedly be adopted to guard against and defeat this singular enterprise.

It has several times happened that an artful and enterprising fellow, by the name of Moody, employed by the British in New York, has succeeded in taking our mail from the post-rider on the road, though he has had some very remarkable escapes. After the interview of General Washington and Count Rochambeau, the British were particularly desirous of obtaining intelligence relative to the result. Accordingly Moody was again despatched to effect the object. Being perfectly well acquainted with the roads and passes, he waylaid the mail for some days in the Jerseys, till at length it was his good fortune to possess himself of that very mail which contained General Washington's despatches to Congress, communicating the information which was the object of their desires. This valuable prize he had the address to bear off to New York in safety.

June 20th.—It is directed in general orders that the whole army at this place march and encamp at Peekskill, leaving the invalids and a small party to garrison West Point. One of the three divisions of the army is to pass the Hudson each day, till all have crossed.

22d.—Our division of the army crossed the Hudson at West Point-landing yesterday, and reached Peekskill at night. We have left our cantonments in a woody mountain, affording a romantic and picturesque scenery of nature clothed in her wild and winter attire, having scarcely the appearance of vegetation. A splendid world is now open to our view, all nature is in animation—the fields and meadows display the beauties of spring, a pleasing variety of vegetables and flowers perfume the air, and the charming music of the feathered tribe delights our ears. But there is a contrast in music. What can compare with that martial band, the drum and fife, bugle-horn and shrill trumpet, which set the war-horse in motion, thrill through every fibre of the human frame, still the groans of the dying soldier, and stimulate the living to the noblest deeds of glory? The full roll of the drum, which salutes the commander-in-chief, the animating beat, which calls to arms for the battle, the reveille, which breaks our slumbers at dawn of day, with "come, strike your tents, and march away," and the evening tattoo, which commands to retirement and repose; these form incomparably the most enchanting music that has ever vibrated on my ear.

23d.—The army is now concentrated to a point in this place, and encamped in two lines, and in the same regular order that the troops usually form in a line of battle, occupying a very large extent of ground, and covering fields of corn, grain and meadows. Our brigade is stationed on the left of the second line. The campaign is now about to be opened, and we expect in a few days that the French army will form a junction with us to coöperate with our troops.

July 1st.—A division of our French allies are on their march from Rhode Island, to unite with us in the service of the campaign. Great preparations are continually making for some important operation, and it is in general conjectured that the object of the campaign is to besiege New York. We are ordered to have four days' provisions cooked, and to march at three o'clock in the morning, leaving all our baggage behind, except a single blanket to each man. It is remarkable that we have so much as four days' provisions on hand.

5th.—The reveille beat at three o'clock on the 2d instant, when we marched, and reached Tarrytown in the evening; the weather being extremely hot, the troops were much fatigued. Halted at Tarrytown about two hours, and then proceeded; marched all night, and at sunrise arrived within two miles of the enemy's works at King's-bridge. Having halted about two hours, a firing of cannon and musketry was heard in front, and we were informed that a party of our troops had engaged the enemy, and we were ordered to advance rapidly to their assistance; but before we could reach the scene of action, the enemy had retired within their strong works. A detachment of continental troops, under command of Major-General Lincoln, went down the North river in boats in the night, to attack the enemy by surprise, or to draw them out to a distance from their works, to afford an opportunity to the commander-in-chief to engage them in the field; but this object could not be accomplished, and a skirmish only ensued, in which both parties suffered some loss, and General Lincoln brought off ten prisoners. We took our repose for the night in the open field, and our tents and baggage having arrived the next day, we pitched our encampment in two lines, on the most advantageous ground, within a few miles of the outposts of the enemy. The French army, under General Rochambeau, have arrived and encamped at a small distance on the left of the Americans.

The French legion of dragoons and infantry, under command of the Duke de Luzerne, arrived, and took their station near our encampment, and appear in true military style; they are a fine looking corps, full of military ardor, and, in conjunction with Colonel Sheldon's dragoons, much important service is expected.

7th.—Our army was drawn up in a line, and reviewed by General Rochambeau, commander-in-chief of the French army, with his Excellency General Washington and other general officers.

10th.—Another review took place in presence of the French ambassador, from Philadelphia; after which, the French army passed a review in presence of the general officers of both armies.

13th.—Notwithstanding the active bustle which attends our present situation, I received an invitation, with a number of officers of our regiment, to dine with a party of French officers in their camp. We were politely received under an elegant marquee: our entertainment consisted of excellent soup, roast-beef, &c., served in French style. The gentlemen appear desirous of cultivating an acquaintance with our officers, but being ignorant of each others' language, we can enjoy but little conversation. The French army exhibit their martial array to the greatest advantage. In the officers we recognize the accomplished gentlemen, free and affable in their manners. Their

military dress and side-arms are elegant; the troops are
under the strictest discipline, and are amply provided with
arms and accoutrements, which are kept in the neatest
order; they are in complete uniform, coats of white broadcloth, trimmed with green, and white under-dress, and on
their heads they wear a singular kind of hat or chapeau.
It is unlike our cocked hats in having but two corners
instead of three, which gives them a very novel appearance. It has been remarked, to their honor, that during
their march from Newport to join our army, their course
has been marked with the most exemplary order and
regularity, committing no depredations, but conducting
towards the inhabitants on their route with great civility
and propriety. We now greet them as friends and allies,
and they manifest a zealous determination to act in unison
with us against the common enemy. This conduct must
have a happy tendency to eradicate from the minds of the
Americans their ancient prejudices against the French
people. They punctually paid their expenses in hard
money, which made them acceptable guests wherever they
passed; and, in fact, the large quantity of solid coin which
they brought into the United States, is to be considered as
of infinite importance at the present period of our affairs.

15th.—Two of the British frigates and several smaller
vessels passed up the North river as far as Tarrytown, in
defiance of our cannon, which were continually playing
on them. Their object appears to be, to seize some of our
small vessels which are passing down the river with supplies for our army. One small sloop, loaded with bread
for the French army, has fallen into their hands.

17th.—A fine corps of light-infantry, selected from the
several New England regiments, is now formed, and put
under the immediate command of Colonel Alexander
Scammel, formerly our adjutant-general. This select corps,
consisting of the most active and soldierly young men and
officers, is intended to march in advance of the main army,
constantly prepared for active and hazardous service.
Colonel Scammel was indulged the liberty of choosing
his own officers, rejecting those whom he deemed unfit
for his enterprising purpose. According to regular detail,
it fell to the lot of Dr. C. to act as surgeon to this corps;
but it was the doctor's misfortune to have one blink eye,

JOHN PAUL JONES.

and not being perfectly active, Colonel Scammel objected to him, and desired that he might be exchanged for one more competent to the duties of the service. In consequence of this, I received a billet from Dr. James Craig, chief physician and surgeon to the army, requesting me to repair to the detachment immediately, and take the place of Dr. C. Colonel Jackson, unwilling to have his regiment left destitute of a surgeon, strongly protested against it; but Colonel Scammel was strenuous, and finally prevailed, and I now enjoy the honor of officiating as surgeon to a fine corps of infantry, commanded by an officer of the first military reputation. Dr. Munson, of the Connecticut line, is my mate; and the medical duties of Colonel Jackson's regiment devolve on Dr. Francis le Baron Goodwin, surgeon's mate, during my absence.

19th.—The British frigates that passed up the North river a few days since, took the advantage of wind and tide to return to New York. A severe cannonade commenced from our battery at Dobbs' ferry, where the river is about three miles wide, and they were compelled to run the gauntlet. They returned the fire as they passed, but without effect. On board the Savage ship-of-war a box of powder took fire, and such was their consternation, that twenty people jumped into the river; among whom was a prisoner on board, who informs us that he was the only man who got on shore, all the others being drowned. He reports also that the Savage was several times hulled by our shot, and was very near sinking. In the evening of the 21st, our army and the French were put in motion, marching with great rapidity through a thick, unfrequented wood and swamps, and through fields of corn and wheat. Passing through a swamp in the night, our rear-guard, with myself and Dr. Munson, lost sight of the main body of the army for more than an hour, and I got a severe fall from my horse. In the morning, we arrived near the enemy's post at Morrissania, but they had taken the alarm, and escaped to New York. Having continued there during the day, we retired in the evening about five or six miles, and lay on the hills near King's-bridge, where we remained unmolested till the night of the 23d, when we returned to our encampment. While near the enemy's lines, the army was drawn up in a line of battle, and General Washington,

18

General Rochambeau, and all the general officers and engineers, were employed in reconnoitering the different positions of the enemy's works in all directions. The position which we now occupy is the neutral ground between the lines, a beautiful fertile country, and the roads and commons as well as the inclosures are loaded with grass, while the deserted houses in ruins, and the prostrate fences, exhibit the melancholy devastation of war.

31st.—Our detachment, under Colonel Scammel, marched last evening down to Phillips' house, near the enemy's works, on a foraging expedition. After our wagons were loaded, we retired into the woods, and lay in ambush, with the hope that the enemy would give us an opportunity to engage them, but they did not make their appearance.

August 13th.—A most tremendous storm of rain came on last night, and continued almost incessantly; about two o'clock in the morning, a sudden gust rent our tents asunder, and whirled them about our ears, leaving us destitute of shelter, and most thoroughly drenched.

15th.—A French soldier, who deserted, and was taken on his way to the enemy, was shot in the French camp.

General orders are now issued for the army to prepare for a movement at a moment's notice. The real object of the allied armies the present campaign has become a subject of much speculation. Ostensibly an investment of the city of New York is in contemplation—preparations in all quarters for some months past indicate this to be the object of our combined operations. The capture of this place would be a decisive stroke, and from the moment such event takes place, the English must renounce all hopes of subjugating the United States. But New York is well fortified both by land and water, and garrisoned by the best troops of Great Britain. The success of a siege must depend entirely on the arrival and coöperation of a superior French fleet. The enemy have a garrison on Staten Island, which is separated from Long Island only by a strait of two miles wide. The capture of this garrison would be a brilliant affair, and would essentially facilitate our operations against New York. General Washington and Count Rochambeau have crossed the North river, and it is supposed for the purpose of reconnoitering the enemy's posts from the Jersey shore. A field for an extensive encampment has been marked out on the Jersey side, and a number of ovens have been erected and fuel provided for the purpose of baking bread for the army. From these combined circumstances we are led to conclude that a part of our besieging force is to occupy that ground. But General Washington possesses a capacious mind, full of resources, and he resolves and matures his great plans and designs under an impenetrable veil of secrecy, and while we repose the fullest confidence in our chief, our own opinions must be founded only on doubtful conjectures. The royal army at New York, have received a reïnforcement of three thousand Germans from Europe.

20th.—According to orders, we commenced our line of march yesterday, a party of pioneers being sent forward to clear the road towards King's-bridge, and we expected immediately to follow in that direction; but an army is a machine, whose motions are directed by its chief. When the troops were paraded for the march, they were ordered to the right about, and, making a retrograde movement up the side of the North river, we have reached King's-ferry, and are preparing to cross the Hudson at this ferry. Our allies are in our rear, and it is probable we are destined to occupy the ground on the Jersey side.

31st.—Colonel Laurens has arrived at head-quarters on his way from Boston to Philadelphia. This gentleman is the son of Mr. Henry Laurens, our ambassador to Holland, who is now confined in the tower of London. We have the pleasing information that he has brought with him from France a large sum of specie for the United States. He reports that the different powers of continental Europe are friendly to the cause in which we are engaged.

Our situation reminds me of some theatrical exhibition, where the interest and expectations of the spectators are continually increasing, and where curiosity is wrought to the highest point. Our destination has been for some time matter of perplexing doubt and uncertainty; bets have run high on one side that we were to occupy the ground marked out on the Jersey shore, to aid in the siege of New York, and on the other, that we are stealing a march on the enemy, and are actually destined to Virginia, in pursuit of the army under Lord Cornwallis. We crossed at King's-ferry, 21st instant, and encamped at Haverstraw. A number of batteaux, mounted on carriages, have followed in our train, supposed for the purpose of conveying the troops over to Staten Island. 22d, Resumed our line of march, passing rapidly through Paramus, Acquackanack, Springfield and Princeton. We have now passed all the enemy's posts, and are pursuing our route with increased rapidity towards Philadelphia; wagons have been prepared to carry the soldiers' packs, that they may press forward with greater facility. Our destination can no longer be a secret. The British army, under Lord Cornwallis, is unquestionably the object of our present expedition. It is now rumored that a French fleet may soon be expected to arrive in Chesapeake bay, to cöoperate with the allied army in that quarter. The great secret respecting our late preparations and movements can now be explained. It was a judiciously concerted stratagem, calculated to menace and alarm Sir Henry Clinton for the safety of the garrison of New York, and induce him to recall a part of his troops from Virginia, for his own defence; or, perhaps, keeping an eye on the city, to attempt its capture, provided that by the arrival of a French fleet, favorable circumstances should present. The deception has proved completely successful; a part of Cornwallis' troops are reported to have returned to New York. His Excellency General Washington, having succeeded in a masterly piece of *generalship*, has now the satisfaction of leaving his adversary to ruminate on his own mortifying situation, and to anticipate the perilous fate which awaits his friend, Lord Cornwallis, in a different quarter. Major General Heath is left commander-in-chief of our army in the vicinity of New York and the highlands, and the menacing aspect of an attack on New York will be continued till time and circumstances shall remove the delusive veil from the eyes of Sir Henry Clinton, when it will probably be too late to afford succour to Lord Cornwallis. To our officers, the inactivity of the royal army in New York is truly unaccountable: they might, without risking a great deal, harass our army on its march, and subject us to irreparable injury; but the royalists are more dexterous in availing themselves of treachery and insurrection, than in effecting valorous achievements. In passing through Princeton, but little time was allowed me to visit the college. This once celebrated seminary is now destitute of students, and the business of education is entirely suspended in consequence of the constant bustle and vicissitudes of war. The little village of Princeton is beautifully situated, and the college edifice is of stone, four stories high, and lighted by twenty-five windows in front in each story. It has suffered considerable injury in being occupied alternately by the soldiers of the two contending armies. Trenton, where we are now encamped for the night, is a much more considerable village, and more advantageously situated, on the north-eastern bank of the Delaware, twenty-seven miles above Philadelphia. This is the town which General Washington has rendered famous to the latest times, by a victory in which he so happily displayed the resources of his genius, in the severe winter of 1776. Great indeed must be the resources of that man who can render himself the most formidable to an enemy, when apparently he is the most destitute of power. General Washington and Count Rochambeau having proceeded to Virginia by land, Major-General Lincoln takes the command of our troops, and the Baron de Viomenil those of the French.

September 8th.—We crossed the Delaware river at Trenton ferry on the 1st instant, and in the afternoon crossed a small river at Shammany's rope ferry. Our boats were pulled across with facility by a rope made fast at each shore. We marched nineteen miles, and encamped at a place called Lower Dublin. 2d, In the afternoon, marched through the city of Philadelphia. The streets being extremely dirty, and the weather warm and dry, we raised a dust like a smothering snow-storm, blinding our eyes and covering our bodies with it; this was not a little mortifying, as the ladies were viewing us from the open windows of every house as we passed through this splendid city. The scene must have been exceedingly interesting to the inhabitants; and, contemplating the noble cause in which we are engaged, they must have experienced in their hearts a glow of patriotism, if not emotions of military ardor. Our line of march, including appendages and attendants, extended nearly two miles. The general officers and their aids, in rich military uniform, mounted on

noble steeds elegantly caparisoned, were followed by their
servants and baggage. In the rear of every brigade were
several field-pieces, accompanied by ammunition carriages.
The soldiers marched in slow and solemn step, regulated
by the drum and fife. In the rear followed a great number of wagons, loaded with tents, provisions and other
baggage, such as a few soldiers' wives and children; though
a very small number of these are allowed to encumber us
on this occasion. The day following, the French troops
marched through the city, dressed in complete uniform
of white broadcloth, faced with green, and besides the
drum and fife, they were furnished with a complete band
of music, which operates like enchantment.*

* The following is extracted from letters published by a French clergyman, in Count Rochambeau's army:

"The arrival of the French army at Philadelphia was more like a
triumph, than simply passing through the place; the troops made a halt
about a quarter of a league from the city, and in an instant were dressed
as elegantly as ever the soldiers of a garrison were on a day of review;
they then marched through the town, with the military music playing
before them, which is always particularly pleasing to the Americans; the
streets were crowded with people, and the ladies appeared at the windows in their most brilliant attire. All Philadelphia was astonished to
see people who had endured the fatigues of a long journey, so ruddy and
handsome, and even wondered that there could possibly be *Frenchmen*
of so genteel an appearance.

"The troops next marched in single file before the Congress and M. le
Chevalier de la Luzerne, minister from the court of France, and afterwards encamped in a large plain contiguous to the river Schuylkill. The
next day after our arrival, the regiment of Soissonnais went through the
exercise of fire-arms; at least twenty thousand persons, and a vast number of carriages, remarkable for their lightness and elegance, added to
the lustre of this exhibition, which was still heightened by the pleasant-
ness of the situation and the remarkable serenity of the day. The rapidity of the military evolutions, the soldierly appearance of the troops
in general, and the exactness of their motions, surprised and enraptured
the beholders.

"We were a good deal amused with a mistake of some of the common
people, who took for a general one of those alert fellows whom our
commanding officers commonly have in their retinue to run up and down
to carry their written orders. His short, tight-bodied coat, his rich waistcoat, with a silver fringe, his rose-colored shoes, his cap, adorned with a
coat-of-arms, and his cane, with an enormous head—all appeared to them
so many tokens of extraordinary dignity. Though he approached his
master, the colonel-commandant, merely to receive and publish his
orders, they imagined that he gave them of his own accord, and directed
the movements of the troops, independently of any superior.

3*d.*—We crossed the river Schuylkill, over a floating bridge, and encamped four miles from Philadelphia, where we continued through the day, to give the men time to rest and wash their clothes. 4th, Marched through Wilmington, eighteen miles. This is a handsome, flourishing

"The President of Congress, the Honorable Thomas McKean, Esquire, in a suit of black velvet, honored this review with his presence. These honest Pennsylvanians differ very considerably from us in the ceremonies of dress, as we differ from them again in our modes of legislation.

"The manœuvres of our troops raised the most flattering expectations in the minds of the spectators; and they did not hesitate to declare that such soldiers were invincible.

"This day was destined for favorable omens. M. le Chevalier de la Luzerne, who on this occasion received his countrymen with the dignity and generosity of the representative of a great monarch, and the frankness and cordiality of an individual, after the review, invited all the officers to dine with him. Hardly were we seated at the table, when an express arrived; a disquieting silence immediately seized every guest —our eyes were fixed on the Chevalier de la Luzerne, every one endeavoring to guess what the message would turn out to be—'Thirty-six ships of the line,' said he, 'commanded by Monsieur le Comte de Grasse, are arrived in Chesapeake bay, and three thousand men have landed, and opened a communication with the Marquis de la Fayette.' Joy and good-humor immediately resumed their place on every countenance. Our impatient leaders began to count the days, and reckon how long it would be before they could have it in their power to face the enemy, and their heated imaginations made the time much shorter than it afterwards proved to be. Healths were next drank; and that of the minister of the marine of France was not forgotten, whose activity and great abilities have paved the way to the most brilliant successes of our fleet; the presence of his son, M. le Comte de Chartre, second colonel of the regiment of Saintonge, added still more to our pleasure and satisfaction.

"Among others, Charles Thomson, the Secretary of Congress, the soul of that political body, came also to receive and present his compliments. His meagre figure, furrowed countenance, his hollow, sparkling eyes, his white strait hair, that did not hang quite so low as his ears, fixed our thorough attention, and filled us with surprise and admiration.

"The important news of the arrival of Count de Grasse was soon spread throughout the city, and echoes of joy were heard from every quarter; some merry fellows, mounted on scaffolds and stages, pronounced funeral orations for Cornwallis, and uttered lamentations on the grief and distress of the tories. The people ran in crowds to the residence of the minister of France; and '*Long live Louis the Sixteenth !*' was the general cry.

"Thus you see the people are universally persuaded of the success of this expedition. Could these flattering hopes be realized, they would hasten a peace, which in our situation, and under the wise and benevolent prince that governs us, would place France in a point of view that has been wholly unknown since the existence of her monarchy."

village, situated on the Delaware river, on a small branch of which is erected eight very large and valuable stone mills, where an immense quantity of wheat is ground and bolted. The wheat is brought in vessels to the very door, and the flour taken off in return. The Rev. Mr. Smith, minister of this place, and Dr. Smith, his brother, politely introduced themselves to me, and I took tea and spent the evening at Dr. Smith's, in social friendship. Marched again on the 5th, and on the 6th arrived at the head of Elk river, Maryland, in the morning, having completed a march of two hundred miles in fifteen days.

An express has now arrived from Virginia, with the pleasing intelligence that Count de Grasse has actually arrived at the mouth of the Chesapeake bay, with a fleet of thirty-six ships of the line, and three thousand land forces, which are landed, and have joined our troops under the Marquis de la Fayette, in Virginia.

The royal army, under Lord Cornwallis, has taken post in Yorktown, situated on York river, in Virginia, where he has constructed strong fortifications for his defence; but his communication by water is now entirely cut off by several French ships stationed at the mouth of the river. Preparation is constantly making for our troops and our allies who have arrived here, to embark at the head of Elk river, whence we shall proceed down the Chesapeake bay to Yorktown, in pursuit of the object of our expedition. About eighty vessels are in readiness, great activity prevails, embarkation has commenced, and our horses are sent round to Virginia by land. It falls to my lot to take passage on board a small schooner, with four other officers and sixty men. She is so deeply laden with cannon, mortars and other ordnance, that our situation will be attended with considerable danger, if rough weather should overtake us.

11th.—Sailed at four o'clock P.M. on board the schooner Glasco, beat against contrary wind down the Elk river, and at sun-rise next morning entered the head of the great Chesapeake bay, eighteen miles from the place of embarkation. The bay at its entrance is six or seven miles wide, and has two rivers which empty into it on the west side— the North-east river and the great Susquehanna, which takes its origin at Lake Otsego, six hundred miles from this bay. Another river, called Sassafras, which empties into the bay on the east side, is navigable to Georgetown, twelve miles. Pool's Island affords a romantic prospect, being about two miles long, and three-quarters of a mile wide, supporting two families. About twelve miles further down, the bay widens to about ten miles, and on the west side is the river Patapsco; at the head of which, twelve miles from its mouth, stands the town of Baltimore, which admits large ships into its capacious and convenient harbor. Nearly opposite to this, Chester river empties into the bay on the eastern shore, and is navigable fifty miles.

The town of Annapolis, the metropolis of Maryland, is situated on the western shore at the mouth of the river Severn, where it falls into the bay. We came to anchor in the harbor at sun-setting, and I accompanied several officers to the coffee-house, and partook of a handsome supper. A very severe shower of rain, with high winds and extreme darkness, obliged us to spend the night on shore. On the 13th, we returned on board at seven o'clock, and proceeded on our voyage before a fresh gale, but had not sailed more than four miles, when we were recalled by express to the harbor of Annapolis. This is in consequence of intelligence of a naval action between the British and French fleets near the mouth of the Chesapeake bay. Our safety requires that we should remain in port till the event of the battle is known. Should the British have obtained the victory, and should they get possession of the Chesapeake bay, we shall be unable to proceed on our voyage, and our expedition will be entirely defeated. Annapolis is a very inconsiderable city, but the buildings are chiefly of brick, and many of them are in a style of elegance and grandeur. The state-house, in the centre of the city, is a most splendid and magnificent piece of architecture; it is topped with a handsome dome; the several apartments are finished in a style surpassing every thing which I have before witnessed. The archives for the security of the public records are fire-proof. It is remarkable that there is not a church in the city, though they have an ordinary building which they occupy for a theatre. We were treated with much politeness and hospitality, and received an invitation to dine at the house of a respectable gentleman. In the evening we attended the theatre, and were entertained by a Mr. Wall, who exhibited Stephens' Lecture on Heads, greatly to the amusement of the audience; after which, Mrs. Wall exhibited a variety of amusing scenes, and her little daughter, of seven years of age, spoke an epilogue, and sung several songs to the admiration of all present.

Information has just reached us that after General Arnold had returned from his depredating expedition to Virginia, he was despatched on a new incursion to Connecticut, his native state. His force consisted of two thousand infantry and three hundred cavalry, accompanied by forty sail of ships and transports. He landed his troops at the mouth of New London harbor, and proceeded to the town. Fort Trumbull not being tenable, was soon evacuated by our people, but Fort Griswold on the other side of the river was courageously defended by Colonel Ledyard and a few militia-men hastily collected. The assault on this fort was made by Colonel Eyre, who was three or four times repulsed, and finally received himself a mortal wound; and Major Montgomery being killed, the command devolved on Major Bromfield, who, by a superior force and much resolution, carried the place at the point of the bayonet. On entering the fort, the British officer inquiring who commanded, Colonel Ledyard answered, "I did, sir, but you do now," and presented him his sword as a prisoner, when the British officer plunged his sword into the body of Colonel Ledyard, and several soldiers assisted with their bayonets in despatching him. An indiscriminate slaughter by the bayonet of those who had surrendered immediately ensued, and seventy-three men were left dead in the fort, about forty wounded, and the same number taken prisoners. Arnold continued on the New London side, suffering the town to be plundered; and by a conflagration, sixty dwelling-houses and eighty-four stores were entirely destroyed. The loss which we sustained was very considerable, consisting of vessels, naval-stores, European goods, provisions, &c., and not less than one hundred inhabitants were deprived of their habitations and all their property. The militia collected, and conducted with great spirit and alacrity in avenging the murder of their friends, and they hastened the retreat of the enemy, after the loss of two officers and forty-six rank and file killed, and eight officers and one hundred and thirty-five rank and file wounded. It is reported that a wagon, loaded with their wounded soldiers, was put in motion from the top of a long and steep ·hill, which in its rapid course struck an apple-tree with such force that the faint and bleeding men received a shock which killed a part of them instantly. It is highly probable that Sir Henry Clinton projected this expedition to Connecticut, in the hope of diverting General Washington from his enterprise against Earl Cornwallis; but this manœuvre will not effect his object.

15th.—The gratifying intelligence is announced that the naval engagement between the two fleets has resulted in the defeat of the British with considerable loss, and the French have now the sole command of the Chesapeake bay. This event is of infinite importance, and fills our hearts with joy, as we can now proceed on our expedition.

16th.—We obeyed the signal for sailing, and passed Sharp's island, which is situated in the middle of the bay, two miles long and one wide; it supports four families. Sent one boat on shore, and procured some poultry and fruit. 18th, Passed the great Potomac, which divides the states of Maryland and Virginia. At its mouth it is about fifteen miles wide; it is navigable for large ships, up to Georgetown, which is one hundred and seventy miles distant, on the Maryland shore, while the city of Alexandria is situated a few miles below it on the Virginia shore. The bay at this place is about thirty miles wide. The wind this afternoon has blown with all the violence of a gale; the bow of our vessel, in ploughing through the billows, is frequently brought under water, which keeps us in perpetual alarm. We passed York river on the western or Virginia shore, fifteen miles from the mouth of which stands Yorktown, where the royal army under Lord Cornwallis is posted, and which it is the object of our expedition to capture. He is completely blockaded by three French ships of the line and several smaller armed vessels lying at the mouth of York river. 20th, Passed Hampton road, and entered James river, which is at its entrance about five miles wide. We enjoyed a distant view of the grand French fleet, riding at anchor at the mouth of the Chesapeake, consisting of thirty-six ships of war, besides

frigates and other armed vessels. This was the most noble
and majestic spectacle I ever witnessed, and we viewed it
with inexpressible pleasure, and the warmest gratitude was
excited in every breast towards our great ally.

22*d*.—Reached the harbor between Jamestown and
Williamsburg, where the greater part of our transports
arrived in the course of the day, and the troops disembarked and encamped on the banks of the river, within
twelve miles of Yorktown. We now congratulated ourselves on having completed our voyage of three hundred
and fifty miles, which, on account of contrary winds and
detention at Annapolis, has occupied twelve days; vessels
with troops are arriving every day. Jamestown is the
place where the English first established themselves in
Virginia, in 1607. Though the most ancient settlement in
America, it cannot now be called a town, there being but
two houses standing on the banks of the river. 25th,
Marched from the landing-place through the city of Williamsburg. This is the capital of Virginia, but in other
respects is of little importance. It is situated on a level
piece of land, at an equal distance between two small
rivers, one of which falls into York, the other into James
river. The city is one mile and a quarter in length, and
contains about two hundred and fifty houses. The main
street is more than one hundred feet in width, and exactly
one mile in length: at one of the extremities, and fronting
the street, is the capitol, or state-house, a handsome edifice,
and at the other end is the college, capable of accommodating three hundred students, but the tumult of war has
broken up the institution. The college is about one hundred and thirty feet in length and forty in breadth, with
two handsome wings, fifty by thirty. Their library is
said to consist of about three thousand volumes. Near
the centre of the city is a large church, and not far from
it the palace, the usual residence of the governor, which
is a splendid building. The water in this vicinity is extremely brackish and disagreeable. This part of the state
of Virginia is celebrated for the excellent tobacco which it
produces, and this is their principal staple commodity,
though the culture of cotton receives some attention. In
dian corn, hemp and flax, are also among the productions
of this state. The population of Virginia is computed at

one hundred and fifty thousand whites, and five hundred thousand blacks. Manual labor, therefore, is performed almost entirely by the latter class, leaving the whites little else to do but to oversee their large estates and to cultivate their minds. This may be one of the principal reasons why it produces so many celebrated statesmen ; as it will be readily admitted that our country · has very few that will equal her Washington's, Patrick Henry's, Randolph's, and many others of the same school.

27th.—We arrived at Yorktown yesterday from Jamestown, and have encamped within one mile of the enemy's line of redoubts.

28th.—The French troops have arrived and encamped on our left. Yorktown is situated on the south bank of the river, about fifteen miles from its entrance into Chesapeake bay. In this little village, Lord Cornwallis, with about seven thousand troops, has taken his station, and is endeavoring to fortify himself against the impending danger of our combined operations. His communication by water is entirely cut off by the French ships of war stationed at the mouth of the river, preventing both his escape and receiving succor from Sir Henry Clinton at New York. The allied army is about twelve thousand strong, exclusive of the militia, under Governor Nelson. The Americans form the right, and the French the left wing of the combined forces, each extending to the borders of the river, by which the besiegers form a half-circle round the town. His Excellency General Washington commands in person, and is assisted by Major-General Lincoln, Baron Steuben, the Marquis de la Fayette, General Knox, &c. The French troops are commanded by General the Count Rochambeau, a brave and experienced officer, having under him a number of officers of distinguished character. Unbounded confidence is reposed in our illustrious commanders, the spirit of emulation and military ardor universally prevails, and we are sanguine in our expectations that a surrender of the royal army must be his lordship's fate.

A cannonade commenced yesterday from the town, by which one man was wounded, and I assisted in amputating his leg. 30th. We were agreeably surprised this morning, to find that the enemy had, during the preceding night, abandoned three or four of their redoubts, and retired within the town, leaving a considerable extent of commanding ground, which might have cost us much labor and many lives to obtain by force. Our light infantry and a party of French were ordered to advance and take possession of the abandoned ground, and to serve as a covering party to our troops who are employed in throwing up breastworks. Considerable cannonading from the besieged in the course of the day, and four militia-men were wounded by a single shot, one of whom died soon after. An occurrence has just been announced which fills our hearts with grief and sorrow. Colonel Alexander Scammel being officer of the day, while reconnoitering the ground which the enemy had abandoned, was surprised by a party of their horse, and after having surrendered, they had the baseness to inflict a wound which we fear will prove mortal; they have carried him into Yorktown.

October 1st and 2d.—Our troops have been engaged in throwing up two redoubts in the night time; on discovery, the enemy commenced a furious cannonade, but it does not deter our men from going on vigorously with their work. Heavy cannon and mortars are continually arriving, and the greatest preparations are made to prosecute the siege in the most effectual manner.

3d and 4th.—A considerable cannonading from the enemy; one shot killed three men, and mortally wounded another. While the Rev. Mr. Evans, our chaplain, was standing near the commander-in-chief, a shot struck the ground so near as to cover his hat with sand. Being much agitated, he took off his hat, and said, "See here, general." "Mr. Evans," replied his excellency, with his usual composure, "you had better carry that home, and show it to your wife and children." Two soldiers from the French, and one from us, deserted to the enemy, and two British soldiers deserted to our camp the same night. The enemy from the want of forage are killing off their horses in great numbers; six or seven hundred of these valuable animals have been killed, and their carcases are almost continually floating down the river. The British are in possession of a place called Gloucester, on the north side of the river, nearly opposite Yorktown; their force consists of one British regiment, and Colonel Tarleton's legion of horse and infantry. In opposition to this force the French legion, under the command of the Duke de Luzerne, and a detachment of French infantry and militia, are posted in that vicinity. Tarleton is a bold and impetuous leader, and has spread terror through the Carolinas and Virginia for some time past. In making a sally from Gloucester yesterday, they were attacked by the French, and defeated with the loss of the commanding officer of their infantry, and about fifty men killed and wounded; among the latter is Tarleton himself. The duke lost three men killed, and two officers and eleven men wounded. It is with much concern we learn that Colonel Scammel died at Williamsburg, of the wound which he received a few days since, when he was taken prisoner; the wound was inflicted after he had surrendered. At the request of General Washington, Lord Cornwallis allowed him to be carried to Williamsburg, where he died this day, universally lamented, as he was while living universally respected and esteemed. The commander-in-chief was well apprised of his merit, and bestowed on him marks of his friendly regard and confidence. For some time he sustained the office of adjutant-general to our army, but preferring a more active command and the post of danger, he was put at the head of a regiment of light-infantry for this enterprising campaign. The British have sent from Yorktown a large number of negroes, sick with the small-pox, probably for the purpose of communicating the infection to our army. Thus our inhuman enemies resort to every method in their power, however, barbarous or cruel, to injure and distress, and thus to gain an advantage over their opposers.

7th.—A large detachment of the allied army, under command of Major-General Lincoln, were ordered out last evening for the purpose of opening intrenchments near the enemy's lines. This business was conducted with great silence and secrecy, and we were favored by Providence with a night of extreme darkness, and were not discovered before day-light. The working party carried on their shoulders fascines and intrenching tools, while a large part of the detachment was armed with the implements of death. Horses, drawing cannon and ordnance, and wagons loaded with bags filled with sand for constructing breastworks,

followed in the rear. Thus arranged, every officer and
soldier knowing his particular station, orders were given
to advance in perfect silence, the distance about one mile.
My station on this occasion was with Dr. Munson, my
mate, in the rear of the troops; and as the music was not
to be employed, about twenty drummers and fifers were
put under my charge to assist me in case of having
wounded men to attend. I put into the hands of a drum-
mer, a mulatto fellow, my instruments, bandages, &c., with
a positive order to keep at my elbow, and not lose sight
of me a moment; it was not long, however, before I found
to my astonishment that he had left me, and gone in pursuit of some rum, carrying off the articles which are indispensable in time of action. In this very unpleasant
predicament, unwilling to trust another, I hastened with
all speed to the hospital, about one mile, to procure another
supply from Dr. Craik; and he desired that if the Marquis
de la Fayette should be wounded, I would devote to him
my first attention. On my return I found Dr. Munson
and my party waiting, but the troops had marched on and
we knew not their route. We were obliged to follow at
random, and in the darkness of night, hazarding our approach to the enemy. Having advanced about half a mile,
of a sudden a party of armed men in white uniform rose
from the ground, and ordered us to stop; they proved to
be the rear-guard of the French. The officer demanded
the countersign, which I was unable to give, and as we
could not understand each others' language, I was detained
under considerable embarrassment till an officer who could
speak English was called, when producing my instruments
and bandages, and assuring the French officer that I was
surgeon to the infantry, he politely conducted me to my
station. Our troops were indefatigable in their labors
during the night, and before day-light they had nearly
completed the first parallel line of nearly two miles in
extent, besides laying a foundation for two redoubts, within
about six hundred yards of the enemy's lines. At day-light
the enemy, having discovered our works, commenced a severe cannonade, but our men being under cover, received
no injury. A French soldier deserted to the enemy; after
which, there was a constant firing against the French lines,
and one officer was killed, and fifteen men were killed or

BURNING OF BRITISH VESSELS.

wounded. In the latter part of the night it rained severely, and being in the open field, cold and uncomfortable, I entered a small hut made of brush, which the enemy had abandoned. Soon after, a man came to the door, and, seeing me standing in the centre, instantly drew his sword, and put himself in an attitude to plunge it into me. I called out *friend, friend,* and he as speedily, to my great joy, responded, "Ah, Monsieur, *friend,*" and returning his sword to its place, he departed. I think he was a French soldier, and it is doubtful whether he or myself was the most frightened.

8th and 9th.—The duty of our troops has been for several days extremely severe: our regiment labors in the trenches every other day and night, where I find it difficult to avoid suffering by the cold, having no other covering than a single blanket in the open field. We erected a battery last night in front of our first parallel, without any annoyance from the enemy. Two or three of our batteries being now prepared to open on the town, his Excellency General Washington put the match to the first gun, and a furious discharge of cannon and mortars immediately followed, and Earl Cornwallis has received his first salutation.

From the 10th to the 15th, a tremendous and incessant firing from the American and French batteries is kept up, and the enemy return the fire, but with little effect. A red-hot shell from the French battery set fire to the Charon, a British 44-gun ship, and two or three smaller vessels at anchor in the river, which were consumed in the night. From the bank of the river, I had a fine view of this splendid conflagration. The ships were enwrapped in a torrent of fire, which spreading with vivid brightness among the combustible rigging, and running with amazing rapidity to the tops of the several masts, while all around was thunder and lightning from our numerous cannon and mortars, and in the darkness of night, presented one of the most sublime and magnificent spectacles which can be imagined. Some of our shells, overreaching the town, are seen to fall into the river, and bursting, throw up columns of water like the spouting of the monsters of the deep. We have now made further approaches to the town, by throwing up a second parallel line, and batteries within

19

about three hundred yards; this was effected in the night, and at day-light the enemy were roused to the greatest exertions; the engines of war have raged with redoubled fury and destruction on both sides, no cessation day or night. The French had two officers wounded, and fifteen men killed or wounded, and among the Americans, two or three were wounded. I assisted in amputating a man's thigh. The siege is daily becoming more and more formidable and alarming, and his lordship must view his situation as extremely critical, if not desperate. Being in the trenches every other night and day, I have a fine opportunity of witnessing the sublime and stupendous scene which is continually exhibiting. The bomb-shells from the besiegers and the besieged are incessantly crossing each others' path in the air. They are clearly visible in the form of a black ball in the day, but in the night, they appear like a fiery meteor with a blazing tail, most beautifully brilliant, ascending majestically from the mortar to a certain altitude, and gradually descending to the spot where they are destined to execute their work of destruction. It is astonishing with what accuracy an experienced gunner will make his calculations, that a shell shall fall within a few feet of a given point, and burst at the precise time, though at a great distance. When a shell falls, it whirls round, burrows, and excavates the earth to a considerable extent, and bursting, makes dreadful havoc around. I have more than once witnessed fragments of the mangled bodies and limbs of the British soldiers thrown into the air by the bursting of our shells; and by one from the enemy, Captain White, of the seventh Massachusetts regiment, and one soldier were killed, and another wounded near where I was standing. About twelve or fourteen men have been killed or wounded within twenty-four hours; I attended at the hospital, amputated a man's arm, and assisted in dressing a number of wounds. The enemy having two redoubts, about three hundred yards in front of their principal works, which enfiladed our intrenchment and impeded our approaches, it was resolved to take possession of them both by assault. The one on the left of the British garrison, bordering on the banks of the river, was assigned to our brigade of light-infantry, under the command of the Marquis de la Fayette. The advanced corps was led on by the intrepid Colonel Hamilton, who had commanded a regiment of light-infantry during the campaign, and assisted by Colonel Gimat. The assault commenced at eight o'clock in the evening, and the assailants bravely entered the fort with the point of the bayonet without firing a single gun. We suffered the loss of eight men killed, and about thirty wounded, among whom Colonel Gimat received a slight wound in his foot, and Major Gibbs, of his excellency's guard, and two other officers, were slightly wounded. Major Campbell, who commanded in the fort, was wounded and taken prisoner, with about thirty soldiers, the remainder made their escape I was desired to visit the wounded in the fort, even before the balls had ceased whistling about my ears, and saw a sergeant and eight men dead in the ditch. A captain of our infantry, belonging to New Hampshire, threatened to take the life of Major Campbell, to avenge the death of his favorite, Colonel Scammel; but Colonel Hamilton interposed, and not a man was killed after he ceased to resist. During the assault, the British kept up an incessant firing of cannon and musketry from their whole line. His Excellency General Washington, Generals Lincoln and Knox, with their aids, having dismounted, were standing in an exposed situation waiting the result. Colonel Cobb, one of General Washington's aids, solicitous for his safety, said to his excellency, "Sir, you are too much exposed here. Had you not better step a little back?" "Colonel Cobb," replied his excellency, "if you are afraid, you have liberty to step back." The other redoubt on the right of the British lines was assaulted at the same time by a detachment of the French, commanded by the gallant Baron de Viomenil. Such was the ardor displayed by the assailants, that all resistance was soon overcome, though at the expense of nearly one hundred men killed and wounded.* Of the defenders of the redoubt, eighteen

---

* The cause of the great loss sustained by the French troops in comparison with that of the Americans, in storming their respective redoubts, was that the American troops when they came to the abatis, removed a part of it with their hands and leaped over the remainder. The French troops on coming up to theirs, waited till their pioneers had cut away the abatis *secundum artem*, which exposed them longer to the galling fire of the enemy. To this cause also is to be ascribed the circumstance, that the redoubt assailed by the Americans, was carried before that at-

were killed, and one captain and two subaltern officers, and forty-two rank and file captured. Our second parallel line was immediately connected with the two redoubts now taken from the enemy, and some new batteries were thrown up in front of our second parallel line, with a covert way, and angling work approaching to less than three hundred yards of their principal forts. These will soon be mantled with cannon and mortars, and when their horrid thundering commences, it must convince his lordship that his post is not invincible, and that submission must soon be his only alternative. Our artillery-men, by the exactness of their aim, make every discharge take effect, so that many of the enemy's guns are entirely silenced, and their works are almost in ruins.

16*th*.—A party of the enemy, consisting of about four hundred men, commanded by Colonel Abercrombie, about four in the morning, made a vigorous sortie against two unfinished redoubts occupied by the French; they spiked up seven or eight pieces of cannon and killed several soldiers, but the French advanced and drove them from the redoubts, leaving several killed and wounded. Our New England troops have now become very sickly; the prevalent diseases are intermittent and remittent fevers, which are very prevalent in this climate during the autumnal months.

17*th*.—The whole of our works are now mounted with cannon and mortars; not less than one hundred pieces of heavy ordnance have been in continual operation during the last twenty-four hours. The whole peninsula trembles under the incessant thunderings of our infernal machines; we have leveled some of their works in ruins, and silenced their guns; they have almost ceased firing. We are so near as to have a distinct view of the dreadful havoc and destruction of their works, and even see the men in their lines tore to pieces by the bursting of our shells. But the scene is drawing to a close. Lord Cornwallis, at length realizing the extreme hazard of his deplorable situation,

tacked by the French troops. The Marquis de la Fayette sent his aid, Major Barbour, through the tremendous fire of the whole line of the British, to inform the Baron Viomenil, that "he was in his redoubt, and to ask the baron where he was." The major found the baron waiting the clearing away the abatis, but sent this answer: "Tell the marquis I am not in mine, but will be in five minutes." He instantly advanced, and was, or nearly so, within his time.

and finding it in vain any longer to resist, has this forenoon come to the humiliating expedient of sending out a
flag, requesting a cessation of hostilities for twenty-four
hours, that commissioners may be appointed to prepare
and adjust the terms of capitulation. Two or three flags
passed in the course of the day, and General Washington
consented to a cessation of hostilities for two hours only,
that his lordship may suggest his proposals as a basis for
a treaty, which being in part accepted, a suspension of
hostilities will be continued till to-morrow.

18th.—It is now ascertained that Lord Cornwallis, to
avoid the necessity of a surrender, had determined on the
bold attempt to make his escape in the night of the 16th,
with a part of his army into the country. His plan was
to leave sick and baggage behind, and to cross with his
effective force over to Gloucester Point, there to destroy
the French legion and other troops, and to mount his infantry on their horses and such others as might be procured, and thus push' their way to New York by land.
A more preposterous and desperate attempt can scarcely
be imagined. Boats were secretly prepared, arrangements
made, and a large proportion of his troops actually embarked and landed on Gloucester Point, when, from a moderate and calm evening, a most violent storm of wind and
rain ensued. The boats with the remaining troops were
all driven down the river, and it was not till the next day
that his troops could be returned to the garrison at York.
At an early hour this forenoon General Washington communicated to Lord Cornwallis the general basis of the
terms of capitulation, which he deemed admissible, and
allowed two hours for his reply. Commissioners were
soon after appointed to prepare the particular terms of
agreement. The gentlemen appointed by General Washington are Colonel Laurens, one of his aid-de-camps, and
Viscount Noaille of the French army. They have this
day held an interview with the two British officers on the
part of Lord Cornwallis, the terms of capitulation are settled, and being confirmed by the commanders of both
armies, the royal troops are to march out to-morrow and
surrender their arms. It is a circumstance deserving of
remark, that Colonel Laurens, who is stipulating for the
surrender of a British nobleman, at the head of a royal

army, is the son of Mr. Henry Laurens, our ambassador
to Holland, who, being captured on his voyage, is now in
close confinement in the tower of London.*

19*th.*—This is to us a most glorious day; but to the
English, one of bitter chagrin and disappointment. Preparations are now making to receive as captives that vindictive, haughty commander, and that victorious army,
who, by their robberies and murders, have so long been a
scourge to our brethren of the Southern states. Being on
horseback, I anticipate a full share of satisfaction in viewing the various movements in the interesting scene. The
stipulated terms of capitulation are similar to those granted
to General Lincoln at Charleston the last year. The captive troops are to march out with shouldered arms, colors
cased, and drums beating a British or German march, and
to ground their arms at a place assigned for the purpose.
The officers are allowed their side-arms and private property, and the generals and such officers as desire it are to
go on parole to England or New York. The marines and
seamen of the king's ships are prisoners of war to the navy
of France; and the land forces to the United States. All
military and artillery stores to be delivered up unimpaired.
The royal prisoners to be sent into the interior of Virginia,
Maryland and Pennsylvania in regiments, to have rations
allowed them equal to the American soldiers, and to have
their officers near them. Lord Cornwallis to man and
despatch the Bonetta sloop-of-war with despatches to Sir
Henry Clinton at New York without being searched, the
vessel to be returned and the hands accounted for. At
about twelve o'clock, the combined army was arranged
and drawn up in two lines extending more than a mile in

* Connected with this transaction there is a concurrence of circumstances so peculiarly remarkable, that I cannot omit to notice them in
this place. Mr. Henry Laurens, who was deputed by Congress as our
ambassador to Holland, was captured and carried into England, and
closely and most rigorously confined in the tower of London. Lord
Cornwallis sustains the office of constable to the tower; of course Mr.
Laurens is his prisoner. The son, Colonel John Laurens, stipulates the
conditions of the surrender of the constable, who becomes our prisoner,
while Mr. Laurens, the father, remains confined in the tower as a prisoner to the captured constable. Congress had proposed that Mr. Laurens
should be received in exchange for General Burgoyne, but the proposal
was rejected by the British government. After Cornwallis was captured, however, he was readily received in exchange for Mr. Laurens.

length. The Americans were drawn up in a line on the
right side of the road, and the French occupied the left.
At the head of the former, the great American commander,
mounted on his noble courser, took his station, attended
by his aids. At the head of the latter was posted the excellent Count Rochambeau and his suite. The French
troops, in complete uniform, displayed a martial and noble
appearance, their band of music, of which the timbrel
formed a part, is a delightful novelty, and produced while
marching to the ground a most enchanting effect. The
Americans, though not all in uniform, nor their dress so
neat, yet exhibited an erect, soldierly air, and every countenance beamed with satisfaction and joy. The concourse
of spectators from the country was prodigious, in point
of numbers was probably equal to the military, but universal silence and order prevailed. It was about two
o'clock when the captive army advanced through the
line formed for their reception. Every eye was prepared
to gaze on Lord Cornwallis, the object of peculiar interest
and solicitude; but he disappointed our anxious expectations; pretending indisposition, he made General O'Hara
his substitute as the leader of his army. This officer was
followed by the conquered troops in a slow and solemn
step, with shouldered arms, colors cased, and drums beating a British march. Having arrived at the head of the
line, General O'Hara, elegantly mounted, advanced to
his excellency the commander-in-chief, taking off his hat,
and apologized for the non-appearance of Earl Cornwallis.
With his usual dignity and politeness, his excellency
pointed to Major-General Lincoln for directions, by whom
the British army was conducted into a spacious field, where
it was intended they should ground their arms. The
royal troops, while marching through the line formed by
the allied army, exhibited a decent and neat appearance,
as respects arms and clothing, for their commander opened
his store, and directed every soldier to be furnished with
a new suit complete, prior to the capitulation. But in
their line of march we remarked a disorderly and unsol-
dierly conduct, their step was irregular, and their ranks
frequently broken. But it was in the field, when they
came to the last act of the drama, that the spirit and pride
of the British soldier was but to the severest test: here

their mortification could not be concealed. Some of the platoon officers appeared to be exceedingly chagrined when giving the word "*ground arms*," and I am a witness that they performed this duty in a very unofficer-like manner; and that many of the soldiers manifested a *sullen temper*, throwing their arms on the pile with violence, as if determined to render them useless. This irregularity, however, was checked by the authority of General Lincoln. After having grounded their arms and divested themselves of their accoutrements, the captive troops were conducted back to Yorktown, and guarded by our troops till they could be removed to the place of their destination. The British troops that were stationed at Gloucester, surrendered at the same time and in the same manner, to the command of the Duke de Luzerne. This must be a very interesting and gratifying transaction to General Lincoln, who, having himself been obliged to surrender an army to a haughty foe the last year, has now assigned him the pleasing duty of giving laws to a conquered army in return, and of reflecting that the terms which were imposed on him are adopted as a basis of the surrender in the present instance. It is a very gratifying circumstance that every degree of harmony, confidence and friendly intercourse subsisted between the American and French troops during the campaign—no contest, except an emulous spirit to excel in exploits and enterprise against the common enemy, and a desire to be celebrated in the annals of history for an ardent love of great and heroic actions. We are not to be surprised that the pride of the British officers is humbled on this occasion, as they have always entertained an exalted opinion of their own military prowess, and affected to view the Americans as a contemptible, undisciplined rabble. But there is no display of magnanimity when a great commander shrinks from the inevitable misfortunes of war; and when it is considered that Lord Cornwallis has frequently appeared in splendid triumph at the head of his army, by which he is almost *adored*, we conceive it incumbent on him cheerfully to participate in their misfortunes and degradations, however humiliating; but it is said he gives himself up entirely to vexation and despair.

20*th*.—In the general orders of this day our commander-

THADDEUS KOSCIUSKO.

in-chief expresses his entire approbation, and his warmest thanks to the French and American officers and soldiers of all descriptions, for the brave and honorable part which they have acted during the siege. He congratulates the combined army on the momentous event which closes the campaign, and which crowns their heads with unfading laurels, and entitles them to the applause and gratitude of their country. Among the general officers whom his excellency particularly noticed, for the important services which they rendered during the siege, are Generals Lincoln, De la Fayette, Steuben, Knox, and Du Portail, his Excellency Count Rochambeau, and several other distinguished French officers. To Governor Nelson, of Virginia, he returned his grateful and sincere acknowledgments for the essential succors afforded by him and the militia under his command. The commander-in-chief, wishing that every heart should participate in the joy of this memorable day, ordered that all those who are under arrest or confinement should be immediately pardoned and set at liberty, a circumstance which I believe has never before occurred in our army. He closed by ordering that divine service shall be performed in the several brigades to-morrow, and recommends that the troops attend with a serious deportment, and with that sensibility of heart which the recollection of the surprising and particular interposition of Providence in our favor claims.

22*d*.—Yesterday being Sunday, our brigade of infantry and the York brigade were drawn up in the field to attend divine service, performed by Mr. Evans. After offering to the Lord of hosts, the God of battles, our grateful homage for the preservation of our lives through the dangers of the siege, and for the important event with which Divine Providence has seen fit to crown our efforts, he preached an excellent and appropriate sermon. Generals Lincoln and Clinton were present. In the design and execution of this successful expedition, our commander-in-chief fairly *out-generaled* Sir Henry Clinton, and the whole movement was marked by consummate military address, which reduced the royal general to a mortifying dilemma that no skill or enterprise could retrieve. A siege of thirteen days, prosecuted with unexampled rapidity, has terminated in the capture of one of the greatest generals of which the

English can boast, and a veteran and victorious army which has for several months past spread terror and desolation throughout the Southern states. The joy on this momentous occasion is universally diffused, and the hope entertained that it will arrest the career of a cruel warfare, and advance the establishment of American Independence. In the progress of the royal army through the state of Virginia the preceding summer, they practised the most abominable enormities, plundering negroes and horses from almost every plantation, and reducing the country to ruin. Among the prodigious assemblage of spectators at the time of surrender, were a number of planters, searching for the property which had been thus purloined from their estates. The famous Colonel Tarleton, mounted on a horse remarkable for elegance and noble appearance, while riding in company with several French officers with whom he was to dine, was met by a gentleman, who instantly recognized the animal as his own property. Tarleton was stopped, and the horse peremptorily demanded; observing a little hesitation, the British General O'Harra, who was present, said, "You had better give him his horse, Tarleton;" on which the colonel dismounted, and delivered the horse to the original proprietor; after which, being remounted on a very miserable animal, he rejoined his company, and the French officers were greatly surprised that he should be so humbly mounted. The British prisoners were all sent off yesterday, conducted by a party of militia on their way to the interior of Virginia and Maryland. I have this day visited the town of York, to witness the destructive effects of the siege. It contains about sixty houses; some of them are elegant, many of them are greatly damaged and some totally ruined, being shot through in a thousand places and honey-combed ready to crumble to pieces. Rich furniture and books were scattered over the ground, and the carcases of men and horses half-covered with earth, exhibited a scene of ruin and horror beyond description. The earth in many places is thrown up into mounds by the force of our shells, and it is difficult to point to a spot where a man could have resorted for safety.

The loss on the part of the French during the siege was fifty killed and one hundred and twenty-seven wounded.

Americans twenty-seven killed and seventy-three wounded, officers included. Cornwallis' account of his loss during the siege is one hundred and fifty-six, three hundred and twenty-six wounded, and seventy missing, probably deserted, total five hundred and fifty-two. The whole number surrendered by capitulation, seven thousand two hundred and forty-seven.* The amount of artillery and military stores, provisions, &c., is very considerable, seventy-five brass and one hundred and sixty-nine iron cannon, seven thousand seven hundred ninety-four muskets; regimental standards, German eighteen, British ten. From the military chest we received two thousand one hundred and thirteen pounds six shillings sterling.

Lord Cornwallis is a very distinguished warrior; he possesses an exalted spirit, is brave and intrepid, and never was there a more zealous champion of his tyrannical master; austere and rigorous in his temper, nothing could be more foreign from his heart than the sympathies of benevolence or generous compassion. Had all the *rebels* in the states but one neck, his lordship would glory in nothing more than an opportunity of *severing* the *jugular vein*. But Cornwallis has fallen! and our country is not subjugated.†

It is proper I should take a retrospect of some events which have marked the conduct of the war of extermination in the Southern states. A singular kind of ferocious animosity has subsisted between the two contending parties, as may be seen by letters from General Greene on

* Another list, which has been published, makes their total loss by death and capture to be eleven thousand eight hundred, including two thousand sailors, one thousand eight hundred negroes, one thousand five hundred tories, eighty vessels, large and small.

† It is asserted in *Gordon's History of the War*, that wherever the army of Lord Cornwallis marched, the dwelling-houses were plundered of every thing that could be carried off. Hundreds of eye-witnesses can prove that his lordship's table was served with plate thus pillaged from private families. By an estimate made at the time, on the best information that could be collected, the state of Virginia lost during Cornwallis' attempts to reduce it, thirty thousand slaves. And it has been computed that one thousand four hundred widows were made by the ravaging hand of war in the single district of Ninety-Six. The whole devastations occasioned by the British army, during the six months previous to their surrender at Yorktown, are supposed to amount to about three millions sterling.

the subject. "The animosity," says this amiable man, "between the whigs and tories of this state renders their situation truly deplorable. Not a day passes but there are more or less who fall a sacrifice to this savage disposition. The whigs seem determined to extirpate the tories, and the tories the whigs. Some thousands have fallen in this way in this quarter, and the evil rages with more violence than ever. If a stop cannot be soon put to these massacres, the country will be depopulated in a few months more, as neither whig nor tory can live." Speaking of a certain party on our side, he says: "This party plunders without mercy, and murders the defenceless people just as private pique, prejudice or personal resentments dictate. Principles of humanity, as well as policy, require that proper measures should be immediately taken to restrain these abuses, heal differences, and unite the people as much as possible. No violence should be offered to any of the inhabitants unless found in arms. The idea of exterminating the tories is no less barbarous than impolitic." Such is the infernal spirit of revenge and bitterness which has caused mutual destruction and wretchedness among the people. But, however atrocious may have been the conduct of some unauthorized partizans on the part of the Americans, the following instance of inhumanity, in the sacrifice of one of the victims of their malicious resentment, is sufficient to stigmatize the British character with eternal infamy. Lord Rawdon and Lieutenant-Colonel Balfour have perpetrated an act which, in all its distressing circumstances, surpasses in enormity and wickedness all others which have come to our knowledge, and which has roused the indignant spirit of every true American to a pitch of desperation. "Colonel Isaac Hayne, during the siege of Charleston, served his country as an officer of militia. After the capitulation, no alternative was left but to abandon his family and property, or to surrender to the conquerors. The small-pox was near his plantation, and he had a wife, six small children, and more than one hundred negroes, all liable to the disease. He concluded that, instead of waiting to be captured, it would be both more safe and more honorable to go within the British lines, and surrender himself a voluntary prisoner. He therefore repaired to Charleston, and offered to bind himself by the honor of an American officer to do nothing prejudicial to the British interest till he should be exchanged. Reports made of his superior abilities and influence, uniformly exerted in the American cause, operated with the conquerors to refuse him a parole, though they were daily accustomed to grant this indulgence to other inhabitants. He was told that he must either become a British subject, or submit to close confinement. To be arrested and detained in the capital, was not to himself an intolerable evil; but to abandon his family, both to the ravages of the small-pox then raging in their neighborhood, and to the insults and depredations of the royalists, was too much for the tender husband and fond parent. To acknowledge himself the subject of a government which he had from principle renounced, was repugnant to his feelings; but, without this, he was cut off from every prospect of a return to his family. In this embarrassing situation, he waited on Dr. Ramsay, with a declaration to the following effect: "If the British would grant me the indulgence which we in the day of our power gave to their adherents, of removing my family and property, I would seek an asylum in the remotest corner of the United States, rather than submit to their government; but, as they allow no other alternative than submission or confinement in the capital, at a distance from my wife and family, at a time when they are in the most pressing need of my presence and support, I must for the present yield to the demands of the conquerors. I request you to bear in mind, that previous to my taking this step, I declare that it is contrary to my inclination, and forced on me by hard necessity. I never will bear arms against my country. My new masters can require no service of me but what is enjoined by the old militia law of the province, which substitutes a fine in lieu of personal service. This I will pay as the price of my protection. If my conduct should be censured by my countrymen, I beg that you would remember this conversation, and bear witness for me, that I do not mean to desert the cause of America."

In this state of perplexity, Colonel Hayne subscribed a declaration of his allegiance to the King of Great Britain; but not without expressly objecting to the clause which required him with *his arms to support the royal government.*

The commandant of the garrison, Brigadier-General Patterson, and James Simpson, Esquire, intendant of the British police, assured him that this would never be required;
and added, further, that when the regular forces could not
defend the country without the aid of its inhabitants, it
would be high time for the royal army to quit it. Having
submitted to the royal government, he was permitted to
return to his family. Notwithstanding what had passed
at the time of his submission, he was repeatedly called on
to take arms against his countrymen, and finally threatened
with close confinement in case of a further refusal. This
he considered as a breach of contract, and it being no
longer in the power of the British to give him that protection which was to be the compensation of his allegiance,
he viewed himself as released from all engagements to
their commanders. The inhabitants of his neighborhood,
who had also revolted, petitioned General Pickens to appoint him to the command of their regiment, which was
done, and the appointment accepted. Hayne fell into
their hands. He was carried to the capital, and confined
in the provost prison, for having resumed his arms after
accepting British protection. At first he was promised a
trial, and had counsel prepared to justify his conduct by
the laws of nations and usages of war; but this was finally
refused, and he was ordered for execution by Lord Rawdon and Lieutenant-Colonel Balfour. The royal Lieutenant-Governor Bull, and a great number of inhabitants,
both royalists and Americans, interceded for his life. The
ladies of Charleston generally signed a petition in his behalf, in which was introduced every delicate sentiment
that was likely to operate on the gallantry of officers or
the humanity of men. His children, accompanied by some
near relations, (the mother had died of the small-pox,)
were presented on their bended knees as humble suitors
for their father's life. Such powerful intercessions were
made in his favor, as touched many an unfeeling heart,
and drew tears from many a hard eye; but Lord Rawdon
and Balfour continued firm in their determination.

The colonel was repeatedly visited by his friends, and
conversed on various subjects with a becoming fortitude.
He particularly lamented that, on principles of retaliation,

his execution would probably be an introduction to the shedding of much innocent blood. He requested those in whom the supreme power was vested, to accommodate the mode of his death to his feelings as an officer; but this was refused. On the last evening of his life he told a friend that he was no more alarmed at the thoughts of death, than at any other occurrence which was necessary and unavoidable.

On receiving his summons, on the morning of August the 4th, to proceed to the place of execution, he delivered to his eldest son, a youth of about thirteen years of age, several papers relative to his case, and said: "Present these papers to Mrs. Edwards, with my request that she should forward them to her brother in Congress. You will next repair to the place of execution, receive my body, and see it decently interred among my forefathers." They took a final leave. The colonel's arms were pinioned, and a guard placed round his person. The procession began from the Exchange in the forenoon. The streets were crowded with thousands of anxious spectators. He walked to the place of execution with such decent firmness, composure and dignity, as to awaken the compassion of many, and command respect from all. When the city-barrier was passed, and the instrument of his catastrophe appeared in full view, a faithful friend by his side observed to him, that he hoped he would exhibit an example of the manner in which an American can die. He answered, with the utmost tranquillity, "I will endeavor to do so." He ascended the cart with a firm step and serene aspect. He inquired of the executioner, who was making an attempt to get up to pull the cap over his eyes, what he wanted. On being informed, the colonel replied, "I will save you the trouble," and pulled the cap over himself. He was afterwards asked whether he wished to say any thing, to which he answered, "I will only take leave of my friends, and be ready." He then affectionately shook hands with three gentlemen, recommending his children to their care, and gave the signal for the cart to move.

Thus fell Colonel Isaac Hayne in the bloom of life, furnishing that example in death, which extorted a confession from his enemies, that though he did not die in a good cause, he must at least have acted from a persuasion of its being so.*

The execution of the worthy Colonel Hayne is univer-sally reprobated as an act of barbarity, justified neither by civil nor military law, and as an unexampled outrage on the principles of morality and Christian benevolence; but in the view of the British commanders, the application of their hackneyed term, *rebel*, sanctions a departure from all laws, both human and divine. In August, 1780, Lord Cornwallis, in addressing one of his officers, says: "I have given orders that all the inhabitants of this province who

* The tragical story of Colonel Hayne is not complete without add-ing, from a recent publication by Alexander Garden, Esq., the following particulars: "Irregularities in the mode of conducting the war, in the highest degree disgraceful to the American cause, had frequently oc-curred. No man lamented them with greater sincerity than Colonel Hayne, for none more anxiously wished the American character to be free from reproach. Soon, then, as solicited by his neighbors, and the inhabitants generally of the district, to resume a hostile position, to be-come their leader, and direct their operations against the enemy, he made an honorable and open declaration: 'that he could only be in-duced to comply with their wishes, by obtaining a solemn promise from all who were to serve under him, that an immediate stop should be put to every unnecessary severity: a desideratum the more to be insisted on, as he was resolved that exemplary punishment should be inflicted on every individual who should indulge in pillage, or in committing any act of inhumanity against the foe.' A copy of the address made to his soldiers on this occasion was found on him at the period of his captivity; but though it forcibly expressed his abhorrence of crime, and was replete with sentiments that did honor to his humanity, it availed not to soften the rigor of persecution, nor in the slightest degree to mitigate the severity of the punishment denounced against him. When the paper which contained this honorable testimony of generous feeling was pre-sented to Major McKenzie, who sat as president of the tribunal before which Colonel Hayne was arraigned, he, with great expression of sensi-bility, requested the prisoner 'to retain it till he should be brought before the court-martial that was to determine his fate,' assuring him 'that the present court were only directed to inquire whether or not he acknowledged himself to be the individual who had taken protection.' It is unnecessary to add, that this trial was never granted. Lord Raw-don reached the city from the interior country, and at his command an order for immediate execution was issued. Little did the sympathy that melted every heart to tenderness—little did the pathetic address of the lovely daughters of the soil, calculated to move even the bosom of ob-duracy—avail. Heedless of the prayers and solicitations of the afflicted friends and relatives, deaf to the cries of his children, who, even with bended knees interceded for mercy, insensible to the dictates of human-ity, his resolution was fixed as adamant, and a hero was sacrificed."

had submitted, and who have taken part in its revolt, shall be punished with the greatest rigor; that they shall be imprisoned, and their whole property taken from them or destroyed. I have ordered, in the most positive manner, that every militia-man who had borne arms with us, and afterwards joined the enemy, shall be immediately hanged; and have now, sir, only to desire that you will take the most vigorous measures to extinguish the rebellion, and that you will obey, in the strictest manner, the directions given in this letter." It is on the authority of the order just quoted that Lord Rawdon and Colonel Balfour justify their cruel execution of Colonel Hayne, and it will be difficult to calculate the number of miserable wretches who have fallen sacrifices to the same relentless spirit; nor are the mandates of Lord Rawdon less sanguinary, as will appear by the following specimen:

Extract of a letter to Colonel Rugely, commanding the British militia, near Camden.

"If attachment to their sovereign will not move the country people to check a crime so disastrous to the service, desertion, it must be my care to *urge them* to their duty, as good subjects, by using invariable severity against every one who shall show so criminal a neglect of the public interest. If any person meet a soldier, straggling without a written pass beyond the piquets, and shall not do his utmost to secure him, or shall not spread an alarm for this purpose, or if any person shall give shelter to soldiers straggling as above mentioned, or shall serve them as a guide, or shall furnish them with passes, or any other assistance, the persons so offending may assure themselves of rigorous punishment, as by *whipping, imprisonment,* or by being sent to serve in the *West Indies,* according as *I* shall think the degree of criminality may require; for I have ordered that every soldier who passes the piquet, shall submit himself to be examined, by any militia-man who has a suspicion of him. If a soldier, therefore, attempts to escape, when ordered by a militia-man to stop, he is immediately to be fired on as a deserter. I will give ten guineas *for the head* of any deserter belonging to the *volunteers of Ireland,* and *five guineas* only if he be brought alive."

But the strong measures which they pursued to crush the *rebellion* has produced a contrary effect, and lighted a flame which rages with tenfold violence, and which will eventually afford an essential aid in the establishment of our Independence.

For some months previous to the capture of Cornwallis, and while his army was traversing the states of the Carolinas and Virginia, he was opposed by the Marquis de la

Fayette with an inferior force. His lordship having received a rëinforcement, was so confident of success against his opponent, that he unguardedly wrote, in a letter which was afterwards intercepted, "*the boy cannot escape me*," but he was disappointed in his sanguine expectations. Cornwallis at one time formed a plan to surprise the marquis while on the same side of James river with himself, but the attempt was prevented by the following incident: The marquis, unapprised of the particular situation of his opponent, contrived to send into his camp a spy to obtain intelligence. A soldier belonging to New Jersey, by the name of Charles Morgan, generally called Charley, agreed to undertake this hazardous service; but insisted that, in case he should be discovered and hanged, the marquis, to secure his reputation, should have it inserted in the New Jersey paper, that he was employed in the service of his commander. Having reached the royal camp, he was soon introduced into his lordship's presence, who inquired the reason of his deserting. Charley replied, "that he had been in the continental service from the beginning, and while under Washington he was well satisfied; but being now commanded by a Frenchman, he was displeased with it, and had quitted the service." His lordship commended and rewarded him for his conduct, and Charley soon commenced the double duty of soldier under the English commander, and a spy in the employment of the marquis, without suspicion. Lord Cornwallis, while in conversation with several of his officers, inquired of Charley how long a time it would take for the marquis to cross James river? Pausing a moment, he replied, "Three hours, my lord." His lordship exclaimed, "Three hours! it will take three days." "No, my lord," said Charley; "the marquis has such a number of boats, and each boat will carry so many men; if you will please to calculate, you will find he can pass in three hours." His lordship, turning to the officers, said, "The scheme will not do." After having obtained the information required, Morgan began to prepare for a return to the marquis, and he prevailed with several British soldiers to desert with him. When challenged by the sentinels, he artfully tampered with them by giving them rum; and, while drinking, he seized their arms, and then compelled them to go; and this brave fellow actually brought off seven deserters to our camp. On his return to head-quarters, the marquis accosted him with, "Well, Charley, have you got back?" "Yes, please your excellency, and have brought seven men with me." Having communicated his information, the marquis offered to reward him, but he declined receiving money; and when it was proposed to promote him to a corporal or sergeant, he replied, "I have ability to discharge the duties of a common soldier, and my character stands fair; but should I be promoted, I may fail, and lose my reputation." He, however, requested that his destitute comrades, who came with him, might be furnished with shoes and clothing, which was readily granted.

A warm action took place early in September, between General Greene and the main body of the royal army, under Colonel Stuart, at Eutaw springs. Though inferior in force, General Greene sought the enemy, and made a furious attack; the battle became general, and continued four hours; it was the hottest and the most bloody, for the numbers engaged, that General Greene ever witnessed; many of the officers combated sword to sword, and the soldiers, rushing together, with the point of the bayonet contended with increased rage and effort for life, for blood, and carnage. A party of the enemy possessed themselves of a three-story brick house and a picketed garden, which gave them considerable advantage, and saved their army from a total rout. In a charge, which decided the fate of the day in our favor, Lieutenant-Colonel Campbell, of the Virginia line, who with undaunted firmness was leading on his brigade, received a mortal wound; and, on being informed that the enemy were flying in all quarters, said, "I die contented." Lieutenant-Colonel Washington had his horse killed under him, was wounded and taken prisoner. The American loss is not less than sixty commissioned officers killed and wounded, one hundred and thirty rank and file killed, and three hundred and forty wounded and missing. The loss on the side of the British is supposed to be fully equal in point of numbers, excepting in officers, and five hundred men, including seventy wounded, which were left, were the next day made prisoners by our army. Victory is claimed by both commanders, but the consequences have proved most disastrous to the enemy;

for the next day Colonel Stuart destroyed a large quantity of stores, abandoned his position, and leaving one thousand stand of arms and seventy wounded men, retired in haste towards Charleston.

31st.—Our troops are now employed in embarking the artillery and stores on board of transports, and we are soon to proceed by water to the head of Elk river, on our way to the North river. Dined with General Hazen, in company with a number of officers, both American and French. Here we enjoyed a profusion of mutual congratulations on our late glorious success, and this was the chief topic of conversation. Lord Cornwallis and his officers, since their capitulation, have received all the civilities and hospitality which it is in the power of their conquerors to bestow. General Washington, Count Rochambeau, and other general officers, have frequently invited them to entertainments, and they have expressed their grateful acknowledgments in return. They cannot avoid feeling the striking contrast between the treatment which they now experience and that which they have bestowed on our prisoners who have unfortunately fallen into their hands. It is a dictate of humanity and benevolence, after sheathing the sword, to relieve and meliorate the condition of the vanquished prisoner.

On one occasion, while in the presence of General Washington, Lord Cornwallis was standing with his head uncovered, his excellency said to him, politely, "My lord, you had better be covered from the cold;" his lordship, applying his hand to his head, replied, "It matters not, sir, what becomes of this *head now.*"

November 3d.—While our soldiers were loading a quantity of bombs and shot on board of transports, a shell burst, by which one man was unfortunately killed and two dangerously wounded. It is much to be lamented that these brave men, whose lives have been preserved through the dangers of the siege, should meet their adverse fate in such a manner. Orders are now received for our regiment of infantry to embark on board the Diligence, a French frigate of thirty-two guns, commanded by Captain Cleoughnaugh, bound up the Chesapeake, to the head of Elk river. Major Nathan Rice commands our regiment.

December.—We sailed from York river on the 4th of November, and in consequence of severe storms and contrary winds, our voyage was very unpleasant, and protracted to sixteen days, which has often been performed in three. Captain Cleoughnaugh and his officers were very polite and accommodating; we dined constantly at the table of the captain, and shared with him in his store of wine, &c. It happened unfortunately that a few days after we left York, four of our soldiers were seized with the small-pox, and having on board about eighty men who were liable to receive the infection, they were with several officers put on the Virginia shore, to march round by land. We disembarked at the head of Elk, on the 20th of November, where we met with our horses, and on the 24th we commenced our march to the highlands, near West Point. Passed through Philadelphia, Trenton, Princeton, Bonbrook and Morristown, and on the 7th instant crossed the Hudson at King's ferry. On account of the inclemency of the season we have suffered exceedingly from cold, wet and fatigue, during our long march. But we return in triumph to rējoin our respective regiments, and enjoy a constant interchange of congratulations with our friends, on the glorious and brilliant success of our expedition, which closes the campaign. This event reflects the highest honor on our combined arms; it will adorn the pages of our history, and we fondly hope it will be attended with the most favorable consequences, in bringing this long-protracted and distressing war to a happy termination. It will be to me a source of inexpressible satisfaction that I have had an opportunity of participating in the siege and capture of a British army. It is among the blessed privileges and richest incidents of my life. I have for several days been afflicted with inflammatory rheumatism, attended with excruciating pains. Having no other covering than canvas tents, and the weather being extremely cold, my sufferings have been almost insupportable; but I have much less reason to complain than to be grateful to a kind Providence, that I have enjoyed uninterrupted health during my seven years of military service.

Since my return, I am happy to learn that my friend Major Trescott, of our regiment, with a detachment of one hundred men, crossed the Sound to Long Island on the 3d of October, and completely surprised the enemy's fort Slonge, making two captains, one lieutenant, and eighteen rank and file prisoners; of the enemy two were killed and two wounded; of the Americans one only was wounded. Two double fortified four-pounders were damaged, one brass three-pounder, with a number of small-arms, ammunition, clothing, English goods, &c., were brought off. This enterprise was conducted with much address and gallantry, •reflecting great honor on the commander and his little party.

By report from the northern department, the British having projected an attack on the frontiers of New York state, were advancing towards Albany through the settlements on the Mohawk river, and committing great depredations among the inhabitants. The party was commanded by Major Ross, and consisted of six hundred regular rangers and Indians. Having, on the 25th of October, advanced as far as Johnstown, they were met by Lieutenant-Colonel Willet, at the head of a regiment of New York levies, and some militia, with about sixty Oneida Indians. This officer has frequently given evidence of his valor and gallantry, and on this occasion he was no less fortunate in his enterprise. Having directed Major Rowly, with a body of militia, by a circuitous movement, to get into the rear of the enemy, he made a vigorous attack in front, and they were soon totally defeated and driven into the wilderness. The next day a party of our people and Indians followed in pursuit till they were worn down by fatigue. It was impossible to ascertain the number of the enemy's slain, but their loss must have been very considerable. Fifty-two prisoners were taken and brought in, and Major Ross, with the remainder of his party, escaped into the barren wilderness, where they must have suffered extremely for want of provisions. The loss on the side of Colonel Willet is one lieutenant and twelve rank and file killed; one captain, two lieutenants, and twenty rank and file wounded. Colonel Willet's victory is rendered more important by the fall of the notorious Major Butler, who has long, as a partizan officer with the savages, been a scourge to the frontier inhabitants. He was wounded by one of our Indians, and on asking for quarters, "Yes,

Cherry-Valley quarter," said the Indian, and immediately despatched him. He alluded to Butler's having refused quarter to our people at Cherry-Valley, in November, 1778. When Congress received General Washington's letter, announcing the surrender of the British army, they resolved, that they would at two o'clock go in procession to the Dutch Lutheran Church, and return thanks to Almighty God, for crowning the allied arms with success, by the surrender of the whole British army, under the command of Earl Cornwallis. They also issued a proclamation for religiously observing throughout the United States the 13th of December, as a day of thanksgiving and prayer. They resolved, that thanks should be given to General Washington, Count Rochambeau, Count de Grasse, and the officers of the different corps, and the men under their command, for their services in the reduction of Lord Cornwallis. Also, resolved, to erect in Yorktown a marble column, adorned with emblems of the alliance between the United States and his Most Christian Majesty, and inscribed with a succinct narrative of the surrender of the British army. Two stands of colors, taken from the royal troops under the capitulation, were presented to General Washington in the name of the United States in Congress assembled; and two pieces of field ordnance, so taken, were by a resolve of Congress to be presented by General Washington to Count Rochambeau, with a short memorandum engraved thereon, that "Congress were induced to present them from considerations of the illustrious part which he bore in effecting the surrender."

The Congress of the United States, the assembly and council of the state of Pennsylvania, and a number of principal gentlemen of various orders, having been invited by the minister of France to be present at the praises offered to Heaven in the Catholic Church, on occasion of the late glorious success of the allied arms, the Abbe Bandole, Almoner to the Embassy of His Most Christian Majesty, ascended the pulpit, and addressed this august assembly in the following discourse; after which a *Te Deum* was sung.

The occasion was in this hemisphere singular and affecting; and the discourse itself is so elegant and animated in the French, so warm with those sentiments of piety and gratitude to our Divine Benefactor, in which good men of all countries accord, and so evidently dictated by the spirit of that new friendship and alliance from which such important advantages have been derived to the rights of America, as must give pleasure to every serious and candid friend to our glorious cause.

"GENTLEMEN: A numerous people assembled to render thanks to the Almighty for his mercies, is one of the most affecting objects, and worthy the attention of the Supreme Being. While camps resound with triumphal acclamations, while nations rejoice in victory and glory, the most honorable office a minister of the altar can fill, is to be the organ by which public gratitude is conveyed to the Omnipotent.

"Those miracles which he once wrought for his chosen people are renewed in our favor; and it would be equally ungrateful and impious not to acknowledge, that the event which lately confounded our enemies, and frustrated their designs, was the wonderful work of that GOD who guards your liberties.

"And who but he could so combine the circumstances which led to success? We have seen our enemies push forward amid perils almost innumerable—amid obstacles almost insurmountable—to the spot which was designed to witness their disgrace; yet they eagerly sought it, as their theatre of triumph! Blind as they were, they bore hunger, thirst, and inclement skies, poured their blood in battle against brave republicans, and crossed immense regions to confine themselves in another Jericho, whose walls were fated to fall before another Joshua. It is he, whose voice commands the winds, the seas, and the seasons, who formed a junction on the same day, in the same hour, between a formidable fleet from the south, and an army rushing from the north, like an impetuous torrent. Who but he, in whose hands are the hearts of men, could inspire the allied troops with the friendship, the confidence, the tenderness of brothers? How is it that two nations, once divided, jealous, inimical, and nursed in reciprocal prejudices, are now become so closely united as to form but one? Worldlings would say, it is the wisdom, the virtue, and moderation of their chiefs—it is a great national interest which has performed this prodigy. They will say, that to the skill of the generals, to the courage of the troops, to the activity of the whole army, we must attribute this splendid success. Ah! they are ignorant that the combining of so many fortunate circumstances is an emanation from the All-perfect Mind; that courage, that skill, that activity bear the sacred impression of him who is divine.

"For how many favors have we not to thank him during the course of the present year? Your union, which was at first supported by justice alone, has been consolidated by your courage, and the knot which ties you together is become indissoluble by the accession of all the states, and the unanimous voice of all the confederates. You present to the universe the noble sight of a society which, founded in equality and justice, secure to the individuals who compose it the utmost happiness which can be derived from human institutions. This advantage, which so many other nations have been unable to procure, even after ages of efforts and misery, is granted by Divine Providence to the United States; and his adorable decrees have marked the present moment for the completion of that memorable, happy revolution which has taken place in this extensive continent. While your councils were thus acquiring new energy, rapid and multiplied successes have crowned your arms in the Southern states.

" We have seen the unfortunate citizens of these states forced from their peaceful abodes; after a long and cruel captivity, old men, women and children thrown, without mercy, into a foreign country. Master of their lands and their slaves, amid his temporary affluence, a superb victor rejoiced in their distresses. But Philadelphia has witnessed their patience and fortitude; they have found here another home, and, though driven from their native soil, they have blessed God that he has delivered them from the presence of their enemy, and conducted them to a country where every just and feeling man has stretched out the helping hand of benevolence. Heaven rewards their virtues. These large states are at once wrested from the foe. The rapacious soldier has been compelled to take refuge behind his ramparts, and oppression has vanished like those phantoms which are dissipated by the morning ray.

"On this solemn occasion, we might renew our thanks to the God of battles for the success he has granted to the arms of your allies and your friends, by land and by sea, through the other parts of the globe. But let us not recall those events, which too clearly prove how much the hearts of our enemies have been hardened. Let us prostrate ourselves at the altar, and implore the God of mercy to suspend his vengeance, to spare them in his wrath, to inspire them with sentiments of justice and moderation, to terminate their obstinacy and error, and to ordain that your victories be followed'by peace and tranquillity. Let us beseech him to continue to shed on the councils of the king, your ally, that spirit of wisdom, of justice, and of courage, which has rendered his reign so glorious.—Let us entreat him to maintain in each of the states that intelligence by which the United States are inspired. Let us return him thanks that a faction, whose rebellion he has corrected, now deprived of support, is annihilated. Let us offer him pure hearts, unsoiled by private hatred or public dissension; and let us, with one will and one voice, pour forth to the Lord that hymn of praise, by which Christians celebrate their gratitude and his glory."

January, 1782.—The huts which we now occupy were erected the last winter by some of the Massachusetts troops, a short distance from the banks of the Hudson, and called New Boston; they afford us a very convenient and comfortable accommodation. Orders having been received for all the troops that have not gone through the small-pox to be inoculated, I commenced this business a few weeks since, and inoculated about two hundred, including women and children. Their accommodations were not such as their circumstances required; we were unprovided with proper articles of diet, and a considerable

number were seized with putrid fever, which proved fatal
in several instances.

March 10*th*.—A singular incident occurred in the sixth
regiment to-day. Two soldiers were eating soup together,
and one forbid the other eating any more; as he did not
desist, his comrade gave him a blow with his fist on the
side of his head, on which he fell to the ground and instantly expired. On close examination, I could discover
no bruise or injury which could enable me to account satisfactorily for his death.

An unhappy controversy has subsisted for some time
between Captain H. and Lieutenant S., both of the first
Massachusetts regiment. Captain H. was esteemed a man
of modest merit and unexceptionable character; he has
long commanded a company, and proved himself brave in
the field and a good disciplinarian. Lieutenant S., though
a good, active officer, is assuming, high-spirited, and values
himself on what he deems the principles of honor and the
gentleman. Having imbibed a strong prejudice against
his captain, and probably calculating on promotion, he
took unjustifiable liberties, and, in violation of honor and
decency, aspersed his character with unfounded calumnies.
The friends of the parties interposed, and endeavored to
effect a reconciliation. S. affected an acquiescence; in
consequence of which, the contention apparently subsided.
But still retaining in his breast the old grudge, he renewed
his calumnies, and was determined to provoke his captain
to a personal combat; and though contrary to his nature
and to his principles, he was compelled to the alternative.
Captain H. obtained a furlough, visited his friends in Massachusetts, made his will, and arranged his worldly affairs.
Having returned to camp, it was agreed to meet in the
field according to the rules of duelling. The tragical result
is, that Captain H. received a mortal wound, and died in
three hours after, and S. escaped with a wound in his arm.
Thus has this imperious young man, to gratify a sordid
passion, sent into eternity a man whom he ought to have
respected as his superior in every point of view—deprived
the public of a valuable officer, and a wife and three children of a husband and father. Barbarous and cruel murderer! you have violated the laws of God and man. Should
you escape punishment in this life, what must be your

doom in the awful day of retribution? The friends of
Captain H. in Massachusetts manifested their abhorrence
of this murderous deed, and endeavored by a legal pro-
cess to bring S. to condign punishment. They procured
a sheriff in the state of New York, where the crime was
committed, who repaired to camp with assistance, took the
opportunity when the regiment was on parade, and demanded of the colonel that S. should be delivered up to
the civil authority. The colonel reluctantly pointed out
the man, the sheriff advanced towards him, and S., soldier
like, unsheathed his sword and stood in defiance. The
sheriff, unaccustomed to the sword, was intimidated, and
finally retired from the field without the prisoner.[*]

April 5th.—Having completed the inoculation of the
soldiers, and attended them through the small-pox, and
my professional duty being considerably diminished, I
have obtained a furlough for forty-five days to visit my
friends in Massachusetts, and shall to-morrow commence
my journey to Boston, in company with my friend Doctor Eustis.

May 30th.—I returned to New Boston last evening from
Boston, having been absent forty-four days, which is one
day short of my furlough; our journey to Boston occupied
nine days, being impeded by foul weather and bad roads.
We were on horseback, attended by a servant, and took
our route through Connecticut and Providence. Here we
spent a pleasant evening with Lieutenant-Governor Bowen;
he and Doctor Eustis engaged in conversation respecting
the properties of coffee; Governor Bowen asserted that it
is a sedative, while the doctor contended for its stimulant
effects, and he certainly had the best of the argument.
Having arrived at Boston, Doctor Eustis kindly introduced
me to his father's family, where I received hospitable and
polite civilities. I proceeded to Plymouth and Barnstable,
where I had the satisfaction of a family interview, after an
absence of four years. Great preparations are making at
West Point, to celebrate the birth of the young Dauphin

---

[*] In the year 1786, a regiment was raised in the state of Massachusetts for the purpose of an Indian expedition. Lieutenant S. presented
his pretensions as a candidate for a commission, but notwithstanding a
respectable recommendation from several general officers, the governor
and council rejected the application with disdain.

of France; being in alliance with his Most Christian Ma jesty, propriety requires that we should celebrate the joyous event of the birth of his first son. His Excellency General Washington has, in general orders, given an invitation to all officers of the army, and they are requested to invite any friends or acquaintance they may have in the country to participate in the grand festival.

On the 6th instant a dangerous mutiny was discovered among the soldiers of the Connecticut line. It had been conducted with so much address and secrecy, that it was on the point of execution before it was divulged. The defection was general in the line: the soldiers had determined at reveille the next morning to have marched from their cantonments with arms, &c., complete, for Fishkill, where they intended to take a number of field-pieces with ammunition and provisions, and proceed to Hartford, and there demand of the Assembly that justice which they consider their due. At the moment the officers were retiring to bed, a faithful soldier, who was a waiter, informed his officer that he could not retire to rest without divulging an event which would assuredly take place the next morning at day-light. The most guilty soldiers were immediately seized and confined, and the ringleader was sentenced to suffer death, which happily frustrated the whole design. It is but just to observe, that the Connecticut line of troops have during the war, except in this instance, conducted in a very exemplary and meritorious manner.

June 1st.—Yesterday was celebrated the birth of the Dauphin of France, by a magnificent festival. The edifice under which the company assembled and partook of the entertainment was erected on the plain at West Point. The situation was romantic, and the occasion novel and interesting. Major Villefranche, an ingenious French engineer, has been employed with one thousand men about ten days in constructing the curious edifice. It is composed of the simple materials which the common trees in this vicinity afford. It is about six hundred feet in length and thirty feet wide, supported by a grand colonnade of one hundred and eighteen pillars, made of the trunks of trees. The covering of the roof consists of boughs, or branches of trees curiously interwoven, and the same materials form the walls, leaving the ends entirely open. On the inside, every pillar was encircled with muskets and bayonets, bound round in a fanciful and handsome manner, and the whole interior was decorated with evergreens, with American and French military colors, and a variety of emblems and devices, all adjusted in such style as to beautify the whole interior of the fabric. This superb structure, in symmetry of proportion, neatness of workmanship, and elegance of arrangement, has seldom perhaps been surpassed on any temporary occasion; it affected the spectators with admiration and pleasure, and reflects much credit on the taste and ability of Major Villefranche. Several appropriate mottos decorated the grand edifice, pronouncing benedictions on the dauphin and happiness to the two allied nations. The whole army was paraded on the contiguous hills on both sides of the river, forming a circle of several miles in open view of the public edifice, and at the given signal of firing three cannon, the regimental officers all left their commands, and repaired to the building to partake of the entertainment which had been prepared by order of the commander-in-chief. At five o'clock, dinner being on the table, his Excellency General Washington and lady and suite, the principal officers of the army and their ladies, Governor Clinton and his lady, and a number of respectable characters from the states of New York and New Jersey, moved from Major-General McDougall's quarters through the line formed by Colonel Crane's regiment of artillery to the arbor, where more than five hundred gentlemen and ladies partook of a magnificent festival. A martial band charmed our senses with music, while we feasted our appetites and gazed with admiration on the illustrious guests and the novel spectacle exhibited to our view. The cloth being removed, thirteen appropriate toasts were drank, each one being announced by the discharge of thirteen cannon and accompanied by music. The guests retired from the table at seven o'clock, and the regimental officers repaired to their respective commands. The arbor was, in the evening, illuminated by a vast number of lights, which being arranged in regular and tasteful order, exhibited a scene vieing in brilliancy with the starry firmament. The officers having rejoined their regiments, thirteen cannon were again fired as a prelude to a general *feu de joie*, which immediately succeeded throughout the whole line of the army on the surrounding hills; and being three times repeated, the mountains resounded and echoed like tremendous peals of thunder, and the flashing from thousands of fire-arms in the darkness of evening, could be compared only to the most vivid flashes of lightning from the clouds. The *feu de joie* was immediately followed by three shouts of acclamation and benediction for the *dauphin*, by the united voices of the whole army on all sides. At half-past eleven o'clock, the celebration was concluded by the exhibition of fire-works, very ingeniously constructed of various figures. His Excellency General Washington was unusually cheerful. He attended the ball in the evening, and with a dignified and graceful air, having Mrs. Knox for his partner, carried down a dance of twenty couple in the arbor on the green grass.

June 20th.—Dined by invitation with Major-General Howe, at his quarters at Robinson's house, with several respectable guests.

23d.—The officers of our regiment prepared an entertainment and invited a respectable party. At three o'clock we repaired to an arbor erected for the occasion, under which a long table was spread and a variety of dishes arranged in proper style; we prided ourselves on our camp dinner, as being almost on a par with that of a country gentleman. A band of military music attended, and we finished with toasts and songs in social glee.

July.—Our brigade moved out of huts on the first instant, and encamped at Nelson's point, on the bank of the Hudson, opposite West Point.

On the 4th, the anniversary of the declaration of our Independence was celebrated in camp. The whole army was formed on the banks of the Hudson on each side of the river. The signal of thirteen cannon being given at West Point, the troops displayed and formed in a line, when a general *feu de joie* took place throughout the whole army.

A most barbarous and horrid transaction of the royal refugees, a few weeks since, has excited universal indignation throughout the army. It is the cruel murder of Captain Joshua Huddy, of New Jersey, who, being commanding officer of a detachment stationed at the block-house in

Monmouth county, was attacked by a party of refugees from New York on Sunday, the 24th March, and after bravely defending himself till he had expended his ammunition, was taken prisoner and carried into New York. He was closely confined till April 8th, when, without even the form of a trial, he was told that he was ordered to be hanged; accordingly, on the 12th, he was carried over to the Jersey shore, by a party of refugees under the direction of one Captain Lippincot, and there hung on a tree, and left with the following label affixed on his breast: "We the refugees, having with grief long beheld the cruel murders of our brethern, and finding nothing but such measures daily carrying into execution—we, therefore, determine not to suffer without taking vengeance for the numerous cruelties; and thus begin, and, I say, may those lose their liberty who do not follow on, and have made use of Captain Huddy as the first object to present to your view; and further determine to hang man for man while there is a refugee existing. *Up goes Huddy for Philip White.*"

The refugees pretend to justify this violent act by asserting that Captain Huddy, some time before, made prisoner of a certain Philip White, of their party, and after having maimed him, broke both his legs, and tauntingly bid him run. But this is a vile falsehood; it has been fully proved that Captain Huddy was closely confined a prisoner at New York *at the time and for many days before White was taken.* A letter dated at Freehold, Monmouth county, 15th April last, and published in the Trenton paper, relates that White was taken the last of March, and after tokens of surrendering as a prisoner, he took up a musket, and killed a son of Colonel Hendrickson; but being taken by some light-horse, and while they were conducting him to Freehold, he again attempted to make his escape; and being called on several times to surrender, and continuing to run, when leaping into a bog impassable by the horse, he received a stroke on his head with a sword which killed him instantly. The above facts were proved by affidavits of the persons who were present, and by the voluntary testimony of one Aaron, who was taken prisoner with the said White. The wanton execution of Captain Huddy so exasperated the inhabitants of that part of New Jersey, that they presented a respectful memorial to General Washington, claiming justice for the murder of one of their fellow-citizens, or retaliation in case justice should be refused. General Washington immediately addressed Sir Henry Clinton on the subject, and assured him that unless the perpetrators of the murder were delivered up, he should be under the painful necessity of retaliating. . In the meantime, all the general officers, and those commanding brigades or regiments, were ordered to assemble at General Heath's quarters, to deliberate and decide on the following questions: 1st, Shall resort be had to retaliation for the murder of Captain Huddy? 2d, On whom shall it be inflicted? 3d, How shall the victim be designated? In order that each officer should be free from all bias and uninfluenced by each other, General Washington ordered that, without conversing on the questions, each one should write his own opinion, and address the same sealed up to the commander-in-chief. By this method his excellency obtained the spontaneous expression of the feelings of each individual officer, and they were unanimously of opinion that retaliation ought to be resorted to; that it should be inflicted on an officer of equal rank with Captain Huddy, and that the victim be designated by lot. Accordingly the painful alternative was adopted: the names of the British captains, our prisoners, were collected, a fair and impartial lot was drawn, and it fell on Captain Asgill, of the British guards, a gentleman of a noble English family, an only son of his parents, and only nineteen years of age, to be the unhappy victim. Next to the execution of Major Andre, this event occasioned the most painful sensations to the mind of the benevolent and humane Washington; his anxiety and poignant distress it is said were very visible. But still, firm and inflexible in his determination to obtain satisfaction, or pursue a course that will tend to deter others from a repetition of crimes so derogatory to the laws of humanity, of war, and of justice, he addressed Congress on the subject, and communicated to that body the New Jersey memorial. They unanimously approved of the firm and judicious conduct of the commander-in-chief, and assured him of their firmest support in his purpose of exemplary retaliation.

General Washington was anxious to alleviate the melancholy condition of Captain Asgill as much as possible, and directed the officer of his guard to treat him with every tender attention and politeness which his rank, fortune, and connexions, together with his unfortunate state, demanded, that is not inconsistent with his perfect security. He ordered also that Captain Ludlow, Asgill's friend, should be permitted to go into New York with such representations as they may please to make to Sir Guy Carleton, who has now succeeded Sir Henry Clinton as commander-in-chief of the British army. Captain Asgill, in addressing General Washington, thus expresses himself: "I cannot conclude this letter without expressing my gratitude to your excellency for ordering Colonel Dayton to favor me as much as my situation will admit of, and in justice to him I must acknowledge the feeling and attentive manner in which these commands have been executed." How awful is the condition of this innocent young gentleman, doomed to suffer an ignominious death for the crime of an infamous miscreant who so justly deserves the halter! Dreadful indeed must be that suspense when one's life is made to poise on a point so acute and delicate that an uncertain contingency shall decide the issue. General Washington having received information by letter, that a court-martial was appointed by Sir Henry Clinton, even before he received the letter of complaint, for the trial of Captain Lippincot and his abettors in the death of Captain Huddy, waited to be apprised of the issue, as Sir Guy Carleton had assured him of the fullest satisfaction. At length, however, the proceedings of the court-martial were communicated, and it was finished by the following declaration: "The court having considered the evidence for and against the captain, and it appearing, that, though Joshua Huddy was executed without proper authority, what the prisoner did, was not the effect of malice or ill-will, but proceeded from a conviction that it was his duty to obey the orders of the board of directors of associated loyalists, and his not doubting their having full authority to give such orders, the court is of opinion that he is *not guilty* of the murder laid to his charge, and therefore acquit him." Never perhaps was there a more complete burlesque on all courts of justice! never a more disgraceful proceeding to exculpate a criminal from merited punishment.

21

It appeared in the course of the trial that Governor Franklin, president of the board of associated loyalists, gave
Lippincot a verbal order to hang Captain Huddy without
a trial, and without a crime alleged against him! The
order is obeyed in the most unfeeling manner, yet the perpetrator is *found not guilty, and therefore acquitted.*   Sir Guy
Carleton requested of General Washington a passport for
Chief-Justice Smith to repair to the American head-quarters in order to lay before the commander-in-chief the
proceedings of the court-martial, with other documents and
explanations which he had no doubt would be satisfactory.
His excellency declined an interview with Mr. Smith, "as
the question is purely of a military nature, and reducible
to the single point whether the perpetrator of the wanton
and cruel murder of Huddy is to be given up, or a British
officer to suffer in his place." But he proposed to send
Major-General Heath to meet a British officer of equal
rank, if agreeable to the English commander. This was
also declined, and it appears that both Sir Henry Clinton
and Sir Guy Carleton disapproved of the acquittal of Lippincot. Sir Guy, in a letter which accompanied the proceedings of the court, expressed in unequivocal terms to
General Washington that, notwithstanding the acquittal,
he reprobated the act, and gave assurances of prosecuting
a further inquiry. Thus stands at present this very unfortunate affair, and Captain Asgill remains in custody to
await the final issue.

In order to avoid breaking the chain of this interesting
narrative, I proceed, in anticipation in point of time, to the
final conclusion of the melancholy catastrophe. General
Washington on the 19th of August made a representation
to Congress respecting the whole business for their consideration, and soon after directed that Captain Asgill be put
on his parole at Morristown, till further orders; and he
was allowed the indulgence of riding for his health and
recreation several miles into the country in any direction,
even within a few miles of the British lines, accompanied
by his friend Major Gordon.

On the 7th of October, General Washington, in a letter
to the secretary of war, expressed his private opinion that
Captain Asgill ought to be liberated from his *duresse*, and
be permitted to return to his friends in England. Suffi-

cient time had now elapsed since the arrest of Captain
Asgill for the distressing intelligence to reach his parents,
and to interest the attention and solicitude of almost all
Europe. The father of young Asgill was languishing with
mortal sickness. Lady Asgill, in the agony of her soul,
with her family in the deepest distress and sorrow, prostrated themselves at the feet of their king and queen, to
implore their compassion and assistance. She next had
recourse to the beneficence of the illustrious sovereigns of
France, through the medium of the celebrated Count de
Vergennes, though the two nations were at war. Her
incomparably pathetic and eloquent letter could not fail
of producing the desired effect: it reached the hearts, and
interested the sympathies of those exalted philanthropists
to whom it was addressed. A letter was immediately
despatched from Count de Vergennes to General Washington, dated July 27th, and this was accompanied by that
which the count had received from Lady Asgill. "Your
excellency," says the count, "will not read this letter (Lady
Asgill's) without being extremely affected. It thus affected
the king and queen, to whom I communicated it. The
goodness of their majesties' hearts induces them to desire
that the inquietudes of an unfortunate mother may be
calmed and her tenderness reässured.—There is one consideration, sir, which, though not decisive, may have an
influence on your resolution. Captain Asgill is doubtless
your prisoner, but he is among those whom the arms of
the king contributed to put into your hands at Yorktown.—Though this circumstance does not operate as a
safeguard, it, however, justifies the interest I permit myself
to take in this affair.—In seeking to deliver Mr. Asgill from
the fate which threatens him, I am far from engaging you
to seek another victim; the pardon, to be perfectly satisfactory, must be entire."—Copies of these letters being
transmitted with one from his excellency to Congress, they
resolved, November 7th, that the commander-in-chief be
directed to set Captain Asgill at liberty. A more grateful
duty could scarcely be assigned; it relieved his mind from
a weight which had long oppressed and preyed on his
spirits. He immediately transmitted to Captain Asgill a
copy of the resolve of Congress, accompanied with a passport for him to go into New York, and also a letter which

closes as follows: "I cannot take leave of you, sir, without
assuring you that, in whatever light my agency in this
unpleasant affair may be viewed, I was never influenced
through the whole of it by sanguinary motives, but by
what I conceived to be a sense of my duty, which loudly
called on me to take measures, however disagreeable, to
prevent a repetition of those enormities which have been
the subject of discussion. And that this important end
is likely to be answered without the effusion of the blood
of an innocent person is not a greater relief to you than
it is, sir, to

"Your most obedient, humble servant,
"GEORGE WASHINGTON."*

* From the "Historical and Literary Memoirs and Anecdotes, selected from
the Correspondence of Baron de Grimm and Diderot:"

"You can well remember the general interest Sir —— Asgill inspired,
a young officer in the English guards, who was made prisoner and condemned to death by the Americans in reprisal for the death of Captain
Huddy, who was hanged by the order of Captain Lippincot. The public
prints all over Europe resounded with the unhappy catastrophe, which
for eight months impended over the life of this young officer. The extreme grief of his mother, the sort of delirium which clouded the mind
of his sister at hearing of the dreadful fate which menaced the life of her
brother, interested every feeling mind in the fate of this unfortunate
family. The general curiosity, with regard to the events of the war,
yielded, if I may so say, to the interest which young Asgill inspired, and
the first question asked of all vessels that arrived from any port in North
America, was always an inquiry into the fate of this young man. It is
known that Asgill was thrice conducted to the foot of the gibbet, and
that thrice General Washington, who could not bring himself to commit
this crime of policy without a great struggle, suspended his punishment;
his humanity and justice made him hope that the English general would
deliver over to him the author of the crime which Asgill was condemned
to expiate. Clinton, either ill obeyed, or insensible to the fate of young
Asgill, persisted in refusing to deliver up the barbarous Lippincot. In
vain the king of England, at whose feet this unfortunate family fell
down, had given orders to surrender up to the Americans the author of
a crime which dishonored the English nation; George III. was not
obeyed. In vain the United States of Holland entreated of the United
States of America the pardon of the unhappy Asgill; the gibbet, erected
in front of his prison, did not cease to offer to his eyes those dreadful
preparatives more awful than death itself. In these circumstances, and
almost reduced to despair, the mother of the unfortunate victim bethought
herself that the minister of a king armed against her own nation might
succeed in obtaining that which was refused to her king. Lady Asgill
wrote to the Count de Vergennes a letter, the eloquence of which, independently of oratorical forms, is that of all people and all languages, because
it derives its power from the first and noblest sentiments of our nature.

The tour of duty at Dobbs' ferry having fallen to our regiment, we marched from Nelson's Point on the 24th,

"The two memorials which are subjoined, merit being preserved as historical monuments.

Letter from Lady Asgill to the Comte de Vergennes.

"SIR: If the politeness of the French court will permit a stranger to address it, it cannot be doubted but that she who unites in herself all the more delicate sensations with which an individual can be penetrated, will be received favorably by a nobleman who reflects honor not only on his nation, but on human nature. The subject on which I implore your assistance, is too heart-rending to be dwelt on; most probably, the public report of it has already reached you; this relieves me from the burthen of so mournful a duty. My son, my only son, dear to me as he is brave, amiable as he is beloved, only nineteen years of age, a prisoner of war, in consequence of the capitulation of Yorktown, is at present confined in America as an object of reprisal.—Shall the innocent share the fate of the guilty? Figure to yourself, sir, the situation of a family in these circumstances. Surrounded as I am with objects of distress, bowed down by fear and grief, words are wanting to express what I feel, and to paint such a scene of misery: my husband, given over by his physicians some hours before the arrival of this news, not in a condition to be informed of it; my daughter attacked by a fever, accompanied with delirium; speaking of her brother in tones of wildness, and without an interval of reason, unless it be to listen to some circumstances which may console her heart. Let your sensibility, sir, paint to you my profound, my inexpressible misery, and plead in my favor; a word, a word from you, like a voice from Heaven, would liberate us from desolation, from the last degree of misfortune. I know how far General Washington reveres your character. Tell him only that you wish my son restored to liberty, and he will restore him to his desponding family; he will restore him to happiness. The virtue and courage of my son will justify this act of clemency. His honor, sir, led him to America; he was born to abundance, to independence, and to the happiest prospects. Permit me, once more, to entreat the interference of your high influence in favor of innocence, and in the cause of justice and humanity. Despatch, sir, a letter from France to General Washington, and favor me with a copy of it, that it may be transmitted from hence. I feel the whole weight of the liberty taken in presenting this request; but I feel confident, whether granted or not, that you will pity the distress by which it was suggested; your humanity will drop a tear on my fault, and blot it out for ever.

"May that Heaven which I implore grant that you may never need the consolation which you have it in your power to bestow on

"THERESA ASGILL."

Second Letter of Lady Asgill to the Comte de Vergennes.

"SIR: Exhausted by long suffering, overpowered by an excess of unexpected happiness, confined to my bed by weakness and languor, bent

crossed the river at King's ferry, and on the 25th encamped near the block-house at this place. This after-

to the earth by what I have undergone, my sensibility alone could supply me with strength sufficient to address you.

"Condescend, sir, to accept this feeble effort of my gratitude. It has
been laid at the feet of the Almighty; and believe me, it has been presented with the same sincerity to you, sir, and to your illustrious sovereigns; by their august and salutary intervention, as by your own, a son
is restored to me, to whom my own life was attached. I have the
sweet assurance that my vows for my protectors are heard by Heaven,
to whom they are ardently offered; yes, sir, they will produce their effect
before the dreadful and last tribunal, where I indulge in the hope that
we shall both appear together; you to receive the recompense of your
virtues; myself, that of my sufferings. I will raise my voice before that
imposing tribunal, I will call for those sacred registers in which your
humanity will be found recorded. I will pray that blessings may be
showered on your head, on him who, availing himself of the noblest
privilege received from God—a privilege no other than divine—has
changed misery into happiness, has withdrawn the sword from the innocent head, and restored the worthiest of sons to the most tender and
unfortunate of mothers.

"Condescend, sir, to accept this last tribute of gratitude due to your
virtuous sentiments. Preserve this tribute, and may it go down to your
posterity as a testimony of your sublime and exemplary beneficence to
a stranger, whose nation was at war with your own; but these tender
affections have not been destroyed by war. May this tribute bear testimony to my gratitude long after the hand that expresses it, with the
heart which at this moment only vibrates with the vivacity of grateful
sentiments, shall be reduced to dust; even to the last day of my existence, it shall beat but to offer all the respect and all the gratitude with
which it is penetrated.   "THERESA ASGILL."

REMARKS.—The Baron de Grimm has unfortunately been led to make
an erroneous statement respecting the treatment of Captain Asgill,
which ought in justice to be corrected. It is difficult to account for his
assertion that, "It is known that Asgill was thrice conducted to the foot
of the gibbet, and thrice General Washington, who could not bring himself to commit this crime of policy without a great struggle, suspended
his punishment;" and again, "the gibbet, erected in front of his prison,
did not cease to offer to his eyes those dreadful preparatives more awful
than death itself." I can with the fullest confidence affirm, that a gibbet
never was erected for Captain Asgill at any period of his confinement, and
that no preparations whatever were made for his execution, except a secure
confinement for a short period, during which the utmost tenderness and
polite civilities were bestowed on him, and for these he expressed his
grateful acknowledgments in his letter to General Washington. It would
be preposterous to suppose that the commander-in-chief could act a
farcical part by exhibiting the machines of death, when it was altogether
problematical whether an execution would be the final resort, and surely
nothing could be less characteristic of Washington, than wantonly to
torture the feelings of a prisoner with the horrors of death.

noon a flag of truce arrived here from New York with despatches for General Washington, which were immediately forwarded to him.

August 5th.—Flags are passing and repassing from this post to New York and back every day, and several gentlemen have been permitted to come out of that city. By the intelligence which they bring, corroborating those which we receive from other sources, commissioners are sent from the court of London to Paris, where they are to meet French and American commissioners for the important purpose of negotiating a general peace. May God grant them success in bringing to America an honorable peace and national independence! A very considerable number of deserters have come out from New York within these few days past.

31st.—The army marched from their different quarters this morning and encamped at Verplank's point in the evening. Part of the troops came down the river in boats, which, being in motion and in regular order on the water, made a most beautiful appearance. I shall to-morrow commence a journey to Philadelphia, for the purpose of receiving a sum of money at the American Bank, for the payment of our regiment.

September 10th.—I returned last evening from Philadelphia, where I met my very respectable friends Dr. Treat and Dr. Benney of the hospital, with whom I dined. Drank tea and spent the evening with Dr. Andrew Craige, our apothecary-general. The next day dined with Mr. James Lovell, lieutenant and adjutant of our regiment. Here I had the pleasure of being introduced to two celebrated characters, Dr. John Jones, of Philadelphia, and the honorable Robert Morris, the great American financier. Dr. Jones formerly resided in the city of New York, where he was "distinguished for his professional merit, urbanity of manners, and moral excellence." As a surgeon, Dr. Jones is considered at the head of the profession in the United States, and his reputation has been considerably extended by a valuable work, entitled, "*Plain Remarks on Wounds and Fractures,*" which he published in the year 1775 for the particular benefit of the surgeons of our army, and which has been received with universal approbation. Mr. Morris stands preeminent as a citizen, mer-

chant and patriot, and the public are greatly indebted to
him for his unrivaled efforts as superintendent of the
finances of the United States, by which the public interest
has been greatly promoted. I waited on Major-General
Lincoln, secretary at war, to obtain an order on the bank
for the money which was the object of my visit, but was
disappointed, as the state of the bank would not admit of
any discount. General Lincoln introduced me to Mr.
Osgood, a member of Congress from Massachusetts.

September 14*th*.—The whole army was paraded under
arms this morning in order to honor his Excellency Count
Rochambeau on his arrival from the southward. The
troops were all formed in two lines, extending from the
ferry, where the count crossed, to head-quarters. A troop
of horse met and received him at King's ferry, and conducted him through the line to General Washington's
quarters, where, sitting on his horse by the side of his
excellency, the whole army marched before him, and paid
the usual salute and honors. Our troops were now in
complete uniform, and exhibited every mark of soldierly
discipline. Count Rochambeau was most highly gratified
to perceive the very great improvement which our army
had made in appearance since he last reviewed them, and
expressed his astonishment at their rapid progress in military skill and discipline. He said to General Washington,
"You have formed an alliance with the King of Prussia.
These troops are Prussians." Several of the principal
officers of the French army, who have seen troops of different European nations, have bestowed the highest encomiums and applause on our army, and declared that they
had seen none superior to the Americans.

16*th*.—Dined with Major-General Howe, with a numbei
of officers of our line, and on the 17th dined with Baron
Steuben in company with Generals Howe, Patterson, and
a number of French officers. The baron is never more
happy than when he is manifesting his generous friendship and benevolence.

October.—Eight battalions have been selected from the
army to perform some grand manœuvres and a review.
The evolutions and firings were performed this day with
that regularity and precision which does them honor, and
which received the full approbation of the numerous

spectators, and of the American and French officers who were present.

30th.—At reveille on the 26th instant, the left wing of our army, under the command of General Heath, decamped from Verplank's point and marched to the highlands; took our lodging in the woods, without covering, and were exposed to heavy rain during a night and day. Thence we crossed the Hudson to West Point, and marched over the mountain called Butter hill; passed the night in the open field, and the next day reached the ground where we are to erect log huts for our winter-quarters, near New Windsor.

November 10*th.*—I attended the funeral of my late worthy friend, Ensign Trant. This young gentleman at the age of eighteen came over from Ireland about two years since, and on his arrival in Boston was appointed an ensign in our regiment. Having a taste for military life, he had acquired considerable reputation as an officer, and was esteemed for his amiable temper and disposition, his liberal and generous sentiments, and his polite and gentlemanly manners. He suffered a lingering illness of eight months. Renouncing all hope of recovery, he conquered the terrors of death, and acquired a remarkable degree of patience and resignation during the last weeks of his extreme suffering. His remains were decently interred in the garrison at West Point, and were followed to the grave by his Excellency General Washington and a very respectable procession.

A melancholy event has recently been announced from South Carolina—Colonel *John Laurens*, a man of estimable value, has been slain in a rencounter with the enemy near Charleston. He was the son of Henry Laurens, Esq., late president of Congress, and our ambassador to Holland. He had been employed on a special mission to France, to obtain a loan for the United States, in which he was successful. The enemy having detached a party into the country to procure provisions, Colonel Laurens, ever foremost in danger, joined the party of continentals as a volunteer, to counteract their object, and while advancing on the enemy with great intrepidity, he received a mortal wound. His death is universally lamented, more especially at this late period, when the contest is supposed to be near a termination. No eulogy can exceed the merit of this noble and very useful officer.

A very extraordinary and melancholy event has recently been announced from England. The ship called the Royal George, of one hundred and eight guns, commanded by Admiral Kempenfelt, being careened on one side to receive some necessary repairs, was by a sudden gust of wind forced over, and her gun-ports being open, she instantly filled with water, and went to the bottom. The admiral himself was writing at his table in the cabin, and with about one thousand souls was lost; among them were about three hundred women and children. Admiral Kempenfelt was about seventy years of age, and was considered, in point of professional knowledge and judgment, one of the first naval officers in Europe. A victualler alongside was swallowed up in the whirlpool occasioned by the sinking of the ship.

The campaign is now brought to a close, and no glorious deeds have been achieved; not a gun has been fired between the two armies during the campaign, and the prospect of peace is so favorable and encouraging, that our Congress have passed a resolve to discharge a considerable part of the army on the 1st day of January next. The supernumerary officers are to retire on the establishment provided by Congress, and are to be entitled to all the emoluments with those who continue in service till peace shall be proclaimed.

December 15*th.*—Dined with my friends Drs. Townsend, Eustis and Adams, at the hospital, in company with Generals Gates and Howe, and their aids, Dr. Cochran, our surgeon-general, and several other officers. Our entertainment was ample and elegant.

19*th.*—I partook of another entertainment at Dr. Eustis' quarters, New Boston. Our guests were General McDougall and his aids, Colonels Jackson, Crane, &c. General Alexander McDougall is the son of a Scotchman, whose employment was that of a milk-man in the city of New York, and the son was sometimes his assistant. The general at an early period was distinguished among those who had adopted the whig principles, and known to be a zealous advocate for freedom. Principle and a sense of duty led him to the field of contest, and in August, 1776, he was by Congress appointed a brigadier-general, and by his intelligence and active spirit he has acquired a reputable standing as a general officer. He displays much of the Scotch character, is affable and facetious, often indulging in pleasantry, and adverting to his national peculiarities and family origin; at the close of which he adds, "Now, gentlemon, you have got the history of Sawney McDougall, the milk-mon's son."

25th.—The time is now approaching when, according to a resolve of Congress, a reduction of the army is to take place, and it is optional with me to continue till peace is actually proclaimed and our army entirely disbanded, or to retire from service on the new establishment, by which I shall be entitled to the same emoluments with those who remain. Having duly deliberated on the subject, I have come to the resolution of bidding a final adieu to the scenes of military life, and have resigned my commission in favor of Dr. Shute. It is with inexpressible reluctance that I contemplate a separation from numerous friends with whom I have so long associated in the most harmcnious and pleasing intercourse. Engaged in the same glorious and honorable cause, encountering together the same perils, suffering unparalleled hardships and privations, and participating in the most interesting scenes and events, our mutual and cherished attachments are no less ardent than the ties of brotherly affection. Friendship formed under such circumstances, and cemented by purity of sentiment, must prove as lasting as our days on earth, and we shall ever cherish a sincere interest in the welfare of the companions of our military career. It will be to me a source of infinite satisfaction during the remainder of my days, that I have shared in the toils and perils of war during seven years and a half, in defence of my country and its freedom, and that the mighty struggle terminates in peace and the establishment of our national Independence. This momentous event should be considered as a rich blessing which Providence bestows on us for the benefit of the present and many future generations. It is incumbent on me to express my unfeigned gratitude to the All-wise Author and Preserver of men, that he has been pleased to confer on me innumerable blessings, and preserved my life and health during a long period while exposed to the greatest hardships and imminent perils.

January 1st, 1783.—This day I close my military career, and quit for ever the toils and vicissitudes incident to the storms of war. To my military companions I bid a final adieu, and hope to enjoy in future the blessings which attend a virtuous course of domestic life. I retire with honorable testimonials from very respectable authority of my punctuality and faithful performance of duty in the various situations which I have been called to occupy, and with a heart fraught with grateful recollections of the kindness and affectionate intercourse which I have experienced from my superiors, and from my numerous companions and associates. While I congratulate my country on the momentous event by which we are about to be elevated to the rank of an Independent Nation, most cordially do I proffer my sympathy for the many lives of inestimable value which have been sacrificed during this ever-memorable contest.

NOTE.—As the materials for the remainder of this work were collected and arranged after I returned from the army, I have thought it proper to change my *running title* from "Military Journal" to "Revolutionary Annals."

REVOLUTIONARY ANNALS.

SOCIETY OF CINCINNATI.

WHILE contemplating a final separation of the officers of the army, the tenderest feelings of the heart had their afflicting operations. It was at the suggestion of General Knox, and with the acquiescence of the commander-in-chief, that an expedient was devised by which a hope is entertained that their long-cherished friendship and social intercourse may be perpetuated, and that at future periods they may annually communicate, and revive a recollection of the bonds by which they were connected. It was on the 10th day of May, 1783, when the officers held their first meeting, at which the Baron Steuben, the senior officer, presided, that Major-General Knox, Brigadier-General Hand, Brigadier-General Huntington and Captain Shaw, were chosen to revise the proposals for the institution, and prepare a copy to be laid before the next meeting, at Baron Steuben's quarters, on the 13th, when the plan for establishing a society was accepted, and is as follows:

"It having pleased the Supreme Governor of the Universe, in the disposition of human affairs, to cause the separation of the Colonies of North America from the dominion of Great Britain, and, after a bloody conflict of eight years, to establish them Free, Independent, and Sovereign States, connected by alliances, founded on reciprocal advantages, with some of the greatest princes and powers of the earth:

"To perpetuate, therefore, as well the remembrance of this vast event, as the mutual friendships which have been formed, under the pressure of common danger, and in many instances cemented by the blood of the parties, the officers of the American army do hereby, in the most solemn manner, associate, constitute and combine themselves into one Society of Friends, to endure so long as they shall endure, or any of their eldest male posterity, and in failure thereof, the collateral branches, who may be judged worthy of becoming its supporters and members.

"The officers of the American army having generally been taken from the citizens of America, possess high veneration for the character of that illustrious Roman, Lucius Quintius Cincinnatus, and being resolved to follow his example, by returning to their citizenship, they think they may with propriety denominate themselves the *Society of the Cincinnati.*

"The following principles shall be immutable, and form the basis of the Society of the Cincinnati:

"An incessant attention to preserve inviolate those exalted rights and liberties of human nature, for which they have fought and bled, and without which the high rank of a rational being is a curse instead of a blessing.

"An unalterable determination to promote and cherish, between the respective states, that union and national honor, so essentially necessary to their happiness, and the future dignity of the American empire.

"To render permanent the cordial affection subsisting among the officers, this spirit will dictate brotherly kindness in all things, and particularly extend to the most substantial acts of beneficence, according to the ability of the society, towards those officers and their families who unfortunately may be under the necessity of receiving it.

"The general society will, for the sake of frequent communications, be divided into state societies, and these again into such districts as shall be directed by the state society.

"The societies of the districts to meet as often as shall be agreed on by the state society; those of the state on the 4th day of July, annually, or oftener if they shall find it expedient; and the general society on the first Monday in May, annually, so long as they shall deem it necessary, and afterwards, at least once in every three years.

"At each meeting, the principles of the institution will be fully considered, and the best measures to promote them adopted.

"The state societies to have a president, vice-president, secretary, treasurer, and assistant-treasurer, to be chosen annually by a majority of votes, at the state meeting.

"In order to form funds which may be respectable, and assist the unfortunate, each officer shall deliver to the treasurer of the state society one month's pay, which shall remain for ever, to the use of the state society; the interest only of which, if necessary, to be appropriated to the relief of the unfortunate.

"The society shall have an order, by which its members shall be known and distinguished, which shall be a medal of gold, of a proper size to receive the emblems, and be suspended by a deep-blue ribband, two inches wide, edged with white, descriptive of the union of America and France."

His Excellency General Washington officiated as president of the general society from its institution, in 1783, till his death, as did Major-General B. Lincoln of the society of Massachusetts. Since his demise, in 1810, Governor Brooks has been annually elected president. Some attempts were made at the first general meeting, in 1784, to alter the constitution of the society, in order that the hereditary succession of the members should be done away, without substituting any means of perpetuating the existence of the society. But a majority of the state societies did not approve this change, and the institution remains as it was originally adopted in 1783. The society of Massachusetts was incorporated by the legislature in the year 1806, and their by-laws provide that persons who claim admission as members in right of succession to a deceased member shall be the oldest male heirs, or collateral branches not under twenty-one years of age. He must make his application to the standing committee in writing, and will be voted in by ballot.

In December, 1782, the officers of the army being apprehensive that they should be disbanded before their accounts should be liquidated and the engagements of government complied with, resolved to memorialize Congress on the subject, and Major-General McDougall, Colonel Ogden and Colonel Brooks were deputed as a committee to wait on that honorable body, requesting their attention to the distresses under which the army labored, and to solicit payment of the money actually due to the army, and security for the commutation of half-pay, stipulated by the resolve of October, 1780, for a sum in gross, which they conceive would be less objectionable than the half-pay establishment. Subsequent to this proceeding, a report was circulated in camp that Congress did not mean to comply with their resolves respecting half-pay, &c. This operated very powerfully on the minds of the officers of the army, and occasioned them to forward an address to Congress, in behalf of themselves and their brethren, the soldiers. They asked for a supply of money, to be forwarded immediately to the army, for a settlement of the accounts of arrearages of pay, and security for what is due; for a commutation of half for *full* pay for a certain number of years, or for a sum in gross, as should be agreed on; for a settlement of accounts, for deficiencies of rations and compensations, and of the deficiencies of clothing and compensations. They conclude their address in these words: "The pressure of evils and injuries in the course of seven long years have made their condition, in many instances, wretched; they therefore entreat that Congress, to convince the army and the world that the Independence of America shall not be placed on the ruin of any particular class of citizens, will point out a mode for immediate redress; and that the disabled officers and soldiers, with the widows and orphans of those who have lost or may lose their lives in the service of their country, may be included, and that some mode be pointed out for the eventual payment of those soldiers who are the subjects of the resolution of Congress of the 15th of May, 1778." In consequence of this address, Congress passed the following resolves, namely:

"That the superintendent of finance be directed, conformably to the measures already taken for that purpose, so soon as the state of the public finances will permit, to make such payment, and in such manner as he shall think proper, till the further order of Congress.

"With respect to the second article of the address, the settlement of accounts of the arrearages of pay, that the several states be called on to complete, without delay, the settlements with their respective lines of the army, up to the first day of August, 1780; and that the superintendent of finance take such measures as shall appear to him most proper for effecting the settlement from this period. That the troops of the United States, in common with all creditors of the same, have an undoubted right to expect security for what shall be found due, and Congress will make every effort in their power to obtain from the respective states substantial funds, adequate to the object of funding the whole debt of the United States, and will enter on an immediate and full consideration of the nature of such funds, and the most likely mode of obtaining them."

The remainder of the report of the committee, on the subject of the address, was referred to a committee of five.

General McDougall and Colonel Ogden, in a letter to General Knox, made known to the army their success; and Colonel Brooks returned to camp to inform them, verbally, of the prospect of commutation, or of obtaining an equivalent for half-pay, which they had proposed in their address. General McDougall continued at Congress on the army business, while the impression of the report which occasioned the address to Congress, however false, remained on the minds of some officers; notwithstanding Congress were doing all that the circumstances of the states would admit to relieve and satisfy the army.

March 10*th.*—In the midst of this perturbed state of affairs in camp, and while the day of final separation was supposed to be near at hand, the following anonymous letter, calculated to exasperate the passions of the moment, was privately circulated:

"TO THE OFFICERS OF THE ARMY.

"GENTLEMEN: A fellow-soldier, whose interest and affections bind him strongly to you—whose past sufferings have been as great, and whose future fortune may be as desperate, as yours—would beg leave to address you.

"Age has its claims, and rank is not without its pretensions to advise; but, though unsupported by both, he flatters himself that the plain language of sincerity and experience will neither be unheard nor unregarded.

"Like many of you he loved private life, and left it with regret. He left it, determined to retire from the field, with the necessity that called him to it, and not till then—not till the enemies of his country, the slaves of power, and the hirelings of injustice, were compelled to abandon their schemes, and acknowledge America as terrible in arms as she had been humble in remonstrance. With this object in view, he has long shared in your toils and mingled in your dangers.—He has felt the cold hand of poverty without a murmur, and has seen the insolence of wealth without a sigh.—But, too much under the direction of his wishes, and sometimes weak enough to mistake desire for opinion, he has till lately—very lately—believed in the justice of his country. He hoped that, as the clouds of adversity scattered, and as the sunshine of peace and better fortune broke in on us, the coldness and severity of government would relax, and that more than justice, that gratitude would blaze forth on those hands which had upheld her, in the darkest stages of her passage from impending servitude to acknowledged independence. But faith has its limits, as well as temper, and there are points beyond which neither can be stretched, without sinking into cowardice or plunging into credulity.—This, my friends, I conceive to be your situation: hurried to the very edge of both, another step would ruin you for ever.— To be tame and unprovoked when injuries press hard on you, is more than weakness; but too look up for kinder usage, without one manly effort of your own, would fix your character, and show the world how richly you deserve those chains you broke. To guard against this evil, let us take a review of the ground on which we now stand, and thence carry our thoughts forward for a moment, into the unexplored field of experiment.

"After a pursuit of seven long years, the object for which we set out is at length brought within our reach—yes, my friends, that suffering courage of yours was active once: it has conducted the United States of America through a doubtful and bloody war. It has placed her in the chair of independency, and peace returns again to bless—who? A country willing to redress your wrongs, cherish your worth, and reward your services? A country courting your return to private life, with tears of gratitude and smiles of admiration, longing to divide with you that independency which your gallantry has given, and those riches which your wounds have preserved? Is this the case? or is it rather a country that tramples on your rights, disdains your cries, and insults your distresses? Have you not more than once suggested your wishes, and made known your wants to Congress?—wants and wishes which gratitude and policy should have anticipated rather than evaded; and have you not lately, in the meek language of entreating memorials, begged from their justice what you could no longer expect from their favor?

22

How have you been answered? Let the letter which you are called to consider to-morrow reply.

"If this, then, be your treatment, while the swords you wear are necessary for the defence of America, what have you to expect from peace, when your voice shall sink, and your strength dissipate by division?—when those very swords, the instruments and companions of your glory, shall be taken from your sides, and no remaining mark of military distinction be left but your wants, infirmities, and scars? Can you, then, consent to be the only sufferers by this revolution, and, retiring from the field, grow old in poverty, wretchedness, and contempt? Can you consent to wade through the vile mire of dependency, and owe the miserable remnant of that life to charity which has hitherto been spent in honor? If you can, go—and carry with you the jest of tories and the scorn of whigs; the ridicule, and, what is worse, the pity of the world. Go—starve, and be forgotten! But if your spirit should revolt at this; if you have sense enough to discover, and spirit enough to oppose tyranny under whatever garb it may assume; whether it be the plain coat of republicanism, or the splendid robe of royalty; if you have not yet learned to discriminate between a people and a cause, between men and principles—awake; attend to your situation, and redress yourselves. If the present moment be lost, every future effort is in vain; and your threats then, will be as empty as your entreaties now.

"I would advise you, therefore, to come to some final opinion on what you can bear, and what you will suffer. If your determination be in any proportion to your wrongs, carry your appeal from the justice, to the fears of government. Change the milk-and-water style of your last memorial; assume a bolder tone—decent, but lively, spirited and determined, and suspect the man who would advise to more moderation and longer forbearance. Let two or three men who can feel as well as write, be appointed to draw up your *last remonstrance;* for I would no longer give it the suing, soft, unsuccessful epithet of memorial. Let it be represented in language that will neither dishonor you by its rudeness, nor betray you by its fears, what has been promised by Congress, and what has been performed—how long and how patiently you have suffered—how little you have asked, and how much of that little has been denied. Tell them that, though you were the first, and would wish to be the last to encounter danger, though despair itself can never drive you into dishonor, it may drive you from the field; that the wound often irritated, and never healed, may at length become incurable; and that the slightest mark of indignity from Congress now must operate like the grave, and part you for ever; that in any political event, the army has its alternative. If peace, that nothing shall separate you from your arms but death; if war, that, courting the auspices and inviting the directions of your illustrious leader, you will retire to some unsettled country, smile in your turn, and 'mock when their fear cometh.' But let it represent, also, that should they comply with the request of your late memorial, it would make you more happy, and them more respectable; that while war should continue, you would follow their standard into the field, and when it came to an end, you would withdraw into the shade of private life, and give the world another subject of wonder and applause; an army victorious over its enemies—victorious over itself."

Alarmed and distressed with this vile attempt to stimulate the army to rash and dangerous proceedings, the commander-in-chief noticed in general orders the anonymous address with his pointed disapprobation, and, with the view of counteracting its effects, requested that the general and field officers, and one from each company, and a proper representation from the staff of the army, would assemble on the 15th instant, to hear the report of the committee deputed by the army to Congress. The next day a second anonymous paper from the same pen appeared as follows:

"Till now, the commander-in-chief has regarded the steps you have taken for redress with good wishes alone; his ostensible silence has authorized your meetings, and his private opinion sanctified your claims. Had he disliked the object in view, would not the same sense of duty which forbade you from meeting on the third day of the week, have forbidden you from meeting on the seventh? Is not the same subject held up for your discussion? and has it not passed the seal of office, and taken all the solemnity of an order? This will give system to your proceedings, and stability to your resolves. It will ripen speculation into fact, and while it adds to the unanimity, it cannot possibly lessen the independency of your sentiments. It may be necessary to add, on this subject, that, from the injunction with which the general orders close, every man is at liberty to conclude that the report to be made to head-quarters is intended for Congress. Hence will arise another motive for that energy which has been recommended; for, can you give the lie to the pathetic descriptions and the more alarming predictions of our friends?"*

* With respect to the author of the Newburgh anonymous letters, suspicion has ever rested on John Armstrong, who at the time of their appearance was a major in the army, and for some time aid-de-camp to Major-General Gates. Though many circumstances conspired to fix this suspicion on Major Armstrong and a few confederates, the real fact has never been established till recently. In the last number of the *United States Magazine*, published in New York, General Armstrong has announced himself to be the author of these notorious letters. In justification of his motives, he maintains "that they were written by himself at the solicitation of his friends, as the chosen organ to express the sentiments of the officers of the army, and were only an *honest* and *manly*, though perhaps an indiscreet endeavor *to support public credit* and do justice to a long-suffering, patient, and gallant soldiery." In the same publication, General Armstrong has thought proper to risk his reputation on the bold and unqualified assertion, that the *slander* propagated and believed for half a century, that two distinguished officers of the revolution had conspired to put down the commander-in-chief, is an *impudent and vile falsehood from beginning to end*. The young reader, who may not be apprised of the circumstances on which the evidence of this conspiracy rests, is referred to the biography of Generals Lee, Gates and Conway, in the Appendix.

On the 15th instant, the convention of officers assembled, and General Gates presided. The commander-in-chief delivered to them the following very interesting and feeling address:

"Gentlemen: By an anonymous summons, an attempt has been made to convene you together. How inconsistent with the rules of propriety, how unmilitary, and how subversive of all order and discipline, let the good sense of the army decide.

"In the moment of this summons, another anonymous production was sent into circulation, addressed more to the feelings and passions than to the judgment of the army. The author of the piece is entitled to much credit for the goodness of his pen; and I could wish he had as much credit for the rectitude of his heart; for, as men see through different optics, and are induced by the reflecting faculties of the mind to use different means to attain the same end, the author of the address should have had more charity than to 'mark for suspicion the man who should recommend moderation and longer forbearance;' or, in other words, who should not think as he thinks, and act as he advises. But he had another plan in view, in which candor and liberality of sentiment, regard to justice and love of country, have no part; and he was right to insinuate the darkest suspicion to effect the blackest design. That the address was designed with great art, and is designed to answer the most insidious purposes; that it is calculated to impress the mind with an idea of premeditated injustice in the sovereign power of the United States, and rouse all those resentments which must unavoidably flow from such a belief; that the secret mover of this scheme, whoever he may be, intended to take advantage of the passions, while they were warmed by the recollection of past distresses, without giving time for cool, deliberative thinking, and that composure of mind which is so necessary to give dignity and stability to measures, is rendered too obvious, by the mode of conducting the business, to need other proof than a reference to the proceedings.

"Thus much, gentlemen, I have thought it incumbent on me to observe to you, to show on what principles I opposed the irregular and hasty meeting which was proposed to have been held on Tuesday last, and not because I wanted a disposition to give you every opportunity, consistently with your own honor and the dignity of the army, to make known your grievances. If my conduct heretofore has not evinced to you that I have been a faithful friend to the army, my declaration of it at this time would be equally unavailing and improper. But as I was among the first who embarked in the cause of our common country; as I have never left your side one moment, but when called from you on public duty; as I have been the constant companion and witness of your distresses, and not among the last to feel and acknowledge your merits; as I have ever considered my own military reputation as inseparably connected with that of the army; as my heart has ever expanded with joy when I have heard its praises, and my indignation has arisen when the mouth of detraction has been opened against it; it can scarcely be supposed at this last stage of the war that I am indifferent to its interests. But how are they to be promoted? The way is plain, says the anonymous addresser: 'If war continues, remove into the unsettled country; there establish yourselves, and leave an ungrateful country to defend itself!' But who are they to defend?—our wives, our children, our farms and other property which we leave behind us? or in this state of hostile separation, are we to take the two first—the latter cannot be removed—to perish in a wilderness, with hunger, cold and nakedness?

"'If peace takes place, never sheath your swords,' says he, 'till you have obtained full and ample justice.' This dreadful alternative of either deserting our country in the extremest hour of her distress, or turning our arms against it, which is the apparent object, unless Congress can be compelled into instant compliance, has something so shocking in it, that humanity revolts at the idea. My God! what can this writer have in view, by recommending such measures? Can he be a friend to the army? Can he be a friend to this country? Rather, is he not an insidious foe—some emissary, perhaps, from New York—plotting the ruin of both, by sowing the seeds of discord and separation between the civil and military powers of the continent? And what a compliment does he pay our understandings,° when he recommends measures, in either alternative, impracticable in their nature? But here, gentlemen, I will drop the curtain, because it would be as imprudent in me to assign my reasons for this opinion, as it would be insulting to your conception to suppose you stood in need of them. A moment's reflection will convince every dispassionate mind of the physical impossibility of carrying either proposal into execution. There might, gentlemen, be an impropriety in my taking notice, in this address to you, of an anonymous production; but the manner in which this performance has been introduced to the army; the effect it was intended to have, together with some other circumstances, will amply justify my observations on the tendency of this writing.

"With respect to the advice given by the author, to suspect the man who shall recommend moderate measures and longer forbearance, I spurn it, as every man who regards that liberty and reveres that justice for which we contend, undoubtedly must; for if men are to be precluded from offering their sentiments on a matter which may involve the most serious and alarming consequences that can invite the consideration of mankind, reason is of no use to us. The freedom of speech may be taken away, and, and, dumb and silent, we may be led, like sheep to the slaughter. I cannot in justice to my own belief, and what I have great reason to conceive is the intention of Congress, conclude this address without giving it as my decided opinion, that that honorable body entertain exalted sentiments of the services of the army, and, from a full conviction of its merits and sufferings, will do it complete justice. That their endeavors to discover and establish funds for this purpose have been unwearied, and will not cease till they have succeeded, I have not a doubt.

"But, like all other large bodies, where there is a variety of different interests to reconcile, their determinations are slow. Why then should we distrust them? and in consequence of this distrust, adopt measures which may cast a shade over that glory which has been so justly acquired, and tarnish the reputation of an army which is celebrated through

all Enrope for its fortitude and patriotism? And for what is this done?
—to bring the object we seek nearer? No ; most certainly, in my opin
ion, it will cast it at a greater distance. For myself, (and I take no
merit in giving the assurance, being induced to it from principles of
gratitude, veracity, and justice, and a grateful sense of the confidence
you have ever placed in me,) a recollection of the cheerful assistance
and prompt obedience I have experienced from you, under every vicissi-
tude of fortune, and the sincere affection I feel for an army I have so
long had the honor to command, will oblige me to declare, in this public and solemn manner, that in the attainment of complete justice for all
your toils and dangers, and in the gratification of every wish, so far as
may be done consistently with the great duty I owe my country, and
those powers we are bound to respect, you may freely command my
services to the utmost extent of my abilities.

"While I give you these assurances, and pledge myself, in the most
unequivocal manner, to exert whatever abilities I am possessed of in
your favor, let me entreat you, gentlemen, on your part, not to take any
measures which, viewed in the calm light of reason, will lessen the dignity and sully the glory you have hitherto maintained. Let me request
you to rely on the plighted faith of your country, and place a full confidence in the purity of the intentions of Congress; that, previous to your
dissolution as an army, they will cause all your accounts to be fairly
liquidated, as directed in the resolutions which were published to you
two days ago; and that they will adopt the most effectual measures in
their power to render ample justice to you for your faithful and meritorious services. And let me conjure you in the name of our common
country, as you value your own sacred honor; as you respect the rights
of humanity ; and as you regard the military and national character of
America; to express your utmost horror and detestation of the man who
wishes, under any specious pretences, to overturn the liberties of our
country; and who wickedly attempts to open the flood-gates of civil
discord, and deluge our rising empire in blood.

"By thus determining, and thus acting, you will pursue the plain and
direct road to the attainment of your wishes; you will defeat the insidious designs of our enemies, who are compelled to resort from open
force to secret artifice. You will give one more distinguished proof of
unexampled patriotism and patient virtue, rising superior to the pressure
of the most complicated sufferings; and you will, by the dignity of your
conduct, afford occasion for posterity to say, when speaking of the glorious example you have exhibited to mankind, 'Had this day been
wanting, the world had never seen the last stage of perfection to which
human nature is capable of attaining.'"

Having finished his incomparable and very efficacious
address, his excellency withdrew, and the convention
unanimously resolved to present him their thanks, and
that he be assured "that the officers reciprocate his affectionate expressions with the greatest sincerity of which
the human heart is capable." After which, General Knox,
Colonel Brooks, and Captain Howard were appointed a

committee to prepare resolutions expressive of the business of the convention, and to report in half an hour. They reported, and the convention—

"*Resolved, unanimously,* That, at the commencement of the present war, the officers of the American army engaged in the service of their country from the purest love and attachment to the rights and liberties of human nature; which motives still exist in the highest degree; and that no circumstances of distress or danger shall induce a conduct that may tend to sully the reputation and glory which they have acquired, at the price of their blood and eight years' faithful services.

"*Resolved, unanimously,* That the army continue to have an unshaken confidence in the justice of Congress and their country, and are fully convinced that the representatives of America will not disband or disperse the army till their accounts are liquidated, the balances accurately ascertained, and adequate funds established for payment; and in this arrangement the officers expect that the half-pay, or a commutation for it, should be efficaciously comprehended.

"*Resolved, unanimously,* That his excellency the commander-in-chief be requested to write to his excellency the president of Congress, earnestly entreating the most speedy decision of that honorable body on the subject of our late address, which was forwarded by a committee of the army, some of whom are waiting on Congress for the result. In the alternative of peace or war, this event would be highly satisfactory, and would produce immediate tranquillity in the minds of the army, and prevent any further machinations of designing men, to sow discord between the civil and military powers of the United States.

"On motion, *Resolved, unanimously,* That the officers of the American army view with abhorrence, and reject with disdain, the infamous propositions contained in a late anonymous address to the officers of the army, and resent with indignation the secret attempts of some unknown persons to collect the officers together, in a manner totally subversive of all discipline and good order.

"*Resolved, unanimously,* That the thanks of the officers of the army be given to the committee who presented to Congress the late address of the army, for the wisdom and prudence with which they have conducted that business; and that a copy of the proceedings of this day be transmitted by the president to Major-General McDougall; and that he be requested to continue his solicitations at Congress, till the objects of his mission are accomplished."

The result of the foregoing proceedings was, by the commander-in-chief, transmitted to Congress, accompanied by an impressive letter, of which the following is an extract:

"That in the critical and perilous moment when the last-mentioned communication was made, there was the utmost danger that a dissolution of the army would have taken place, unless measures similar to those recommended had been adopted, will not admit of a doubt. That the adoption of the resolution granting half-pay for life has been attended with all the happy consequences I had foretold, so far as respected the good of the service, let the astonishing contrast between the state of the army at this instant and at the former period determine.

"And that the establishment of funds, and security of the payment of all the just demands of the army will be the most certain means of pre serving the national faith and future tranquillity of this extensive conti nent, is my decided opinion. By the preceding remarks, it will readily be imagined that, instead of retracting and reprehending, from further experience and reflection, the mode of compensation so strenuously urged in the inclosures, I am more and more confirmed in the sentiment, and if in the wrong, suffer me to please myself with the grateful delusion. For if, besides the simple payment of their wages, a further compensation is not due to the sufferings and sacrifices of the officers, then have I been mistaken indeed. If the whole army have not merited whatever a grateful people can bestow, then have I been beguiled by prejudice, and built opinion on the basis of error. If this country should not in the event perform every thing which has been requested in the late memorials to Congress, then will my belief become vain, and the hope that has been excited void of foundation. And if, as has been suggested for the purpose of inflaming their passions, the officers of the army are to be the only sufferers by this revolution; if, retiring from the field, they are to grow old in poverty, wretchedness, and contempt; if they are to wade through the vile mire of dependency, and owe the miserable remnant of that life to charity which has hitherto been spent in honor, then shall I have learned what ingratitude is—then shall I have realized a tale which will embitter every moment of my future life. But I am under no such apprehensions; a country rescued by their arms from impending ruin, will never leave unpaid the debt of gratitude."

"G. WASHINGTON."

March 22d.—Congress at length came to the following resolutions:

"Whereas the officers of the several lines, under the immediate command of his Excellency General Washington, did by their late memorial transmitted, represent to Congress that the half-pay granted by sundry resolutions was regarded in an unfavorable light by the citizens of some of the states, who would prefer a compensation for a limited term of years, or by a sum in gross, to an establishment for life; and did, on this account, solicit a commutation of their half-pay for an equivalent, in one of the modes above mentioned, in order to remove all subjects of dissatisfaction from the minds of their fellow-citizens: And whereas Congress are desirous, as well of gratifying the reasonable expectations of the officers of the army, as of removing all objections which may exist in any part of the United States to the principles of the half-pay establishment, for which the faith of the United States has been pledged; persuaded that these objections can only arise from the nature of the compensation, not from any indisposition to compensate those whose services, sacrifices, and sufferings, have so justly a title to the approbation and rewards of their country: Therefore—

"*Resolved*, That such officers as are now in service, and shall continue therein to the end of the war, shall be entitled to receive the amount of five years' full pay in money, or securities on interest at six per cent. per annum, as Congress shall find most convenient, instead of the half-pay promised for life, by the resolution of the 21st day of October, 1780, the said securities to be such as shall be given to the creditors of the United States. *Provided*, that it be at the option of the lines of the respective states to accept or refuse the same. And provided, also, that their election shall be signified to Congress, through the commander-in-chief, from the lines under his immediate command within two months; and through the commanding officer of the Southern army, from those under his command, within six months, from the date of this resolution.

"That the same computation shall extend to the corps not belonging to the lines of particular states, and who are entitled to half-pay for life as aforesaid; the acceptance or refusal to be determined by corps, and to be signified in the same manner, and within the same time as above mentioned.

"That all officers belonging to the hospital department, who are entitled to half-pay by the resolution of the 17th day of January, 1781, may collectively agree to accept or refuse the aforesaid commutation, signifying the same through the commander-in-chief, within six months from this time.

"That such officers as have retired at different periods, entitled to half-pay for life, may, collectively in each state in which they are inhabitants, accept or refuse the same; their acceptation or refusal to be signified by agents, authorized for this purpose, within six months from this period. That with respect to such retiring officers, the commutation, if accepted, shall be in lieu of whatever may be now due to them, since the time of their retiring from service, as well as of what might hereafter become due, and that as soon as their acceptance shall be signified, the superintendent of finance be, and he is hereby, directed to take measures for the settlement of their accounts accordingly, and to issue to them certificates bearing interest at six per cent.

"That all officers entitled to half-pay for life, not included in the preceding resolution, may also collectively agree to accept or refuse the aforesaid commutation, signifying the same within six months from this time."

April 18th.—The commander-in-chief thus addressed the army on the cessation of hostilities:

"The commander-in-chief orders the cessation of hostilities, between the United States of America and the King of Great Britain, to be publicly proclaimed to-morrow at twelve o'clock, at the New Building; and that the proclamation which will be communicated herewith, be read to-morrow evening, at the head of every regiment and corps of the army; after which, the chaplains, with the several brigades, will render thanks to Almighty God for all his mercies, particularly for his overruling the wrath of man to his own glory, and causing the rage of war to cease among the nations."

Though the proclamation before alluded to extends only to the prohibition of hostilities, and not to the annunciation of a general peace, yet it must afford the most rational and sincere satisfaction to every benevolent mind, as it puts a period to a long and doubtful contest—stops the effusion of human blood—opens the prospect to a more splendid scene—and, like another morning-star, promises the approach of a brighter day than has hitherto illuminated this western hemisphere! On such a happy day— a day which is the harbinger of peace—a day which completes the eighth year of the war, it would be ingratitude not to rejoice; it would be insensibility not to participate in the general felicity.

"The commander-in-chief, far from endeavoring to stifle the feelings of joy in his own bosom, offers his most cordial congratulations on the occasion, to all the officers of every denomination, to all the troops of the United States in general, and in particular to those gallant and persevering men who had resolved to defend the rights of their invaded country so long as the war should continue; for these are the men who ought to be considered as the pride and boast of the American army, and who, crowned with well-earned laurels, may soon withdraw from the field of glory to the more tranquil walks of civil life.

"While the general recollects the almost infinite variety of scenes through which we have passed with a mixture of pleasure, astonishment, and gratitude—while he contemplates the prospects before us with rapture—he cannot help wishing that all the brave men, of whatever condition they may be, who have shared in the toils and dangers of effecting this glorious revolution, of rescuing millions from the hand of oppression, and of laying the foundation of a great empire, might be impressed with a proper idea of the dignified part they have been called to act, under the smiles of Providence, on the stage of human affairs; for happy, thrice happy, shall they be pronounced hereafter, who have contributed any thing, who have performed the meanest office in erecting this stupendous *fabric of Freedom and Empire*, on the broad basis of independency; who have assisted in protecting the rights of human nature, and establishing an asylum for the poor and oppressed of all nations and religions.

"The glorious task for which we first flew to arms being thus accomplished—the liberties of our country being fully acknowledged and firmly secured by the smiles of Heaven on the purity of our cause, and the honest exertions of a feeble people, determined to be free, against a powerful nation disposed to oppress them—and the character of those who have persevered through every extremity of hardship, suffering, and danger, being immortalized by the illustrious appellation of the *Patriot Army*—nothing now remains but for the actors of this mighty scene to preserve a perfect, unvarying consistency of character through the very last act; to close the drama with applause; and to retire from the military theatre with the same approbation of angels and men, which have crowned all their former virtuous actions.

"For this purpose, no disorder or licentiousness must be tolerated; every considerate and well-disposed soldier must remember it will be absolutely necessary to wait with patience till peace shall be declared, or Congress shall be enabled to take proper measures for the security of the public stores, &c. So soon as these arrangements shall be made, the general is confident there will be no delay in discharging, with every mark of distinction and honor, all the men enlisted for the war, who will then have faithfully performed their engagements with the public. The general has already interested himself in their behalf; and he thinks he need not repeat the assurances of his disposition to be useful to them on the present, and every other proper occasion. In the mean time, he is determined that no military neglects or excesses shall go unpunished while he retains the command of the army.

"The adjutant-general will have such working parties detailed to assist in making the preparation for a general rejoicing as the chief engineer, with the army, shall call for; and the quarter-master-general will also furnish such materials as he may want. The quarter-master-general will, without delay, procure such a number of discharges to be printed as will be sufficient for all the men enlisted for the war; he will please to apply to head-quarters for the form.

"An extra ration of liquor to be issued to *every man to-morrow, to drink perpetual peace, independence and happiness to the United States of America.*"

The officers of the army, by their committee, prepared the following address to the commander-in-chief:

"Sir: It is difficult for us to express the regret we feel at being obliged again to solicit your excellency's attention and patronage. Next to the anguish which the prospect of our own wretchedness excites in our breasts, is the pain which arises from the knowledge of your anxiety on account of those men who have been the sharers of your fortunes, and have had the honor of being your companions through the various vicissitudes of the war. Nothing, therefore, but necessity could induce us to a representation which we know must give you concern.

"Your excellency has so intimate a knowledge of the condition of the army, as to render a particular delineation unnecessary. As you have been a witness of our sufferings during a war uncommon in its nature, and unparalleled in many circumstances attending it; so you are now, sir, no less a witness of the unequal burden which has fallen on us, from the want of that provision to which, from our assiduous and unremitting services, we conceive we are entitled. Having recently expressed our sense of what was due to our distress; having repeated to your excellency the confidence we had that our accounts would be liquidated, the balances ascertained, and adequate funds provided for payment, previous to our being dispersed or disbanded; having seen with pleasure the approbation which Congress gave our reliance, it is with a mixture of astonishment and chagrin that we view the late resolve of Congress, by which the soldiers for the war, and a proportionate number of officers, are to be furloughed without any one of those important objects being accomplished; and, to complete the scene of woe, are to be compelled to leave the army without the means of defraying the debts we have necessarily incurred in the course of service, or even of gratifying those menials in the pittance which is their due; much less to carry with us that support and comfort to our families, of which, from our long military services, they have been deprived. No less exposed to the insults of the meanest followers of the army, than to the arrests of the sheriff—deprived of the ability to assist our families, and without an evidence that any thing is due to us for our services, and consequently without the least prospect of obtaining credit for even a temporary subsistence, till we can get into business—to what quarter can we look? We take the liberty to say this, sir, only to your excellency; and, from the sincerity of our hearts, we do it no less from a persuasion of the efficacy of your further efforts in our favor, than from the kind assurances you have been pleased to give us of your support.

"To your excellency, then, we make one appeal, and in the most solemn manner, from that abhorrence of oppression and injustice which first unsheathed our swords; from the remembrance of the common dangers through which we have passed; and from the recollection of those astonishing events which have been effected by our united efforts —permit us to solicit your further aid, and to entreat that the order of the 2d instant, founded on the act of Congress of the 26th of May last, may be suspended or varied in its operation, so far as that no officer or soldier be obliged to receive a furlough till that honorable body can be apprised of the wretched situation into which the army must be plunged by a conformity to it; that your excellency will endeavor to prevail on Congress—nay, that on the principles of common justice, you will insist that neither officer nor soldier be compelled to leave the field till a liquidation of accounts can be effected, till the balances are ascertained, certificates for the sums due given, including the commutation of half-pay to the officers and gratuity of eighty dollars to the soldiers; and till a supply of money can be furnished, sufficient to carry us from the field of glory, with honor to ourselves and credit to our country. We still wish to believe that that country, to which we have been so long devoted, will never look with indifference on the distresses of those of her sons who have so essentially contributed to the establishment of freedom, the security of property, and the rearing of an empire.

"In the name and behalf of the generals and officers commanding regiments and corps, in the cantonment on Hudson's river,

"I have the honor to be, with the highest respect,

"Your Excellency's most obedient servant,

"*July 5th*, 1783."   "W. HEATH, Major-General, *President.*

To the foregoing address General Washington was pleased to make an affectionate reply, in which, among other things, he observes, that as furloughs in all services are considered as a matter of indulgence and not of compulsion—as Congress, he is persuaded, entertain the best disposition towards the army—and as he apprehends in a short time the two principal articles of complaint will be removed—he will not hesitate to comply with the wishes of the army with respect to furloughs, &c. He cannot but hope, he observes, that the notes will soon arrive, and that the settlement of accounts may be completed in a very few days. In the mean time, he shall have the honor of laying the sentiments of the generals and officers before Congress; they are expressed in so decent, candid and affecting a manner, that he is certain every mark of attention will be paid to them. In his letter to the president of Congress, inclosing the address of the officers, and his answer, his excellency observes:

"These inclosures will explain the distresses which resulted from the measures now carrying into execution, in consequence of the resolution of the 26th of May; but the sensibility, occasioned by a parting scene, under such peculiar circumstances, will not admit of description! While I consider it a tribute of justice on this occasion to mention the temperate and orderly behavior of the whole army, and particularly the accommodating spirit of the officers, in arranging themselves to the command of the battalions, which will be composed of the three years' men; permit me to recall to mind all their former sufferings and merits, and to recommend their reasonable request to the early and favorable notice of Congress."

19*th*.—On the completion of eight years from the memorable battle of Lexington, the proclamation of the Congress for a cessation of hostilities was published at the door of the public building, followed by three huzzas; after which, a prayer was offered to the Almighty Ruler of the world, by the Rev. Mr. Ganno, and an anthem was performed by voices and instruments.

On the 29th of June, about eighty new-levy soldiers of the Pennsylvania line, who had been stationed at Lancaster, in defiance of their officers, marched to Philadelphia to seek a redress of their supposed grievances from the executive council of the state. They proceeded to the barracks in the city, where were quartered some other soldiers, who joined them, amounting to about three hundred in the whole. The day following, these insurgent troops, with fixed bayonets and drums beating, marched to the state-house, the seat of Congress and of the supreme executive council of Pennsylvania. They placed sentinels at every door, sent in a written message to the president and council, and threatened to let loose an enraged soldiery on them, if they were not gratified as to their demands within twenty minutes. Though no other insult was offered to Congress, this *duresse* continued about three hours.

Congress resolved that the authority of the United States had been grossly insulted by the armed soldiers; that their committee confer with the executive council; and that in case it should appear to the committee that there is no satisfactory ground for expecting adequate exertions by the state of Pennsylvania for supporting the dignity of the federal government, the president, on the advice of the committee, should summon the members of Congress to meet on Thursday, the 26th, at Trenton or Princeton, and that the secretary at war should communicate to the commander-in-chief the state and disposition of the mutineers, that he might take immediate measures for suppressing them. Congress now found it expedient to separate, and rëassemble at Princeton. The commander-in-chief, on receiving information of this shameful outrage, instantly detached fifteen hundred men, under command of Major-General Howe, to quell the mutiny and punish the most guilty. Before his arrival, however, they had dispersed without bloodshed. A number were brought to trial, and two sentenced to suffer death, and four others to receive corporeal punishment. The commander-in-chief, on this occasion, addressed the president of Congress in the feeling language which follows:

"While I suffer the most poignant distress in observing that a handful of men, contemptible in numbers, and equally so in point of service, if the veteran troops from the southward have not been seduced by their example, and who are not worthy to be called soldiers, should disgrace themselves and their country, as the Pennsylvania mutineers have done, by insulting the sovereign authority of the United States, and that of their own; I feel an inexpressible satisfaction, that even this behavior cannot stain the name of the American soldiery. It cannot be imputable to, or reflect dishonor on the army at large; but, on the contrary, it will, by the striking contrast it exhibits, hold up to public view the other troops in the most advantageous point of light. On taking all the circumstances into consideration, I cannot sufficiently express my surprise and indignation at the arrogance, the folly, and the wickedness of the mutineers; nor can I sufficiently admire the fidelity, the bravery and patriotism, which must for ever signalize the unsullied character of the other corps of our army. For when we consider that these Pennsylvania levies, who have now mutinied, are recruits, and soldiers of a day, who have not borne the heat and burden of the war, and who can have in reality very few hardships to complain of; and when we at the same time recollect that those soldiers who have lately been furloughed from this army are the veterans who have patiently endured hunger, nakedness, and cold; who have suffered and bled without a murmur, and who,

with perfect good order, have retired to their homes, without a settlement of their accounts, or a farthing of money in their pockets; we shall
be as much astonished at the virtues of the latter, as we are struck with
horror and detestation at the proceedings of the former; and every candid mind, without indulging ill-grounded prejudices, will undoubtedly
make the proper discrimination."

On the 2d of November, 1783, General Washington
issued his farewell orders to the armies of the United
States. Having taken notice of the proclamation of Congress of October 18th, he said:

"It only remains for the commander-in-chief to address himself once
more, and that for the last time, to the armies of the United States,
however widely dispersed the individuals who composed them may be,
and to bid them an affectionate, a long farewell. But before the commander-in-chief takes his final leave of those he holds most dear, he
wishes to indulge himself a few moments in calling to mind a slight
review of the past. He will then take the liberty of exploring with his
military friends their future prospects—of advising the general line of
conduct which, in his opinion, ought to be pursued, and he will conclude
the address by expressing the obligations he feels himself under for the
spirited and able assistance he has experienced from them in the performance of an arduous office.

"A contemplation of the complete attainment, at a period earlier than
could have been expected, of the object for which we contended, against
so formidable a power, cannot but inspire us with astonishment and
gratitude. The disadvantageous circumstances, on our part, under which
the war was undertaken, can never be forgotten. The signal interpositions of Providence, in our feeble condition, were such as could scarcely
escape the attention of the most unobserving; while the unparalleled
perseverance of the armies of the United States, through almost every
possible suffering and discouragement, for the space of eight long years,
was little short of a standing miracle."

His closing words are: "And being now to conclude
these his last public orders, to take his ultimate leave in
a short time of the military character, and to bid adieu to
the armies he has so long had the honor to command, he
can only again offer in their behalf his recommendations
to their grateful country, and his prayers to the God of
armies. May ample justice be done them here, and may
the choicest of Heaven's favors, both here and hereafter,
attend those who, under the divine auspices, have secured
innumerable blessings for others! With these wishes, and
this benediction, the commander-in-chief is about to retire
from service. The curtain of separation will soon be
drawn, and the military scene to him will be closed for
ever."—The definitive treaty of peace was signed on the

23d of September, and Congress, having ratified it, they issued a proclamation to disband their army. This proclamation purports, "that part of the army which stood engaged to serve during the war, and by several acts of Congress had been furloughed, should be absolutely discharged after the 3d of November from said service, and that the further service in the field of the officers deranged, and on furlough, are now dispensed with, and they have permission to retire from service, no more to be called to command," &c. In their proclamation, Congress give their thanks to the army for their exertions in the cause of America and the common rights of mankind. The mode of disbanding the army was well calculated to prevent any disorders, which might have been the consequence of dismissing a large number of men in a body. The advice of their beloved commander-in-chief, and the resolves of Congress to pay and compensate them in such manner as the ability of the United States would permit, operated to keep them quiet and prevent tumult. Painful indeed was the parting scene; no description can be adequate to the tragic exhibition. Both officers and soldiers, long unaccustomed to the affairs of private life, turned loose on the world to starve and to become a prey to vulture speculators. Never can that melancholy day be forgotten when friends, companions for seven long years in joy and in sorrow, were torn asunder, without the hope of ever meeting again, and with prospects of a miserable subsistence in future. Among other incidents, peculiarly affecting on this occasion, were the lamentations of women and children, earnestly entreating that those with whom they had been connected in the character of husband and father, would not withdraw from them the hand of kindness and protection, and leave them in despair; but in several instances the reply was, No; "we took you as *companions during the war*, and now we are destitute of the means of support, and you must provide for yourselves."

November 25th.—The British army evacuated New York, and the American troops, under General Knox, took possession of the city. Soon after, General Washington and Governor Clinton, with their suite, made their public entry into the city on horseback, followed by the lieutenant-governor and the members of council, for the temporary government of the Southern district, four abreast. General Knox and the officers of the army, eight abreast; citizens on horseback, eight abreast; the speaker of the assembly and citizens on foot, eight abreast. The governor gave a public dinner, at which the commander-in-chief, and other general officers were present. The arrangements for the whole business were so well made and executed, that the most admirable tranquillity succeeded through the day and night. On Monday the governor gave an elegant entertainment to the French · ambassador, the Chevalier de la Luzerne; General Washington, the principal officers of New York state and of the army, and upwards of a hundred gentlemen, were present. Magnificent fire-works, infinitely exceeding every thing of the kind before seen in the United States, were exhibited at the Bowling Green in Broadway, on the evening of Tuesday, in celebration of the definitive treaty of peace. They commenced by a dove descending with the *olive branch*, and setting fire to a marron battery. On Tuesday noon, December 4th, the principal officers of the army assembled at Francis' tavern, to take a final leave of their much-loved commander-in-chief. Soon after, his excellency entered the room. His emotions were too strong to be concealed. Filling a glass, he turned to them, and said, "With a heart full of love and gratitude, I now take leave of you. I most devoutly wish that your latter days may be as prosperous and happy as your former ones have been glorious and honorable." Having drank, he added, "I cannot come to each of you to take my leave, but shall be obliged to you, if each of you will come and take me by the hand." General Knox, being nearest, turned to him. Incapable of utterance, Washington, *in tears*, grasped his hand, embraced and kissed him. In the same affectionate manner he took leave of each succeeding officer. In every eye was the tear of dignified sensibility; and not a word was articulated to interrupt the eloquent silence and tenderness of the scene. Leaving the room, he passed through the corps of light-infantry, and walked to White Hall, where a barge waited to convey him to Paulus' Hook. The whole company followed in mute and solemn procession, with dejected countenances, testifying feelings of delicious melancholy which no language can

23

describe. Having entered the barge, he turned to the
company, and, waving his hat, bid them a silent adieu.
They paid him the same affectionate compliment, and after
the barge had left them, returned in the same solemn
manner to the place where they had assembled. The
passions of human nature were never more tenderly agitated than in this interesting and distressful scene.

General Washington now repaired to Annapolis, where
Congress were in session, to whom he resigned his commission, which eight years before he had received from
this honorable body. On the 23d of December, the day
appointed for the very interesting transaction, a vast concourse of spectators attended. The gallery was filled with
a group of ladies, and some graced the floor of Congress.
The governor, council and legislature of Maryland, several
general officers, the consul general of France, and numerous citizens of Annapolis were present. Congress were
seated and covered, as representatives of the sovereignty
of the union; the spectators were uncovered and standing.
The general was introduced to a chair by the secretary,
who, after a decent interval, ordered silence. A short
pause ensued, when the honorable Thomas Mifflin, the
president, informed the general that "the United States
in Congress assembled were prepared to receive his communications." On which, he rose with dignity, and delivered this address:

"MR. PRESIDENT: The great events on which my resignation depended, having at length taken place, I now have the honor of offering
my sincere congratulations to Congress, and of presenting myself before
them, to surrender into their hands the trust committed to me, and to
claim the indulgence of retiring from the service of my country.

"Happy in the confirmation of our independence and sovereignty, and
pleased with the opportunity afforded the United States of becoming a
respectable nation, I resign with satisfaction the appointment I accepted
with diffidence—a diffidence in my abilities, to accomplish so arduous a
task, which, however, was superseded by a confidence in the rectitude
of our cause, the support of the supreme power of the union, and the
patronage of Heaven.

"The successful termination of the war has verified the most sanguine
expectations: my gratitude for the interpositions of Providence, and the
assistance I have received from my countrymen, increase with every review of the momentous contest.

"While I respect my obligations to the army in general, I should do
injustice to my own feelings not to acknowledge in this place the peculiar services and distinguished merits of the persons who have been

attached to my person during the war. It was impossible the choice of confidential officers to compose my family should have been more fortunate. Permit me, sir, to recommend in particular those who have continued in the service to the present moment, as worthy of the favorable notice and patronage of Congress.

"I consider it as an indispensable duty to close this last solemn act of my official life by commending the interests of our dearest country to the protection of Almighty God, and those who have the superintendence of them to his holy keeping.

"Having now finished the work assigned me, I retire from the great theatre of action; and bidding an affectionate farewell to this august body, under whose orders I have long acted, I here offer my commission, and take my leave of all the employments of public life."

This address being ended, General Washington advanced, and delivered his commission into the hands of the President of Congress, who replied as follows:

"The United States, in Congress assembled, receive with emotions too affecting for utterance the solemn resignation of the authorities under which you have led their troops with success through a perilous and doubtful war.

"Called on by your country to defend its invaded rights, you accepted the sacred charge before it had formed alliances, and while it was without friends or a government to support you.

"You have conducted the great military contest with wisdom and fortitude, invariably regarding the rights of the civil power, through all disasters and changes. You have, by the love and confidence of your fellow-citizens, enabled them to display their martial genius, and transmit their fame to posterity; you have persevered till these United States, aided by a magnanimous king and nation, have been enabled, under a just Providence, to close the war in safety, freedom, and independency; on which happy event we sincerely join you in congratulations.

"Having defended the standard of liberty in this new world; having taught a lesson useful to those who inflict, and to those who feel oppression, you retire from the great theatre of action with the blessings of your fellow-citizens; but the glory of your virtues will not terminate with your military command: it will continue to animate remotest ages. We feel, with you, our obligations to the army in general, and will particularly charge ourselves with the interest of those confidential officers who have attended your person to this affecting moment.

"We join you in commending the interests of our dearest country to the protection of Almighty God, beseeching him to dispose the hearts and minds of its citizens to improve the opportunity afforded them of becoming a happy and respectable nation; and for you we address to Him our earnest prayers, that a life so beloved may be fostered with all his care; that your days may be happy, as they have been illustrious, and that he will finally give you that reward which this world cannot give."

It is impossible to conceive that greater honor can be conferred on any man, than to receive the united acknowledgments of three millions of people, assembled by their representatives, declaring to all the world that he has been the temporal saviour of his country! His mind was powerful and enlightened, his devotion to his country fervent, his sacrifices great and important, and his triumphs noble and splendid; and his memory will be blessed and immortal!

It has been estimated that the loss of lives in the various armies of the United States, during the war, is not less than seventy thousand. The numbers who died on board of the horrid prison-ships of the enemy cannot be calculated. It is, however, confidently asserted, that no less than eleven thousand of our brave soldiers died on board the one called the *Jersey prison-ship*, only! This dreadful mortality is universally attributed to the cruel treatment which they received while crowded together in close confinement.

The loss to Great Britain is two large armies captured by the United States, exclusively of many thousands killed and taken in various actions during the war; thirteen colonies dismembered from her, and an increase of her national debt, in seven years, one hundred and twenty millions.

The *United States* have *gained* that independence and liberty for which they contended, and find their debt to be less than forty-five millions of dollars, which is short of ten millions of pounds sterling! This long-protracted warfare, waged in behalf of American freedom, is now triumphantly terminated, and a sanctuary sacred to civil and religious liberty will be opened in this western hemisphere.

Extract of a Circular Letter from his Excellency George Washington, Commander-in-Chief of the Armies of the United States of America, to the Governors of the several States.

"HEAD-QUARTERS, *Newburgh, June*, 18, 1783.

"For my own part, conscious of having acted, while a servant of the public, in the manner I conceived best suited to promote the real interests of my country; having, in consequence of my fixed belief, in some measure pledged myself to the army that their country would finally do them complete and ample justice, and not willing to conceal any instance of my official conduct from the eyes of the world, I have thought proper to transmit to your excellency the inclosed collection of papers, relative to the half-pay and commutation granted by Congress to the officers of the army.

"From these communications, my decided sentiment will be clearly comprehended, together with the conclusive reasons which induced me at an early period to recommend the adoption of this measure in the most earnest and serious manner. As the proceedings of Congress, the army, and myself are open to all, and contain, in my opinion, sufficient information to remove the prejudice and errors which may have been entertained by any, I think it unnecessary to say any thing more than just to observe, that the resolutions of Congress, now alluded to, are as undoubtedly and absolutely binding on the United States, as the most solemn acts of confederation or legislation.

"As to the idea, which I am informed has in some instances prevailed, that the half-pay and commutation are to be regarded merely in the odious light of a pension, it ought to be exploded for ever: That provision should be viewed as it really was, a reasonable compensation offered by Congress, at a time when they had nothing else to give, to officers of the army for services then to be performed: It was the only means to prevent a total dereliction of the service; it was a part of their hire—I may be allowed to say, it was the price of their blood and of your independency; it is therefore more than a common debt; it is a debt of honor; it can never be considered as a pension or gratuity, nor canceled till it is fairly discharged."

For the following sketch I am indebted to the Hon. William Eustis, a highly respectable surgeon in the hospital department during the revolutionary war:

COLONEL JOHN CRANE, AND OTHERS.

The mechanics of Boston and its vicinity may take a just pride in having furnished from their ranks some of the bravest and most useful officers of the revolutionary army, and, among them, no one more brave or more useful than John Crane.

In adverting to the sources whence they derived their knowledge of discipline and of service, our first object is to show, from facts and experience, the utility and importance of a well-organized militia, and to defend this invaluable institution from the reproaches of the ignorant and assuming, who would sap the foundation of the national defence; and secondly, to inspire the young mechanics with zeal in the military profession, that like their predecessors they may become the able and substantial defenders of their country.

Previous to the war of the revolution, there was in Boston a company of artillery, commanded by Captain Adino Paddock, by profession a chaise-maker. It was composed principally, if not altogether, of the mechanics of Boston, and was distinguished by its superior discipline, by the exactness of its manœuvres and the accuracy of its firings. Paddock had tory connexions, adhered to the British, went to England, was consulted repeatedly by the British ministry, and was invested with the military command of the island of Guernsey. In this company were raised Colonel John Crane, Colonel (now General) Ebenezer Stevens, with others, all of whose names are not recollected. Crane and Stevens were house-carpenters, Perkins was a shoe-maker, Seward a hatter, Popkins a tailor, Allen a sail-maker, Carnes a rope-maker, Lillie a cooper, Johnson a painter, Treat a cooper, Burbeck a ——, Hall a mason, D. Bryant a chair-maker, Cook a butcher, Thomas a cooper, and Allen a sail-maker.

The greater part of these with others formed a regiment of artillery, not exceeded in discipline, valor, and usefulness by any regiment in service. Crane was made a major in 1775. An uneducated man, he had all the pride and ambition of a soldier. He was constitutionally bold and daring, courting danger wherever it was to be found.

In 1775, when Boston was besieged, his station was in Roxbury. On Boston neck a breastwork was constructed, and so soon as cannon could be procured they were mounted. Crane had the command, spent a great part of his time there, and was never more delighted than when he was permitted to fire on the British intrenchment. Our stock of powder was then small. It was on this theatre that he first displayed an undaunted courage, and a knowledge of the art of gunnery, not often displayed by old artillery officers. He repeatedly dismounted the cannon in the embrasures of the British works, killing and wounding their men. After the evacuation of Boston, he marched to New York. Whenever a British ship-of-war appeared in the East or North rivers, or any firing was heard, Crane was on horseback, and galloped to the scene of action. Being reproached on an occasion when he exposed himself alone, riding through Greenwich-street, under the constant broadsides of a passing ship, he replied, "The shot is not cast which is to kill me."

Not long after, a frigate run up the East river, and anchored on the Long Island side, near Corlaer's hook. Four field-pieces were ordered to annoy her. They were only six-pounders. Crane, as usual, was present, and pointed the pieces. His sight was remarkably true—his aim was sure. He had from habit and the acuteness of his vision the faculty of seeing a cannon-ball on its passage through the air. A falling shot from the ship he kenned in a direction to strike, as he thought, the lower part of his body. Not having time to change his position in any other way, he whirled himself round on one foot; the ball struck the other foot while raised in the air, carrying away the great toe and ball of the foot. Thus ended his usefulness for the campaign. He was afterwards removed to New Jersey, and, surviving the perils of a partial jaw-lock, so far recovered as to go home on furlough. He returned the next spring, and continued in service till the peace.

The nature of this work will not allow us to follow him through the remainder of his career; but we cannot refrain from stating a closing anecdote, illustrative of his independent spirit. He had been among the number of those who thought the army had been neglected by the country, and spake as he felt, indignantly, at the treatment they had received. A board of general and field officers, with two hospital surgeons, were appointed to examine the wounded officers and soldiers in camp at the close of the war, and to report the rate of compensation to which they were severally entitled. A friend and brother-officer, who well knew the nature of his wound, waited on Colonel Crane, represented to him that, on his return to private life, his activity of mind and body would lead him to some kind of labor, and that having lost the ball of his foot, the bones would come through the cicatrix, and his wound open again, asking the favor of him to walk over, and suffer his foot to be inspected. Stamping the wounded foot on the floor, he replied, indignantly, "No, sir; they never shall say that I eat their bread when I have done serving them."

He entered afterwards on active and laborious business, and prospered for a number of years, met with adverse circumstances, his wound broke out again, he could no longer labor. After many years he came to the friend who had admonished him of the consequences of his wound, and said to him, with tears in his eyes, "My friend, I am now a humbled man, you may do with me as you please." He was immediately placed on the pension-list, but did not live a year to enjoy his pension.

The important services of Major Stevens, who commanded the artillery under General Gates, in the campaign of 1777, are well known.

There are anecdotes relative to many others of them, illustrative of their bravery in the field, and of their magnanimity and general usefulness during the war which we have not room to particularize. One, however, we cannot in justice omit. David Bryant, bred a chair-maker in Boston, and afterwards a lieutenant in the artillery, was a man of small stature, but remarkable for the strictness of discipline which he observed from the earliest period of the war. At the close of the battle of Brandywine, he was hard pressed by the enemy, and was mortally wounded. His men hovered round him to take care of him. He addressed them in the following words: "My lads, it is over with me; leave me, but don't leave the pieces." His words were electric; they saved their pieces, and brought him off on the trail. He died in the American camp.

To the above catalogue of worthies may be added Colonel Paul Revere; his occupation was that of a gold-smith. He was a very active and influential patriot at the commencement of the revolution, associated with a number of mechanics, who watched with a vigilant eye every movement of the British, and promptly communicated intelligence to the proper authority. In the evening preceding the 19th of April, 1775, Colonel Revere was one of the first who discovered that a British detachment was ordered on an expedition into the country, and with the utmost despatch repaired to Lexington, spreading the alarm among the militia, and giving notice to Messrs. Hancock and Adams, who were then at the house of the clergyman in that town, that they might escape the impending danger. Colonel Revere was afterwards appointed to command a regiment of artillery in the militia, and was on the unfortunate Penobscot expedition in the summer of 1779. He was through life esteemed for unimpeachable integrity, attachment to correct political principles, and as a useful citizen. He died in Boston, in 1818, in his eighty-fourth year.

Dr. John Thomas is a respectable regimental surgeon. He possesses a remarkable faculty of mimicry, and no person in New England can tell a Yankee story with more genuine humor. An occurrence at head-quarters is thus related by a gentleman who was present. General Washington seldom smiles; I never saw him laugh but once; it was after the preliminaries of peace were signed, and at a Yankee story told by Dr. Thomas. The doctor being invited to dine at head-quarters, one of the aids requested the general's permission for him to repeat the dialogue between two New England men who had visited the French camp. In doing this, he repeated quaint speeches and remarks in a manner so inimitably ludicrous, that no one but his excellency could contain his gravity. At length he added, "What, said Jonathan, do you think Chambeau's soldiers call a hat? the tarnation fools, they call it a chappeau! Why, and be darn'd to them, can't they call it a hat and adone with it?" The general could no longer refrain; he burst into a fit of laughter. There is not perhaps another man who can boast of exciting laughter in General Washington.

Captain Houdin, commonly pronounced Udang, is a Frenchman of singular manners and character, and ludicrous in his personal appearance, being rather tall, but slender; his features are sharp and irregular, complexion dark, with small jet-black eyes. His long hair is brought in a braid to the top of his head, which is constantly covered with powder; he is never seen without his small-sword, nor in conversation without a display of vanity and affectation. He converses in broken English, with rapid articulation, often perverting words from their legitimate meaning. Dr. Thomas and Udang have at command an inexhaustible fund of merriment and humor, and Udang once said to the doctor, "You can take me off better than I can myself." On a return from Boston, in 1780, he related some incidents that occurred to him, which have frequently been repeated to aid in festive mirth. Some wag, knowing his vanity and affectation of consequence, had employed a negro wench to make a familiar address to him in some public place. This was a severe mortification, and destroyed all the comforts of his visit. In answer to an inquiry how he liked Boston, this vexation was uppermost in his mind. "I like Boston very well, all but one d—d madam nig." On being pressed further, he related the particulars with all the action and irritation that the reality occasioned. One gentleman said to me,

Will you take a walk to the market—twas one very fine market—de poult, de geese, ebery ting—one very fine *assortiment*—*dere* it was I hear somebody say behind, '*How do you do, Captain Udang?*' I looked round; one black bish say again, making reverence, '*I hope you be well, Captain Udang.*' Who be you speak to me in de market? 'You forget,' she say, 'I was your sweetheart in '77.' Hol you tongue, you d—d rascal bish. You speak to me in de market, when I am wid gentlemen, I cut off your head, I will, you rascal wench. I was so asham, I put de hat over my eyes and run right home tro five tousand people. Next day some gentlemen tell me who own the black bish dat spoke to me in de market, and advise me to tell de mistress. I go to the house, and knock, knock—by by door open, '*How do you do, Captain Udang*'—de same black bish rascal dat spoke to me in de market. Who own you? Tell you mistress one gentleman officer wish to see her. Madam, say I, do you own dat d—d madam nig, dat spoke to me in de market. She say, if you had not been too familiar with my negro wench, she would not spoke to you in de market. I say, 'You be one d—d rascal yourself, madam.'"

There is, among many good anecdotes related of Monsieur, one that shows the simplicity of the man, and is characteristic of the times. Before and at the period of the adoption of the federal constitution, great excitement existed in many parts of the country against many of its leading provisions, much mischief was predicted, and the irritated spirit of party could discern nothing but the most odious features and destructive tendencies. Houdin, on whom principles and opinions set rather loosely, was a zealous anti-federalist. After the new government was adopted, he was among the first to apply to the war department for an office. With no very favorable indication in his manner, General Knox inquired, "Do you expect patronage under that system of government that you have every where assailed?" "Ah, general," says Monsieur, "I tot it was popular; I meant noting." This honest simplicity availed him with the frank and generous mind of Knox, more than a hypocritical, canting affectation of patriotism. He received the appointment of conductor of *military stores*, which he held till his death.

APPENDIX.

NOTE I.—*See Page* 102.

GENERAL BURGOYNE, in his defence, after his arrival in England, as commander of the Northern expedition, has paid a just tribute of praise to American bravery. Adverting to the action of the 19th of September, he says: "Few actions have been characterized by more obstinacy in attack or defence. The British bayonet was repeatedly tried ineffectually. Eleven hundred British soldiers, foiled in these trials, bore incessant fire from a succession of fresh troops, in superior numbers, for above four hours; and after a loss of above a third of their number, and in one of the regiments above two-thirds, forced the enemy at last. Of a detachment of a captain and forty-eight artillery-men, the captain and thirty-six men were killed or wounded. The tribute of praise due to such troops, will not be wanting in this generous nation." His observations respecting the action of the 7th of October, are expressed in the following energetic and feeling language: "The losses in the action were uncommonly severe. Sir Francis Clark, my aid-de-camp, had originally recommended himself to my attention by his talents and diligence. As service and intimacy opened his character more, he became endeared to me by every quality that can create esteem. I lost in him a useful assistant, an amiable companion, an attached friend; the state was deprived by his death of one of the fairest promises of an able general.

"The fate of Colonel Ackland, taken prisoner, and then supposed to be mortally wounded, was a second source of anxiety. General Frazer was expiring.

"In the course of the action, a shot had passed through

my hat, and another had torn my waistcoat. I should be sorry to be thought at any time insensible to the protecting hand of Providence; but I ever more particularly consid ered a soldier's hair-breadth escapes as incentives to duty, a marked renewal of the trust of being, for the due purposes of a public station; and under this reflection, to lose our fortitude, by giving way to our affections, to be diverted by any possible self-emotion from meeting a present exigency with our best faculties, were at once dishonor and impiety."

General Frazer died of his wounds on the 8th instant. Before his death, he requested that his body might be carried, without parade, by the officers of his own corps to the great redoubt, and there buried. About sun-set the corpse was carried up the hill, and necessarily passed in view of both armies. Generals Burgoyne, Phillips, and Reidesel placed themselves in the humble procession. As General Gates was not made acquainted with the intended solemnity, a constant cannonade was kept up by our people, directed to the hill, where the ceremony was performed. From the pen of General Burgoyne, we have the following eloquent delineation of the melancholy scene: "The incessant cannonade during the solemnity, the steady attitude and unaltered voice with which the clergyman officiated, though frequently covered with dust, which the shot threw up on all sides of him; the mute, but expressive mixture of sensibility and indignation on every countenance; these objects will remain to the last of life on the mind of every man who was present. The growing duskiness added to the scenery, and the whole marked a character of this juncture, that would make one of the finest subjects for the pencil of a master that the field ever exhibited. To the canvas and to the page of a more important historian, gallant friend! I consign thy memory. There may thy talents, thy manly virtues, their progress and their period, find due distinction; and long may they survive, long after the frail record of my pen shall be forgotten!"

The following appropriate lines are from the elegant pen of Mrs. Morton:

> To gallant Gates, in war serenely brave,
> The tide of fortune turns its refluent wave;

Forced by his arm, the bold invaders yield
The prize and glory of the well-fought field;
Bleeding and lost the captured *Ackland* lies,
While leaden slumbers seal his *Frazer's* eyes;
Frazer! whose deeds unfading glories claim,
Endear'd by virtue, and adorn'd by fame.

LADY ACKLAND.—*See Page* 110.

FURTHER particulars respecting the affecting story of this distinguished lady have since appeared; and from the writings of General Burgoyne and other sources I extract the following. She accompanied Major Ackland to Canada in 1776, and was called to attend on him while sick in a miserable hut at Chamblee. In the expedition to Ticonderoga, in 1777, she was positively enjoined not to expose herself to the risk and hazards which might occur on that occasion; but Major Ackland, having received a wound in the battle of Hubberton, she crossed Lake Champlain to pay her attention to him. After this, she followed his fortune, and shared his fatigue, while traversing the dreary, woody country to Fort Edward. Here the tent in which they lodged took fire by night, from which they escaped with the utmost difficulty. During the action of the 19th of September, she was exposed to great fatigue, and inexpressible anxiety for the fate of her husband, being advanced in the front of the battle. On the 7th of October, during the heat of the conflict, Lady Ackland took refuge among the wounded and dying; her husband, commanding the grenadiers, was in the most exposed part of the action, and she in awful suspense awaiting his fate. The Baroness Reidesel, and the wives of two other field-officers, were her companions in painful apprehension. One of these officers was soon brought in dangerously wounded, and the death of the other was announced. It was not long before intelligence was received that the British army was defeated, and that Major Ackland was desperately wounded and taken. The next day she proposed to visit her husband in the American camp. General Burgoyne observes, "Though I was ready to believe, for I had experienced, that patience and fortitude in a supreme degree were to be found, as well as every other virtue, under the most tender form, I was astonished at this proposal. After so long an agitation of the spirits, exhausted not only for want of rest, but abso lutely want of food, drenched in rain for twelve hours together, that a woman should be capable of delivering herself to the enemy, probably in the night, and uncertain into what hands she might fall, appeared an effort above human nature. The assistance I was enabled to give was small indeed; I had not even a cup of wine to offer her; but I was told she had found from some kind and fortunate hand a little rum and dirty water. All I could furnish to her was an open boat and a few lines written on dirty and wet paper to General Gates, recommending her to his protection.—It is due to justice, at the close of this adventure, to say, that she was received and accommodated by General Gates, with all the humanity and respect that her rank, her merits, and her fortunes deserved.

"Let such as are affected by these circumstances of alarm, hardship and danger, recollect that the subject of them was a woman of the most tender and delicate frame; of the gentlest manners; habituated to all the soft elegancies and refined enjoyments that attend high birth and fortune; and far advanced in a state in which the tender cares, always due to the sex, become indispensably necessary. Her mind alone was formed for such trials."

The adventures of Lady Ackland have been a theme for the display of the poetic talents of the accomplished lady of Perez Morton, Esq. It is regretted that the limits of this production will not admit of more than the following lines, and those on the preceding page, from that excellent poem:

> "'Twas now the time, when twilight's misty ray
> Drops the brown curtain of retiring day;
> The clouds of heaven, like midnight mountains, lower,
> Waft the wild blast, and dash the drizzly shower:
> Through the wet path her restless footsteps roam,
> To where *the leader* spread his spacious dome;
> Low at his feet she pours the desperate prayer—
> 'Give my lost husband to my soothing care:
> Give me, in yonder solitary cave,
> With duteous love, his burning wounds to lave,
> On the warm pillow, which this breast supplies,
> Catch his faint breath, and close his languid eyes,
> Or in his cause my proffer'd life resign,
> Mine were his blessings, and his pains are mine.'"

NOTE II.—*See Page* 112.

THE following sketch, borrowed from the *Memoirs of General Wilkinson,* is too highly interesting to be omitted; every reader of taste will be gratified with the perusal, and, for myself, I owe to General Wilkinson only an apology for the liberty I have taken.

Extract from the Baroness Reidesel's Narrative.

"As we had to march still further, I ordered a large calash to be built, capable of holding my three children, myself, and two female servants; in this manner we moved with the army in the midst of the soldiery, who were very merry, singing songs, and panting for action. We had to travel through almost impassable woods and a most picturesque and beautiful country, which was abandoned by its inhabitants, who had repaired to the standard of General Gates; they added much to his strength, as they were all good marksmen, and fitted by habit for the species of warfare the contending parties were then engaged in—and the love of their country inspired them with more than ordinary courage. The army had shortly to encamp; I generally remained about an hour's march in the rear, where I received daily visits from my husband; the army was frequently engaged in small affairs, but nothing of importance took place; and as the season was getting cold, Major Williams of the artillery proposed to have a house built for me with a chimney, observing that it would not cost more than five or six guineas, and that the frequent change of quarters was very inconvenient to me; it was accordingly built, and was called the Block-house from its square form and the resemblance it bore to those buildings.

"On the 19th of September, an affair happened which, though it turned out to our advantage, yet obliged us to halt at a place called Freeman's farm; I was an eye-witness to the whole affair, and as my husband was engaged in it, I was full of anxiety, and trembled at every shot I heard; I saw a great number of the wounded, and, what added to the distress of the scene, three of them were brought into the house in which I took shelter; one was a Major Harnage of the sixty-second British regiment, the husband of a lady of my acquaintance; another was a lieutenant, married to a lady with whom I had the honor to be on terms of intimacy, and the third was an officer of the name of Young.

"In a short time afterwards I heard groans proceeding from a room near mine, and knew they must have been occasioned by the sufferings of the last-mentioned officer, who lay writhing with his wounds.

"His mournful situation interested me much, and the more so, because the recollection of many polite attentions, received from a family of that name during my visit to England, was still forcibly impressed on my mind. I sent to him, and begged him to accept my best services, and afterwards furnished him with food and refreshments; he expressed a great desire to see me, politely calling me his benefactress. I accordingly visited him, and found him lying on a little straw, as he had lost his equipage. He was a young man, eighteen or nineteen years of age, and really the beloved nephew of the Mr. Young, the head of the family I have mentioned, and the only son of his parents. This last circumstance was what he lamented most; as to his pain, he thought lightly of it. He had lost much blood, and it was thought necessary to amputate the leg; but this he would not consent to, and of course a mortification took place. I sent him cushions and coverings, and my female friends sent him a mattress. I redoubled my attention to him, and visited him every day, for which I received a thousand wishes for my happiness. At last his limb was amputated, but it was too late, and he died the following day. As he lay in the next room to me, and the partition was very thin, I distinctly heard his last sigh, when his immortal part quitted its frail tenement, and, I trust, winged its way to the mansions of eternal bliss.

"But severer trials awaited us, and on the 7th of October our misfortunes began; I was at breakfast with my husband, and heard that something was intended. On the same day I expected Generals Burgoyne, Phillips and Frazer to dine with us. I saw a great movement among the troops; my husband told me it was merely a reconnoisance, which gave me no concern, as it often happened. I walked out of the house, and met several Indians in their war dresses, with guns in their hands. When I asked them where they were going, they cried out, 'War! war!' meaning that they were going to battle. This filled me with apprehension, and I had scarcely got home before I heard reports of cannon and musketry, which grew louder by degress, till at last the noise became excessive. About four o'clock in the afternoon, instead of the guests whom I expected, General Frazer was brought on a litter, mortally wounded. The table, which was already set, was instantly removed, and a bed placed in its stead for the wounded general. I sat trembling in a corner; the noise grew louder, and the alarm increased; the thought that my husband might perhaps be brought in, wounded in the same manner, was terrible to me, and distressed me exceedingly. General Frazer said to the surgeon, 'Tell me if my wound is mortal; do not flatter me.' The ball had passed through his body, and, unhappily for the general, he had eaten a very hearty breakfast, by which the stomach was distended, and the ball, as the surgeon said, had passed through it. I heard him often exclaim, with a sigh, 'Oh, fatal ambition! Poor General Burgoyne! Oh, my poor wife!' He was asked if he had any request to make, to which he replied, that, 'If General Burgoyne would permit it, he should like to be buried at six o'clock in the evening, on the top of a mountain, in a redoubt which had been built there.' I did not know which way to turn: all the other rooms were full of sick. Towards evening I saw my husband coming. Then I forgot all my sorrows, and thanked God that he was spared to me. He ate in great haste with me and his aid-de-camp, behind the house. We had been told that we had the advantage over the enemy, but the sorrowful faces I beheld told a different tale, and before my husband went away he took me aside, and said every thing was going very badly; that I must keep myself in readiness to leave the place, but not to mention it to any one. I made the pretence that I would move the next morning into my new house, and had every thing packed up ready.

"Lady Ackland had a tent not far from our house; in this she slept, and the rest of the day she was in the camp. All of a sudden a man came to tell her that her husband was mortally wounded and taken prisoner; on hearing

24

this she became very miserable; we comforted her by tell
ing her that the wound was only slight, and at the same
time advised her to go over to her husband, to do which,
she would certainly obtain permission, and then she would
attend him herself; she was a charming woman, and very
fond of him. I spent much of the night in comforting
her, and then went again to my children, whom I had put
to bed. I could not go to sleep, as I had General Frazer
and all the other wounded gentlemen in my room, and I
was sadly afraid my children would wake, and by their
crying disturb the dying man in his last moments, who
often addressed me, and apologized '*for the trouble he gave
me.*' About three o'clock in the morning I was told that
he could not hold out much longer; I had desired to be
informed of the near approach of this sad crisis, and I then
wrapped up my children in their clothes, and went with
them into the room below. About eight o'clock in the
morning *he died.* After he was laid out, and his corpse
wrapped up in a sheet, we came again into the room, and
had this sorrowful sight before us the whole day, and, to
add to the melancholy scene, almost every moment some
officer of my acquaintance was brought in wounded. The
cannonade commenced again; a retreat was spoken of, but
not the smallest motion was made towards it. About four
o'clock in the afternoon, I saw the house which had just
been built for me in flames, and the enemy was now not
far off. We knew that General Burgoyne would not refuse the last request of General Frazer, though, by his
acceding to it, an unnecessary delay was occasioned, by
which the inconvenience of the army was much increased.
At six o'clock the corpse was brought out, and we saw
all the generals attend it to the mountain; the chaplain,
Mr. Brudenell, performed the funeral service, rendered
unusually solemn and awful from its being accompanied
by constant peals from the enemy's artillery. Many cannon-balls flew close by me, but I had my eyes directed
towards the mountain,* where my husband was standing,
amidst the fire of the enemy, and of course I could not
think of my own danger.

"General Gates afterwards said that, if he had known

* The height occupied by Burgoyne on the 18th, which ran parallel
with the river till it approached General Gates' camp.

it had been a funeral, he would not have permitted it to be fired on.

"So soon as the funeral-service was finished, and the grave of General Frazer was closed, an order was issued that the army should retreat. My calash was prepared, but I would not consent to go before the troops. Major Harnage, though suffering from his wounds, crept from his bed, as he did not wish to remain in the hospital, which was left with a flag of truce. When General Reidesel saw me in the midst of danger, he ordered my women and children to be brought into the calash, and intimated to me to depart without delay. I still prayed to remain, but my husband, knowing my weak side, said, 'Well, then, your children must go, that at least they may be safe from danger.' I then agreed to enter the calash with them, and we set off at eight o'clock.

"The retreat was ordered to be conducted with the greatest silence; many fires were lighted, and several tents left standing; we travelled continually during the night. At six o'clock in the morning we halted, which excited the surprise of all; General Burgoyne had the cannon ranged and counted; this delay seemed to displease every body, for if we could only have made another good march, we should have been in safety. My husband, quite exhausted with fatigue, came into my calash, and slept for three hours. During that time, Captain Willoe brought me a bag full of bank notes, and Captain Grismar his elegant watch, a ring, and a purse full of money, which they requested me to take care of, and which I promised to do to the utmost of my power. We again marched, but had scarcely proceeded an hour before we halted, as the enemy was in sight; it proved to be only a reconnoitering party of two hundred men, who might easily have been made prisoners, if General Burgoyne had given proper orders on the occasion.

"The Indians had now lost their courage, and were departing for their homes; these people appeared to droop much under adversity, and especially when they had no prospect of plunder. One of my waiting-women was in a state of despair, which approached to madness; she cursed and tore her hair, and when I attempted to reason with her, and to pacify her, she asked me if I was not grieved at our situation, and on my saying I was, she tore her cap off her head and let her hair drop over her face, saying to me, 'It is very easy for you to be composed and talk: you have your husband with you; I have none; and what remains to me but the prospect of perishing or losing all I have!' I again bade her take comfort, and assured her I would make good whatever she might happen to lose; and I made the same promise to Ellen, my other waiting-woman, who, though filled with apprehensions, made no complaints.

"About evening we arrived at Saratoga; my dress was wet through and through with rain, and in this state I had to remain the whole night, having no place to change it; I, however, got close to a large fire, and at last lay down on some straw. At this moment General Phillips came up to me, and I asked him why he had not continued our retreat, as my husband had promised to cover it and bring the army through? 'Poor, dear woman,' said he, 'I wonder how, drenched as you are, you have the courage still to persevere and venture further in this kind of weather! I wish,' continued he, 'you was our commanding-general; General Burgoyne is tired, and, means to halt here to-night and give us our supper.'

"On the morning of the 7th, at ten o'clock, General Burgoyne ordered the retreat to be continued, and caused the handsome houses and mills of General Schuyler to be burned; we marched, however, but a short distance, and then halted. The greatest misery at this time prevailed in the army, and more than thirty officers came to me, for whom tea and coffee was prepared, and with whom I shared all my provisions, with which my calash was in general well supplied; for I had a cook who was an excellent caterer, and who often in the night crossed small rivers and foraged on the inhabitants, bringing in with him sheep, small pigs, and poultry, for which he very often forgot to pay, though he received good pay from me so long as I had any, and was ultimately handsomely rewarded. Our provisions now failed us for want of proper conduct in the commissary's department, and I began to despair. About two o'clock in the afternoon we again heard a firing of cannon and small-arms; instantly all was alarm, and every thing in motion. My husband told me to go to a house not far off; I immediately seated myself in my calash, with my children, and drove off; but scarcely had we reached it before I discovered five or six armed men on the other side of the Hudson; instinctively I threw my children down in the calash, and then concealed myself with them; at this moment the fellows fired and wounded an already wounded English soldier, who was behind me. Poor fellow! I pitied him exceedingly, but at this moment had no means or power to relieve him. A terrible cannonade was commenced by the enemy, which was directed against the house in which I sought to obtain shelter for myself and children, under the mistaken idea that all the generals were in it. Alas! it contained none but wounded and women; we were at last obliged to resort to the cellar for refuge, and in one corner of this I remained the whole day, my children sleeping on the earth with their heads in my lap; and in the same situation I passed a sleepless night.—Eleven cannon-balls passed through the house, and we could distinctly hear them roll away. One poor soldier, who was lying on a table for the purpose of having his leg amputated, was struck by a shot, which carried away his other; his comrades had left him, and when we went to his assistance we found him in a corner of the room, into which he had crept, more dead than alive, scarcely breathing. My reflections on the danger to which my husband was exposed now agonized me exceedingly, and the thoughts of my children and the necessity of struggling for their preservation alone sustained me.

"The ladies of the army who were with me were Mrs. Harnage, a Mrs. Kennels, the widow of a lieutenant who was killed, and the lady of the commissary. Major Harnage, his wife, and Mrs. Kennels, made a little room in a corner with curtains to it, and wished to do the same for me, but I preferred being near the door, in case of fire. Not far off, my women slept, and opposite to us three English officers, who, though wounded, were determined not to be left behind: one of them was Captain Green, an aid-de-camp to Major-General Phillips, a very valuable officer and most agreeable man. They each made me a most sacred promise not to leave me behind, and in case of sudden retreat, that they would each of them take one of my children on his horse, and for myself, one of my husband's was in constant readiness.

"Our cook, whom I have before mentioned, procured us our meals, but we were in want of water, and I was often obliged to drink wine and to give it to my children. It was the only thing my husband took, which made our faithful Hunter, Rockel, express one day his apprehensions that 'the general was weary of his life, or fearful of being taken, as he drank so much wine.' The constant danger which my husband was in, kept me in a state of wretchedness,' and I asked myself if it was possible I should be the only happy one, and have my husband spared to me unhurt, exposed as he was to so many perils. He never entered his tent, but laid down whole nights by the watch-fires; this alone was enough to have killed him, the cold was so intense.

"The want of water distressed us much. At length, we found a soldier's wife who had courage enough to fetch us some from the river, an office nobody else would undertake, as the Americans shot at every person who approached it; but out of respect for her sex they never molested her.

"I now occupied myself through the day in attending the wounded; I made them tea and coffee, and often shared my dinner with them, for which they offered me a thousand expressions of gratitude. One day a Canadian officer came to our cellar, who had scarcely the power of holding himself upright, and we concluded he was dying for want of nourishment; I was happy in offering him my dinner, which strengthened him and procured me his friendship. I now undertook the care of Major Bloomfield, another aid-de-camp of General Phillips; he had received a musket-ball through both cheeks, which in its course had knocked out several of his teeth, and cut his tongue; he could hold nothing in his mouth; the matter which ran from his wound almost choked him, and he was not able to take any nourishment except a little soup, or something liquid; we had some Rhenish wine, and in the hope that the acidity of it would cleanse his wound, I gave him a bottle of it; he took a little now and then, and with such effect that his cure soon followed. Thus I added another to my stock of friends, and derived a satisfaction which, in the midst of sufferings, served to tranquillize me and diminish their acuteness.

"One day General Phillips accompanied my husband, at the risk of their lives, on a visit to us, who, after having witnessed our situation, said to him, 'I would not for ten thousand guineas come again to this place; my heart is almost broken.'

"In this horrid situation we remained six days; a cessation of hostilities was now spoken of, and eventually took place; a convention was afterwards agreed on; but one day a message was sent to my husband, who had visited me and was reposing in my bed,*to attend a council of war, where it was proposed to break the convention: but, to my great joy, the majority were for adhering to it. On the 16th, however, my husband had to repair to his post, and I to my cellar; this day fresh beef was served out to the officers, who till now had only had salt provisions, which was very bad for their wounds. The good woman who brought us water, made us an excellent soup of the meat, but I had lost my appetite, and took nothing but crusts of bread dipped in wine. The wounded officers, my unfortunate companions, cut off the best bit and presented it to me on a plate. I declined eating any thing, but they contended that it was necessary for me to take nourishment, and declared they would not touch a morsel till I afforded them the pleasure of seeing me partake. I could no longer withstand their pressing invitations, accompanied as they were by assurances of the happiness they had in offering me the first good thing they had in their power, and I partook of a repast rendered palatable by the kindness and good-will of my fellow-sufferers, forgetting for the moment the misery of our apartment, and the absence of almost every comfort.

"On the 17th of October, the convention was completed. General Burgoyne and the other generals waited on the American General Gates; the troops laid down their arms, and gave themselves up prisoners of war! And now the good woman who had supplied us with water at the hazard of her life, received the reward of her services; each of us threw a handful of money into her apron, and she got altogether about twenty guineas. At such a moment as this, how susceptible is the heart of feelings of gratitude!

"My husband sent a message to me to come over to him with my children. I seated myself once more in my dear calash, and then rode through the American camp. As I passed on, I observed (and this was a great consolation to me) that no one eyed me with looks of resentment, but that they all greeted us, and even showed compassion in their countenances at the sight of a woman with small children. I was, I confess, afraid to go over to the enemy, as it was quite a new situation to me. When I drew near the tents, a handsome man approached and met me, *took my children from the calash, and hugged and kissed them, which affected me almost to tears.* 'You tremble,' said he, addressing himself to me; 'be not afraid.' 'No,' I answered; 'you seem so kind and tender to my children, it inspires me with courage.' He now led me to the tent of General Gates, where I found Generals Burgoyne and Phillips, who were on a friendly footing with the former. Burgoyne said to me, 'Never mind; your sorrows have now an end.' I answered him, 'that I should be reprehensible to have any cares, as he had none;' and I was pleased to see him on such a friendly footing with General Gates. All the generals remained to dine with General Gates.

"The same gentleman who received me so kindly, now came and said to me, 'You will be very much embarrassed to eat with all these gentlemen; come with your children to my tent, where I will prepare for you a frugal dinner, and give it with a free will.' I said, 'You are certainly a husband and a father, you have shown me so much kindness.' I now found that he was *General Schuyler.* He treated me with excellent smoked tongue, beef-steaks, potatoes, and good bread and butter! Never could I have wished to eat a better dinner; I was content: I saw all around me were so likewise; and, what was better than all, my husband was out of danger. When we had dined, he told me his residence was at Albany, and that General Burgoyne intended to honor him as his guest, and invited myself and children to do so likewise. I asked my husband how I should act; he told me to accept the invitation. As it was two days' journey there, he advised me to go to a place which was about three hours' ride distant. General Schuyler had the politeness to send with me a French officer, a very agreeable man, who commanded the reconnoitering party, of which I have before spoken; and when he had escorted me to the house where I was to remain, he turned back again. In the house, I found a French surgeon, who had under his care a Brunswick officer, who was mortally wounded, and died some few days afterwards. The Frenchman boasted much of the care he took of his patient, and perhaps was skillful enough as a surgeon, but otherwise was a mere simpleton; he was rejoiced when he found out I could speak his language, and began to address many empty and impertinent speeches to me. He said, among other things, he could not believe that I was a general's wife, as he was certain a woman of such rank would not follow her husband; he wished me to remain with him, as he said it was better to be with the conquerors than the conquered. I was shocked at his impudence, but dared not show the contempt and disdain I felt for him, because it would deprive me of a place of safety. Towards evening he begged me to take a part of his chamber. I told him I was determined to remain in the room with the wounded officer; whereon he attempted to pay me some stupid compliments. *At this moment the door opened, and my husband with his aid-de-camp entered.* I then said, 'Here, sir, is my husband,' and at the same time eyed him with scorn, whereon he retired abashed; nevertheless he was *so polite* as to offer his chamber to us.

"Some days after this we arrived at Albany, where we so often wished ourselves; but we did not enter it as we expected we should—victors! We were received by the *good General Schuyler, his wife, and daughters*, not as enemies, but kind friends, and they treated us with the most marked attention and politeness, as they did General Burgoyne, who had caused General Schuyler's beautifully finished house to be burned. In fact, they behaved like persons of exalted minds, who determined to bury all recollection of *their own* injuries in the contemplation of *our* misfortunes. General Burgoyne was struck with General Schuyler's generosity, and said to him, 'You show me great kindness, though I have done you much injury.' 'That was the fate of war,' replied the brave man; 'let us say no more about it.'"

NOTE III.—*See Page* 126.

MR. BUSHNELL'S squadron of kegs, committed to the Delaware in 1777, produced an unprecedented alarm among the British fleet at Philadelphia, and the singular catastrophe was, by the Hon. Francis Hopkinson, made a subject of the following song, which has been, and ever will be, celebrated for the brilliancy of its wit and humor:

THE BATTLE OF THE KEGS, A SONG.

TUNE—*Moggy Lawder.*

Gallants, attend, and hear a friend
  Trill forth harmonious ditty;
Strange things I'll tell, which late befell
  In Philadelphia city.

'Twas early day, as poets say,
  Just when the sun was rising,
A soldier stood on log of wood,
  And saw a sight surprising.

As in a maze he stood to gaze—
  The truth can't be denied, sir—
He spied a score of kegs or more
  Come floating down the tide, sir.

A sailor, too, in jerkin blue,
  The strange appearance viewing,
First damn'd his eyes, in great surprise,
  Then said, "Some mischief's brewing:

"These kegs now hold the rebels bold,
  Pack'd up like pickled herring;
And they're come down t' attack the town
  In this new way of ferrying."

The soldier flew; the sailor too;
  And scared almost to death, sir,
Wore out their shoes to spread the news,
  And ran till out of breath, sir.

Now up and down, throughout the town,
  Most frantic scenes were acted;
And some ran here, and some ran there,
  Like men almost distracted.

Some fire cried, which some denied,
  But said the earth had quaked:
And girls and boys, with hideous noise,
  Ran through the town half-naked.

Sir William* he, snug as a flea,
   Lay all this time a snoring;
Nor dreamt of harm, as he lay warm
   In bed with Mrs. L——ng.†

Now in a fright he starts upright,
   Awaked by such a clatter;
He rubs both eyes, and boldly cries,
   "For God's sake, what's the matter?"

At his bed-side he then espied
   Sir Erskine‡ at command, sir;
Upon one foot he had one boot,
   And t'other in his hand, sir.

"Arise! arise!" Sir Erskine cries;
   "The rebels—more's the pity—
Without a boat, are all on float,
   And ranged before the city.

The motley crew, in vessels new,
   With Satan for their guide, sir,
Pack'd up in bags, or wooden kegs,
   Come driving down the tide, sir:

Therefore prepare for bloody war;
   These kegs must all be routed,
Or surely we despised shall be,
   And British courage doubted."

The royal band now ready stand,
   All arranged in dread array, sir,
With stomachs stout, to see it out,
   And make a bloody day, sir.

The cannons roar from shore to shore,
   The small arms make a rattle:
Since wars began, I'm sure no man
   E'er saw so strange a battle.

The rebel vales, the rebel dales,
   With rebel trees surrounded,
The distant woods, the hills and floods,
   With rebel echoes sounded.

* Sir William Howe.

† The wife of Joshua Loring, a refugee from Boston, made commissary of prisoners by General Howe. "The consummate cruelties practised on the American prisoners under his administration, almost exceed the ordinary powers of human invention. The conduct of the Turks in putting all prisoners to death, is certainly much more rational and humane, than that of the British army for the first three years of the American war, or till after the capture of Burgoyne."

‡ Sir William Erskine.

The fish below swam to and fro,
    Attack'd from every quarter;
"Why sure," thought they, "the devil's to pay
    "'Mongst folks above the water."

The kegs, 'tis said, though strongly made
    Of rebel staves and hoops, sir,
Could not oppose their pow'rful foes,
    The conqu'ring British troops, sir.

From morn to night these men of might
    Display'd amazing courage:
And when the sun was fairly down,
    Retired to sup their porridge.

A hundred men, with each a pen,
    Or more, upon my word, sir,
It is most true, would be too few
    Their valor to record, sir.

Such feats did they perform that day,
    Upon these wicked kegs, sir,
That years to come, if they get home,
    They'll make their boasts and brags, sir.

● NOTE IV.—*See Page* 259.

THE following is an abstract of an interesting narrative taken from the travels of the late Dr. Dwight:

After the failure of the expedition against the British garrison at Penobscot, General Peleg Wadsworth was appointed in the spring of 1780 to the command of a party of state troops in Camden, in the District of Maine. At the expiration of the period for which the troops were engaged, in February following, General Wadsworth dismissed his troops, retaining six soldiers only as his guard, and he was making preparations to depart from the place. A neighboring inhabitant communicated his situation to the British commander at Penobscot, and a party of twenty-five soldiers, commanded by Lieutenant Stockton, was sent to make him a prisoner. They embarked in a small schooner, and landing within four miles of the general's quarters, they were concealed at the house of one Snow, a methodist preacher, professedly a friend to him, but really a traitor, till eleven o'clock in the evening, where they made their arrangements for the attack on the gen-

eral's quarters. The party rushed suddenly on the sentinel, who gave the alarm, and one of his comrades instantly
opened the door of the kitchen, and the enemy were so near
as to enter with the sentinel. The lady of the general, and
her friend Miss Fenno, of Boston, were in the house at the
time, and Mrs. Wadsworth escaped from the room of her
husband into that of Miss Fenno. The assailants soon
became masters of the whole house, except the room where
the general was, and which was strongly barred, and they
kept up a constant firing of musketry into the windows
and doors, except into those of the ladies' room. General
Wadsworth was provided with a pair of pistols, a blunderbuss and a fusee, which he employed with great dexterity,
being determined to defend himself to the last moment.
With his pistols, which he discharged several times, he
defended the windows of his room and a door which opened
into the kitchen. His blunderbuss he snapped several
times, but unfortunately it missed fire. He then seized
his fusee, which he discharged on some who were breaking
through one of the windows, and obliged them to flee.
He next defended himself with his bayonet, till he received
a ball through his left arm, when he surrendered, which
terminated the contest. The firing, however, did not cease
from the kitchen till the general unbarred the door, when
the soldiers rushed into the room, and one of them who
had been badly wounded, pointing a musket at his breast,
exclaimed, with an oath, " You have taken my life, and I
will take yours." But Lieutenant Stockton turned the
musket, and saved his life. The commanding officer now
applauded the general for his admirable defence, and assisted in putting on his clothes, saying, "You see we are in a
critical situation: you must excuse haste." Mrs. Wadsworth
threw a blanket over him, and Miss Fenno applied a handkerchief closely round his wounded arm. In this condition,
though much exhausted, he, with a wounded American
soldier, was directed to march on foot, while two British
wounded soldiers were mounted on a horse taken from the
general's barn. They departed in great haste. When they
had proceeded about a mile, they met, at a small house, a
number of people who had collected, and who inquired
if they had taken General Wadsworth. They said no,
and added, that they must leave a wounded man in their

care, and if they paid proper attention to him they should be compensated, but if not, they would burn down their house; but the man appeared to be dying. General Wadsworth was now mounted on the horse behind the other wounded soldier, and was warned that his safety depended on his silence. Having crossed over a frozen mill-pond, about a mile in length, they were met by some of their party who had been left behind. At this place they found the British privateer which brought the party from the fort. The captain, on being told that he must return there with the prisoner and the party, and seeing some of his men wounded, became outrageous, and damned the general for a rebel, demanded how he dared to fire on the king's troops, and ordered him to help launch the boat, or he would put his hanger through his body. The general replied that he was a prisoner, and badly wounded, and could not assist in launching the boat. Lieutenant Stockton, on learning of this abusive treatment, in a manner honorable to himself, told the captain that the prisoner was a gentleman, had made a brave defence, and was to be treated accordingly; and added, that his conduct should be represented to General Campbell. After this, the captain treated the prisoner with great civility, and afforded him every comfort in his power. General Wadsworth had left the ladies in the house, not a window of which escaped destruction. The doors were broken down, and two of the rooms were set on fire; the floors covered with blood, and on one of them lay a brave old soldier, dangerously wounded, begging for death, that he might be released from misery. The anxiety and distress of Mrs. Wadsworth was inexpressible, and that of the general was greatly increased by the uncertainty in his mind respecting the fate of his little son, only five years old, who had been exposed to every danger by the firing into the house, but he had the happiness afterwards to hear of his safety. Having arrived at the British post, the capture of General Wadsworth was soon announced, and the shore thronged with spectators, to see the man who, through the preceding year, had disappointed all the designs of the British in that quarter; and loud shouts were heard from the rabble which covered the shore; but when he arrived at the fort, and was conducted into the officers' guard-room, he was treated with politeness. General Campbell, the commandant of the British garrison, sent his compliments to him and a surgeon to dress his wounds, assuring him that his situation should be made comfortable. The next morning, General Campbell invited him to breakfast, and at table paid him many compliments on the defence he had made, observing, however, that he had exposed himself in a degree not perfectly justifiable. General Wadsworth replied that, from the manner of the attack, he had no reason to suspect any design of taking him alive, and that he intended therefore to sell his life as dearly as possible. "But, sir," said General Campbell, "I understand that the captain of the privateer treated you very ill; I shall see that matter set right." He then informed the prisoner that a room in the officers' barracks within the fort was prepared for him, and that he should send his orderly-sergeant daily to attend him to breakfast and dinner at his table. Having retired to his solitary apartment, and while his spirits were extremely depressed by a recollection of the past, and by his present situation, he received from General Campbell several books of amusement, and soon after a visit from him, kindly endeavoring to cheer the spirits of his prisoner by conversation. Not long after, the officers of the party called, and among others the redoubtable captain of the privateer, who called to ask pardon for what had fallen from him when in a passion; adding, that it was not in his nature to treat a gentleman prisoner ill; that the unexpected disappointment of his cruise had thrown him off his guard, and he hoped that this would be deemed a sufficient apology. This General Wadsworth accepted. At the hour of dining he was invited to the table of the commandant, where he met with all the principal officers of the garrison, and from whom he received particular attention and politeness. General Wadsworth soon made application to the commandant for a flag of truce, by which means he could transmit a letter to the governor of Massachusetts, and another to Mrs. Wadsworth. This was granted, on the condition that the letter to the governor should be inspected. The flag was intrusted to Lieutenant Stockton, and on his return, the general was relieved from all anxiety respecting his wife and family. General Campbell and the officers of the

garrison continued their civilities for some time, and endeavored by books and personal visits to render his situation as pleasant as circumstances would admit of. At the
end of five weeks, his wound being nearly healed, he requested of General Campbell the customary privilege of
a parole, and received, in reply, that his case had been
reported to the commanding officer at New York, and
that no alteration could be made till orders were received
from that quarter. In about two months, Mrs. Wadsworth
and Miss Fenno arrived, and General Campbell and some
of the officers contributed to render their visit agreeable
to all concerned. About the same time, orders were received from the commanding general at New York, which
were concealed from General Wadsworth, but he finally
learned that he was not to be paroled nor exchanged, but
was to be sent to England as a rebel of too much consequence to be at liberty. Not long afterwards Major
Benjamin Burton, a brave and worthy man, who had
served under General Wadsworth the preceding summer,
was taken and brought into the fort, and lodged in the
same room with General Wadsworth. He had been informed that both himself and the General were to be sent,
immediately after the return of a privateer now out on a
cruise, either to New York or Halifax, and thence to
England. The prisoners immediately resolved to make a
desperate attempt to effect their escape. They were confined in a grated room in the officers' barracks within the
fort. The walls of this fortress, exclusively of the depth
of the ditch surrounding it, were twenty feet high, with
fraising on the top, and *chevaux de frise* at the bottom.
Two sentinels were always in the entry, and their door,
the upper part of which was of glass, might be opened by
these watchmen whenever they thought proper, and was
actually opened at seasons of peculiar darkness and silence.
At the exterior doors of the entries, sentinels were also
stationed, as were others in the body of the fort, and at
the quarters of General Campbell. At the guard-house, a
strong guard was daily mounted. Several sentinels were
stationed on the walls of the fort, and a complete line
occupied them by night. Without the ditch, glacis and
abatis, another complete set of soldiers patroled through
the night also. The gate of the fort was shut at sun-set,

and a piquet-guard was placed on or near the isthmus leading from the fort to the main land.

The room in which they were confined was railed with boards. One of these they determined to cut off, so as to make a hole large enough to pass through, and then to creep along till they should come to the next or middle entry; and then lower themselves down into this entry by a blanket. If they should not be discovered, the passage to the walls of the fort was easy. In the evening, after the sentinels had seen the prisoners retire to bed, General Wadsworth got up, and, standing in a chair, attempted to cut with his knife the intended opening, but soon found it impracticable. The next day, by giving a soldier a dollar, they procured a gimblet. With this instrument they proceeded cautiously and as silently as possible to perforate the board, and in order to conceal every appearance from their servants and from the officers their visitors, they carefully covered the gimblet-holes with chewed bread. At the end of three weeks their labors were so far completed that it only remained to cut with a knife the parts which were left to hold the piece in its place. When their preparations were finished, they learned that the privateer in which they were to embark was daily expected. In the evening of the 18th of June, a very severe storm of rain, with great darkness and almost incessant lightning came on. This the prisoners considered as the propitious moment. Having extinguished their lights, they began to cut the corners of the board, and in less than an hour the intended opening was completed. The noise which the operation occasioned was drowned by the rain falling on the roof. Major Burton first ascended to the ceiling, and pressed himself through the opening. General Wadsworth next, having put the corner of his blanket through the hole, and made it fast by a strong wooden skewer, attempted to make his way through, standing on a chair below, but it was with extreme difficulty that he at length effected it, and reached the middle entry. From this he passed through the door, which he found open, and made his way to the wall of the fort, and had to encounter the greatest difficulty before he could ascend to the top. He had now to creep along the top of the fort between the sentry boxes at the very moment when the

25

relief was shifting sentinels, but the falling of heavy rain kept the sentinels within their boxes, and favored his escape. Having now fastened his blanket round a picket at the top, he let himself down through the *chevaux de frise* to the ground, and in a manner astonishing to himself made his way into the open field. Here he was obliged to grope his way among rocks, stumps and brush in the darkness of night, till he reached the cove; happily the tide had ebbed, and enabled him to cross the water, about a mile in breadth and not more than three feet deep. About two o'clock in the morning General Wadsworth found himself a mile and a half from the fort, and he proceeded through a thick wood and brush to the Penobscot river, and after passing some distance along the shore, being seven miles from the fort, to his unspeakable joy he saw his friend Burton advancing towards him. Major Burton had been obliged to encounter in his course equal difficulties with his companion, and such were the incredible perils, dangers and obstructions which they surmounted, that their escape may be considered almost miraculous. It was now necessary they should cross the Penobscot river, and very fortunately they discovered a canoe with oars on the shore suited to their purpose. While on the river they discovered a barge with a party of British from the fort in pursuit of them, but by taking an oblique course, and plying their oars to the utmost, they happily eluded the eyes of their pursuers, and arrived safe on the western shore. After having wandered in the wilderness for several days and nights, exposed to extreme fatigue and cold, and with no other food than a little dry bread and meat, which they brought in their pockets from the fort, they reached the settlements on the river St. George, and no further difficulties attended their return to their respective families.

NOTE V.

THERE is a particular transaction in the history of our revolutionary war, which was known only to General Washington and a single confidential officer, the gallant Major Lee, commander of a corps of cavalry. As the story is particularly interesting, and as it has never been disclosed to the public by any historian, except by Major Lee in his valuable memoirs, I cannot resist the temptation of enriching this work with the narration, in the words of the respectable author.

" Lately, John Champe, sergeant-major of the legion of cavalry, who had been for several months considered by the corps a deserter, returned. This high-minded soldier had been selected to undertake a very difficult and perilous project, the narration of which is due to his merit, as well as to the singularity of his progress.

"The treason of General Arnold, the capture of Andre, with intelligence received by Washington, through his confidential agents in New York, communicating that many of his officers, and especially a major-general named to him, were connected with Arnold, could not fail to seize the attention of a commander even less diligent and zealous. It engaged his mind entirely, exciting sensations the most anxious, as well as unpleasant. The moment he reached the army, then under the orders of Major-General Greene, encamped in the vicinity of Tappan, he sent for Major Lee, posted with the light troops some distance in front. This officer repaired to head-quarters with celerity, and found the general in his marquee alone, busily engaged in writing. So soon as Lee entered, he was requested to take a seat, and a bundle of papers, lying on the table, was given him for perusal. In these much information was detailed, tending to prove that Arnold was not alone in the base conspiracy just detected, but that the poison had spread; and that a major-general, whose name was not concealed, was certainly as guilty as Arnold himself. This officer had enjoyed, without interruption, the confidence of the commander-in-chief throughout the war; nor did there exist a single reason in support of the accusation. It altogether rested on the intelligence derived from the papers before him. Major Lee, personally acquainted with the accused, could not refrain from suggesting the probability, that the whole was a contrivance of Sir Henry Clinton, in order to destroy that confidence between the commander and his officers, on which the success of military operations depend. This suggestion, Washington replied, was plausible, and deserved due consideration.

It had early occurred to his own mind, and had not been slightly regarded; but his reflections settled in a conclusion not to be shaken, as the same suggestion applied to no officer more forcibly than a few days ago it would have done to General Arnold, known now to be a traitor.

"Announcing this result of his meditations with the tone and countenance of a mind deeply agitated, and resolved on its course, Lee continued silent, when the general proceeded: 'I have sent for you, in the expectation that you have in your corps individuals capable and willing to undertake an indispensable, delicate, and hazardous project. Whoever comes forward on this occasion, will lay me under great obligations personally; and in behalf of the United States, I will reward him amply. No time is to be lost; he must proceed, if possible, this night. My object is to probe to the bottom the afflicting intelligence contained in the papers you have just read, to seize Arnold, and by getting him, to save Andre. They are all connected. While my emissary is engaged in preparing means for the seizure of Arnold, the guilt of others can be traced; and the timely delivery of Arnold to me, will possibly put it into my power to restore the amiable and unfortunate Andre to his friends. My instructions are ready, in which you will find my express orders that Arnold is not to be hurt; but that he be permitted to escape, if to be prevented only by killing him, as his public punishment is the only object in view. This you cannot too forcibly press on whoever may engage in the enterprise; and this fail not to do. With my instructions are two letters, to be delivered as ordered, and here are some guineas for expenses.'

"Major Lee, replying, said, that he had little or no doubt but that his legion contained many individuals daring enough for any operation, however perilous; but that the one in view required a combination of qualities not easily to be found, unless in a commissioned officer, to whom he could not venture to propose an enterprise, the first step to which was desertion; that though the sergeant-major of the cavalry was in all respects qualified for the delicate and adventurous project, and to him it might be proposed without indelicacy, as his station did not interpose the obstacle before stated; yet it was very probable

that the same difficulty would occur in his breast, to remove which would not be easy, if practicable.

"Washington was highly pleased with finding that a
non-commissioned officer was deemed capable of executing
his views; as he had felt extreme difficulty in authorizing
an invitation to officers, who generally are, and always
ought to be, scrupulous and nice in adhering to the course
of honor. He asked the name, the country, the age, the
size, length of service, and character of the sergeant.

"Being told his name—that he was a native of Loudon
county in Virginia; about twenty-four years of age—that
he had enlisted in 1776—rather above the common size,
full of bone and muscle, with a saturnine countenance,
grave, thoughtful and taciturn—of tried courage and inflexible perseverance, and as likely to reject an overture coupled with ignominy as any officer in the corps; a commission
being the goal of his long and anxious exertions, and certain on the first vacancy.

"The general exclaimed that he was the very man for
the business; that he must undertake it; and that going
to the enemy by the instigation and at the request of his
officer was not desertion, though it appeared to be so; and
he enjoined that this explanation, as coming from him,
should be pressed on Champe; and that the vast good in
prospect should be contrasted with the mere semblance of
doing wrong, which he presumed could not fail to conquer
every scruple. Major Lee assured the general that every
exertion would be assayed on his part to execute his
wishes; and, taking leave, returned to the camp of the
light corps, which he reached about eight o'clock at night.
Sending instantly for the sergeant-major, he introduced
the business in the way best calculated, as he thought, to
produce his concurrence; and dilated largely on the very
great obligations he would confer on the commander-in-
chief, whose unchanging and active beneficence to the
troops had justly drawn to him their affection, which
would be merely nominal, if, when an opportunity should
offer to any individual of contributing to the promotion
of his views, that opportunity was not zealously embraced.
That the one now presented to him had never before occurred, and in all probability would never occur again,
even should the war continue for ages; it being most rare

for these distinct consequences, all of primary weight, to be comprised within a single operation, and that operation necessarily to be intrusted to one man, who would want but one or two associates in the active parts of its execution. That the chance of detection became extremely narrow, and consequently that of success enlarged. That by succeeding in the safe delivery of Arnold, he not only gratified his general in the most acceptable manner, but he would be hailed as the avenger of the reputation of the army, stained by foul and wicked perfidy; and, what could not but be highly pleasing, he would be the instrument of saving the life of Major Andre, soon to be brought before a court of inquiry, the decision of which could not be doubted, from the universally known circumstances of the case, and had been anticipated in the general's instructions. That by investigating with diligence and accuracy the intelligence communicated to him, he would bring to light new guilt, or he would relieve innocence, as was most probable, from distrust; quieting the torturing suspicions which now harrowed the mind of Washington, and restoring again to his confidence a once-honored general, possessing it at present only ostensibly, as well as hush doubts affecting many of his brother-soldiers.

"In short, the accomplishment of so much good was in itself too attractive to be renounced by a generous mind; and when connected with the recollection of the high honor which the selection shed on him as a soldier, he ought not—he must not pause. The discourse was followed by a detail of the plan, with a wish that he would enter on its execution instantly. Champe listened with deep attention, and with a highly-excited countenance; the perturbations of his breast not being hid even by his dark visage. He briefly and modestly replied, that no soldier exceeded him in respect and affection for the commander-in-chief, to serve whom he would willingly lay down his life; and that he was sensible of the honor conferred by the choice of him for the execution of a project all over arduous; nor could he be at a loss to know to whom was to be ascribed the preference bestowed, which he took pleasure in acknowledging, though increasing obligations before great and many. That he was charmed with the plan. Even its partial success would lead to great good; as it would give peace to the general's mind, and do justice, as he hoped, to innocence. Full success, added powerful and delicious personal incitements, as well as the gratification of the general and army. He was not, he said, deterred by the danger and difficulty which was evidently to be encountered, but he was deterred by the ignominy of desertion, to be followed by the hypocrisy of enlisting with the enemy; neither of which comported with his feelings, and either placed an insuperable bar in his way to promotion. He concluded by observing, if any mode could be contrived free from disgrace, he would cordially embark in the enterprise. As it was, he prayed to be excused; and hoped that services, always the best in his power to perform, faithfully executed, did entitle his prayer to success.

"The objections at first apprehended, now to be combated, were extended to a consequence which had not suggested itself. Lee candidly admitted that he had expected the first objection made, and that only; which had been imparted to the general, who gave to it full consideration, and concluded by declaring that the crime of desertion was not incurred; as no act done by the soldier at the request of the commander-in-chief could be considered as desertion, and that an action so manifestly praiseworthy as that to be performed, when known, would dissipate by its own force the reflections excited by appearances, which no doubt would be acrimonious, leaving the actor in full enjoyment of the future rich rewards of his virtue. That the reflecting mind ought not to balance between the achievement of so much good, and the doing wrong in semblance only; to which Major Lee subjoined, that when in consequence of the general's call on him for a soldier capable and willing to execute a project so tempting to the brave, he considered himself and corps highly honored; and that he should consider himself reduced to a mortifying condition, if the resistance to the undertaking compelled him to inform the general that he must recur to some other corps to provide an agent to execute this necessary and bold enterprise. He entreated the sergeant to ask himself what must be the sensations of his comrades, if a soldier from some other corps should execute the enterprise, when they should be told that the glory transferred to the regi-

ment of which he was one, might have been enjoyed by
the legion, had not Sergeant Champe shrunk from the
overture made to him by his general, rather than reject
scruples too narrow and confined to be permitted to inter-
fere with grand and virtuous deeds.

"The *esprit du corps* could not be resisted, and, united
to his inclination, it subdued his prejudices, and he declared
his willingness to conform to the wishes of the general;
relying, as he confidently did, that his reputation would
be protected by those who had induced him to undertake
the enterprise, should he be unfortunate in the attempt.

"The instructions were read to him, and every distinct
object presented plainly to his view, of which he took
notes so disguised as to be understood only by himself.
He was particularly cautioned to use the utmost circumspection in delivering his letters, and to take care to with-
hold from the two individuals, addressed under feigned
names, knowledge of each other; for though both had
long been in the confidence of the general, yet it was not
known by one that the other was so engaged. He was
further urged to bear in constant recollection the solemn
injunction so pointedly expressed in the instructions to
Major Lee, of forbearing to kill Arnold in any condition
of things.

"This part of the business being finished, the major's
and sergeant's deliberations were turned to the manner
of the latter's desertion; for it was well known to both
that to pass the numerous patroles of horse and foot crossing from the stationary guards, was itself difficult, which
was now rendered more so by parties thrown occasionally
beyond the place called Liberty-pole, as well as by swarms
of irregulars, induced sometimes to venture down to the
very point of Paulus' Hook with the hope of picking up
booty. Evidently discernible as were the difficulties in
the way, no relief could be administered by Major Lee,
lest it might induce a belief that he was privy to the
desertion, which opinion getting to the enemy would involve the life of Champe. The sergeant was left to his
own resources and to his own management, with the declared determination that in case his departure should be
discovered before morning, Lee would take care to delay
pursuit as long as was practicable.

"Giving to the sergeant three guineas, and presenting his best wishes, he recommended him to start without delay, and enjoined him to communicate his arrival in New York as soon thereafter as might be practicable. Champe, pulling out his watch, compared it with the major's, reminding the latter of the importance of holding back pursuit, which he was convinced would take place in the course of the night, and which might be fatal, as he knew that he should be obliged to zigzag in order to avoid the patroles, which would consume time. It was now nearly eleven. The sergeant returned to camp, and taking his cloak, valise and orderly-book, he drew his horse from the picket, and, mounting him, put himself on fortune. Lee, charmed with his expeditious consummation of the first part of the enterprise, retired to rest. Useless attempt! the past scene could not be obliterated; and, indeed, had that been practicable, the interruption which ensued would have stopped repose.

"Within half an hour Captain Carnes, officer of the day, waited on the major, and with considerable emotion told him that one of the patrole had fallen in with a dragoon, who, being challenged, put spur to his horse, and escaped, though instantly pursued. Lee, complaining of the interruption, and pretending to be extremely fatigued by his ride to and from head-quarters, answered as if he did not understand what had been said, which compelled the captain to repeat it. 'Who can the fellow that was pursued be?' inquired the major; adding, 'a countryman, probably.' 'No,' replied the captain; 'the patrole sufficiently distinguished him to know that he was a dragoon; probably one from the army, if not certainly one of our own.' This idea was ridiculed from its improbability, as, during the whole war, but a single dragoon had deserted from the legion. This did not convince Carnes, so much stress was it now the fashion to lay on the desertion of Arnold, and the probable effect of his example. The captain withdrew to examine the squadron of horse, whom he had ordered to assemble in pursuance of established usage on similar occasions. Very quickly he returned, stating that the scoundrel was known, and was no less a person than the sergeant-major, who was gone off with his horse, baggage, arms and orderly-book—so presumed, as neither the one nor the other could be found. Sensibly affected at the supposed paseness of a soldier extremely respected, the captain added that he had ordered a party to make ready for pursuit, and begged the major's written orders.

"Occasionally this discourse was interrupted, and every idea suggested which the excellent character of the sergeant warranted, to induce the suspicion that he had not deserted, but had taken the liberty to leave camp with a view to personal pleasure; an example, said Lee, too often set by the officers themselves, destructive as it was of discipline, opposed as it was to orders, and disastrous as it might prove to the corps in the course of service.

"Some little delay was thus interposed; but it being now announced that the pursuing party was ready, Major Lee directed a change in the officer, saying that he had a particular service in view, which he had determined to intrust to the lieutenant ready for duty, and which probably must be performed in the morning. He therefore directed him to summon Cornet Middleton for the present command. Lee was induced thus to act, first to add to the delay, and next from his knowledge of the tenderness of Middleton's disposition, which he hoped would lead to the protection of Champe, should he be taken. Within ten minutes Middleton appeared to receive his orders, which were delivered to him, made out in the customary form, and signed by the major. 'Pursue so far as you can with safety Sergeant Champe, who is suspected of deserting to the enemy, and has taken the road leading to Paulus' Hook. Bring him alive, that he may suffer in the presence of the army; but kill him if he resists, or escapes after being taken.'

"Detaining the cornet a few minutes longer in advising him what course to pursue—urging him to take care of the horse and accoutrements, if recovered—and enjoining him to be on his guard, lest he might, by his eager pursuit, improvidently fall into the hands of the enemy—the major dismissed Middleton, wishing him success. A shower of rain fell soon after Champe's departure, which enabled the pursuing dragoons to take the trail of his horse; knowing, as officer and trooper did, the make of their shoes, whose impression was an unerring guide.*

* The horses being all shod by our own farriers, the shoes were made in the same form; which, with a private mark annexed to the fore shoes, and known to the troopers, pointed out the trail of our dragoons to each other, which was often very useful.

"When Middleton departed, it was a few minutes past twelve, so that Champe had only the start of rather more than an hour—by no means so long as was desired. Lee became very unhappy, not only because the estimable and gallant Champe might be injured, but lest the enterprise might be delayed; and he spent a sleepless night. The pursuing party during the night was, on their part, delayed by the necessary halts to examine occasionally the road, as the impression of the horse's shoes directed their course; this was unfortunately too evident, no other horse having passed along the road since the shower. When the day broke, Middleton was no longer forced to halt, and he passed on with rapidity. Ascending an eminence before he reached the Three Pigeons, some miles on the north of the village of Bergen, as the pursuing party reached its summit, Champe was descried not more than half a mile in front. Resembling an Indian in his vigilance, the sergeant at the same moment discovered the party, to whose object he was no stranger, and, giving spur to his horse, he determined to outstrip his pursuers. Middleton at the same instant put his horses to the top of their speed; and being, as the legion all were, well acquainted with the country, he recollected a short route through the woods to the bridge below Bergen, which diverged from the great road just after you gain the Three Pigeons. Reaching the point of separation, he halted, and dividing his party, directed a sergeant with a few dragoons to take the near cut, and possess with all possible despatch the bridge, while he with the residue, followed Champe; not doubting but that Champe must deliver himself up, as he would be inclosed between himself and his sergeant. Champe did not forget the short cut, and would have taken it himself, but he knew it was the usual route of our parties when returning in the day from the neighborhood of the enemy, properly preferring the woods to the road. He consequently avoided it; and, persuaded that Middleton would avail himself of it, wisely resolved to relinquish his intention of getting to Paulus' Hook, and to seek refuge from two British galleys, lying a few miles to the west of Bergen.

"This was a station always occupied by one or two galleys, and which it was known now lay there. Entering the village or Bergen, Champe turned to his right, and disguising his change of course as much as he could by taking the beaten streets, turning as they turned, he passed through the village, and took the road towards Elizabeth town Point. Middleton's sergeant gained the bridge, where he concealed himself, ready to pounce on Champe, when he came up; and Middleton, pursuing his course through Bergen, soon got also to the bridge, when, to his extreme mortification, he found that the sergeant had slipped through his fingers. Returning up the road, he inquired of the villagers of Bergen whether a dragoon had been seen that morning preceding his party. He was answered in the affirmative, but could learn nothing satisfactory as to the route he had taken. While engaged in inquiries himself, he spread his party through the village to strike the trail of Champe's horse, a resort always recurred to. Some of his dragoons hit it, just as the sergeant, leaving the village, got in the road to the point. Pursuit was renewed with vigor, and again Champe was descried. He, apprehending the event, had prepared himself for it, by lashing his valise, containing his clothes and orderly-book, on his shoulders, and holding his drawn sword in his hand, having thrown away its scabbard. This he did to save what was indispensable to him, and to prevent any interruption to his swimming from the scabbard, should Middleton, as he presumed, when disappointed at the bridge, take the measures adopted by him. The pursuit was rapid and close, as the stop occasioned by the sergeant's preparations for swimming had brought Middleton within two or three hundred yards. As soon as Champe got abreast of the galleys, he dismounted, and running through the marsh to the river, plunged into it, calling on the galleys for help. This was readily given; they fired on our horse, and sent a boat to meet Champe, who was taken in and carried on board, and conveyed to New York with a letter from the captain of the galley, stating the past scene, all of which he had seen.

"The horse with his equipments, the sergeant's cloak and sword scabbard, were recovered; the sword itself, being held by Champe till he plunged into the river, was lost, as Middleton found it necessary to retire without searching for it.

"About three o'clock in the evening our party returned;

and the soldiers, seeing the horse, well known to them, in our possession, made the air resound with exclamations that the scoundrel was killed.

"Major Lee, called by this heart-rending annunciation from his tent, saw the sergeant's horse led by one of Middleton's dragoons, and began to reproach himself with the blood of the highly-prized, faithful, and intrepid Champe. Stifling his agony, he advanced to meet Middleton, and became somewhat relieved as soon as he got near enough to discern the countenance of his officer and party. There was evidence in their looks of disappointment, and he was quickly relieved by Middleton's information that the sergeant had effected his escape with the loss of his horse, and narrated the particulars just recited.

"Lee's joy was now as full as, the moment before, his torture had been excruciating. Never was a happier conclusion. The sergeant escaped unhurt, carrying with him to the enemy undeniable testimony of the sincerity of his desertion—cancelling every apprehension before entertained, lest the enemy might suspect him of being what he really was.

"Major Lee imparted to the commander-in-chief the occurrence, who was sensibly affected by the hair-breadth escape of Champe, and anticipated with pleasure the good effect sure to follow the enemy's knowledge of its manner.

"On the fourth day after Champe's departure, Lee received a letter from him, written the day before in a disguised hand, without any signature, and stating what had passed, after he got on board the galley, where he was kindly received.

"He was carried to the commandant of New York as soon as he arrived, and presented the letter addressed to this officer from the captain of the galley. Being asked to what corps he belonged, and a few other common questions, he was sent under care of an orderly-sergeant, to the adjutant-general, who, finding that he was sergeant-major of the legion of horse, heretofore remarkable for their fidelity, he began to interrogate him. He was told by Champe that such was the spirit of defection which prevailed among the American troops, in consequence of Arnold's example, that, he had no doubt, if the temper was properly cherished, Washington's ranks would not only be greatly thinned, but that some of his best corps would leave him. To this conclusion, the sergeant said; he was led by his own observations, and especially by his knowledge of the discontents which agitated the corps to which he had belonged. His size, place of birth, his form, countenance, color of his hair, the corps in which he had served, with other remarks in conformity to the British usage, was noted in a large folio book. After this was finished, he was sent to the commander-in-chief, in charge of one of the staff, with a letter from the adjutant-general. Sir Henry Clinton treated him very kindly, and detained him more than an hour, asking him many questions, all leading—first to know to what extent this spirit of defection might be pushed by proper incitements—what were the most operating incitements—whether any general officers were suspected by Washington as concerned in Arnold's conspiracy, or any other officers of note—who they were, and whether the troops approved or censured Washington's suspicions—whether his popularity in the army was sinking, or continued stationary. What was Major Andre's situation—whether any change had taken place in the manner of his confinement—what was the current opinion of his probable fate—and whether it was thought Washington would treat him as a spy. To these various interrogations, some of which were perplexing, Champe answered warily; exciting, nevertheless, hopes that the adoption of proper measures to encourage desertion, of which he could not pretend to form an opinion, would certainly bring off hundreds of the American soldiers, including some of the best troops, horse as well as foot. Respecting the fate of Andre, he said he was ignorant, though there appeared to be a general wish in the army that his life should not be taken; and that he believed it would depend more on the disposition of Congress, than on the will of Washington.

"After this long conversation ended, Sir Henry presented Champe with a couple of guineas, and recommended him to wait on General Arnold, who was engaged in raising an American legion in the service of his majesty. He directed one of his aids to write to Arnold by Champe, stating who he was, and what he had said about the disposition in the army to follow his example, which was very soon done; it was given to the orderly attending on Champe, to be presented with the deserter to General Arnold. Arnold expressed much satisfaction on hearing from Champe the manner of his escape, and the effect of Arnold's example; and concluded his numerous inquiries by assigning quarters to the sergeant—the same as were occupied by his recruiting-sergeants.

"He also proposed to Champe to join his legion, telling him he could give to him the same station he had held in the rebel service, and promising further advancement when merited. Expressing his wish to retire from war, and his conviction of the certainty of his being hung if ever taken by the rebels, he begged to be excused from enlistment; assuring the general that, should he change his mind, he would certainly accept his offer. Retiring to the assigned quarters, Champe now turned his attention to the delivery of his letters, which he could not effect till the next night, and then only to one of the two *incogniti* to whom he was recommended. This man received the sergeant with extreme attention, and, having read the letter, assured Champe that he might rely on his faithful coöperation in doing every thing in his power consistently with his safety, to guard which required the utmost prudence and circumspection. The sole object in which the aid of this individual was required, regarded the general and others of our army, implicated in the information sent to Washington by him. To this object Champe urged his attention, assuring him of the solicitude it had excited, and telling him that its speedy investigation had induced the general to send him into New York. Promising to enter on it with zeal, and engaging to send out Champe's letters to Major Lee, he fixed the time and place for their next meeting, when they separated.

"Lee made known to the general what had been transmitted to him by Champe, and received in answer directions to press Champe to the expeditious conclusion of his mission, as the fate of Andre would be soon decided, when little or no delay could be admitted in executing whatever sentence the court might decree. The same messenger who brought Champe's letter, returned with the ordered communication. Five days had nearly elapsed after reaching New York, before Champe saw the confidant to whom only the attempt against Arnold was to be intrusted. This person entered with promptitude into the design, promising his cordial assistance. To procure a proper associate to Champe was the first object, and this he promised to do with all possible despatch. Furnishing a conveyance to Lee he again heard from Champe, who stated what I have related, with the additional intelligence that he had that morning, the last of September, been appointed one of Arnold's recruiting-sergeants, having enlisted the day before with Arnold; and that he was induced to take this afflicting step, for the purpose of securing uninterrupted ingress and egress to the house which the general occupied, it being indispensable to a speedy conclusion of the difficult enterprise which the information he had just received had so forcibly urged. He added, that the difficulties in his way were numerous and stubborn, and that his prospect of success was by no means cheering. With respect to the additional treason, he asserted that he had every reason to believe that it was groundless; that the report took its rise in the enemy's camp, and that he hoped soon to clear up this matter satisfactorily. The pleasure which the first part of this communication afforded was damped by the tidings it imparted respecting Arnold, as on his speedy delivery depended Andre's relief. The interposition of Sir Henry Clinton, who was extremely anxious to save his much-loved aid-de-camp, still continued; and it was expected the examination of witnesses and the defence of the prisoner would protract the decision of the court of inquiry, now assembled, and give sufficient time for the consummation of the project committed to Champe. A complete disappointment took place from a quarter unforeseen and unexpected. The honorable and accomplished Andre, knowing his guilt, disdained defence, and prevented the examination of witnesses, by confessing the character in which he stood. On the next day, the 2d of October, the court again assembled, when every doubt that could possibly arise in the case having been removed by the previous confession, Andre was declared to be a spy, and condemned to suffer accordingly.

"The sentence was executed on the subsequent day in the usual form, the commander-in-chief deeming it improper to interpose any delay. In this decision he was warranted by the very unpromising intelligence received from Champe—by the still existing implication of other officers in Arnold's conspiracy—by a due regard to public opinion—and by real tenderness to the condemned.

"Neither Congress nor the nation could have been with propriety informed of the cause of the delay, and without such information it must have excited in both alarm and suspicion. Andre himself could not have been intrusted with the secret, and would consequently have attributed the unlooked-for event to the expostulation and exertion of Sir Henry Clinton, which would not fail to produce in his breast expectations of ultimate relief; to excite which would have been cruel, as the realization of such expectation depended only on a possible but improbable contingency. The fate of Andre, hastened by himself, deprived the enterprise committed to Champe of a feature which had been highly prized by its projector, and which had very much engaged the heart of the individual chosen to execute it.

"Washington ordered Major Lee to communicate what had passed to the sergeant, with directions to encourage him to prosecute with unrelaxed vigor the remaining objects of his instructions, but to intermit haste in the execution only so far as was compatible with final success.

"This was accordingly done, by the first opportunity, in the manner directed. Champe deplored the sad necessity which occurred, and candidly confessed that the hope of enabling Washington to save the life of Andre, who had been the subject of universal commiseration in the American camp, greatly contributed to remove the serious difficulties which opposed his acceding to the proposition when first propounded. Some documents accompanied this communication, tending to prove the innocence of the accused general; they were completely satisfactory, and did credit to the discrimination, zeal and diligence of the sergeant. Lee inclosed them immediately to the commander-in-chief, who was pleased to express the satisfaction he derived from the information, and to order the major to wait on him the next day; when the whole subject was reexamined, and the distrust heretofore entertained of the

26

accused was for ever dismissed.* Nothing now remained
to be done but the seizure and safe delivery of Arnold.
To this object Champe gave his undivided attention; and
on the 19th of October, Major Lee received from him a
very particular account of the progress he had made, with
the outlines of his plan. This was without delay submitted to Washington; with a request for a few additional
guineas. The general's letter,† written on the same day,

* *Copy of a Letter from General Washington to Major Lee, in his own
hand-writing, dated*
"OCTOBER 23d, 1780.

"DEAR SIR: I am very glad your letter of this date has given strength
to my conviction of the innocence of the gentleman who was the subject
of your inquiry. I want to see you on a particular piece of business.
If the day is fair, and nothing of consequence intervenes, I will be at
the marquis' quarters at ten o'clock to-morrow. If this should not happen, I shall be glad to see you at head-quarters.

"I am, dear sir, your most obedient servant,
"G. WASHINGTON."

† *Copy of a Letter from General Washington to Major Lee in his own
hand-writing.*
"HEAD-QUARTERS, *October 20th,* 1780.

"DEAR SIR: The plan proposed for taking A——d, the outlines of
which are communicated in your letter, which was this moment put into
my hands without date, has every mark of a good one. I therefore agree
to the promised rewards; and have such entire confidence in your management of the business, as to give it my fullest approbation; and leave
the whole to the guidance of your own judgment, with this express stipulation and pointed injunction, that he, A——d, is brought to me alive.

"No circumstance whatever shall obtain my consent to his being put
to death. The idea which would accompany such an event, would be
that ruffians had been hired to assassinate him. My aim is to make a
public example of him; and this should be strongly impressed on those
who are employed to bring him off. The sergeant must be very circum-
spect;—too much zeal may create suspicion, and too much precipitancy
may defeat the project. The most inviolable secrecy must be observed
on all hands. I send you five guineas; but I am not satisfied of the propriety of the sergeant's appearing with much specie. This circumstance
may also lead to suspicion, as it is but too well known to the enemy
that we do not abound in this article.

"The interviews between the party, in and out of the city, should be
managed with much caution and seeming indifference; or else the fre-
quency of their meetings, &c., may betray the design, and involve bad
consequences; but I am persuaded you will place every matter in a
proper point of view to the conductors of this interesting business, and
therefore I shall only add, that
"I am, dear sir, &c., &c.
"G. WASHINGTON."

20th October, evinces his attention to the minutiæ of business, as well as his immutable determination to possess Arnold alive, or not at all. This was his original injunction, which he never omitted to enforce on every proper occasion.

"Major Lee had an opportunity, in the course of the week, of writing to Champe, when he told him that the rewards which he had promised to his associates would be certainly paid on the delivery of Arnold; and in the mean time, small sums of money would be furnished for casual expenses, it being deemed improper that he should appear with much, lest it might lead to suspicion and detection. That five guineas were now sent, and that more would follow when absolutely necessary.

" Ten days elapsed before Champe brought his measures to conclusion, when Lee received from him his final communication, appointing the third subsequent night for a party of dragoons to meet him at Hoboken, when he hoped to deliver Arnold to the officer. Champe had, from his enlistment into the American legion, (Arnold's corps,) every opportunity he could wish to attend to the habits of the general. He discovered that it was his custom to return home about twelve every night, and that previous to going to bed he always visited the garden. During this visit the conspirators were to seize him, and, being prepared with a gag, intended to have applied the same instantly.

" Adjoining the house in which Arnold resided, and in which it was designed to seize and gag him, Champe had taken off several of the palings and rēplaced them so that with care and without noise he could readily open his way to the adjoining alley. Into this alley he meant to have ccnveyed his prisoner, aided by his companion, one of two associates who had been introduced by the friend to whom Champe had been originally made known by letter from the commander-in-chief, and with whose aid and counsel he had so far conducted the enterprise. His other associate was with the boat prepared at one of the wharves on the Hudson river to receive the party.

" Champe and his friend intended to have placed themselves each under Arnold's shŏulder, and to have thus borne him through the most unfrequented alleys and streets to the boat; representing Arnold, in case of being questioned, as a drunken soldier whom they were conveying to the guard-house.

"When arrived at the boat, the difficulties would be all surmounted, there being no danger nor obstacle in passing to the Jersey shore. These particulars, so soon as known to Lee, were communicated to the commander-in-chief, who was highly gratified with the much-desired intelligence. He directed Major Lee to meet Champe, and to take care that Arnold should not be hurt. The day arrived, and Lee with a party of dragoons left camp late in the evening, with three led accoutred horses; one for Arnold, one for the sergeant, and the third for his associate, never doubting the success of the enterprise, from the tenor of the last-received communication. The party reached Hoboken about midnight, where they were concealed in the adjoining wood—Lee with three dragoons stationing himself near the river-shore. Hour after hour passed—no boat approached. At length the day broke, and the major retired to his party, and with his led horses returned to camp, when he proceeded to head-quarters to inform the general of the much-lamented disappointment, as mortifying as inexplicable. Washington having perused Champe's plan and communication, had indulged the presumption that at length the object of his keen and constant pursuit was sure of execution, and did not dissemble the joy such conviction produced. He was chagrined at the issue, and apprehended that his faithful sergeant must have been detected in the last scene of his tedious and difficult enterprise.

"In a few days Lee received an anonymous letter from Champe's patron and friend, informing him that on the day preceding the night fixed for the execution of the plot, Arnold had removed his quarters to another part of the town, to superintend the embarkation of troops, preparing, as was rumored, for an expedition to be directed by himself; and that the American legion, consisting chiefly of American deserters, had been transferred from their barracks to one of the transports; it being apprehended that if left on shore till the expedition was ready, many of them might desert. Thus it happened that John Champe, instead of crossing the Hudson that night, was safely de-

JOHN ADAMS.

posited on board one of the fleet of transports, whence he never departed till the troops under Arnold landed in Virginia! nor was he able to escape from the British army till after the junction of Lord Cornwallis at Petersburg, when he deserted, and proceeding high up into Virginia, he passed into North Carolina, near the Sama towns, and, keeping in the friendly districts of that state, safely joined the army soon after it had passed the Congaree in pursuit of Lord Rawdon.

"His appearance excited extreme surprise among his former comrades, which was not a little increased when they saw the cordial reception he met with from the late major, now Lieutenant-Colonel Lee. His whole story soon became known to the corps, which reproduced the love and respect of officer and soldier, heretofore invariably entertained for the sergeant, heightened by universal admiration of his late daring and arduous attempt.

"Champe was introduced to General Greene, who very cheerfully complied with the promises made by the commander-in-chief, so far as in his power; and having provided the sergeant with a good horse and money for his journey, sent him to General Washington, who munificently anticipated every desire of the sergeant, and presented him with his discharge from further service,* lest he might in the vicissitudes of war fall into the enemy's hands; when, if recognized, he was sure to die on the gibbet."

* When General Washington was called by President Adams to the command of the army, prepared to defend the country from French hostility, he sent to Lieutenant-Colonel Lee, to inquire for Champe; being determined to bring him into the field at the head of a company of infantry. Lee sent to Loudon county, where Champe settled after his discharge from the army; when he learned that the gallant soldier had removed to Kentucky, where he soon after died.

BIOGRAPHICAL SKETCHES.

MAJOR-GENERAL ISRAEL PUTNAM.

THE life of this patriot and hero has been portrayed by the able and impartial hand of the late General David Humphreys, and a brief sketch, chiefly from that work, must suffice for the present purpose. General Putnam was born at Salem, Massachusetts, on the 7th day of January, 1718. He was indebted to nature, more than education, for a vigorous constitution, for mental endowments, and for that undaunted courage and active enterprise which were his prominent characteristics. Much confidence was reposed in his military prowess and judgment, and he was remarkable for a faithful perseverance in all the duties of his station, and for the most undeviating principles of honor, humanity and benevolence. In the year 1739, he removed to Pomfret, in Connecticut, where he applied himself to the art of agriculture. His biographer, as a display of character in early life, has recorded an instance of his bold attack of a wolf while in her den; but as the story has been frequently promulgated, it need not be repeated in this place. When, in the year 1755, the war between England and France broke out in America, Putnam was appointed to the command of a company of rangers, and was distinguished for his active services as a partizan officer. In 1757, he was promoted to a majority, and being in a warm and close engagement with a party of French and savages, he had discharged his fuzee several times, when at length it missed fire while the muzzle was pressed against the breast of a large and well-proportioned Indian. This adversary, with a tremendous war-whoop, sprang forward with his lifted hatchet, and compelled him to surrender; and having bound him fast to a tree returned to the battle. For a considerable time the tree to which Major Putnam was tied was directly between the fires of the two parties, than which no conceivable situation could be more deplorable. The balls flew incessantly from each side, many struck the tree, while some passed through the sleeves and skirts of his coat. In this state of jeopardy, unable to move his body, to stir his limbs, or even to incline his head, he remained more than an hour—so equally balanced and so obstinate was the fight! At one moment, while the battle swerved in favor of the enemy, a young savage chose an odd way of discovering his humor. He found Putnam bound. He might have despatched him at a blow. But he loved better to excite the terrors of the prisoner by hurling a tomahawk at his head, or rather it should seem his object was to see how near he could throw it without touching him.—The weapon struck in the tree a number of times at a hair's-breadth from the mark. When the Indian had finished his amusement, a French bas-officer, a much more inveterate savage by nature, though descended from so humane and polished a nation, perceiving Putnam, came to him, and, levelling a fuzee within a foot of his breast, attempted to discharge it—it missed fire. Ineffectually did the intended victim solicit the treatment due to his situation, by repeating that he was a prisoner of war. · The degenerate Frenchman did not understand the language of honor or of nature; deaf to their voice, and dead to sensibility, he violently and repeatedly pushed the muzzle of his gun against Putnam's rib's, and finally gave him a cruel blow on the jaw with the butt-end of his piece. After this dastardly deed he left him.

At length the enemy was driven from the field of battle, and, as they were retiring, Putnam was untied by the Indian who had made him prisoner, and whom he afterwards called master. Having been conducted to some distance from the place of action, he was stripped of his coat, vest, stockings and shoes; loaded with as many of the packs of the wounded as could be piled on him, strongly pinioned, and his wrists tied as closely together as they could be pulled with a cord. After he had marched through no pleasant paths, in this painful manner, for many a tedious mile, the party, who were excessively fatigued, halted to breathe. His hands were now immoderately swelled from the tightness of the ligature, and the pain had become intolerable. His feet were so much scratched, that the blood dropped fast from them. Exhausted with bearing a burden above his strength, and frantic with torments exquisite beyond endurance, he intreated the Irish interpreter to implore, as the last and only grace he desired of the savages, that they would knock him on the head, and take his scalp at once, or loose his hands. A French officer, instantly interposing, ordered his hands to be unbound, and some of the packs to be taken off. By this time the Indian who captured him and had been absent with the wounded, coming up, gave him a pair of moccasins, and expressed great indignation at the unworthy treatment his prisoner had suffered.

That savage chief again returned to the care of the wounded, and the Indians, about two hundred in number, went before the rest of the party to the place where the whole were that night to encamp. They took with them Major Putnam, on whom, besides innumerable other outrages, they had the barbarity to inflict a deep wound with the tomahawk in the left cheek. His sufferings were in this place to be consummated. A scene of horror, infinitely greater than had ever met his eyes before, was now preparing. It was determined to roast him alive. For this purpose they led him into a dark forest, stripped him naked, bound him to a tree, and piled dry brush, with other fuel, at a small distance, in a circle round him. They accompanied their labors, as if for his funeral dirge, with screams and sounds, inimitable but by savage voices. Then they set the piles on fire. A sudden shower damped the rising flame. Still they strove to kindle it; at last the blaze ran fiercely round the circle. Major Putnam soon began to feel the scorching heat. His hands were so tied that he could move his body. He often shifted sides as the fire approached. This sight, at the very idea of which, all but savages must shudder, afforded the highest diversion to his inhuman tormentors, who demonstrated the delirium of their joy by corresponding yells, dances and gesticulations. He saw clearly that his final hour was inevitably come. He summoned all his resolution, and composed his mind, so far as the circumstances could admit, to bid an eternal farewell to all he held most dear. To quit the world would scarcely have cost a single pang; but for the idea of home, but for the remembrance of domestic endearments, of the affectionate partner of his soul, and of their beloved offspring. His thought was ultimately fixed on a happier state of existence, beyond the tortures he was beginning to endure. The bitterness of death, even of that death which is accompanied with the keenest agonies, was, in a manner, past—nature, with a feeble struggle, was quitting its last hold on sublunary things—when a French officer rushed through the crowd, opened a way by scattering the burning brands, and unbound the victim. It was Molang himself—to whom a savage, unwilling to see another human victim immolated, had run and communicated the tidings. That commandant spurned and severely reprimanded the barbarians, whose nocturnal powwas and hellish orgies he suddenly ended. Putnam did not want for feeling or gratitude. The French commander, fearing to trust him alone with them, remained till he could safely deliver him into the hands of his master.

The savage approached his prisoner kindly, and seemed to treat him with particular affection. He offered him some hard biscuit; but finding that he could not chew them, on account of the blow he had received from the Frenchman, this more humane savage soaked some of the biscuit in water, and made him suck the pulp-like part. Determined, however, not to lose his captive, the refreshment being finished, he took the moccasins from his feet, and tied them to one of his wrists; then directing him to lie down on his back on the bare ground, he stretched one arm to its full length, and bound it fast to a young tree; the other arm was extended and bound in the same manner—his legs were stretched apart, and fastened to two saplings. Then a number of tall, but slender poles were cut down, which, with some long bushes, were laid across his body from head to foot: on each side lay as many Indians as could conveniently find lodging, in order to prevent the possibility of his escape. In this disagreeable and painful posture he remained till morning. During the night, (the longest and most dreary conceivable,) our hero used to relate that he felt a ray of cheerfulness come casually across his mind, and could not even refrain from smiling when he reflected on this ludicrous group for a painter, of which he himself was the principal figure.

The next day he was allowed his blanket and moccasins, and permitted to march without carrying any pack or receiving any insult. To allay his extreme hunger, a little bear's-meat was given, which he sucked through his teeth. At night the party arrived at Ticonderoga, and the prisoner was placed under the care of a French guard. The savages, who had been prevented from glutting their diabolical thirst for blood, took this opportunity of manifesting their malevolence for the disappointment by horrid grimaces and angry gestures; but they were suffered no more to offer violence or personal indignity to him.

After having been examined by the Marquis de Montcalm, Major Putnam was conducted to Montreal by a French officer, who treated him with the greatest indulgence and humanity.

At this place were several prisoners. Colonel Peter Schuyler, remarkable for his philanthropy, generosity and friendship, was of the number. No sooner had he heard of Major Putnam's arrival, than he went to the interpreter's quarters, and inquired whether he had a Provincial major in his custody? He found Major Putnam in a comfortless condition—without coat, waistcoat, or hose—the remnant of his clothing miserably dirty and ragged—his beard long and squalid—his legs torn by thorns and briers—his face gashed with wounds and swollen with bruises. Colonel Schuyler, irritated beyond all sufferance at such a sight, could scarcely restrain his speech within limits consistent with the prudence of a prisoner and the meekness of a Christian. Major Putnam was immediately treated according to his rank, clothed in a decent manner, and supplied with money by this liberal and sympathetic patron of the distressed, and by his assistance he was soon after exchanged.

In the year 1760, Major Putnam was promoted to the rank of lieutenant-colonel, and served under General Amherst in the conquest of Canada. He embraced numerous opportunities of achieving feats of valor, and was particularly honored by his general for the promptitude and ability with which he acquitted himself of his arduous duty. "Colonel Putnam, at the expiration of ten years from his first receiving a commission, after having seen as much service, endured as many hardships, encountered as many dangers, and acquired as many laurels, as any officer of his rank, with great satisfaction laid aside his uniform and returned to his plough." No character stood fairer in the public eye for integrity, bravery and patriotism. It was proverbially said, as well by British as Provincial officers, that, in a service of great peril and hardship, from 1755 to 1763, "*he dared to lead where any dared to follow.*"

At the commencement of hostilities between the colonies and the mother-country, Colonel Putnam, on hearing of the battle at Lexington, left his plough in the middle of the field, and, without changing his clothes, repaired to Cambridge, riding in a single day one hundred miles. He was soon appointed a major-general in the provincial army, and, returning to Connecticut, he made no delay in bringing on a body of troops. Not long after his appointment, the commander of the British army, unwilling that so valuable an officer should act in opposition, privately conveyed to him a proposal that if he would quit the *rebel* party, he might rely on being made a major-general in the British establishment, and receiving a great pecuniary compensation for his services; but he spurned the offer. "On the 16th of June, 1775, it was determined in a council of war, at which General Putnam assisted, that a fortified post should be established at or near Bunker-hill. General Putnam marched with the first detachment and commenced the work; he was the principal agent or engineer who traced the lines of the redoubt, and he continued most, if not all the night with the workmen: at any rate, he was on the spot before sun-rising in the morning, and had taken his station on the top of Bunker-hill, and participated in the *danger* as well as the glory of that day."*

A Letter from the Hon. Judge Grosvenor, of Pomfret, Connecticut.

"Being under the command of General Putnam, part of our regiment, and a much larger number of Massachusetts troops, under Colonel Pres-

* In the spring of the year 1818 an account of the battle of Bunker-hill was publishdd in the Port Folio by Henry Dearborn, Esq., major-general in the army of the United States, in which he animadverts on the conduct of General Putnam with great severity. To this production Daniel Putnam, Esq., son of the late general, has published a rejoinder from which I have taken the testimonials which follow.

cott, were ordered to march on the evening of the 16th of June, 1775, to Breed's-hill, where, under the immediate superintendence of General Putnam, ground was broken and a redoubt formed. On the following day, the 17th, dispositions were made to deter the advance of the enemy, as there was reason to believe an immediate attack was intended. General Putnam during the period was extremely active, and directed principally the operations. All were animated, and their general inspired confidence by his example. The British army, having made dispositions for landing at Morton's Point, were covered by the fire of shot and shells from Copp's-hill in Boston, which it had opened on our redoubt early in the morning, and continued the greater part of the day. At this moment a detachment of four lieutenants, of which I was one, and one hundred and twelve men, selected the preceding day from General Putnam's regiment, under Captain Knowlton, were by the general ordered to take post at a rail-fence on the left of the breastwork that ran north from the redoubt to the bottom of Breed's-hill. This order was promptly executed, and our detachment, in advancing to the post, took one rail-fence and placed it against another, as a partial cover, nearly parallel with the line of the breastwork, and extended our left nearly to Mystic river. Each man was furnished with *one pound* of *gun-powder* and *forty-eight balls*. This ammunition was received, however, prior to marching to Breed's-hill. In this position our detachment remained till a second division of British troops landed, when they commenced a fire of their *field artillery* of several rounds, and particularly against the rail-fence; then formed in columns, advanced to the attack, displayed in line at about the distance of musket-shot, and commenced firing. At this instant our whole line opened on the enemy, and so precise and fatal was our fire, that in the course of a short time they gave way, and retired in disorder out of musket-shot, leaving before us many killed and wounded. There was but a short respite on the part of the British, as their lines were soon filled up and led against us, when they were met as before, and forced back with great loss. On reinforcements joining the enemy, they made a direct advance on the redoubt, and being successful, which our brave Captain Knowlton perceiving, ordered a retreat of his men, *in which he was sustained by two companies under the command of Captains Clark and Chester.* The loss in our detachment I presume was nearly equal. Of my own immediate command of thirty men and one subaltern, there were *eleven killed and wounded;* among the latter was myself, though not so severely as to prevent my retiring. *At the rail-fence there was not posted any corps save our own, under Knowlton, at the time the firing commenced; nor did I hear of any other being there, till long after the action.* Other troops, it is said, were ordered to join us, but refused doing so. Of the officers on the ground, the most active within my observation were General Putnam, Colonel Presscott, and Captain Knowlton; but no doubt there were many more, equally brave and meritorious, who must naturally have escaped the eye of one attending to his own immediate command.

"Thus you have a brief statement of my knowledge of the action, without descending to particulars. To conclude, it is matter of surprise, even of astonishment to me, my dear sir, that I am called on to state my opinion of the character of your honored father, General Putnam, who was ever the first in public life at the post of honor and danger, and who, in his private conduct, was excelled by none. Look but at his services in the French and Indian wars from 1755 to 1763, and finally at those of the revolution, and you will need no proof to refute the calumny of common defamers.

"With respect, I am, yours, truly,   "THOMAS GROSVENOR.
"Colonel Daniel Putnam."

The following is a letter from Colonel John Trumbull, of New York, an officer of distinction in the revolutionary war, and now a celebrated historical painter, employed in his profession by the government of the United States, dated, New York, 30th of March, 1818:

"In the summer of 1786, I became acquainted in London with Colonel *John Small*, of the British army, who had served in America many years, and had known General Putnam intimately during the war of Canada, from 1756 to 1763. From him I had the two following anecdotes respecting the battle of Bunker-hill. I shall nearly repeat his words: Looking at the picture which I had then almost completed, he said: 'I don't like the situation in which you have placed my old friend Putnam; you have not done him justice. I wish you would alter that part of your picture, and introduce a circumstance which actually happened, and which I can never forget. When the British troops advanced the second time to the attack of the redoubt, I with other officers was in front of the line to encourage the men; we had advanced very near the works undisturbed, when an irregular fire like a *feu de joie* was poured in on us; it was cruelly fatal. The troops fell back, and when I looked to the right and left, I saw not one officer standing. I glanced my eye to the enemy, and saw several young men levelling their pieces at me; I knew their excellence as marksmen, and considered myself gone. At this moment my old friend Putnam rushed forward, and striking up the muzzles of their pieces with his sword, cried out, 'For God's sake, my lads, don't fire at that man!—I love him as I do my brother.' We were so near each other that I heard his words distinctly. He was obeyed; I bowed, thanked him, and walked away unmolested.'

"The other anecdote relates to the death of General Warren. At the moment when the troops succeeded in carrying the redoubt and the Americans were in full retreat, General Howe, who had been hurt by a spent ball, which bruised his ankle, was leaning on my arm. He called suddenly to me: 'Do you see that elegant young man who has just fallen?—do you know him?' I looked to the spot to which he pointed: 'Good God, sir, I believe it is my friend Warren.' 'Leave me then instantly—run—keep off the troops—save him if possible.'—I flew to the spot. 'My dear friend,' I said to him, 'I hope you are not badly hurt.' He looked up, seemed to recollect me, smiled, and died! A musket-ball had passed through the upper part of his head. Colonel Small had the character of an honorable, upright man, and could have no conceivable motive for deviating from truth in relating these circumstances to me; I therefore believe them to be true. You remember, my dear sir, the viper biting the file. The character of your father for courage, humanity,

generosity and integrity is too firmly established, by the testimony of those who *did know him*, to be tarnished by the breath of one who confesses that he *did not*. Accept, my dear sir, this feeble tribute to your father's memory, from one who *knew* him, *respected* him, *loved* him—and who wishes health and prosperity to you and all the good man's posterity.   "JOHN TRUMBULL.
"Daniel Putnam, Esquire."

"I shall make no comment," says Colonel Putnam, "on the first anecdote by Colonel Small, except that the circumstances were related by General Putnam, without any essential alteration, soon after the battle; and that there was an interview of the parties on the lines between Prospect and Bunker-hill, at the request of Colonel Small, not long afterwards."

It is very apparent that General Washington reposed great confidence in the skill and judgment of General Putnam, or he would not have intrusted him with the command of the city of New York at the moment when it was expected that the whole of the British land and naval forces would attempt to take possession of that city. On the 29th of March, 1776, the commander-in-chief gave to General Putnam the following orders and instructions: "You will, no doubt, make the best despatch in getting to New York; on your arrival there, you will assume the command, and immediately proceed in continuing to execute the plan proposed by Major-General Lee, for fortifying that city, and securing the passes of the East and North rivers. If, on consultation with the brigadier-generals and engineers, any alteration in that plan is thought necessary, you are at liberty to make it, cautiously avoiding to break in too much on his main design, unless where it may be apparently necessary so to do, and that by the general voice and opinion of the gentlemen above mentioned. You will meet the quarter-master-general, Colonel Mifflin, and commissary-general, Colonel Trumbull, at New York. As these are both men of excellent talents in their different departments, you will do well to give them all the authority and assistance they require; and should a council of war be necessary, it is my direction that they assist at it. Your *long service and experience* will, better than my particular directions at this distance, point out to you the works most proper to be first raised, and your *perseverance, activity and zeal* will lead you, without my recommending it, to exert every nerve to disappoint the enemy's designs."

"The faithful execution of the duties here enjoined were acknowledged by the commander-in-chief after his arrival in New York, and his thanks were publicly expressed in general orders. Two days before the battle of Flatbush, in consequence of the sickness of that excellent officer, Major-General Greene, who had commanded on Long Island, General Putnam was ordered to the command of that post, and assisted in the arduous and complicated difficulties of that masterly retreat. In the memorable and distressing *flight* of the American army through New Jersey, in 1776, General Putnam was always near—always the friend, the supporter, and confidant of his beloved chief; and the moment after reaching the western bank of the Delaware with the rear of the army, he was ordered to Philadelphia, to fortify and defend that city against a meditated attack. When, in the summer of 1777, Fort Montgomery was captured by the enemy, and it was determined to erect another fortification on the banks of the Hudson for the defence of that river, the commander-in-chief left it wholly to the judgment of General Putnam to fix on the spot, who decided in favor of West Point; and, as his biographer has remarked, 'it is no vulgar praise to say, that to him belongs the glory of having chosen this rock of our military salvation.'"

As an instance of the decision of his temper, the following is deserving of notice. A man by the name of Nathan Palmer was detected in General Putnam's camp, who, on trial, was found to be a lieutenant in the tory new levies. Governor Tryon, their commander, addressed General Putnam, and reclaimed Palmer as a British officer, and threatened vengeance in case he should be executed. This drew from him a reply in the following laconic style:

"SIR: Nathan Palmer, a lieutenant in your king's service, was taken in my camp as a *spy*,—he was tried as a *spy*,—he was condemned as a *spy*,—and you may rest assured, sir, that he shall be hanged as a *spy*.

"I have the honor to be, &c.   "ISRAEL PUTNAM.

"His Excellency Governor Tryon.

"P. S. Afternoon. He is hanged."

In December, 1779, while on his return from Connecticut to head-quarters, this venerable man was attacked by a paralytic affection, under which he languished till the 19th of May, 1790, when his honorable and useful life was brought to a final close. The qualities of his mind were sincerity, generosity and an invincible sense of duty. The moral virtues, and duties of piety and pure religion, were objects of his serious reflection, and the late Rev. Dr. Dwight, in his Travels, has eulogized these as eminent traits in his character.

Extract of a Letter from Gen. Washington to Gen. Putnam, dated

"HEAD-QUARTERS, *2d June*, 1783.

"DEAR SIR: Your favor of the 20th of May I received with much pleasure. For I can assure you that, among the many worthy and meritorious officers with whom I have had the happiness to be connected in service through the course of this war, and from whose cheerful assistance in the various and trying vicissitudes of a complicated contest, the name of Putnam is not forgotten; nor will it be, but with that stroke of time which shall obliterate from my mind the remembrance of all those toils and fatigues through which we have struggled for the preservation and establishment of the rights, liberties, and independence of our country. Your congratulations on the happy prospect of peace and independent security, with their attendant blessings to the United States, I receive with great satisfaction; and beg you will accept a return of my gratulations to you, on this auspicious event—an event in which, great as it is in itself, and glorious as it will probably be in its consequences, you have a right to *participate largely, from the distinguished part you have contributed towards its attainment.* I anticipate with pleasure the day, and I trust not far off, when I shall quit the busy scenes of military employment, and retire to the more tranquil walks of domestic life. In that, or whatever other situation Providence may dispose of my future days, *the remembrance of the many friendships and connexions I have had the* happiness to contract with the gentlemen of the army, will be one of my most grateful reflections.

"Under this contemplation, and impressed with the sentiments of benevolence and regard, I commend you, my dear sir, my other friends, and, with them, the interests and happiness of our dear country, to the *keeping and protection of Almighty God.*

"I have the honor to be, &c., &c.

"GEORGE WASHINGTON.

"To the Hon. Major-General Putnam."

The following eulogium was pronounced at the grave of General Putnam by Dr. A. Waldo:

"Those venerable relics! once delighted in the endearing domestic virtues which constitute the excellent neighbor—husband—parent—and worthy brother! liberal and substantial in his friendship;—unsuspicious —open—and generous; just and sincere in dealing; a benevolent citizen of the world—he concentrated in his bosom the noble qualities of an Honest Man.

"Born a *Hero*—whom nature taught and cherished in the lap of innumerable toils and dangers, he was terrible in battle! But, from the amiableness of his heart—when carnage ceased, his humanity spread over the *field*, like the refreshing zephyrs of a summer's evening! The prisoner—the wounded—the sick—the forlorn—experienced the delicate sympathy of *this Soldier's Pillar*. The poor and the needy of every description, received the charitable bounties of *this* Christian Soldier.

"He pitied littleness—loved goodness—admired greatness, and ever aspired to its glorious summit! The friend, the servant, and almost unparalleled lover of his country;—worn with honorable age, and the former toils of *war*—Putnam rests from his labors!

"'Till mouldering worlds and trembling systems burst!
When the last trump shall renovate his dust—
Still by the mandate of eternal truth,
His soul will flourish in immortal youth!'

"'This all who knew him, know; this all who loved him tell.'"

Dr. Dwight penned a very excellent inscription, which is engraved on his tomb, but our narrow limits must apologize for its omission in this place.

MAJOR-GENERAL WILLIAM HEATH.

MAJOR-GENERAL WILLIAM HEATH was a native of Roxbury, Massachusetts, and was from his youth a cultivator of the soil, which was his favorite pursuit. He was not conversant with general literature; but, being particularly attached to the study of military tactics, he acquired a knowledge of modern warfare in its various branches and duties.

At an early period of the opposition of the colonies to the unjust and oppressive measures of the British ministry, he was an active militia officer, and assiduously engaged in organizing and disciplining the companies of militia and minute-men. In the year 1775, being ranked among the patriots and advocates for liberty, he was by the Provincial Congress commissioned as a brigadier-general.

During the siege of Boston, he was in commission as a general officer, but on no occasion distinguished for enterprise or important services. When General Washington contemplated an attack on Boston, General Heath was offered the command of a division, but he declined the hazardous service. In August, 1776, he was by Congress promoted to the rank of major-general in the continental

27

army, and in the campaign of that year he commanded a division near the enemy's lines at King's-bridge and Morrisania. During the year 1777, and till November, 1778, he was the commanding officer of the Eastern department, and his head-quarters were at Boston. Here devolved on him the very arduous duties of superintendent of the convention troops, captured with General Burgoyne at Saratoga, which were quartered at Cambridge. This station required a character of uncommon firmness and decision, and had General Heath been destitute of these qualities, he would have been subjected to the grossest impositions and indignities, from the haughty Generals Burgoyne and Phillips, and the perverse temper of their soldiery. These officers, lofty in spirit, and of high rank and character, now chagrined by a state of captivity, occasioned to General Heath a series of difficulties and vexations. He soon, however, convinced them that he was neither deficient in spirit nor ignorant of his duty, as a military commander. In all his proceedings with these turbulent captives, he supported the authority of Congress and the honor and dignity of the command reposed in him; and he received the entire approbation of that honorable body, to whom he was amenable for his conduct. In the most interesting and critical circumstances in which a general could possibly be place.'   iformly exhibited a prudence, animation, decision, ...u firmness which have done him honor, and fully justified the confidence reposed in him.

The cordial and most explicit approbation of the army, the inhabitants of this town, the army and navy of our illustrious ally, the government of this state, his excellency the commander-in-chief, and of Congress, added to the consciousness of his having discharged his trust with fidelity, must in a great measure have alleviated the fatigues incident to his arduous station, and compensated the loss of his health, so much impaired by an incessant attention to business.* In June, 1779, General Heath was elected by Congress a commissioner of the Board of War, with a salary of four thousand dollars per annum, and allowed to retain his rank in the army, which he declined, preferring to participate in active operations in the field.

* *Continental Journal*, printed at Boston, November 12th, 1778.

In the summer of 1780, he was directed by the commander-in-chief to repair to Rhode Island, to make arrangements for the reception of the French fleet and army, which
were expected soon to arrive. In his interview with the
Count Rochambeau and other officers of the French army
and navy, he proffered his friendly civilities, and contributed all in his power to their comfortable accommodation,
which was productive of a mutual and lasting friendship
between them. Indefatigable attention to duty, in the
various stations assigned him, was a prominent trait in his
character. In May, 1781, General Heath was directed by
the commander-in-chief to repair to the New England
states, to represent to their respective executives the distressing condition of our army, and to solicit a speedy
supply of provisions and clothing, in which he was successful. As senior major-general, he was more than once
commander of the right wing of our army, and during the
absence of the commander-in-chief, at the siege of Yorktown, he was intrusted with the command of the main
army, posted at the highlands and vicinity, to guard the
important works on the Hudson. On the 24th of June,
1784, hostilities having ceased between the two armies,
General Washington addressed a letter to General Heath,
expressing his thanks for his meritorious services, and his
real affection and esteem, and on the same day they took
their final leave.

General Heath was corpulent and bald-headed, which
occasioned some of the French officers to observe that he
resembled the Marquis of Granby, and he appeared always
pleased with the comparison. As an officer of parade and
discipline, he was respectable; but for valorous achievements, we look in vain for his laurels. Had it been his
destiny, however, to encounter the perils of a conflict in
the field of blood, no one can say with what adroitness he
would have played the hero.

Immediately after the close of the war, General Heath
was called again into public service in civil life, and continued to hold a seat, either in the legislature or in the
council of Massachusetts, till the county of Norfolk was
established, in 1793, when he was appointed by Governor
Hancock judge of probate and a justice of the court of
common pleas; the latter office he did not accept; in the

former he continued till his death. He was also a member of the state convention which ratified the federal constitution. All these offices he discharged with assiduity, affability and impartiality, and to the general satisfaction of his fellow-citizens.

He had formed his opinion of human nature on the most favorable examples, and to the close of life had a strong regard to popular opinion. He repeatedly allowed himself to be held up and voted for, for the office of governor and lieutenant-governor of the commonwealth, and at one period had, no doubt, a willingness and desire to hold one of these offices. In 1806 he was elected lieutenant-governor. His refusal of the office was matter of surprise to many, and was by some imputed to an unwillingness to serve with Governor Strong; while it was well known to those most intimate with him to be owing to his disapprobation of the conduct of the legislature of that year, in their memorable attempt to defeat the voice of the people, by setting aside Governor Strong's election.

He was more than once an elector of president and vice-president of the United States, and gave his vote to those who undertook to appropriate to themselves the name *republican*, till the election preceding his death, when he withheld his vote from Mr. Madison, on account of his recommending the declaration of war in 1812, and sanctioning the measures which preceded and followed this event, and which caused the general wholly to withdraw his confidence from that administration.

Such was General Heath's public life. His private one was retired and domestic, amiable, orderly, and industrious, but not remarkable for hospitality, or a liberal appropriation of property to public purposes. He died at Roxbury, January 24th, 1814, aged seventy-seven years.

MAJOR-GENERAL BENJAMIN LINCOLN.

GENERAL LINCOLN deserves a high rank in the fraternity of American heroes. He was born in Hingham, Massachusetts, January 23d, (O. S.) 1733. His early education was not auspicious to his future eminence, and his vocation was that of a farmer, till he was more than forty years of age, though he was commissioned as a magistrate, and elected a representative in the state legislature. In the year 1775, he sustained the office of lieutenant-colonel of militia, and having espoused the cause of his country as a firm and determined whig, he was elected a member of the Provincial Congress, and one of the secretaries of that body, and also a member of the committee of correspondence. In 1776 he was appointed by the council of Massachusetts a brigadier, and soon after a major-general, and he applied himself assiduously to training and preparing the militia for actual service in the field, in which he displayed the military talent which he possessed. In October, he marched with a body of militia, and joined the main army at New York. The commander-in-chief, from a knowledge of his character and merit, recommended him to Congress as an excellent officer, and in February, 1777, he was by that honorable body created a major-general on the continental establishment. For several months he commanded a division, or detachments in the main army, under Washington, and was in situations which required the exercise of the utmost vigilance and caution, as well as firmness and courage. Having the command of about five hundred men in an exposed situation near Bound Brook, through the neglect of his patroles, a large body of the enemy approached within two hundred yards of his quarters undiscovered; the general had scarcely time to mount and leave the house before it was surrounded. He led off his troops, however, in the face of the enemy, and made good his retreat, though with the loss of about sixty men, killed and wounded. One of his aids with the general's baggage and papers fell into the hands of the enemy, as did also three small pieces of artillery. In July, 1777, General Washington selected him to join the northern army, under the command of General Gates, to oppose the advance of General Burgoyne. He took his station at Manchester, in Vermont, to receive and form the New England militia, as they arrived, and to order their march to the rear of the British army. He detached Colonel Brown with five hundred men on the 13th of September to the landing at Lake George, where he succeeded in surprising the enemy, and took possession of two hundred batteaux, liberated one hundred American prisoners, and captured two hundred and ninety-three of the enemy, with the loss of only three killed and five wounded. This enterprise was of the highest importance, and contributed essentially to the glorious event which followed. Having detached two other parties to the enemy's posts at Mount Independence and Skenesborough, General Lincoln united his remaining force with the army under General Gates, and was the second in command. During the sanguinary conflict on the 7th of October, General Lincoln commanded within our lines, and at one o'clock the next morning he marched with his division to relieve the troops that had been engaged, and to occupy the battle-ground, the enemy having retreated. While on this duty he had occasion to ride forward some distance, to reconnoitre, and to order some disposition of his own troops, when a party of the enemy made an unexpected movement, and he approached within musket-shot before he was aware of his mistake. A whole volley of musketry was instantly discharged at him and his aids, and he received a wound by which the bones of his leg were badly fractured, and he was obliged to be carried off the field. The wound was a formidable one, and the loss of his limb was for some time apprehended. He was for several months confined at Albany, and it became necessary to remove a considerable portion of the main bone before he was conveyed to his house at Hingham; and under this painful surgical operation, the writer of this being present, witnessed in him a degree of firmness and patience not to be exceeded. I have known him, says Colonel Rice, who was a member of his military family, during the most painful operation by the surgeon, while bystanders were frequently obliged to leave the room, entertain us with some pleasant anecdote, or story, and draw forth a smile from his friends. His wound continued several years in an ulcerated state, and by the loss of the bone the limb was shortened, which occasioned lameness during the remainder of his life. General Lincoln certainly afforded very important assistance in the capture of Burgoyne, though it was his unfortunate lot, while in active duty, to be disabled before he could participate in the capitulation. Though his recovery was not complete, he repaired to head-quarters in the following August, and was joyfully received by the commander-in-chief, who well knew how to appreciate his merit. It was from a devel-opment of his estimable character as a man, and his talent as a military commander, that he was designated by Con-gress for the arduous duties of the chief command in the southern department, under innumerable embarrassments. On his arrival at Charleston, December, 1778, he found that he had to form an army, to provide supplies, and to arrange the various departments, that he might be able to cope with an enemy consisting of experienced officers and veteran troops. This, it is obvious, required a man of superior powers, indefatigable perseverance, and uncon-querable energy. Had not these been his inherent quali-ties, Lincoln must have yielded to the formidable obstacles which opposed his progress. About the 28th of Decem-ber, General Prevost arrived with a fleet and about three thousand British troops, and took possession of Savannah, after routing a small party of Americans, under General Robert Howe. General Lincoln immediately put his troops in motion, and took post on the eastern side of the river, about twenty miles from the city; but he was not in force to commence offensive operations till the last of February. In April, with the view of covering the upper part of Georgia, he marched to Augusta; after which Prevost, the British commander, crossed the river into Carolina, and marched for Charleston. General Lincoln, therefore, re-crossed the Savannah, and followed his route, and on his arrival near the city, the enemy had retired from before it during the previous night. A detachment of the enemy, supposed to be about six hundred men, under Lieutenant-Colonel Maitland, being posted at Stone-Ferry, where they had erected works for their defence, General Lincoln re-solved to attack them, which he did on the 19th of June. The contest lasted one hour and twenty minutes, in which he lost one hundred and sixty men killed and wounded, and the enemy suffered about an equal loss. Their works were found to be much stronger than had been represented, and our artillery proving too light to annoy them, and the enemy receiving a reinforcement, our troops were obliged to retire.

The next event of importance which occurred with our general, was the bold assault on Savannah, in conjunction with the Count D'Estaing. General Prevost had again possessed himself of that city, and Count D'Estaing arrived with his fleet and armament in the beginning of September, 1779. Having landed nearly three thousand French troops, General Lincoln immediately united about one thousand men to his force. The prospect of success was highly flattering, but the enemy exerted all their efforts in strengthening their lines, and after the count had summoned the garrison, and while Prevost was about to arrange articles of capitulation, he received a rëinforcement. It was now resolved to attempt the place by a regular siege, but various causes occasioned a delay of several days, and when it commenced, the cannonade and bombardment failed of producing the desired effect, and the short time allowed the count on our coast, was quite insufficient for reducing the garrison by regular approaches. The commanders concluded, therefore, to make an effort on the works by assault. On the 9th of October, in the morning, the troops were led on by D'Estaing and Lincoln, united, while a column led by Count Dillon missed their route in the darkness, and failed of the intended cöoperation. Amidst a most appalling fire of the covered enemy, the allied troops forced the abatis, and planted two standards on the parapets. But being overpowered at the point of attack, they were compelled to retire; the French having seven hundred, the Americans two hundred and forty killed and wounded. The Count Pulaski, at the head of a body of our horse, was mortally wounded. General Lincoln next repaired to Charleston, and endeavored to put that city in a posture of defence, urgently requesting of Congress a rëinforcement of regular troops, and additional supplies, which were but partially complied with. In February, 1780, General Sir Henry Clinton arrived, and landed a formidable force in the vicinity; and on the 10th of March encamped in front of the American lines at Charleston. Considering the vast superiority of the enemy, both in sea and land forces, it might be questioned whether prudence and correct judgment would dictate an attempt to defend the city; it will not be supposed, however, that the determination was formed without the most mature deliberation, and for reasons perfectly justifiable. It is well known that the general was in continual expectation of an augmentation of strength by rëinforcements. On the 10th of April, the enemy having made some advances, summoned the garrison to an unconditional surrender, which was promptly refused. A heavy and incessant cannonade was sustained on each side, till the 11th of May, when the besiegers had completed their third parallel line, and having made a second demand of surrender, a capitulation was agreed on.

"Having received," says the general, "an address from the principal inhabitants, and from a number of the country militia, desiring that I would accept the terms; and a request from the lieutenant-governor and council, that the negotiation might be renewed; the militia of the town having thrown down their arms; our provisions, saving a little rice, being exhausted; the troops on the line being worn down by fatigue, having for a number of days been obliged to lay on the banquette; our harbor closely blocked up; completely invested by land by nine thousand men at least, the flower of the British army, besides the large force they could at all times draw from the marine, and aided by a great number of blacks in their laborious employments; the garrison at this time, exclusive of sailors, but little exceeding two thousand five hundred men, part of whom had thrown down their arms; the citizens in general discontented, the enemy being within twenty yards of our lines, and preparing to make a general assault by sea and land; many of our cannon dismounted, and others silenced for want of shot; a retreat being judged impracticable, and every hope of timely succor cut off, we were induced to offer and accede to the terms executed on the 12th of May." It is to be lamented that, with all the judicious and vigorous efforts in his power, General Lincoln was requited only by the frowns of fortune, whereas had he been successful in his bold enterprise and views, he would have been crowned with unfading laurels. But notwithstanding a series of disappointments and unfortunate occurrences, he was censured by no one, nor was his judgment or merit called in question. He retained his popularity and the confidence of the army, and was considered as a most zealous patriot, and the bravest of soldiers. "The motives and feelings that prompted General Lincoln rather to risk a siege than to evacuate Charleston were most honorable to him as a man and a soldier. There

was such a balance of reasons on the question, as under the existing circumstances should exempt his decision from blame or distrust. He could not calculate on the despondence and inactivity of the people who should come to his succor. The suspense and anxiety, the toil and hazard attending the siege, gave the fullest scope to his wisdom, patience and valor. His exertions were incessant. He was on the lines night and day, and for the last fortnight never undressed to sleep."* Notwithstanding this unfortunate termination of his command, so established was the spotless reputation of the vanquished general, that he continued to enjoy the undiminished respect and confidence of the Congress, the army, and the commander-in-chief.†
"Great praise is due to General Lincoln," says Dr. Ramsay, "for his judicious and spirited conduct in baffling for three months the greatly superior force of Sir Henry Clinton and Admiral Arburthnot. Though Charleston and the Southern army were lost, yet, by their long-protracted defence, the British plans were not only retarded but deranged, and North Carolina was saved for the remainder of the year 1780."

General Lincoln was admitted to his parole, and in November following he was exchanged for Major-General Phillips, a prisoner of the convention of Saratoga. In the campaign of 1781, General Lincoln commanded a division under Washington, and at the siege of Yorktown he had his full share of the honor of that brilliant and auspicious event. The articles of capitulation stipulated for the same honor in favor of the surrendering army, as had been granted to the garrison of Charleston. General Lincoln was appointed to conduct them to the field where their arms were deposited, and received the customary submission. In the general order of the commander-in-chief the day after the capitulation, General Lincoln was among the general officers whose services were particularly mentioned. In October, 1781, he was chosen by Congress secretary at war, retaining his rank in the army. In this office he continued till October, 1783, when his proffered resignation was accepted by Congress as follows:

* Notice of General Lincoln in the *Collection of the Historical Society*, vol. 3d, second series, from which I have made other extracts.
† *Lee's Memoirs of the War in the Southern Department.*

"*Resolved*, That the resignation of Major-General Lincoln, as secretary of war for the United States, be accepted in consideration of the earnest desire which he expresses, the objects of the war being so happily accomplished, to retire to private life, and that he be informed that the United States in Congress assembled entertain a high sense of his perseverance, fortitude, activity and meritorious services in the field, as well as of his diligence, fidelity and capacity in the execution of the office of secretary at war, which important trust he has discharged to their entire approbation."

Having relinquished the duties and cares of a public employment, he retired, and devoted his attention to his farm; but in 1784, he was chosen one of the commissioners and agents on the part of the state to make and execute a treaty with the Penobscot Indians. When in the year 1786–7, the authority of our state government was in a manner prostrated, and the country alarmed by a most audacious spirit of insurrection, under the guidance of Shays and Day, General Lincoln was appointed by the governor and council to command a detachment of militia, consisting of four or five thousand men, to oppose their progress, and compel them to a submission to the laws. He marched from Boston on the 20th of January, into the counties of Worcester, Hampshire, and Berkshire, where the insurgents had erected their standard. They were embodied in considerable force, and manifested a determined resistance, and a slight skirmish ensued between them and a party of militia under General Shepherd. Lincoln, however, conducted with such address and energy, that the insurgents were routed from one town to another, till they were completely dispersed in all directions; and by his wise and prudent measures the insurrection was happily suppressed without bloodshed, excepting a few individuals who were slain under General Shepherd's command. At the May election, 1787, General Lincoln was elected lieutenant-governor by the legislature, having had a plurality of votes by the people. He was a member of the convention for ratifying the federal constitution, and in the summer of 1789, he received from President Washington the appointment of collector of the port of Boston, which office he sustained till, being admonished by the increasing infirmities of age, he requested permission to resign, about two years before his death. In 1789, he was appointed one of the commissioners to treat with the Creek Indians on the frontiers of the Southern states, and in 1793 he was one of the commissioners to effect a peace with the Western Indians. The subject of this memoir received from the University of Cambridge the honorary degree of Master of Arts. He was one of the first members of the American Academy of Arts and Sciences, and a member of the Massachusetts Historical Society, and he contributed by his pen to the stock of useful materials for their respective publications. Having, after his resignation of the office of collector, passed about two years in retirement and in tranquillity of mind, but experiencing the feebleness of age, he received a short attack of disease, by which his honorable life was terminated on the 9th of May, 1810, aged 77 years. The following tribute is on the records of the society of Cincinnati:

"At the annual meeting in July, 1810, Major-General John Brooks was chosen president of the society, to supply the place of our venerable and much-lamented president, General Benjamin Lincoln, who had presided over the society from the organization thereof, in 1783, to the 9th of May, 1810, the day of his decease, with the entire approbation of every member, and the grateful tribute of his surviving comrades, for his happy guidance and affectionate attentions during so long a period."

General Lincoln in his very nature was unsusceptible of the spirit of envy. Whoever achieved a noble action to the honor and advantage of his country, whether as a patriot or soldier, was with him the man of merit and the theme of eulogy, though it might eclipse his own fame. He was universally respected as one of the best of men, of ardent patriotism, and of heroic courage. Major-General Knox, whose candor and discriminating judgment no one will deny, was known to estimate next to Washington in military talents, Generals Greene and Lincoln. Colonel Nathan Rice, a respectable officer, who was a member of his military family, observes, that the sacrifice of as much domestic happiness as falls to the lot of men, to serve his country, would seem to place his patriotism beyond suspicion. The firmness and zeal with which he rendered this service during her struggle, the coolness with which he met danger, his fortitude under bodily pain, privation and disappointments, and the confidence reposed in him by the commander-in-chief, all strongly evince that his country had not misjudged in elevating him to the distinguished rank he held in the army. While at Purysburgh, on the Savannah river, a soldier named Fickling, having been detected in frequent attempts to desert, was tried and sentenced to be hanged. The general ordered the execution. The rope broke; a second was procured, which broke also; the case was reportèd to the general for directions. "Let him run," said the general, "I thought he looked like a scape-gallows."* Regularity both in business and his mode of living were peculiar traits in his character; habitually temperate, and accustomed to sleep unconfined to time or place. In conversation he was always correct and chaste; on no occasion uttering any thing like profanity or levity on serious subjects, and when others have indulged in these respects in his presence, it was ever re-

---

* Major Garden, in his *Anecdotes of the American Revolution*, relates this story with some addition. It happened that as Fickling was led to execution, the surgeon-general of the army passed accidentally on his way to his quarters, which were at some distance. When the second rope was procured, the adjutant of the regiment, a stout and heavy man, assayed by every means to break it, but without effect. Fickling was then haltered and again turned off, when, to the astonishment of the by-standers, the rope untwisted, and he fell a second time uninjured to the ground. A cry for mercy was now general throughout the ranks, which occasioned Major Ladson, aid-de-camp to General Lincoln, to gallop to head-quarters to make a representation of facts, which were no sooner stated than an immediate pardon was granted, accompanied with an order that he should instantaneously be drummed, with every mark of infamy, out of camp, and threatened with instant death if he ever should be found attempting to approach it. In the interim, the surgeon-general had established himself at his quarters in a distant barn, little doubting but that the catastrophe was at an end, and Fickling quietly resting in his grave. Midnight was at hand, and he was busily engaged in writing, when, hearing the approach of a footstep, he raised his eyes, and saw with astonishment the figure of the man who had in his opinion been executed, slowly and with haggard countenance approaching towards him. "How! how is this?" exclaimed the doctor; "whence come you? what do you want with me? were you not hanged this morning?" "Yes, sir," replied the resuscitated man; "I am the wretch you saw going to the gallows, and who was hanged." "Keep your distance," said the doctor; "approach me not till you say why you come here." "Simply, sir," said the supposed spectre, "to solicit food. I am no ghost, doctor. The rope broke twice while the executioner was doing his office, and the general thought proper to pardon me." "If that be the case," rejoined the doctor, "eat and be welcome; but I beg of you in future to have a little more consideration, and not intrude so unceremoniously into the apartment of one who had every right to suppose you an inhabitant of the tomb."

ceived by him with such marked disapprobation of countenance, as to draw from them an instantaneous apology,
and regret for the offence. Having, while collector, appointed a violent party-man to a place of profit merely
from motives of benevolence, he had frequently, with
many others, abused the general, calling him "a damned
old rascal." On the first opportunity, the general said to
him, "So Mr. ——, you say I am a damned old rascal;
you might have spared the damned," without adding a
word more; but it was expressed in a manner that prevented a reply; nor did he remove him from office. In
the various characters of parent, husband and master, I
ever held him up, says Colonel Rice, as a model of perfection. The law of kindness ever dwelt on his tongue.

This memoir will be concluded by some brief extracts
from the *Historical Collections:*

"In General Lincoln's character, strength and softness, the estimable
and amiable qualities, were happily blended. His mind was quick and
active, yet discriminating and sound. He displayed a fund of thought
and information, derived from select though limited reading, from careful
observation of men and things, from habits of thinking, and from conversation. A degree of enthusiasm or exultation of feeling on the objects of his pursuit belonged to his temperament, but it was under the
control of good sense and sober views. He was patient and cool in
deliberation; in execution, prompt and vigorous. He was conspicuous
for plain, strict, inflexible integrity, united, however, with prudence, candor, and a compassionate disposition. As a military commander, he was
judicious, brave, determined, indefatigable. His distinguished merit in
this character was never denied, while all have not agreed in opinion on
some of his plans in the southern command. Being a soldier of the
revolution, he had to anticipate the effect of experience, and might commit mistakes. He was surrounded by difficulties; he met extraordinary
disappointments in his calculations of supplies and succors. In the
principal instances which issued unfortunately, the storming of Savannah
and the siege of Charleston, he had but a choice of evils; and whichever
way he decided, the course rejected would have seemed to many persons
more eligible. General Lincoln was a federalist of the Washington
school. He experienced the benefit of his weight of character and the
sense entertained by the community of his public services, in being suffered to retain his office of collector.

"Religion exerted its full influence over the mind and conduct of
General Lincoln. He was a Christian of the Anti-sectarian, Catholic,
or liberal sect. He was firm in his faith, serious and affectionate in his
piety, without superstition, fanaticism or austerity. He was from early
manhood a communicant, and for a great part of his life a deacon of the
church. He never shunned an avowal of his belief, nor feared to appear
what he was, nor permitted the reality of his convictions to remain in

doubt. The person and air of General Lincoln betokened his military vocation. He was of middle height and erect, broad-chested and muscular, in his latter years corpulent, with open intelligent features, a venerable and benign aspect. His manners were easy and unaffected, but courteous and polite."

In all his transactions, both public and private, his mind was elevated above all sordid or sinister views, and our history will not perhaps record many names more estimable than was that of General Lincoln.

FREDERICK WILLIAM AUGUSTUS BARON DE STEUBEN,

Knight of the Order of Fidelity in Germany, and Major-General in the Army of the United States.

THIS highly distinguished personage was a Prussian officer, aid-de-camp to the great Frederick, and held the rank of lieutenant-general in the army of that consummate commander. He arrived in America December, 1777, and presented himself with his credentials to Congress, proffering his services in our army without any claim to rank, and requested permission only to render such assistance as might be in his power, in the character of a volunteer. In thus devoting himself to our cause, he made an immense sacrifice, by relinquishing his honorable station and emoluments in Europe. Congress voted him their thanks for his zeal and the disinterested tender of his services, and he joined the main army under General Washington at Valley Forge. His qualifications for a teacher of the system of military tactics were soon manifested; having for many years practised on the system which the king of Prussia had introduced into his own army. In May, 1778, by the strong recommendation of the commander-in-chief, Congress appointed him inspector-general with the rank of major-general. He commenced his duties as inspector, beginning with the officers, who were formed into separate bodies, frequently exercised and instructed in the various movements and evolutions, when manœuvring battalions, brigades, or divisions of the army. He exerted all his powers for the establishment of a regular system of discipline, economy, and uniformity among our heterogeneous bodies of soldiers. In the discharge of this duty, and to effect his favorite object, he encountered obstacles to which a less zealous spirit would have yielded as insurmountable. By his superior talents, indefatigable industry, and perseverance, he rendered a service to our army, without which it could not have attained to a con dition capable of achieving honor and glory in the face of European veteran troops. Charmed with the neat and soldierly appearance of those who had profited by his instructions and duly improved in the art of discipline, and equally detesting the soldier whose awkward and unmilitary conduct betrayed his negligence, there never was a review but the baron rewarded the one with more than praise, and censured the other, whether officer or soldier, with a severity equal to his deserts. While reviewing our regiment, he noticed in the ranks a very spruce young lad, handsomely formed, standing erect, with the air of a genteel soldier, his gun and equipments in perfect order. The baron, struck with his military appearance, patted him under his chin to elevate his head still more erect, viewed him with a smile, and said, "How long have you been a soldier? You are one pretty soldier in miniature. How old are you?" "Seventeen, sir." "Have you got a wife?" Then calling to the colonel, said, "Colonel Jackson, this is one fine soldier in miniature."

The baron composed a complete system of exercise and discipline, which was approved by the commander-in-chief, and ordered by Congress to be published and adopted in our army. Colonel William North and Colonel Walker were aids-de-camp and members of his family, between whom there existed a mutual attachment and affection, pure as parent and sons.* The baron was distinguished

* Colonel North at an early age volunteered his services in the bold and perilous enterprise undertaken by General Arnold in the autumn of 1775, to penetrate to Canada through the unexplored wilderness from Kennebec, and was among the miserable sufferers who apprehended the horrors of death in the wilderness. When Colonel Henry Jackson raised his regiment in the state of Massachusetts, this gentleman was commissioned as commander of a company in this regiment, in which he served with honor till he was appointed aid-de-camp to Baron Steuben. By the amiable qualities of his heart, his ingratiating and gentlemanly manners, he won the affection of the baron, by whom he was treated with the favor of an adopted son. After the close of the war he was appointed major-general of militia in the state of New York, and he has recently transferred his residence to New London, in Connecticut. It is chiefly by the aid of his pen that I am enabled to furnish this tribute to the memory of his justly-celebrated patron.

BARON STEUBEN.

for his adherence to the principles of political integrity and moral virtue. His heart was replete with generous sentiments and the purest benevolence.

After General Arnold treacherously deserted his post at West Point, the baron never failed to manifest his indignation and abhorrence of his name and character, and while inspecting Colonel Sheldon's regiment of light-horse, the name of Arnold struck his ear. The soldier was ordered to the front: he was a fine looking fellow; his horse and equipments in excellent order. "Change your name, brother-soldier; you are too respectable to bear the name of a traitor." "What name shall I take, general?" "Take any other name; mine is at your service." Most cheerfully was the offer accepted, and his name was entered on the roll as Steuben. He or his children now enjoy land given to him in the town of Steuben by the baron. This brave soldier met him after the war. "I am well settled, general," said he, "and have a wife and son; I have called my son after you, sir." "I thank you, my friend. What name have you given the boy?" "I called him Baron—what else could I call him?"

The baron's office as inspector did not preclude him the privilege of command in the line according to his rank, and at one period he was commander of a separate detachment in Virginia, to oppose the ravages of the enemy in that quarter. It was with great difficulty that men could be procured for the service; every man was considered as an acquisition. The baron was too honest to suffer an imposition to be practised on the public. A regiment had been collected, and was paraded on the point of marching, when a well-looking man on horseback, and as it appeared his servant on another, rode up and informed the baron that he had brought him a recruit. "I thank you, sir," said the baron, "with all my heart; you have arrived in a happy moment. Where is your man, colonel?"—for he was colonel in the militia. "Here, sir," ordering his boy to dismount. The baron's countenance changed; his aids saw and feared the approaching storm. A sergeant was ordered to measure the lad, whose shoes when off discovered something by which his stature had been increased. The baron, patting the child's head with his hand, trembling with rage, asked him how old he was? He was

28

very young—quite a child. "Sir," said he to the militia colonel, "you must have supposed me to be a rascal." "Oh! no, baron, I did not." "Then, sir, I suppose you to be a rascal, an infamous rascal, thus to attempt to cheat your country. Sergeant, take off this fellow's spurs, and place him in the ranks, that we may have a man able to serve, instead of an infant whom he would basely have made his substitute! Go, my boy; take the colonel's spurs and horse to his wife; make my compliments, and say, her husband has gone to fight for the freedom of his country, as an honest man should do!" And instantly ordered, "Platoons! to the right, wheel! forward march!" Colonel Gaskins, who commanded the regiment, fearing the consequences, after marching some distance, allowed the man to escape, who immediately made application to the civil authority for redress; but Governor Jefferson, Mr. Madison, and others, not doubting the purity of the baron's motive, and fully appreciating his honest zeal, prevented any disagreeable results attending this high-handed exertion of military power. At the siege of Yorktown the baron was in the trenches at the head of his division, and received the first overture of Lord Cornwallis to capitulate. At the relieving hour next morning, the Marquis de la Fayette approached at the head of his division, to relieve him. The baron refused to quit the trenches, assigning as a reason the etiquette in Europe, that the offer to capitulate had been made during his tour of duty, and that it was a point of honor of which he would not deprive his troops to remain in the trenches till the capitulation was signed or hostilities recommenced. The dispute was referred to the commander-in-chief, and the baron was permitted to remain till the British flag was struck. While on this duty the baron, perceiving himself in danger from a shell thrown from the enemy, threw himself suddenly into the trench· General Wayne, in the jeopardy and hurry of the moment, fell on him; the baron, turning his eyes, saw it was his brigadier. "I always knew you were brave, general," said he; "but I did not know you were so perfect in every point of duty: you cover your general's retreat in the best manner possible."

"I have great delight," says Major Garden, "in relating an anecdote which I received from General Walter Stewart; the truth of which may be relied on." After the capture of Yorktown, the superior officers of the allied army vied with each other in acts of civility and attention to the captive Britons. Lord Cornwallis and his family were particularly distinguished. Entertainments were given in succession by all the major-generals, with the exception of Baron Steuben. He alone withheld an invitation, not from a wish to be particular, nor that his heart was closed to the attentions due to misfortunes. His soul was superior to prejudice; and, as a soldier, he tenderly sympathized in their fate, while poverty denied the means of displaying that liberality towards them which had been shown by others. Such was his situation, when, calling on Colonel Stewart, and informing him of his intention to entertain the British commander-in-chief, he requested that he would advance him a sum of money as the price of his favorite charger. "'Tis a good beast," said the baron, "and has proved a faithful servant through all the dangers of the war; but, though painful to my heart, we must part." Colonel Stewart, to prevent a step that he knew must be attended with great loss, and still greater inconvenience, immediately tendered his purse, recommending, should the sum it contained prove insufficient, the sale or pledge of his watch. "My dear friend," said the baron, "'tis already sold. Poor North was sick, and wanted necessaries. He is a brave fellow, and possesses the best of hearts. The trifle it brought is set apart for his use. My horse must go; so no more, I beseech you, to turn me from my purpose. I am a major-general in the service of the United States, and my private convenience must not be put in the scale with the duty which my rank calls on me imperiously to perform." A very friendly intercourse subsisted between the officers of the French army and those of our own, and dining invitations could not always be reciprocated on our part for want of the means. "I can stand it no longer," said the baron; "we are continually dining with these gentlemen, and such is our penury that, except at head-quarters, they receive no invitations in return. "Take," said he to one of his people, "take the silver spoons and forks, and sell them; it is not republican to eat with silver forks, and it is the part of a gentleman to pay his debts. They shall have

one good dinner, if I eat my soup with a wooden spoon
for ever after."

The baron returned to the northward, and remained
with the army, continually employed till the peace in per-
fecting his discipline. The adroitness, and, above all, the
silence with which his manœuvres were performed, was
remarked with astonishment by the officers of the French
army. The Marquis de la Val de Montmorency, a brigadier-general, said to the baron, "I admire the celerity and
exactitude with which your men perform, but what I cannot conceive is the profound silence with which they
manœuvre." "I don't know, Monsieur le Marquis, whence
noise should proceed, when even my brigadiers dare not
open their mouths but to repeat the orders."

The French troops were exceedingly loud in their evolutions and marches, and Mons. la Val at all times louder
than the rest. On a subsequent occasion, designed to
show the high degree of expertness at which our officers
and soldiers had arrived, the baron was asked by one of
the French generals what manœuvres he intended to perform. On being informed, "Yes," replied the French
chief, "I have seen particularly the last you mention performed by the Prussians in Silesia, but with a very complex
addition," which he explained. "But you will recollect,
general, that we are not quite Prussians." After his guests
had retired, the baron said, "I will let these Frenchmen
know that we can do what the Prussians can, and what
their army cannot do. I will save those gentlemen who
have not been in Silesia the trouble of going there; they
may come to Verplank's Point next week for instruction."
They came, chiefs and subalterns, and every thing was
done in the finest style, to their real or pretended admiration. Here General North indulges his honorable feelings
in the following apostrophe: "Alas! when I think of time
past, of that day, and look to that eminence on which
General Washington's marquee was pitched, in front of
which stood that great man, firm in the consciousness of
virtue, surrounded by French nobles and the chiefs of his
own army; when I cast my eyes, then lighted up with
soldierly ambition, hope and joy, along that lengthened
line, my brothers all! endeared by ties made strong by
full communion in many a miserable, many a joyous hour,

my heart sinks at the view! Who, how few of all that
brilliant host, is left; these few are tottering on the con-
fines of the grave! The baron's tent that day was filled,
and more than filled, with Frenchmen. 'I am glad,' said
he, 'to pay some part of the dinner debt we owe our
allies.'" "On the eve of returning to the northward from
Virginia," continues General North, "I was sick, and unable to accompany the baron: he divided his purse with
me, the whole contents of which were two half-joes; his
watch and silver spoons and forks, brought from Germany,
were already disposed of. 'I must go,' said the baron; 'I
must leave you, my son; but I leave you among a people
where we have found the door of every house wide open;
where the heart of every female is full of tenderness and
virtue. Quit this deleterious spot, the instant you are
able; there is my sulkey, and here is half of what I have.
God bless you! I can no more.' Nor could he: the feelings of friends in such a moment, and under such circumstances, may possibly be conceived, but not expressed. A
journey of three hundred miles was before him; a single
piece of gold in his purse. Are other instances necessary
to unfold the texture of his heart?—how many have I
written on my own! There is, I trust, a book in which
they, every one of them, are entered, to the credit of his
account with Heaven."

General Washington had a high esteem for the baron,
and was fully sensible of his worth and merits. On all
proper occasions Congress were urged in his behalf, and
from time to time he received of money, good and bad,
sums which some narrow-minded men thought much too
large, though he proved satisfactorily that he had given
up a salary of five hundred and eighty guineas a year in
Europe. But what sums—how much—could have been
enough for one who searched around for worthy objects,
whose wants might be relieved? "Never did a review or
an inspection pass without rewards in money to soldiers
whose arms were in the highest order. Never was his
table unfilled with guests if furnished with provisions.
Officers of rank, men most prominent for knowledge and
attention to their duty, were marked for invitation; but the
gentlemen of his family were desired to complete the list

with others of inferior grade. 'Poor fellows,' said he, 'they have field officers' stomachs, without their rations.'"

The baron was rough as the ocean in a storm when great faults were committed; but if, in a sudden gust of passion, he had injured, the redress was ample. I recollect that at a review near Morristown, a Lieutenant Gibbons, a brave and good officer, was arrested on the spot, and ordered into the rear, for a fault which it afterwards appeared another had committed. At a proper moment, the commander of the regiment came forward, and informed the baron of Mr. Gibbons' innocence, of his worth, and of his acute feelings under this unmerited disgrace. "Desire Lieutenant Gibbons to come to the front, colonel." "Sir," said the baron, to the young gentleman, "the fault which was made, by throwing the line into confusion, might, in the presence of an enemy, have been fatal. I arrested you as its supposed author, but I have reason to believe that I was mistaken, and that in this instance you were blameless; I ask your pardon: return to your command; I would not deal unjustly by any, much less by one whose character as an officer is so respectable." All this passed with the baron's hat off, the rain pouring on his venerable head!—Do you think there was an officer, a soldier who saw it, unmoved by affection and respect? Not one.

In the company of ladies, the baron always appeared to peculiar advantage. At the house of the respectable Mrs. Livingston, mother of the late Chancellor, where virtue, talent, and modest worth of every kind met a welcome reception, the baron was introduced to a Miss Sheaf, an amiable and interesting young lady. "I am very happy," said he, "in the honor of being presented to you, mademoiselle, though I see it is at an infinite risk; I have from my youth been cautioned to guard myself against *mischief*, but I had no idea that her attractions were so powerful."

Dining at head-quarters with Robert Morris, Esq., and other gentlemen, Mr. Morris complained bitterly of the miserable state of the treasury. "Why," said the baron, "are you not financier?—why do you not continue to create funds?" "I have done all I can; it is not possible for me to do more." "But you remain financier, though without finances?" "Yes." "Well, then, I do not think you are so honest a man as my cook. He came to me one day at Valley Forge, and said, 'Baron, I am your cook, and you have nothing to cook but a piece of lean beef, which is hung up by a string before the fire. Your negro wagoner can turn the string and do as well as I can. You have promised me ten dollars a month; but as you have nothing to cook, I wish to be discharged, and not longer be chargeable to you.' That is an honest fellow, Morris."

Though never perfectly master of our language, the baron understood and spoke it with sufficient correctness. He would sometimes on purpose miscall names, and blend or adopt words similar in sound, dissimilar in meaning. Dining at head-quarters, which he did frequently, Mrs. Washington asked what amusement he had recourse to now that the certainty of peace had relaxed his labors? "I read, my lady, and write, and chess, and yesterday for the first time I went a fishing. My gentlemen told me it was a very fine business to catch fish, and I did not know but that this new trade might, by and by, be useful to me —but I fear I never can succeed—I sat in the boat three hours, it was exceedingly warm, and I caught only two fish; they told me it was fine sport." "What kind of fish did you take, baron?" "I am not sure, my lady, but I believe one of them was a whale." "A whale, baron, in the North river!" "Yes, I assure you, a very fine whale, my lady;—it was a whale, was it not?" appealing to one of his aids. "An eel, baron." "I beg your pardon, my lady, but that gentleman certainly told me it was a whale." General Washington, now that his mind was comparatively at ease, enjoyed a pleasantry of this kind highly.

For the proper understanding of the following *bon mot* of General Washington, it must be mentioned that at Tatawa falls there was a miserable, deformed object, who had lain in his cradle for twenty-seven years. His head was eighteen inches in length, and the rest of his body twenty-seven inches. He received numerous visitors, among whom was his excellency, who asked him whether he was a whig or tory? He answered, as he had been taught, *that he had never taken an active part on either side.**

"A worthy gentleman and lady came out of New York

* See page 204 of this volume.

after the preliminaries of peace were signed, to visit their friends, and resided in the neighborhood of Baron Steuben, by whom the whole party, together with his excellency and lady, were invited to dine. 'It is proper,' said the baron, 'that your excellency should be apprised that Mr. —— and his lady from New York are to dine with me, and perhaps, sir, you may not choose to meet Mr. ——.' 'Oh, baron,' said the general, laughing, 'there is no difficulty on that point. Mr. —— is very like the big-headed boy at Tatawa, *he never has taken an active part.*' This was allowed to be a most adroit *coup de sabre* by those who knew the gentleman, though it is doubted whether, if he had heard it, he would have felt the stroke."

"At the disbandment of the revolutionary army, when inmates of the same tent, or hut, for seven long years, were separating, and probably for ever; grasping each other's hand, in silent agony, I saw the baron's strong— endeavors to throw some ray of sunshine on the gloom to mix some drop of cordial with the painful draught. To go, they knew not whither; all recollection of the art to thrive by civil occupations lost, or to the youthful never known. Their hard-earned military knowledge worse than useless, and with their badge of brotherhood, a mark at which to point the finger of suspicion—ignoble, vile suspicion!—to be cast out on a world, long since by them forgotten. Severed from friends, and all the joys and griefs which soldiers feel! Griefs while hope remained— when shared by numbers, almost joys! To go in silence and alone, and poor and hopeless; it was too hard! On that sad day, how many hearts were wrung! I saw it all, nor will the scene be ever blurred or blotted from my view. To a stern old officer, a Lieutenant-Colonel Cochran, from the Green Mountains, who had met danger and difficulty almost in every step from his youth, and from whose furrowed visage a tear till that moment had never fallen; the good baron said—what could be said to lessen deep distress. 'For myself,' said Cochran, 'I care not—I can stand it; but my wife and daughters are in the garret of that wretched tavern. I know not where to remove, nor have I means for their removal!' 'Come, my friend,' said the baron, 'let us go—I will pay my respects to Mrs. Cochran and your daughters, if you please.' I followed to the loft, the lower rooms being all filled with soldiers, with drunkenness, despair and blasphemy. And when the baron left the poor unhappy cast-aways, he left hope with them, and all he had to give." "A black man, with wounds unhealed, wept on the wharf (for it was at Newburgh where this tragedy was acting): there was a vessel in the stream, bound to the place where he once had friends. He had not a dollar to pay his passage, and he could not walk. Unused to tears, I saw them trickle down this good man's cheeks as he put into the hands of the black man the last dollar he possessed. The negro hailed the sloop, and cried, 'God Almighty bless you, master baron!'

"What good and honorable man, civil or military, before the accursed party-spirit murdered friendships, did not respect and love the baron? Who most? Those who knew him best. After the peace, the baron retired to a farm in the vicinity of New York, where, with forming a system for the organization and discipline of the militia, books, chess, and the frequent visits of his numerous friends, he passed his time as agreeably as a frequent want of funds would permit. The state of New Jersey had given him a small improved farm, and the state of New York gave him a tract of sixteen thousand acres of land in the county of Oneida. After the general government was in full operation, by the exertions of Colonel Hamilton, patronized and enforced by President Washington, a grant of two thousand five hundred dollars per annum was made to him for life. The summers were now chiefly spent on his land, and his winters in the city. His sixteen thousand acres of land were in the uncultivated wilderness; he built a convenient log house, cleared sixty acres, parceled out his land on easy terms to twenty or thirty tenants, distributed nearly a tenth of the tract in gifts to his aids-de-camp and servants, and sat himself down to a certain degree contented without society, except that of a young gentleman, who read to and with him. He ate only at dinner, but he ate with strong appetite. In drinking, he was always temperate; indeed, he was free from every vicious habit. His powers of mind and body were strong, and he received to a certain extent a liberal education. His days were undoubtedly shortened by his sedentary mode of life. He was seized with an apoplexy, which in a few hours was fatal. Agreeably to his desire, often expressed, he was wrapped in his cloak, placed in a plain coffin, and hid in the earth, without a stone to tell where he lies. A few neighbors, his servants, the young gentleman his late companion, and one on whom for fifteen years his countenance never ceased to beam with kindness, followed to the grave. It was in a thick, a lonely wood; but, in a few years after, a public highway was opened near or over the hallowed sod! Colonel Walker snatched the poor remains of his dear friend from sacrilegious violation, and gave a bounty to protect the grave in which he laid them from rude and impious intrusion. He died in 1795, in the sixty-fifth year of his age.

"Some few years previous to the baron's death, a pious gentleman of the city of New York, who had a great affection for him, told me, with strong marks of joy, that they had passed the evening and a part of the last night together; that the baron confessed his full belief in Jesus Christ, with sure and certain hope, through him, of a blessed immortality. 'From the life our dear friend has led, in camps and in the gay world,' said the good man, 'I feared; and you do not know what joy I feel, in the belief that he will be well to all eternity!' The baron was a member of the Reformed German Church, in New York."

General North, from the impulse of his own affectionate and grateful feelings, erected a handsome monument with an appropriate inscription in the Reformed German Church in New York to the memory of his illustrious patron and friend, and these pages accord with the views of that memorial in transmitting to posterity a renowned hero, whose name and invaluable labors should never be forgotten.

What remained of the baron's estate, excepting one thousand dollars and his library, which he willed to a youth whose father had rendered essential service in the war, and whose education he generously charged himself with, was bequeathed to his two affectionate aids-de-camp.

MARQUIS DE LA FAYETTE, MAJOR-GENERAL.

THE name and character of this illustrious French nobleman, will occupy a conspicuous place in our revolutionary annals, and be honored by posterity, no less for his enthusiastic love of liberty, than for his heroism and military renown. There is something truly romantic in the history of this celebrated personage. In the year 1776, at the immature age of nineteen, he espoused the cause of the Americans, and nobly resolved to afford our country all possible assistance by his personal services and influence. At this era the affairs of America were bordering on despair, and were represented in France as so deplorable that it might be supposed sufficient to repress the most determined zeal. Reports were propagated in that country that our army, reduced to a mere rabble, was flying before an army of thirty thousand regulars, nor was this very wide from the reality. In consequence of this, our commissioners found it impossible to procure a vessel to convey the marquis and their own despatches to Congress; they could not therefore feel justified in encouraging his bold contemplated enterprise. This embarrassment, however, had the effect of increasing rather than of restraining his youthful ardor and heroism. He imparted to the commissioners his determination to purchase and fit out a vessel to convey himself and their despatches to America. This project was deemed so extraordinary and important, that it did not fail to engage universal attention. The French court had not then declared even a friendly intention towards America, but, on the contrary, was extremely cautious of giving offence to the British government. Orders were therefore given prohibiting the departure of this nobleman, and vessels were even despatched to the West Indies to intercept him, in case he should take that route. The marquis was well apprised that he exposed himself to the loss of his fortune by the laws of France; and that, should he fall into the hands of the English on his passage, he would be liable to a confinement of uncertain duration, and without a prospect of being exchanged. These considerations however, did not deter him from the attempt; and, bidding adieu to his amiable consort and numerous endeared connexions, and trusting to good fortune to favor his elopement, he embarked, and in due time arrived safe in Charleston, in the summer of 1776. He landed soon after the noble defence made by General Moultrie at the fort on Sullivan's island. Charmed with the gallantry displayed by that general and his brave troops, the marquis presented him with clothing, arms and accoutrements for one hundred men. He met with a cordial reception from our Congress, and they immediately accepted his proffered services. He insisted that he would receive no compensation, and that he would commence his services as a volunteer. This noble philanthropist was received into the family of the commander-in-chief, where a strong mutual attachment was contracted, and he has often been called the adopted son of Washington. July 31st, 1777, Congress resolved, that, "Whereas the Marquis de la Fayette, out of his great zeal to the cause of liberty in which the United States are engaged, has left his family and connexions, and at his own expense come over to offer his services to the United States without pension or particular allowance, and is anxious to risk his life in our cause—*Resolved*, That his service be accepted, and that, in consideration of his zeal, illustrious family and connexions, he have the rank and commission of major-general in the army of the United States."

At the battle of Brandywine, September, 1777, the marquis exhibited full proof of his undaunted bravery and military character, and received a wound in his leg. In May, 1777, with a select corps of two thousand five hundred men, he crossed the Schuylkill, and took post about twelve miles in front of our army at Valley Forge. A Quaker, in whose house he was to lodge, sent information to the enemy, who formed an instantaneous design of surprising him. General Gray, on the night of the 19th of May, marched with seven thousand men, and by a skillful movement got into the marquis' rear, while another detachment was advancing to his front. The marquis fortunately gained intelligence of their approach, and by a prompt decision effected his retreat, and recrossed the river in season to defeat the design of the enemy. Had they succeeded, it must not only have proved fatal to the marquis and his detachment, but placed the remainder of

MAJOR GENERAL WILLIAM MOULTRIE.

our army in a situation of extreme hazard. In August, 1778, the marquis repaired to Rhode Island, to assist in the expedition under Major-General Sullivan, in conjunction with the French fleet, and he received the particular approbation and applause of Congress for his judicious and highly important services. In January, 1779, the marquis embarked at Boston, on a voyage to France, and was subjected to imminent danger from a conspiracy among the sailors, a great part of whom were British. He returned in May, 1780, bringing the joyful intelligence that a French fleet and army would soon arrive on our coast. Through his great zeal for the cause of the United States, he exerted his influence with his government, no longer fearful of giving offence to the English, to afford money and troops and other important succors. He was soon put at the head of a select corps of light-infantry for the service of the campaign. This afforded him a new opportunity for the display of his munificence. He presented to every officer under his command an elegant sword, and his soldiers were clothed in uniform, principally at his expense. He infused into this corps a spirit of pride and emulation, viewing it as one formed and modeled according to his own wishes, and as deserving his highest confidence. They were the pride of his heart and he the idol of their regard; constantly panting for an opportunity of accomplishing some signal achievement worthy of his and their character. This corps was pronounced equal to any that could be produced in any country. In December, 1780, he marched with one thousand two hundred light-infantry for Virginia, to counteract the devastations of Arnold and Phillips. He made a forced march of two hundred miles, and prevented General Phillips' possessing himself of Richmond, and secured the stores of that place. At one period there was not a single pair of shoes in his whole command, and such was his zeal and generous spirit, and such the confidence and respect of the people, that he was enabled to borrow of the merchants of Baltimore two thousand guineas on his own credit, with which he purchased shoes and other necessary articles for his troops. The marquis was employed in watching the motions of Lord Cornwallis in Virginia, with an inferior force; in this arduous duty he displayed the judgment, skill, and prudence of a veteran, with the ardor of youth. In a skirmish near Jamestown, not a man in the whole detachment was more exposed, and one of his horses was killed.

Lord Cornwallis having encamped near Jamestown, the Marquis La Fayette sent General Wayne with the Pennsylvania troops to take their station within a small distance of the British army, and watch their motions. The two advanced parties were soon engaged, and General Wayne drove that of the enemy back to their lines; and, without stopping there, attacked the whole British army, drawn up in order of battle, and charged them with bayonets. The action was extremely severe for the little time it lasted, but the disproportion of numbers was so great, that the enemy was on the point of surrounding our troops, when the marquis arrived in person, just time enough to order a retreat, by which they were rescued from their hazardous situation, after suffering considerable loss.

General Henry Lee, in his *Memoirs of the War in the Southern States*, eulogizes the character and conduct of La Fayette, when compelled to fly before the British commander, in the following language:

"In this period of gloom, of disorder and of peril, La Fayette was collected and undismayed. With zeal, with courage, and with sagacity, he discharged his arduous duties; and, throughout his difficult retreat, was never brought even to array but once in order for battle.—Invigorating our councils by his precepts; dispelling our despondency by his example; and encouraging his troops to submit to their many privations, by the cheerfulness with which he participated in their wants; he imparted the energy of his own mind to the country, and infused his high-toned spirit into the army."

Great encomiums were passed on the marquis for his humanity and goodness in visiting and administering to the relief of the wounded soldiers. Lord Cornwallis having received a reïnforcement, was so confident of success against his young antagonist, that he imprudently said in a letter which was intercepted, "*the boy cannot escape me.*" He planned the surprise of the marquis while on the same side of James river with himself; but in this he was baffled by means of a spy, whom the marquis sent into the enemy's camp to obtain some necessary intelligence.* A combination of talents and skill defeated all the energies of physical power. During the siege of Lord Cornwallis at Yorktown,

* See page 300 of this volume, for further particulars.

the marquis was among the most active and intrepid of the general officers, and he commanded a detachment of our light-infantry, which successfully assaulted the British redoubt on the right of our lines. Previous to his departure from Yorktown, he issued his last orders to his favorite corps of infantry, in which are contained the following expressions:

"In the moment the major-general leaves this place, he wishes once more to express his gratitude to the brave corps of light-infantry, who for nine months past have been the companions of his fortunes. He will never forget that, with them alone, of regular troops, he had the good fortune to manœuvre before an army which after all its reductions is still six times superior to the regular force he had at that time."

The marquis now perceiving that the mighty contest for American independence, in which he had been so nobly engaged, was near its completion, was about to return with the well-earned laurels on his brow to his king and country. Congress resolved, November 23d, 1781, " that major-general the Marquis de la Fayette be informed that on a review of his conduct throughout the past campaign, and particularly during the period in which he had the chief command in Virginia, the many new proofs which present themselves of his zealous attachment to the cause he has espoused, and of his judgment, vigilance, gallantry and address in its defence, have greatly added to the high opinion entertained by Congress of his merit and military talents." During his military career in America, the marquis displayed that patriotism, integrity, humanity, and every other virtue which characterize real greatness of soul. His manners being easy, affable and engaging, he was particularly endeared to the officers and soldiers under his command; they admired, loved, and revered him as their guide and support when in peril, and their warmest friend when in perplexity and trouble. The most affectionate attachment subsisted between him and the illustrious chief under whose banners it was his delight to serve, and whose language was, "This nobleman unites to all the military fire of youth, an uncommon maturity of judgment." His very soul burned with the spirit of enterprise, and he manifested a disinterestedness and devotion to the cause of freedom, ever to be admired and applauded by a grateful people. He ever discovered, both in design and execution, those traits of genius, and that intuitive knowledge of tactics, which designate the great man and the successful warrior. The people of the United States are fully apprised of their high obligations to him, and their history will transmit the name of La Fayette with grateful acknowledgments to the latest posterity. It is gratifying to learn that Congress granted him a valuable tract of land, as a compensation in part for his disinterested patriotism and important services.

When in December, 1784, the marquis was about to take his final departure from America, Congress appointed a committee, consisting of one member from each state, to receive him, and in the name of Congress to take leave of him in such manner as might strongly manifest their esteem and regard for him. That they be instructed to assure him that Congress continue to entertain the same high sense of his abilities and zeal to promote the welfare of America, both here and in Europe, which they have frequently expressed and manifested on former occasions. That the United States regard him with particular affection, and will not cease to feel an interest in whatever may concern his honor and prosperity, and that their best and kindest wishes will always attend him. Congress resolved also that a letter be written to his Most Christian Majesty, expressive of the high sense which the United States, in Congress assembled, entertain of the zeal, talents, and meritorious services of the Marquis de la Fayette, and recommending him to the favor and patronage of his majesty. The marquis made a very respectful and affectionate reply, in which he expressed the lively feelings of a heart devoted to the welfare of our rising empire, and gratefully acknowledged that, at a time when an inexperienced youth, he was favored with his respected friend's paternal adoption. He thus concludes his address:

"May this immense temple of freedom ever stand as a lesson to oppressors, an example to the oppressed, a sanctuary for the rights of mankind; and may these happy United States attain that complete splendor and prosperity which will illustrate the blessings of their government, and for ages to come rejoice the departed souls of its founders. Never can Congress oblige me so much as when they put it in my power in every part of the world to the latest day of my life to gratify the attachment which will ever rank me among the most zealous and respectful servants of the United States."

MAJOR-GENERAL HORATIO GATES.

GENERAL GATES was a native of England, and was educated to the military profession. He was an officer under the unfortunate Braddock, in the expedition against Fort du Quesne, in the year 1755, and who, after receiving a dangerous wound, was, with the illustrious Washington, among the few officers who escaped with life on that memorable occasion. When the American colonies were forced to assume a hostile attitude, Gates had been for some time a resident in Virginia, and having evinced his zeal and attachment to the violated rights of his adopted country, and sustaining a high military reputation, he was by Congress appointed adjutant-general, with the rank of brigadier, and he accompanied General Washington to our camp at Cambridge, in July, 1775. On the retreat of our forces from Canada, the chief command in that department was conferred on him in June, 1776. He continued the retreat of our army from Crown Point to Ticonderoga, which did not fully accord with the views of Congress and the commander-in-chief. The British forces having retired to winter-quarters in Canada, Gates marched with a detachment of his command, and joined the main army in Jersey, in the autumn of that year. His sphere .of action was not brilliant or splendid, till his mighty achievement in the capture of Burgoyne at Saratoga; nor is he justly and exclusively entitled to the full measure of applause acquired by that most glorious victory; the magnanimous General Schuyler,* whom he superseded in command, had, by his indefatigable industry, and almost unprecedented labors, raised the most formidable impediments to the march of Burgoyne, which tended more than is generally imagined to facilitate the conquest made by the northern army.

* MAJOR-GENERAL PHILIP SCHUYLER.—It has been observed that neither history'nor biography has rendered justice to this highly-meritorious character. He possessed a clear understanding, a strong mind, a humane and generous disposition. No individual could have contributed more largely, by his vigilance and efficiency, to augment the obstacles to the march of the British army to Fort Edward. His name should be enrolled with the renowned band of military patriots and heroes, that posterity may know the eminent services which his splendid talents conferred on his country.

29

When General Gates succeeded to the command of the
northern army, August, 1777, Generals Schuyler and St.
Clair were suffering, though most unjustly, the public
odium by the evacuation of Ticonderoga, and their successor in command was in high repute and confidence with
his officers and soldiers. Burgoyne's right wing, under
St. Leger, had been cut off at Fort Stanwix, and his left
at Bennington, by General Stark. Our army was daily
increasing in numbers, and considerably exceeded the
strength of the enemy, and our troops were greatly invig-
orated with courage, and determined on victory. Every
circumstance, in fact, was auspicious to a successful issue.
Burgoyne still perceived that, in proportion as he advanced,
obstacles multiplied on every side. Having at length
surmounted almost insuperable difficulties, he passed the
Hudson, and advanced to Saratoga. Gates also advanced
to Stillwater, and boldly faced his formidable foe; and on
the 19th of September a sanguinary conflict ensued. Both
parties firm and unyielding, both attained the high honors
of the brave, but neither bore the palm of a complete
victory from the field. While Burgoyne's loss was irretrievable, the force and the ardor of his antagonist were
continually augmenting. Every day's delay now increased
the heavy embarrassments of Burgoyne, while time threw
additional advantages into the hands of his spirited opponent; till at length it became obvious that retreat or victory was his unavoidable alternative; but, on trial, it was
proved, to his utter dismay, that neither resource was at
his command. On the 7th of October, the two opposing
armies rushed again to the field of slaughter, and both
were satiated with blood and carnage. The British army
were repulsed in every direction, and its commander was
led to the painful conviction that a more disastrous fate
awaited him. Burgoyne, now driven to the brink of despair—his forces disabled, his provisions exhausted, and a
victorious adversary opposing him in front— resolved on
a rapid retreat, but on exploring the route, behold, his
adversary was there!
    The dreaded crisis had now arrived, when a capitulation
was alone practicable. Articles not very dishonorable to
the vanquished enemy were acceded to, and General Gates
enjoyed the ineffable satisfaction of receiving in submission

the once-victorious chief. To the honor of General Gates, it is mentioned that the captured troops were directed to a sequestered spot to ground their arms, that their feelings might not be wounded in the presence of our army, though it deprived the latter of a satisfaction in which they were justly entitled to participate. An interesting narrative of the first interview between the victor and the captured officers is thus given by Adjutant-General Wilkinson:

"General Burgoyne proposed to be introduced to General Gates, and we crossed the Fishkill, and proceeded to head-quarters on horseback, General Burgoyne in front with his Adjutant-General Kingston, and his aids-de-camp, Captain Lord Petersham and Lieutenant Wilford, behind him; then followed Major-General Phillips, the Baron Reidesel, and the other general officers and their suites according to rank. General Gates, advised of Burgoyne's approach, met him at the head of his camp—Burgoyne in a rich royal uniform, and Gates in a plain blue frock. When they approached nearly within sword's length, they reined up and halted. I then named the gentlemen, and General Burgoyne, raising his hat most gracefully, said, 'The fortune of war, General Gates, has made me your prisoner;' to which the conqueror, returning a courtly salute, promptly replied, 'I shall always be ready to bear testimony that it has not been through any fault of your excellency.' Major-General Phillips then advanced, and he and General Gates saluted, and shook hands with the familiarity of old acquaintances. The Baron Reidesel and other officers were introduced in their turn."

General Gates was remarkable for his humanity to prisoners, and a desire to mitigate the sufferings of the unfortunate. Among the objects in distress who claimed his attention was Lady Ackland, whose husband was wounded and captured during the battle of the 7th of October. General Gates bestowed on her the care and tenderness of a parent. In reply to a letter from General Burgoyne in her behalf, he says: "The respect due to her ladyship's rank, the tenderness due to her person and sex, were sufficient recommendations to entitle her to my protection. I am surprised that your excellency should think that I could consider the greatest attention to Lady Ackland in the light of an obligation."*

General Gates received the thanks of Congress, and a gold medal, as a memorial of their gratitude. Great was the credit which he acquired by this momentous event, universal joy pervaded the country, and all ranks were ready to vie with each other in their homage to the for-

* For a history of this lady, see pages 110 and 359.

tunate conqueror. It was not long after, that the wonderful discovery was supposed to be made, that the illustrious
Washington was incompetent to the task of conducting
the operations of the American army, and that General
Gates, if elevated to the important station of commander-
in-chief, would speedily meliorate the condition of our
affairs. A discontented party in Congress, with a few
interested individuals in our army, constituted the faction
hostile to the saviour of his country. General Gates himself was strongly suspected of more than a passive acquiescence, and there were those who imputed to him a
principal agency in the affair, which, however, he promptly
disavowed. Had the project succeeded, it would in all
probability have sealed the ruin of our army and sacrificed
the glorious cause of our country. But all the *eclat* which
General Gates had acquired, and all the splendor of his
name, were insufficient to proselyte a single officer to his
interest. He was not endowed with that dignity and with
those illustrious qualities which were requisite to command
the confidence and reverence of the army as the successor
of the much-beloved Washington. I am assured by Governor Brooks that, being in company with a number of
respectable officers at Valley Forge when the subject was
canvassed, General Weedon, of Virginia, with great vehe-
mence declared, that should General Gates be preferred to
the chief command, he never would serve under him, but
would absolutely resign his commission and quit the service, and all present were in unison with him in opinion.

A private correspondence was maintained between the
intriguing General Conway and General Gates, criticising
and reprobating the measures pursued by General Washington, and in one of Conway's letters he ascribes our
want of success to a weak general and bad counsellors.
General Gates, on finding that General Washington had
been apprised of this correspondence, addressed his excellency, requesting that he would disclose the name of his
informant; and, extraordinary as it may appear, in violation of the rules of decorum, he addressed the commander-
in-chief on a subject of extreme delicacy in an open letter,
transmitted to the President of Congress. His pretence
was, that some of the members of that body might aid in
detecting the person who made the communication. Gen-

eral Washington, however, made no hesitancy in disclosing
the name and the circumstances which brought the affair
to light. General Gates then, with inexcusable disingen-
uousness, attempted to vindicate the conduct of Conway,
and to deny that his letter contained the reprehensible
expressions in question, but utterly refused to produce the
original letter. This subject, however, was so ably and
candidly discussed by General Washington, as to cover
his adversary with shame and humiliation, and he was glad
to discontinue the investigation. It was thought to be
inexcusable in General Gates that he neglected to communicate to the commander-in-chief an account of so
important an event as the capture of the British army at
Saratoga, but left his excellency to obtain information by
common report. In November, 1777, Congress having
new-modeled the board of war, appointed General Gates
the president, and he entered on the duties of the office,
but retained his rank in the army. The subject of this
sketch was destined to experience, in a remarkable manner, the humiliating vicissitudes of fortune. He had the
conducting of the most prosperous and the most disastrous
of the military enterprises in the war. In June, 1780,
General Gates was by Congress vested with the chief command of our army in the Southern States. In a general
battle at Camden,* August 15th, being the first and only
encounter which he had with Lord Cornwallis, he suffered
a total defeat, and was obliged to fly from the enemy for
personal safety; and thus was the prediction of General
Lee, when Gates was vested with the command, that his
Northern laurels would be exchanged for *Southern willows*,
verified. It would, however, be great injustice to attribute
the misfortune altogether to the commander, under his
peculiar circumstances; a large proportion of his force
consisted of raw militia, who were panic-struck, and fled
at the first fire; their rout was absolute and irretrievable.
It may be observed, nevertheless, that his conduct in some

---

* In the disastrous battle at Camden, the Baron de Kalb, a brave and
experienced Prussian officer, and major-general in our service, was unfortunately slain. It was said that this heroic officer cautioned General
Gates against a general action, under present circumstances. His exit
was marked with unfading glory, and his distinguished merit was gratefully
acknowledged by Congress, in erecting a monument to his memory.

respects on this occasion did not meet the approbation of those who must be admitted as competent judges of the military operations of that fatal day. Proudly calculating on the weight of his name, and too confident in his own superiority, he slighted the counsel which he ought to have respected; and hurrying impetuously into the field of battle, his tide of prosperity ebbed as fast at Camden as it had flowed at Saratoga.

The plot to supplant General Washington is established beyond question, and it will be only sufficient to quote the following extracts from the letters of the two purest patriots and men that have ever lived, to satisfy of its truth those who are not familiar with the events of that period. Patrick Henry, writing on the subject to General Washington, says:

"While you face the armed enemies of our liberty in the field, and, by the favor of God, have been kept unhurt, I trust your country will never harbor in her bosom the miscreant who would ruin her best supporter. I wish not to flatter; but when arts unworthy honest men are used to defame and traduce you, I think it not amiss, but a duty, to assure you of that estimation in which the public hold you. Not that I think any testimony I can bear is necessary for your support or private satisfaction, for a bare recollection of what is past must give you sufficient pleasure in every circumstance of life. But I cannot help assuring you, on this occasion, of the high sense of gratitude which all ranks of men, in this your native county, bear to you. It will give me sincere pleasure to manifest my regards, and render my best services to you or yours. I do not like to make a parade of these things, and I know you are not fond of it; however, I hope the occasion will plead my excuse."

To which General Washington replies:

"The anonymous letter with which you were pleased to favor me was written by * * * * * * * * * * * *, so far as I can judge from a similitude of hands. * * * '* * * *

"My caution to avoid any thing that could injure the service prevented me from communicating, except to a very few of my friends, the intrigues of a faction which I know was formed against me, since it might serve to publish our internal dissensions; but their own rest'ess zeal to advance their views has too clearly betrayed them, and made concealment on my part fruitless. I cannot precisely mark the extent of their views, but it appeared in general that General Gates was to be exalted on the ruin of my reputation and influence. This I am authorized to say from undeniable facts in my possession, from publications, the evident scope of which could not be mistaken, and from private detractions industriously circulated. * * * * * * * * * * * *, it is generally supposed, bore the second part in the cabal; and General

PATRICK HENRY.

Conway, I know, was a very active and malignant partizan; but I have good reason to believe that their machinations have recoiled most sensibly on themselves."

Yet, in the face of the evidence of the fact, General Armstrong recently avows that "the *slander* propagated and believed for half a century, that two distinguished officers of the army of the revolution had conspired to put down the commander-in-chief, *is an impudent and vile falsehood from beginning to end.*"

General Gates was displaced from his command by order of Congress, and his conduct subjected to the inquiry of a special court, which resulted in his acquittal, but his Saratoga laurels had faded, and he was unable to retrieve his suffering fame.

"It was the general opinion that General Gates was not treated by Congress with that delicacy, or indeed gratitude, that was due to an officer of his acknowledged merit. He, however, received the order of his supersedure and suspension, and resigned the command to General Greene with becoming dignity." General Greene asserted that if there was any mistake in the conduct of Gates, it was in hazarding an action at all against such superior force.

He was reïnstated in his military command in the main army in 1782, but the great scenes of war were now passed, and he could only participate in the painful scene of a final separation.

In the midst of his misfortune General Gates was called to mourn the afflictive dispensation of Providence in the death of his only son. Major Garden, in his excellent publication, has recorded the following affecting anecdote, which he received from Dr. William Reed:

"Having occasion to call on General Gates, relative to the business of the department under my immediate charge, I found him traversing the apartment which he occupied, under the influence of high excitement; his agitation was excessive—every feature of his countenance, every gesture betrayed it. Official despatches, informing him that he was superseded, and that the command of the Southern army had been transferred to General Greene, had just been received and perused by him. His countenance, however, betrayed no expression of irritation or resentment; it was sensibility alone that caused his emotion. An open letter, which he held in his hand, was often raised to his lips, and kissed with devotion, while the exclamation repeatedly escaped them, 'Great man! Noble, generous procedure!' When the tumult of his mind had subsided, and his thoughts found utterance, he, with strong expression of feeling, exclaimed, 'I have received this day a communication from the commander-in-chief, which has conveyed more consolation to my bosom, more ineffable delight to my heart, than I had believed it possible for it ever to have felt again. With affectionate tenderness he sympathizes with me in my domestic misfortunes, and condoles with me on the loss I have sustained by the recent death of an only son; and then with peculiar delicacy, lamenting my misfortune in battle, assures me that his confidence in my zeal and capacity is so little impaired, that the command of the right wing of the army will be bestowed on me so soon as I can make it convenient to join him.'"

When the revolution was completed, General Gates retired to his plantation in Virginia, where he continued about seven years, when he with his wife took up his final residence in the neighborhood of New York. In civil life General Gates was a zealous partizan, but he was always disappointed in his ambitious views. In 1800, he was elected to the New York legislature to answer the purpose of a party, and withdrew again to private life as soon as that purpose was answered. During the federal administration of the general government, he was found in the ranks of the opposite or minor party, which excluded him altogether from a share of the honors and emoluments which it was in the power of his former illustrious military leader to bestow. "A few years before his death he generously gave freedom to his slaves, making provision for the old and infirm, while several testified their attachment to him by remaining in his family. In the characteristic virtue of planters'. hospitality, Gates had no competitor, and his reputation may well be supposed to put this virtue to a hard test." "He had a handsome person, and was gentlemanly in his manners, remarkably courteous to all, and carrying good-humor sometimes beyond the nice limit of dignity. To science, literature or erudition, however, he made no pretensions, but gave indisputable marks of a social, amiable, benevolent disposition. He died without posterity at his abode near New York, on the 10th day of April, 1806, aged seventy-eight years."

BRIGADIER-GENERAL JOHN STARK.

GENERAL STARK was a native of Londonderry, in New Hampshire, and was born August 17th, 1728. When at the age of twenty-one years, he was, while on a hunting excursion, surprised and captured by the Indians, and remained four months a prisoner in their hands. He was captain of a company of rangers in the provincial service during the French war of 1755, and was with the British general, Lord Howe, when he was killed in the storming the French lines at Ticonderoga, in July, 1758. At the close of that war he retired, with the reputation of a brave and vigilant officer. When the report of Lexington battle reached him, he was engaged at work in his saw-mill. Fired with indignation and a martial spirit, he immediately seized his musket, and with a band of heroes proceeded to Cambridge. The morning after his arrival, he received a colonel's commission; and availing himself of his own popularity, and the enthusiasm of the day, in two hours he enlisted eight hundred men! On the memorable 17th of June, at Breed's-hill, Colonel Stark, at the head of his back-woodsmen of New Hampshire, poured on the enemy that deadly fire, from a sure aim, which effected such remarkable destruction in their ranks, and compelled them twice to retreat. During the whole of this dreadful conflict, Colonel Stark evinced that consummate bravery and intrepid zeal which entitle his name to honor and perpetual remembrance in the pages of our history. After the British evacuated Boston, Colonel Stark joined our northern army while retreating from Canada, and he had the command of a party of troops who were employed in fortifying the post of Mount Independence. We next find him at Trenton, in December, 1776, where he shared largely in the honors of that ever-memorable battle under Washington, when the Hessians were captured. But Stark reached the climax of his fame when, in one of the darkest and most desponding periods of the American war, he achieved a glorious victory over the enemy at Bennington. General Burgoyne, after possessing himself of Ticonderoga in July, 1776, and while advancing at the head of his victorious army towards Albany, conceived the design of

APPENDIX.

taking by surprise a quantity of stores which our people had deposited at Bennington. For this enterprise he despatched a German officer, Lieutenant-Colonel Baum, with one thousand five hundred soldiers and one hundred Indians, with two field-pieces. Stark was at that time brigadier-general of militia, and was in the vicinity with about one thousand four hundred brave men from New Hampshire. He advanced towards the enemy, and drew up his men in a line of battle. Colonel Baum, deeming it imprudent to engage with his present force, halted his troops, and sent an express to Burgoyne for a rëinforcement, and in the mean time entrenched and rendered himself as defensible as possible.

General Burgoyne immediately despatched Colonel Breyman, with about one thousand troops, to rëinforce Colonel Baum; but a heavy rain and bad roads prevented his arrival in season. General Stark, on the 16th of August, planned his mode of attack, and a most severe action ensued, which continued about two hours, with an incessant firing of musketry and the enemy's field-artillery. Colonel Baum defended himself with great bravery till he received a mortal wound, and his whole party was defeated. It was not long after, that Colonel Breyman appeared with his rëinforcement, and another battle ensued, which continued obstinate on both sides till sunset, when the Germans yielded, and the victory on our side was complete, the trophies of which were four brass field-pieces and more than seven hundred prisoners. For a more particular detail of this enterprise, see page 93 of this volume. Congress, on the 4th of October following, passed a resolve of thanks to General Stark, and the officers and troops under his command, for their brave and successful attack and signal victory, and that Brigadier Stark be appointed a brigadier-general in the army of the United States. General Stark volunteered his services under General Gates at Saratoga, and assisted in the council which stipulated the surrender of General Burgoyne, nor did he relinquish his valuable services till he could greet his native country as an Independent Empire. General Stark was of the middle stature, not formed by nature to exhibit an erect, soldierly mien. His manners were frank and unassuming, but he manifested a peculiar sort of eccentricity and negligence, which precluded all display of personal dignity, and seemed to place him among those of ordinary rank in life. But, as a courageous and heroic soldier, he is entitled to high rank among those who have been crowned with unfading laurels, and to whom a large share of glory is justly due. His character as a private citizen was unblemished, and he was ever held in respect. For the last few years of his life, he enjoyed a pecuniary bounty from the government. He lived to the advanced age of ninety-three years, eight months and twenty-four days, and died May 8th, 1822.

MAJOR-GENERAL JOHN SULLIVAN.

GENERAL SULLIVAN has a claim to honorable distinction among the general officers of the American army. Before the revolution, he had attained to eminence in the profession of the law in New Hampshire. But indulging a laudable ambition for military glory, he relinquished the fairest prospects of fortune and fame, and, on the commencement of hostilities, appeared among the most ardent patriots and intrepid warriors. He was a member of the first Congress, in 1774; but, preferring a military commission, he was in 1775 appointed a brigadier-general of the American army, then at Cambridge, and soon obtained the command on Winter-hill. The next year he was ordered to Canada, and, on the death of General Thomas, the command of the army devolved on him. The situation of our army in that quarter was inexpressibly distressing, destitute of clothing, dispirited by defeat and constant fatigue, and a large proportion of the troops sick with the small-pox, which was attended by an unprecedented mortality. By his great exertions and judicious management he meliorated the condition of the army, and obtained general applause. On his retiring from that command, July 12, 1776, the field-officers thus addressed him: "It is to you, sir, the public are indebted for the preservation of their property in Canada; it is to you we owe our safety thus far. Your humanity will call forth the silent tear and the grateful ejaculation of the sick. Your universal impartiality will force the applause of the wearied soldier." In August, 1776, he was promoted to the rank of major-general, and soon after was, with Major-General Lord Stirling, captured by the British in the battle on Long Island. General Sullivan being paroled, was sent by General Howe with a message to Congress; after which, he returned to New York. In September he was exchanged for Major-General Prescott. We next find him in command of the right division of our troops, in the famous battle at Trenton, and he acquitted himself honorably on that ever-memorable day

In August, 1777, without the authority of Congress or the commander-in-chief, he planned and executed an expedition against the enemy on Staten Island. Though the enterprise was conducted with prudence and success in part, it was said by some to be less brilliant than might have been expected, under his favorable circumstances; and as that act was deemed a bold assumption of responsibility, and reports to his prejudice being in circulation, a court of inquiry was ordered to investigate his conduct. The result was an honorable acquittal. Congress resolved that the result so honorable to General Sullivan is highly pleasing to Congress, and that the opinion of the court be published, in justification of that injured officer. In the battles at Brandywine and at Germantown, in the autumn of 1777, General Sullivan commanded a division, and in the latter conflict his two aids were killed, and his own conduct was so conspicuously brave, that General Washington in his letter to Congress concludes with encomiums on the gallantry of General Sullivan, and the whole right wing of the army who acted immediately under the eye of his excellency. In August, 1778, General Sullivan was sole commander of an expedition to the island of Newport, in coöperation with the French fleet under the Count D'Estaing. The Marquis de la Fayette and General Greene volunteered their services on the occasion. The object of the expedition was defeated, in consequence of the French fleet being driven off by a violent storm. By this unfortunate event the enemy were encouraged to engage our army in battle, in which they suffered a repulse, and General Sullivan finally effected a safe retreat to the main. This retreat, so ably executed, without confusion, the loss of baggage or stores, increased the military reputation of General Sullivan, and redounds to his honor as a skilful commander.

The bloody tragedy acted at Wyoming, in 1778, had determined the commander-in-chief, in 1779, to employ a large detachment from the continental army to penetrate into the heart of the Indian country, to chastise the hostile tribes and their white associates and adherents, for their cruel aggressions on the defenceless inhabitants. The command of this expedition was committed to Major-General Sullivan, with express orders to destroy their settlements, to ruin their crops, and make such thorough devastations as to render the country entirely uninhabitable for the present, and thus to compel the savages to remove to a greater distance from our frontiers. General Sullivan had under his command several brigadiers and a well-chosen army, to which were attached a number of friendly Indian warriors. With this force he penetrated about ninety miles through a horrid, swampy wilderness and barren mountainous deserts, to Wyoming, on the Susquehannah river, thence by water to Tioga, and possessed himself of numerous towns and villages of the savages. During this hazardous expedition, General Sullivan and his army encountered the most complicated obstacles, requiring the greatest fortitude and perseverance to surmount. He explored an extensive tract of country, and strictly executed the severe but necessary orders he had received. A considerable number of Indians were slain, some were captured, their habitations were burned, and their plantations of corn and vegetables laid waste in the most effectual manner. "Eighteen villages, a number of detached buildings, one hundred and sixty thousand bushels of corn, and those fruits and vegetables which conduce to the comfort and subsistence of man, were utterly destroyed. Five weeks were unremittingly employed in this work of devastation." On his return from the expedition, he and his army received the approbation of Congress. It is remarked on this expedition by the translator of M. Chastelleux's Travels, an Englishman then resident in the United States, that the instructions given by General Sullivan to his officers, the order of march he prescribed to his troops, and the discipline he had the ability to maintain, would have done honor to the most experienced ancient or modern generals. At the close of the campaign of 1779, General Sullivan, in consequence of impaired health, resigned his commission in the army. Congress, in accepting of his resignation, passed a resolve, thanking him for his past services. His military talents and bold spirit of enterprise, were universally acknowledged. He was fond of display, and his personal appearance and dignified deportment commanded respect. After his resignation, he resumed his professional pursuits at the bar, and was much distinguished as a statesman, politician, and patriot. He acquired very considerable proficiency in general literature, and an extensive knowledge of men and the world. He received from Harvard University a degree of Master of Arts, and from the University of Dartmouth a degree of Doctor of Laws. He was one of the convention that formed the state constitution for New Hampshire, was chosen into the first council, and was afterwards elected chief magistrate in that state, and held the office for three years. In September, 1789, he was appointed judge of the District court for the District of New Hampshire, and continued in the office till his death, in 1795.

MAJOR-GENERAL THOMAS CONWAY,

Knight of the Order of St. Louis.

THIS gentleman was born in Ireland, and went with his parents to France, at the age of six years, and was from his youth educated to the profession of arms. He had obtained considerable reputation as a military officer and as a man of sound understanding and judgment. He arrived from France with ample recommendations, and Congress appointed him a brigadier-general in May, 1777. He soon became conspicuously inimical to General Washington, and sought occasions to traduce his character. In this he found support from a faction in Congress, who were desirous that the commander-in-chief should be superseded. The Congress not long after elected General Conway to the office of inspector-general to our army, with the rank of major-general, though he had insulted the commander-in-chief, and justified himself in doing so. This gave umbrage to the brigadiers over whom he was promoted, and they remonstrated to Congress against the proceeding, as implicating their honor and character. Conway, now smarting under the imputation of having instigated a hostile faction against the illustrious Washington, and being extremely unpopular among the officers in general, and finding his situation did not accord with his feelings and views, resigned his commission, without having commenced the duties of inspector. He was believed to be an unprincipled intriguer, and after his resignation, his calumny and detraction of the commander-in-chief, and the army generally, was exercised with unrestrained virulence and outrage.

No man was more zealously engaged in the scheme of elevating General Gates to the station of commander-in-chief. His vile insinuations and direct assertions in the public newspapers and in private conversation, relative to the incapacity of Washington to conduct the operations of the army, received countenance from several members of Congress, who were induced to declare their want of confidence in him, and the affair assumed an aspect threatening the most disastrous consequences. Conway maintained a correspondence with General Gates on the subject, and in one of his letters he thus expresses himself: "Heaven has been determined to save your country, or a weak general and bad counsellors would have ruined it." He was himself at that time one of the counsellors, against whom he so basely inveighs. Envy and malice ever are attendant on exalted genius and merit. But the delusion was of short continuance; the name of Washington proved unassailable, and the base intrigue of Conway recoiled with bitterness on his own head. General Cadwallader, of Pennsylvania, indignant at the attempt to vilify the character of Washington, resolved to avenge himself on the aggressor, in personal combat. In Major Garden's *Anecdotes of the Revolutionary War*, &c., we have the following detailed particulars of the duel:

"The parties having declared themselves ready, the word was given to proceed. General Conway immediately raised his pistol, and fired with great composure, but without effect. General Cadwallader was about to do so, when a sudden gust of wind occurring, he kept his pistol down, and remained tranquil. 'Why do you not fire, General Cadwallader?' exclaimed Conway. 'Because,' replied General Cadwallader 'we came not here to trifle. Let the gale pass, and I shall act my part

'You shall have a fair chance of performing it well,' rejoined Conway, and immediately presented a full front. General Cadwallader fired, and his ball entered the mouth of his antagonist; he fell directly forward on his face. Colonel Morgan, running to his assistance, found the blood spouting from behind his neck, and, lifting up the club of his hair, saw the ball drop from it. It had passed through his head, greatly to the derangement of his tongue and teeth, but did not inflict a mortal wound. As soon as the blood was sufficiently washed away to allow him to speak, General Conway, turning to his opponent, said, good-humoredly, 'You fire, general, with much deliberation, and certainly with a great deal of effect,' The calls of honor being satisfied, all animosity subsided, and they parted, free from all resentment."

General Conway, conceiving his wound to be mortal, and believing death to be near, acted honorably, in addressing to General Washington, whom he had perfidiously slandered, the following letter of apology:

"PHILADELPHIA, *February 23d*, 1778.

"SIR: I find myself just able to hold my pen during a few minutes, and take this opportunity of expressing my sincere grief for having done, written, or said any thing disagreeable to your excellency. My career will soon be over; therefore justice and truth prompt me to declare my last sentiments. You are in my eyes the great and good man. May you long enjoy the love, esteem and veneration of these states, whose liberties you have asserted, by your virtues!

"I am, with the greatest respect,

"Your Excellency's most obedient and humble servant,

"THS. CONWAY."

MAJOR-GENERAL CHARLES LEE.

GENERAL LEE was an original genius, and one of the most eccentric and extraordinary characters of the age. His brilliant talents, military prowess, and extensive intelligence, would have entitled him to preëminence in the days of chivalry. He could dignify with honor an elevated station, and it was not difficult for him to degrade his rank by indulging in a malignant, sordid passion for personal satire and invective. From the qualities and manners of a gentleman, he could descend to the level of a querulous clown. The profession of arms was his delight from infancy, and he was commissioned at the early age of eleven years. In the year 1762, he bore a colonel's commission, and served under General Burgoyne in Portugal, where he signalized himself by his martial skill and active enterprises. He afterwards served as an aid-de-camp to his Polish majesty, with the rank of major-general. He exhausted every valuable treatise, both ancient and modern, on the military art, and his capacious mind was stored with knowledge on every subject which he could collect from reading, conversation and extensive travelling in Europe. He was honored with the acquaintance of princes and noblemen, yet his manners were rude and singular, partly from nature and partly from affectation. To his strong powers of intellect, he added literary accomplishments, and the knowledge of six languages beside his own. As a statesman, he appeared to be influenced by an innate principle of republicanism; an attachment to these principles was implanted in the constitution of his mind, and he espoused the cause of America as a champion of her emancipation from oppression. He pertinaciously opposed every oppressive measure of the British cabinet towards the American colonies, even while he was in their service. On his arrival in this country, he became daily more enthusiastic in the cause of liberty, and he travelled rapidly through the colonies, animating, both by conversation and his eloquent pen, to a determined and persevering resistance to British tyranny. Thus he acquired a large share of popularity, and his presence among the people at this crisis was considered as a most fortunate and propitious omen. He probably expected to have become the first in military rank in America, but in 1775, he accepted a commission of second major-general from our Congress, having previously resigned that which he held in the British service, and relinquished his half-pay. He accompanied General Washington to join the troops assembled near Boston, in July, 1775, and he was considered as a real acquisition to our cause. In the spring of 1776 he was ordered to New York, to take the command and to fortify that city for defence. Not long after, he was appointed to the command of the southern department, and in his travels through the country, he received every testimony of high respect from the people. General Sir Henry Clinton and Sir Peter Parker, with a powerful fleet and army, attempted the reduction of Charleston while he was in command. The fleet anchored within half-musket-shot of the fort on Sullivan's island, where

30

Colonel Moultrie, one of the bravest and most intrepid of men, commanded. A tremendous engagement ensued on the 28th of June, 1776, which lasted twelve hours without intermission. The whole British force was completely repulsed, after suffering an irreparable loss. General Lee and Colonel Moultrie received the thanks of Congress for their signal bravery and gallantry. Our hero had now reached the pinnacle of his military glory, the *eclat* of his name alone appeared to enchant and animate the most desponding heart.

But here we pause to contemplate the humiliating reverse of human events. He returned to the main army in October, and in marching at the head of a large detachment through the Jerseys, having, from a desire of retaining a separate command, delayed his march several days in disobedience of express orders from the commander-in-chief, he was guilty of most culpable negligence in regard to his personal security. He took up his quarters two or three miles from the main body, and lay for the night, December 13th, 1776, in a careless, exposed situation. Information of this being communicated to Colonel Harcourt, who commanded the British light-horse, he proceeded immediately to the house, fired into it, and obliged the general to surrender himself a prisoner. They mounted him on a horse in haste, without his cloak or hat, and conveyed him in triumph to New York. A splendid triumph indeed it was, for next to Washington he was the most highly prized as a captive by the British, who considered him as the soul of the American army, and at that juncture of our affairs a more grievous loss, Washington thought, could not have been sustained. The commander-in-chief greatly lamented his capture, as he entertained a high opinion of his martial skill, and he was apprehensive that the British general would treat him with indignity and rigor. Not having any prisoner of his rank, his excellency immediately proposed to exchange for him five Hessian field-officers, captured at Trenton, which is equivalent to the rank of major-general. The British commander affected to consider Lee as a deserter from his majesty's service, and refused to listen to proposals for an exchange, but treated him with all the rigor of a state criminal of the first magnitude. This compelled the

American commander, by order of Congress, to retaliate on the persons of five Hessian officers, and also on Colonel Campbell, who was now committed to a dungeon. After the capture of General Burgoyne and his army, the enemy relaxed in their rigorous treatment, and General Lee was soon exchanged for Major-General Prescott. It is next to be seen in what manner General Lee terminated his career in the continental service. In the battle at Monmouth on the 28th of June, 1778, he commanded the van of the American troops, with orders from the commander-in-chief to attack the retreating enemy. Instead of obeying this order, he conducted in an unworthy manner, and greatly disconcerted the arrangements of the day. His excellency, advancing to the field of battle, met him in his disorderly retreat, and accosted him with strong expressions of disapprobation. Lee, incapable of brooking even an implied indignity, and unable to restrain the warmth of his resentment, used improper language in return, and some irritation was excited on both sides for the moment. Lee on the same day addressed two letters to the commander-in-chief, couched in disrespectful language, and with an air of defiance solicited a trial for his conduct, in consequence of which he was immediately put under arrest. A court-martial, of which Lord Stirling was president, was ordered for his trial on the following charges: 1st, For disobedience of orders in not attacking the enemy on the 28th of June, agreeably to repeated instructions. 2d, For misbehaviour before the enemy on the same day, by making an unnecessary, disorderly and shameful retreat. 3d, For disrespect to the commander-in-chief, in two letters, dated July 1st and June 28th. The letter dated July 1st was so dated my mistake; it was written June 28th. The court found him guilty on all the charges, and sentenced him to be suspended from any command in the armies of the United States of America for the term of twelve months. He made a masterly defence, and endeavored to prove that any other course than that pursued would have given the enemy great advantage, and hazarded the destruction of our army. In his adversity General Lee was not altogether destitute of advocates as respects the affair of Monmouth; they allege that, were it not for the disrespectful letters to his excellency, Lee would have been acquitted, and the degree of punishment seems in some measure to justify this opinion. If he had been proved fully guilty of all the charges, a suspension for one year would be inadequate to the magnitude of the crime. It appears also that Congress did not without some demur sanction the sentence of the court-martial. When at length their confirmation of the sentence was promulgated, it was like a mortal wound to the lofty, aspiring spirit of General Lee. Pointing to his dog, he exclaimed, "Oh, that I was that animal! that I might not call man my brother." He became outrageous, and from that moment he was more open and virulent in his attack on the character of the commander-in-chief, and did not cease in his unwearied endeavors, both in his conversation and writings, to lessen his reputation in the estimation of the army and the public. He was an active abettor of General Conway in his calumny and abuse of General Washington, and they were believed to be in concert in their vile attempts to supersede his excellency in the supreme command. With the hope of effecting his nefarious purpose, he published a pamphlet, replete with scurrilous imputations unfavorable to the military talents of the commander-in-chief; but this with his other malignant allegations were consigned to contempt. At length Colonel Laurens, one of General Washington's aids, unable longer to suffer this gross abuse of his illustrious friend, demanded of Lee that satisfaction which custom has sanctioned as honorable. A rencounter accordingly ensued, and Lee received a wound in his side. Lee, now finding himself abandoned by his friends, degraded in the eye of the public, and despised by the wise and virtuous, retired to his sequestered plantation in Virginia. In this spot, secluded from all society, he lived in a sort of hovel, without glass windows or plastering, or even a decent article of house furniture; here he amused himself with books and dogs. On January 10th, 1780, Congress resolved that Major-General Lee be informed that they have no further occasion for his services in the army of the United States. In the autumn of 1782, wearied with his forlorn situation and broken spirit, he resorted to Philadelphia, and took lodgings in an ordinary tavern. He was soon seized with a disease of the lungs, and, after a few days' confinement, he terminated his mortal course, a martyr to chagrin and disappointment, October 2d, 1782. The last words which he was heard to utter, were, "Stand by me, my brave grenadiers!" The citizens of Philadelphia were much affected with his unexpected death, and his funeral was attended by a large concourse of people, the clergy of different denominations, the president and members of Congress, and of the assembly of Pennsylvania, the minister of France and his secretary, General Baron de Viomenil, the minister of War, and several other officers of distinction, both of the French and of the American army.

General Lee was rather above the middle size, "plain in his person, even to ugliness, and careless in his manners, even to a degree of rudeness; his nose was so remarkably aquiline, that it appeared as a real deformity. His voice was rough, his garb ordinary, his deportment morose. He was ambitious of fame, without the dignity to support it. In private life, he sunk into the vulgarity of the clown." His remarkable partiality for dogs was such, that a number of these animals constantly followed in his train, and the ladies complained that he allowed his *canine adherents* to follow him into the parlor, and not unfrequently a favorite one might be seen on a chair next his elbow at table.

In the year 1776, when our army lay at White Plains, Lee resided near the road which General Washington frequently passed, and he one day with his aids called and took dinner; after they had departed, Lee said to his aids, "You must look me out other quarters, or I shall have Washington and his puppies calling till they eat me up." The next day he ordered his servant to write with chalk on the door, "No victuals cooked here to-day." The company, seeing the hint on the door, passed with a smile at the oddity of the man. "The character of this person," says one who knew him well, "is full of absurdities and qualities of a most extraordinary nature. His understanding was great, his memory capacious, and his fancy brilliant. He was a correct and elegant classical scholar, and both wrote and spoke his native language with perspicuity, force and beauty. From these circumstances he was at times a most agreeable and instructive companion. His temper was naturally sour and severe. He was seldom seen to laugh, and scarcely to smile. The history of his life is

little less than the history of disputes, quarrels and duels
in every part of the world. He was vindictive to his
enemies. His avarice had no bounds. He never went
into a public and seldom into a private house where he
did not discover some marks of ineffable and contemptible
meanness. He grudged the expense of a nurse in his last
illness, and died in a small dirty room in the Philadelphia
tavern, called the *Canastoga Wagon,* attended by no one
but a French servant, and Mr. Oswald the printer, who
once served as an officer under him. He was both impious
and profane. In his principles, he was not only an infidel,
but he was very hostile to every attribute of the Diety.
His morals were exceedingly debauched. His appetite
was so whimsical, as to what he ate and drank, that he
was at all times and in all places a most troublesome and
disagreeable guest. His judgment in war was generally
sound. He was extremely useful to the Americans in the
beginning of the revolution, by inspiring them with military ideas and a contempt for British discipline and valor.
It is difficult to say whether the active and useful part he
took in the contest arose from personal resentment against
the king of Great Britain, or from a regard to the liberties
of America. It is certain he reprobated the French alliance and republican forms of government after he retired
from the American service. He was in the field brave in
the highest degree, and, with all his faults and oddities,
was beloved by his officers and soldiers. He was devoid
of prudence, and used to call it a *rascally virtue.* Two
virtues he possessed in an eminent degree, sincerity and
veracity. He was never known to deceive or desert a
friend, and he was a stranger to equivocation, even where
his safety or character was at stake. It was notorious that
General Lee was a man of unbounded personal ambition;
and, conscious of his European education, and preeminent
military talents and prowess, be affected a superiority over
General Washington, and constantly aimed at the supreme
command, little scrupulous as to the means employed to
accomplish his own advancement. In reference to his base
detraction, General Washington, in a letter to a friend, said:

"What cause is there for such a profusion of venom as he is emitting
on all occasions?—a simple narration of facts would defeat all his asser
tions, notwithstanding they are made with an effronterv which few men

do, and, for the honor of human nature, ought to possess."—"If this gentleman is envious of my station, and conceives that I stand in his way to preferment, I can assure him, in most solemn terms, that the first wish of my soul is to return to that peaceful retirement, and domestic ease and happiness, whence I came. To this end all my labors have been directed, and for this purpose have I been more than four years a perfect slave, endeavoring, under as many embarrassing circumstances as ever fell to any man's lot to encounter, and as pure motives as any man was ever influenced by, to promote the cause and service I had embarked in."
—*Garden's Anecdotes.*

The following is an extract from General Lee's will:

"I desire most earnestly that I may not be buried in any church or church-yard, or within a mile of any Presbyterian or Anabaptist Meeting House, for since I have resided in this country, I have kept so much bad company while living, that I do not choose to continue it when dead."

Thomas Paine once said of Lee, that "he was above all monarchs, and below all scum."

MAJOR-GENERAL BENEDICT ARNOLD.

THIS extraordinary man is already recorded in our revolutionary history, in the character of a valiant and intrepid officer, and in the next page as a sordid and infamous traitor to his country. He was a native of Connecticut, where he was known as a half-bred apothecary, a retailer, a skipper, and a jockey. Under pretence of bankruptcy, he committed perjury with the view of defrauding his creditors. But his mind was formed for bold and desperate enterprise, and he was chosen captain of a militia company of volunteers. On hearing of the battle at Lexington, he marched with his company, and arrived at head-quarters, at Cambridge, about the last of April, 1775, where he was promoted to a colonel. He immediately repaired to the vicinity of Lake Champlain, and united with Colonel Allen and his party, who were preparing to execute their plan for taking possession of the Britsh garrison at Ticonderoga. This enterprise was crowned with success, without bloodshed, and an immense quantity of valuable ordnance and munitions of war was taken for the use of our army. After which, he proceeded down the lake to St. John's in a small schooner, and seized by surprise an armed sloop of superior force, which he brought off with several prisoners. In September follow-ing, Colonel Arnold was invested with the command of eleven hundred men, destined on a very extraordinary and arduous expedition—no less than penetrating through the unexplored wilderness to Quebec, by the route of Kennebec river. Colonel Burr, late vice-president of the United States, was with his party. The expedition was attended by the most distressing circumstances which can be imagined, during which Arnold conducted with unex-ampled resolution, and the soldiers exercised the greatest fortitude and patience, and accomplished an undertaking almost incredible. The men were obliged to drag their batteaux over falls, up rapid streams, over carrying places, and to march through morasses, thick woods, and over mountains for about three hundred and twenty miles. A part of the detachment, consisting of about three hundred men, under Colonel Enos, returned to Cambridge to avoid absolute starvation in the wilderness. Some of those who persevered were compelled to feed on dogs, which they devoured without sparing legs or skin, and also their cart-ridge boxes, leather breeches and shoes. Colonel Arnold appears to have defeated his own object by an imprudent act. He intrusted to a transient Indian a letter to a friend in Quebec; the Indian betrayed his trust, and delivered the letter to the British commandant, who immediately adopted measures for defence and to oppose their march. In December, 1775, Colonel Arnold having reached the vicinity of Quebec, was second in command under General Montgomery, and led a party in the boldest and most spirit-ed manner to the attack of the city of Quebec, by escalade, where he received a wound by a musket-ball in his leg, and the brave Montgomery was slain. In January, 1776, Arnold was promoted to the rank of brigadier, and had the command of the miserable remains of our army, and retreated to Crown Point. He took from merchants at Montreal goods to a very considerable amount, under cir-cumstances which implicated his honor and character. He ordered Colonel Hazen to take charge of the goods; but, conceiving that they were taken unjustly from the proprietors, he refused to comply. On the retreat of the army, part of the goods were pillaged, in consequence of which Colonel Hazen was subjected to a trial, but was honorably acquitted. This affair excited much indignation among several respectable officers, who, having received abusive treatment from Arnold, demanded of General Gates, who now commanded in chief, that he should be arrested and brought to trial; but Gates, viewing him as a brave and valuable officer, was determined that he should command our fleet on Lake Champlain, and therefore waived all complaints exhibited against him. After Arnold was invested with the command of our fleet, Sir Guy Carleton proceeded up Lake Champlain with a superior force, and a furious contest ensued. No man could have conducted with more intrepid bravery than did General Arnold. By his valorous conduct he acquired the highest applause; but being overpowered, he was obliged to retreat with the Congress galley, which he commanded, and four gondolas, which he ran on shore and blew up in despite of every effort of the enemy to prevent it. He even displayed a nice point of honor in keeping his flag flying, and not quitting his galley till she was in flames, that the enemy should not board and strike the American flag. In April, 1777, General Tryon commanded an expedition from New York, consisting of about two thousand men, to destroy a deposit of stores at Danbury, in Connecticut. General Arnold by a forced march reached the scene of action, and with his usual impetuosity engaged the enemy; and, when within a few yards, a whole platoon was leveled at him, by which his horse was killed. A soldier was advancing to thrust his bayonet through him, when with great presence of mind he took his pistols from his holsters, and shot him down. Having mounted another horse, that also was shot through his neck. Congress resolved, that a horse properly caparisoned be presented to General Arnold, as a token of their approbation of his gallant conduct, in which he had one horse killed and another wounded. In May following, he was created a major-general. When, in August, 1777, General St. Leger invested Fort Stanwix, General Arnold marched, at the head of a detachment from Fort Edward, to raise the siege; but the enemy, alarmed at his approach, abandoned the enterprise before his arrival. In September a serious difference took place between him and General Gates, who commanded our army at Saratoga. A conscious superiority on one side, and an arrogant temper on the other, sufficed to render the contention almost irreconcilable. The consequence was, that Arnold in a rage requested to be discharged from under the command of General Gates, and the latter immediately gave him a passport to repair to General Washington's head-quarters, though a battle with Burgoyne was daily expected. He postponed his departure, however, till the sanguinary conflict at Bemis's heights commenced, October 7th, when he betrayed great agitation and wrath. Rushing into the field of battle, and acting the part of a desperado, he exposed himself in the most rash and intemperate manner. In the heat of the action, when our troops were gaining advantage, General Arnold ordered Lieutenant-Colonel Brooks, at the head of his regiment, to force the German lines, which was instantly obeyed, and they boldly entered at the sallyport together, where Arnold received a wound in his leg, and his horse was killed under him. He had so little control of his mind, that while brandishing his sword in animating the officers and soldiers, he struck Captain Pettingill and Captain Brown, and wounded one of them on his head, without assigning any cause These gentlemen the next day requested Colonel Brooks to accompany them to Arnold's quarters, to demand an explanation. He disavowed all recollection of the fact, and denied that he had struck an officer; but when convinced of it, readily offered the required apology. It is but justice to confess, that by his military phrenzy, or romantic heroism, Arnold contributed to the honor and success of the day. General Washington had a high sense of his gallantry, and presented him a pair of elegant pistols. After the evacuation of Philadelphia by the British army, General Arnold was intrusted with the command in that city. Here his display of connubial gallantry, as in the field his martial spirit, was crowned with honor and success. His addresses were auspiciously received, and he was honored with the hand of the then celebrated Miss Shippen, one of the most elegant and accomplished ladies in the city, but of a tory family. His whole soul now appeared to be engaged in the promotion of his own interest and aggrandizement. He occupied the house of Governor Penn, the best in the city, and this he furnished in a rich and splendid style.

His carriage and equipage were equally splendid, and he rioted in the luxury and pageantry of a nobleman "Proud of the trappings of office, and ambitious of an ostentatious display of wealth and greatness, the certain mark of a narrow mind, he had wasted the plunder acquired at Montreal, where his conduct had been remarkably reprehensible, and had dissipated the rich harvest of peculation he had reaped at Philadelphia, where his rapacity had no bounds. He deliberately seized every thing he could lay his hands on in the city, to which he could affix an idea that it had been the property of the disaffected party, and converted it to his own use."*

Unmindful of his military station, he engaged in various speculations and in privateering, in both of which he was unfortunate. He made exorbitant demands on government, in compensation for public services, and made bitter complaints against Congress, pretending that he suffered injustice from their hands. The commissioners appointed to liquidate his accounts, rejected a large proportion of his demands, as being unjust and unfounded, and for which he deserved severe reprehension. He was charged by the citizens of Philadelphia with gross acts of extortion, and of peculating on the public funds; and he was at length so notorious for his follies and vices, and so audacious in his reproaches against what he termed the ingratitude of his country, that the general voice demanded an investigation of his conduct. The government of Pennsylvania, as well as many respectable citizens, exhibited formal charges against him, and Congress directed that he should be arrested, and tried by a court-martial. He was sentenced to be reprimanded by the commander-in-chief, which being approved by Congress, was carried into execution accordingly. The emoluments of his office, with all his embezzlements, proved inadequate to his exigencies, and his funds being exhausted, he was unable to meet the demands of his creditors. Thus he evinced a mind destitute of both moral principle and political integrity. Rebuffed and mortified in his vicious pursuits, he became soured and disaffected to our government and cause, and the most malevolent and rancorous spirit agitated his unprincipled bosom, restrained by a want of opportunity to

* *History of the American Revolution* by Mrs. M. Warren.

indulge his revenge. At the opening of the campaign in June, 1780, the commander-in-chief offered him the command of the left wing of our army, to which his rank entitled him; but this he declined, under the pretext that the wound which he received at Saratoga, rendered him incapable of active service in the field. He solicited the station of commander of the garrison at West Point, and in this request he was indulged by the commander-in-chief, who still had confidence in him as a military officer. He was now invested with a situation which furnished him with the meditated opportunity of executing his treasonable purpose, and avenging himself on his country and the glorious cause of freedom. He engaged in a secret correspondence with Sir Henry Clinton, and actually agreed to put him in possession of the important garrison at West Point.

The British general, appreciating the importance of the acquisition, immediately closed with him for the stipulated sum of ten thousand pounds sterling, and sent Major John Andre, his adjutant-general and aid-de-camp, to negotiate the arrangement for the surrender of the post. A British sloop-of-war, called the Vulture, conveyed him up the North river within twelve miles of West Point, and in the night of the 21st of September, 1780, by direction of General Arnold, this gentleman was brought on shore, under the fictitious name of John Anderson. Arnold received him on the beach, and conducted him to the house of Joshua Smith, within our lines, and the night was spent in ripening the infamous plot for execution. The following night it was attempted to reconduct him on board the Vulture; but the boatmen who had been seduced to bring him on shore, utterly refused to perform the service, and a return to New York by land was the only alternative. Arnold furnished him with numerous papers, containing all the necessary information respecting the garrison, and a passport, naming him John Anderson, on public business, with which he proceeded on his journey.

Having reached Tarrytown, on his route, Andre was suddenly arrested by three militia-men, who, finding the above-mentioned papers concealed in his boots, immediately delivered them into the hands of Lieutenant-Colonel Jameson, the commanding officer on our lines. With the view of giving Arnold an opportunity to escape, Andre had the address to induce Colonel Jameson to inform him by letter that John Anderson was taken on his way to New York. On this being received by express, the guilty traitor, struck with the pressing danger of his situation, instantly informed his wife that he had received some letters which obliged him to flee his country for ever, and desired her to retire and remain in her chamber. He now called earnestly for a horse, and mounted the first that presented; and, instead of the usual path, he took a shorter route, riding down a very steep and dangerous precipice to the landing. This has since been called "Traitor's-hill." The barge being in readiness, he sprang into it, and ordered the boatmen to proceed down the river, and he was soon on board the Vulture, which Andre two nights before had left, and which immediately sailed with her prize for New York. Arnold was apprised that General Washington, being on his return from a journey to Hartford, intended to visit him that day, and he was momentarily expected. Accordingly his excellency arrived soon after Arnold had absconded; and not finding him at his quarters, he passed over the river to West Point, to view the works, and with the expectation of finding him at his post; but being disappointed, he returned to Arnold's quarters, where he still found that no one could account for his absence. But in a few hours despatches arrived from Colonel Jameson, announcing the capture of Major Andre, and this was accompanied by his own letter of confession. The mysterious affair was now developed. Arnold's treason and elopement admitted at once of explanation. An officer was immediately sent to our fort at Verplank's Point, with orders to fire at Arnold's barge; but it was too late; she had already reached the Vulture. In about an hour and a half after Arnold had absconded, Dr. Eustis, who had charge of the hospital in the vicinity, was called to the assistance of Mrs. Arnold, whose situation was alarming. He found her at the head of the stair-case, in great dishabille, her hair disheveled, knowing no one, and frantic in the arms of her maid and Arnold's two aids, struggling to liberate herself from them. She was carried back to her chamber, and fell into convulsions, which lasted several hours. In a lucid interval, she inquired of the doctor if General Washington was in the house, expressing a wish to see him. Believing that she intended to say something which would explain the secret of Arnold's unaccountable absence, he hastened below, gave notice of her request, and conducted the general to her chamber, who remained no longer than to hear her deny that he was General Washington, and to witness the return of her distraction. When Arnold deserted his post, a corporal, by name James Lurvey, was the coxswain of his barge. After their arrival on board the Vulture, and Arnold had held an interview with the officers in the cabin, he came on deck, and said to his bargemen, " My lads, I have quitted the *rebel army*, and joined the standard of his Britannic Majesty. If you will join me, I will make sergeants and corporals of you all; and for you, James, I will do something more." Indignant at the offer, Lurvey promptly replied, " No, sir; one coat is enough for me to wear at a time!"—a worthy example of fidelity in the corporal, and a cutting sarcasm on the guilty traitor. Two only of the crew remained, and they were British deserters. The brave corporal, with the remainder of the men, returned; not, however, in the barge; Arnold had the meanness to retain that for his own use, and gave them a miserable boat in exchange.

After his arrival on board the Vulture, he addressed to General Washington the following letter:

" *On board the Vulture, September 25th,* 1780.

"SIR: The heart which is conscious of its own rectitude, cannot attempt to palliate a step which the world may censure as wrong. I have ever acted from a principle of love to my country, since the commencement of the present unhappy contest between Great Britain and the colonies; the same principle of love to my country actuates my present conduct, however it may appear inconsistent to the world, who very seldom judge right of any man's actions.

" I have no favor to ask for myself; I have too often experienced the ingratitude of my country to attempt it; but from the known humanity of your excellency, I am induced to ask your protection for Mrs. Arnold, from every insult and injury that the mistaken vengeance of my country may expose her to. It ought to fall only on me: she is as good and as innocent as an angel, and is incapable of doing wrong. I beg she may be permitted to return to her friends in Philadelphia, or to come to me, as she may choose; from your excellency I have no fears on her account, but she may suffer from the mistaken fury of the country.

"I have to request that the inclosed letter may be delivered to Mrs. Arnold, and she permitted to write to me.

"I have also to ask that my clothes and baggage, which are of little consequence, may be sent to me. If required, their value shall be paid in money.

"I have the honor to be, with great regard and esteem,
"Your Excellency's most obedient, humble servant.
"B. ARNOLD.
"His Excellency General Washington.

"N. B. In justice to the gentlemen of my family, Colonel Varrick, and Major Frank, I think myself in honor bound to declare, that they, as well as Joshua Smith, Esquire, who I know is suspected, are totally ignorant of any transactions of mine that they had reason to believe were injurious to the public."

Mrs. Arnold was permitted to go unmolested to her husband at New York, and to take her chariot with her. Arnold had the audacity to remonstrate to General Washington against the execution of Major Andre, and to attempt to intimidate him by threats of retaliation, should the unfortunate prisoner suffer; but his excellency treated both the traitor and his affrontive letters with sovereign contempt. He next published an address to the people of the United States, in which he pretended to ascribe his defection from the American cause to principle, of which it is well known that he ever has been destitute. He attempts to vindicate his conduct by the ridiculous pretence that he was actuated by motives favorable to the interests of his country by bringing the war to a speedy termination, as though the destiny of America was doomed to be at his disposal, and that he was authorized to decide the fate of millions. In his artful address he labored to palliate his own guilt and to influence others to follow his vile example. He execrated with peculiar bitterness our alliance with France, and accused Congress of tyranny and usurpation, and a total disregard of the interest and welfare of the people. Not satisfied with this insidious appeal to the people, he addressed by proclamation "the officers and soldiers of the continental army, who had the real interest of their country at heart, and who were determined to be no longer the tools and dupes of Congress or of France." As inducement to the American officers and soldiers to desert the cause which they had embraced, he represented that the corps of cavalry and infantry which he was authorized to raise, would be on the same footing with the other troops in the British service; that he would with pleasure advance those whose valor he had witnessed, and that the private men who might join him should receive a bounty of three guineas each, besides payment at their full value for horses, arms, and accoutrements. He endeavored to paint in lively colors the deplorable condition of our country, and to reprobate our Congress as oppressors, and their authority as tyrannical. "You are promised liberty," he exclaims, "but is there an individual in the enjoyment of it, saving your oppressors? Who among you dare speak or write what he thinks against the tyranny which has robbed you of your property, imprisons your persons, drags you to the field of battle, and is daily deluging your country with your blood?" Again, "what is America now but a land of widows, orphans, and beggars? As to you who have been soldiers in the continental army, can you at this day want evidence that the funds of your country are exhausted, or that the managers have applied them to their own private uses? In either case, you surely can no longer continue in their service with honor and advantage. Yet you have hitherto been their supporters in that cruelty which, with an equal indifference to yours, as well as to the labor and blood of others, is devouring a country that from the moment you quit their colors will be redeemed from their tyranny." These proclamations failed of the effect which they were designed to produce; and notwithstanding all the hardships, sufferings and irritations which the Americans were called to encounter, "Arnold remains the solitary instance of an American officer who abandoned the side first embraced in the contest, and turned his sword on his former companions in arms." "I am mistaken," says Washington in a letter to a friend, "if at this time Arnold is undergoing the torments of a mental hell. From some traits of his character which have lately come to my knowledge, he seems to have been so hacknied in crime—so lost to all sense of honor and shame—that while his faculties still enable him to continue his sordid pursuits, there will be no time for remorse." "This man," says Hamilton, "is in every sense despicable. In addition to the scene of knavery and prostitution during his command at Philadelphia, which the late seizure of his papers has unfolded, the history of his command at West Point is a history of little as well as of great villanies. He practised every dirty act of peculation, and even stooped to connexions with the sutlers of the garrison to defraud the public." A respectable officer, in a letter to a friend, speaks of Arnold in the following language: "It is not possible for human nature to receive a greater quantity of guilt than he possesses. Perhaps there is not a single obligation, moral or divine, but what he has broken through. It is discovered now that, in his most early infancy, hell marked him for her own, and infused into him a full proportion of her own malice. His late apostacy is the summit of his character. He 'began his negotiations with the enemy, to deliver up West Point to them, long before he was invested with the command of it, and whilst he was still in Philadelphia; after which, he solicited the command of that post from the ostensible cause that the wound in his leg incapacitated him for an active command in the field."

His papers contain the most authentic and incontestable proofs of his crime, and that he regarded his important employments only as affording him opportunities to pillage the public with impunity. The crimes of this unprincipled conspirator are thus summed up: Treason, avarice, hypocrisy, ingratitude, barbarity, falsehood, deception, peculation and robbery. He aimed to plunge a dagger into the bosom of his country, which had raised him from the obscurity in which he was born, to honors which never could have been the object even of his hopes. He robbed his country at the time of her deepest distress, having directed his wife to draw all she could from the commissaries' store, and sell or store it, though at a time when the army was destitute of provisions. He robbed the soldiers when they were in want of necessaries, and defrauded his own best friends who trusted and had rendered him the most essential services. He spoke contemptuously of our allies, the French, and his illiberal abuse of every character opposed to his fraudulent and wicked transactions exceeds all description. For the sake of human nature it were to be wished that a veil could for ever be thrown over such a vile example of depravity and wickedness.

An effigy of Arnold, large as life, was constructed by an artist at Philadelphia, and seated in a cart, with the figure of the devil at his elbow, holding a lantern up to the face

31

of the traitor to show him to the people, having his name and crime in capital letters. The cart was paraded the whole evening through the streets of the city, with drums and fifes playing the Rogue's March, with other marks of infamy, and was attended by a vast concourse of people. The effigy was finally hanged, for the want of the original, and then committed to the flames. Yet this is the man on whom the British have bestowed ten thousand pounds sterling as the price of his treason, and appointed to the rank of brigadier-general in their service. It could scarcely be imagined that there was an officer of honor left in that army, who would debase himself and his commission by serving under or ranking with *Benedict Arnold!*

In January, 1781, Arnold was by Sir Henry Clinton invested with the command of one thousand seven hundred men, supported by a naval force, on an expedition to Virginia, where he committed extensive ravages on the rivers and along the unprotected coast, plundering the plantations to the extent of his power. According to report, he shipped off a cargo of negroes, which he had stolen, to Jamaica, and sold them for his own emolument. Having taken an American captain prisoner, he inquired of him what the Americans would do with him if he should fall into their hands; the officer replied, they would cut off the leg that was wounded at Saratoga, and bury it with the honors of war, and hang the remainder of his body on a gibbet. In September, 1781, Arnold was again vested with a command, and sent on a predatory expedition against New London, in Connecticut, his native state. After taking possession of the fort, they made a merciless slaughter of the men who defended it, and destroyed an immense quantity of provisions, stores and shipping; sixty dwelling-houses and eighty-four stores were destroyed, and about one hundred inhabitants were deprived of their habitations, and most of them of their all. This terminated the career of this monster of wickedness in America. At the close of the war, he accompanied the royal army to England. "The contempt that followed him through life," says a late elegant writer,* "is further illustrated by the speech of the present Lord Lauderdale, who, perceiving Arnold on the right hand of the king, and near his

* Alexander Garden, Esquire.—*Anecdotes of the Revolutionary War.*

person, as he addressed his, parliament, declared, on his
return to the Commons, that, however gracious the language he had heard from the throne, his indignation could
not but be highly excited at beholding, as he had done,
his majesty supported by a traitor." "And on another
occasion, Lord Surrey, since duke of Norfolk, rising to
speak in the House of Commons, and perceiving Arnold
in the gallery, sat down with precipitation, exclaiming, 'I
will not speak while that man' (pointing to him) 'is in
the house.'"

He purchased in England a quantity of goods which
he brought over to New Brunswick; the store and goods
took fire, and the whole were consumed; but according
to report they were insured to a much greater amount
than their real value. After this event, no further laurels
remained for him to achieve; he rēcrossed the Atlantic,
and died in London, June 14th, 1801.

SKETCH OF THE LIFE OF GENERAL KNOX.

AMONG those of our countrymen, who most zealously
engaged in the cause of liberty, few sustained a rank more
deservedly conspicuous than General Knox. He was one
of those heroes, of whom it may be truly said, that he lived
for his country.

The ardor of his youth and the vigor of his manhood
were devoted to acquiring its liberty and establishing its
prosperity. Born in Boston, July, 1750, his childhood and
youth were employed in obtaining the best education that
the justly-celebrated schools of his native town afforded.
In very early life he opened a book-store, for the enlarge-
ment of which he soon formed an extensive correspondence
in Europe; but little time elapsed before, at the call of
his country, he relinquished this lucrative and increasing
business. Indebted to no adventitious aid, his character
was formed by himself; the native and vigorous principles
of his own mind made him what he was. Distinguished
among his associates, from the first dawn of manhood, for
a decided predilection to martial exercises, he was at the
age of eighteen selected by the young men of Boston as
one of the officers of a company of grenadiers—a company

so distinguished for its martial appearance, and the precision of its evolutions, that it received the most flattering encomium from a British officer of high distinction.

This early scene of his military labors served but as a school for that distinguished talent which afterward shone with lustre, in the most brilliant campaigns of an eight-years' war: through the whole of which, he directed the artillery with consummate skill and bravery.

His heart was deeply engaged in the cause of freedom; he felt it to be a righteous cause, and to its accomplishment yielded every other consideration. When Britain declared hostilities, he hesitated not a moment what course he should pursue. No sordid calculation of interest retarded his decision. The quiet of domestic life, the fair prospect of increasing wealth, and even the endearing claims of family and friends, though urged with the most persuasive eloquence, had no power to divert the determined purpose of his mind.

In the early stages of British hostility, though not in commission, he was not an inactive spectator. At the battle of Bunker-hill, as a volunteer, he was constantly exposed to danger, in reconnoitering the movements of the enemy, and his ardent mind was engaged with others in preparing those measures that were ultimately to dislodge the British troops from their boasted possession of the capital of New England.

Scarcely had we began to feel the aggressions of the British arms, before it was perceived that, without artillery, of which we were then destitute, the most important objects of the war could not be accomplished. No resource presented itself, but the desperate expedient of procuring it from the Canadian frontier. To attempt this, in the agitated state of the country, through a wide extent of wilderness, was an enterprise so replete with toil and danger, that it was hardly expected any one would be found hardy enough to encounter its perils. Knox, however, saw the importance of the object; he saw his country bleeding at every pore, without the power of repelling her invaders; he saw the flourishing capital of the North in the possession of an exulting enemy, that we were destitute of the means essential to their annoyance, and formed the daring and generous resolution of supplying the army with ordnance, however formidable the obstacles that might oppose him. Young, robust and vigorous, supported by an undaunted spirit, and a mind ever fruitful in resources, he commenced his mighty undertaking, almost unattended, in the winter of 1775, relying solely for the execution of his object on such aid as he might procure from the thinly-scattered inhabitants of the dreary region through which he had to pass. Every obstacle of season, roads, and climate were surmounted by determined perseverance; and a few weeks, scarcely sufficient for a journey so remote, saw him return laden with ordnance and the stores of war —drawn in defiance of every obstacle over the frozen lakes and mountains of the north. Most acceptable was this offering to our defenceless troops, and most welcome to the commander-in-chief, who well knew how to appreciate a service so important. This expedition stamped the character of him who performed it for deeds of enterprise and daring. He received the most flattering testimony of approbation from the commander-in-chief and from Congress, and was in consequence of this important service appointed to the command of the artillery, of which he had thus laid the foundation, in which command he continued with increasing reputation through the Revolutionary War.

Among the incidents that occurred during the expedition to Canada, was his accidental meeting with the unfortunate Andre, whose subsequent fate was so deeply deplored by every man of feeling in both nations. His deportment as a soldier and gentleman so far interested General Knox in his favor, that he often afterward expressed the most sincere regret that he was called by duty to act on the tribunal that pronounced his condemnation.

During the continuance of the war, the corps of artillery was principally employed with the main body of the army, and near the person of the commander-in-chief, and was relied on as an essential auxiliary in the most important battles.

There was perhaps no period of the war when the American cause assumed an aspect so precarious as in the autumn of 1777. Philadelphia, then the centre and capital of our country—preëminent for its wealth, its population, and its trade—a place most distinguished for the progress of the arts, was destined to fall within the grasp of our haughty foe. In the campaign that preceded its occupation by the British, General Knox was a conspicuous actor, eager for the contest, yet compelled with his brave companions to lament that the equipments of our army were unequal to the heroic spirits of its soldiers. Trenton and Princeton witnessed his enterprise and valor. At that critical period of our affairs, when hope had almost yielded to despair, and the great soul of Washington trembled for his country's freedom, Knox was one of those that strengthened his hand and encouraged his heart. At that awful moment, when the tempest raged with its greatest fury, he, with Greene and other heroes, stood as Pillars of the Temple of Liberty, till the fury of the storm was past. .

The letters of General Knox, still extant, written in the darkest periods of the revolution, breathe a spirit of devotedness to the cause in which he had embarked, and a firm reliance on the favor of Divine Providence; from a perusal of those letters it is evident that he never yielded to despondency, but, in the most critical moments of the war, confidently anticipated its triumphant issue.

In the bloody fields of Germantown and Monmouth, without derogating from the merits of others, it may be said that during the whole of these hard-fought battles, no officer was more distinguished for the discharge of the arduous duties of his command. In the front of the battle he was seen animating his soldiers, and pointing the thunder of their cannon. His skill and bravery were so conspicuous on the latter occasion, that he received the particular approbation of the commander-in-chief, in general orders issued by him the day succeeding that of the battle, in which he says, that "the enemy have done them the justice to acknowledge that no artillery could be better served than ours." But his great exertions on that occasion, together with the extreme heat of the day, produced the most alarming consequences to his health. To these more important scenes, his services were not confined; with a zeal devoted to our cause, he was ever at the post of danger; and the immortal hero, who stands first on the list of heroes and of men, has often expressed his sense of their services. In every field of battle where Washington fought, Knox was by his side. The confidence of the commander-in-chief, inspired by early services, was thus matured by succeeding events. There can be no higher testimony to his merits than that, during a war of so long continuance, passed almost constantly in the presence of Washington, he uniformly retained his confidence and esteem, which at their separation had ripened into friendship and affection. The parting interview between General Knox and his illustrious and beloved chief, after the evacuation of New York, by the British, and Knox had taken possession of it at the head of a detachment of our army, was inexpressibly affecting. The hour of their separation having arrived, Washington, incapble of utterance, grasped his hand, and embraced him in silence and in tears. His letters, to the last moment of his life, contain the most flattering expressions of his unabated friendship. Honorable to himself as had been the career of his revolutionary services, new laurels were reserved for him at the siege of Yorktown.—To the successful result of this memorable siege, the last brilliant act of our revolutionary contest, no officer contributed more essentially than the commander of the artillery. His animated exertions, his military skill, his cool and determined bravery in this triumphant struggle, received the unanimous approbation of his brethren in arms, and he was immediately created major-general by Congress, at the recommendation of the commander-in-chief, with the concurrence of the whole army.

The capture of Lord Cornwallis closed the contest, and with it his military life. Having contributed so essentially to the successful termination of the war, he was selected as one of the commissioners to adjust the terms of peace, which service he performed, in conjunction with his colleagues, much to the satisfaction of his country. He was deputed to receive the surrender of the city of New York, and soon after appointed to the command of West Point. It was here that he was employed in the delicate and arduous duty of disbanding the army, and inducing a soldiery, disposed to turbulence by their privations and sufferings, to retire to domestic life, and resume the peaceful character of citizens.

It is a fact most honorable to his character that, by his

countenance and support, he rendered the most essential aid to Washington, in suppressing that spirit of usurpation which had been industriously fomented by a few unprincipled and aspiring men, whose aim was the subjugation of the country to a military government. No hope of political elevation—no flattering assurances of aggrandizement—could tempt him to build his greatness on the ruin of his country.

The great objects of the war being accomplished, and peace restored to our country, Gen. Knox was early, under the confederation, appointed secretary of war by Congress, in which office he was confirmed by President Washington, after the establishment of the federal government. The duties of this office were ultimately increased, by having those of the navy attached to them—to the establishment of which his counsel and exertions eminently contributed. He differed in opinion from some other members of the cabinet on this most interesting subject.—One of the greatest men* whom our country has produced, has uniformly declared that he considered America much indebted to his efforts for the creation of a power which has already so essentially advanced her respectability and fame.

Having filled the office of the war department for eleven years, he obtained the reluctant consent of President Washington to retire, that he might give his attention to the claims of a numerous and increasing family. This retirement was in concurrence with the wishes of Mrs. Knox, who had accompanied him through the trying vicissitudes of war, shared with him its toils and perils, and who was now desirous of enjoying the less busy scenes of domestic life. A portion of the large estates of her ancestor, General Waldo, had descended to her, which he by subsequent purchase increased till it comprised the whole Waldo Patent, an extent of thirty miles square, and embracing a considerable part of that section of Maine which now constitutes the counties of Lincoln, Hancock, and Penobscot. To these estates he retired from all concern in public life, honored as a soldier and beloved as a man, devoting much of his time to their settlement and improvement. He was induced repeatedly to take a share in the government of the state, both in the house of rep-

* President Adams.

resentatives and in the council—in the discharge of whose several duties, he employed his wisdom and experience with the greatest assiduity. At that time Maine and Massachusetts composed one great and powerful state. His enlarged and liberal policy, as a legislator, was manifested on every question on which he acted, and in every debate in which he took a part. While at the council board of Massachusetts, on all public political questions, his opinions had great weight with Governor Strong, at that period the worthy chief magistrate of the commonwealth. Though independent and firm in his political sentiments, like Strong, he was disposed to conciliate those who differed from him in opinion, and was wholly free from the spirit of intolerance.

In 1798, when the French insults and injuries towards this country called for resistance, he was one of those selected to command our armies, and to protect our liberty and honor from the expected hostilities of the French Directory: happily for our country, their services were not required.

Retired from the theatre of active life, he still felt a deep interest in the prosperity of his country. To that portion of it which he had chosen for his residence, his exertions were more immediately directed. His views, like his soul, were bold and magnificent; his ardent mind could not wait the ordinary course of time and events; it outstripped the progress of natural improvement. Had he possessed a cold, calculating mind, he might have left behind him the most ample wealth; but he would not have been more highly valued by his country, or more beloved by his friends.—He died at Montpelier, his seat in Thomaston, 25th of October, 1806, from sudden internal inflammation, at the age of fifty-six, from the full vigor of health.

The great qualities of General Knox were not merely those of the hero and the statesman; with these were combined those of the elegant scholar and the accomplished gentleman. There have been those as brave and as learned, but rarely a union of such valor with so much urbanity —a mind so great, yet so free from ostentation.

In sketching the life of such a man, it is not the least interesting part to recall his private virtues. Long will he be remembered as the ornament of every circle in

which he moved—as the amiable and enlightened com
panion, the generous friend, the man of feeling and benevolence. His conversation was animated and cheerful, and
he imparted an interest to every subject that he touched.
In his gayest moments he never lost sight of dignity; he
invited confidence, but repelled familiarity. His imagination was brilliant, his conceptions lofty; and no man ever
possessed the power of embodying his thoughts in more
vigorous language; when ardently engaged, they were
peculiarly bold and original, and you irresistibly felt in
his society that his intellect was not of the ordinary class.
Yet no man was more unassuming—none more delicately
alive to the feelings of others. He had the peculiar talent
of rendering all who were with him happy in themselves;
and no one ever more feelingly enjoyed the happiness of
those around him. Philanthropy filled his heart; in his
benevolence there was no reserve—it was as diffusive as
the globe, and extensive as the family of man. His feelings were strong and exquisitely tender. In the domestic
circle they shone with peculiar lustre: here, the husband,
the father and the friend, beamed in every smile—and if
at any time a cloud overshadowed his own spirit, he strove
to prevent its influence from extending to those that were
dear to him. He was frank, generous, and sincere; and
in his intercourse with the world, uniformly just. His
house was the seat of elegant hospitality, and his estimate
of wealth, was its power of diffusing happiness. To the
testimony of private friendship, may be added that of less
partial strangers, who have borne witness both to his public
and private virtues. Lord Moira, who is now perhaps the
greatest general that England can boast of, has in a late
publication spoken in high terms of his military talents.
Nor should the opinion of the Marquis Chattelleux be
omitted: "As for General Knox," he says, "to praise him
for his military talents alone, would be to deprive him of
half the eulogium he merits; a man of understanding,
well informed, gay, sincere and honest—it is impossible
to know without esteeming him, or to see without loving
him—thus have the English, without intention, added to
the ornaments of the human species, by awakening talents
where they least wished or expected." Judge Marshall
also, in his *Life of Washington*, thus speaks of him·

"Throughout the contest of the revolution, this officer had continued at the head of the American artillery, and, from being colonel of a regiment, had been promoted to the rank of major-general. In this important station he had preserved a high military character, and on the resignation of General Lincoln, had been appointed secretary of war. To his great services, and to unquestionable integrity, he was admitted to unite a sound understanding; and the public judgment as well as that of the chief magistrate, pronounced him in all respects competent to the station he filled. The president was highly gratified in believing that his public duty comported with his private inclination, in nominating General Knox to the office which had been conferred on him under the former government."—As a proof of their estimation of his literary attainments, the president and trustees of Dartmouth College conferred on him the degree of Doctor of Laws.

Perhaps in no instance of his life was his warmth of heart and strength of attachment more fully exemplified than at the closing interview of the principal leaders of the war, when they were about to take a final leave of each other, never probably to meet again. It was most natural that the recollection of the past scenes should awaken the liveliest emotions: the bosom of the soldier is the residence of honor and of feeling, and no man cherished them more fondly than Knox. He proposed to his brethern in arms that some course should be adopted to keep alive the generous attachment which was the fruit of their long intercourse and mutual toils and dangers; the proposal accorded with the feelings of the principal officers of the army, who united in forming the *Cincinnati*, a society whose object was to cement and perpetuate the friendship of its founders, and transmit the same sentiment to their descendants. Pure as are believed to have been the motives of those who associated in forming this society, there were not wanting some who, from ignorance or illiberality, professed to doubt the purity of its character and the correctness of its objects. But it is a fact, derived from the highest authority,* that it had, from its commencement, the unqualified approbation of the commander-in-chief, expressed in the most decided language. Such sanction

* Governor Brooks.

as that of Washington could not fail to do away every suspicion of its unfairness, and to establish the rectitude of its motives and principles.

General Knox was a supporter of Christian institutions, and contributed much, by his liberality and his example, to promote the preaching of the gospel. It always appeared to afford him the highest pleasure to bear testimony to the excellence of Christianity, and he often expressed his firm belief that its exalted principles were intended to correct the heart and to purify the life; to make man what he ought to be in this world, and to prepare him for the more elevated enjoyments of the future. He most firmly believed in the immortality and the immateriality of the soul.

From his reflections on religion, committed by him to paper, it is evident that his thoughts were often and intensely employed on the all-important concerns of a future state of existence; that he firmly believed in an overruling Providence, and that he was created and sustained by its power and goodness. He considered the order, harmony and beauty of creation, as affording the most convincing proof of wisdom and design. He thought the universal distribution of blessings among mankind, furnished conclusive evidence of the goodness of the Being from whose bounty they flow. But it was a subject on which he reasoned for himself, unfettered by the arrogant dogmas of the churchmen, or the metaphysical subtleties of the schools. He expressed exalted pleasure in the full conviction that the arm of Almighty Power was extended for the protection of the whole family of man, without respect to Jew or Gentile. The exclusive pretensions of the various sects and denominations in the church, he considered the fruits of human invention, and altogether unworthy the wisdom of the Almighty Mind.

Elevated by the aspirations of his own exalted mind, he believed our residence on this globe, which he considered but an atom in creation, as only the commencement of a progressive state of existence, still rising toward perfection from sphere to sphere, till, by successive gradations of intellectual and moral improvement, we are prepared for the presence and enjoyment of the All-perfect Being who created us.